New Financing for Distressed Businesses in the Context of Business Restructuring Law

Sanford U. Mba

New Financing for Distressed Businesses in the Context of Business Restructuring Law

Springer

Sanford U. Mba
Legal Studies
Central European University
Budapest, Hungary

ISBN 978-3-030-19748-3 ISBN 978-3-030-19749-0 (eBook)
https://doi.org/10.1007/978-3-030-19749-0

This Springer imprint is published by the registered company Springer Nature Switzerland AG.
The registered company address is: Gewerbestrasse 11, 6330 Cham, Switzerland

To Professor Tibor Tajti, Adeline, Ugo,
Nathan and the memory of James I. Mba.

Acknowledgments

As one will see, a recurring motif in this book is debt. Even the author is not spared. The difference, however (and thankfully), is that what I owe, I owe in gratitude, a world of gratitude.

I am in great debt of gratitude to the Central European University (CEU), an institution devoted to academic excellence, critical thinking, and the open society, which I have had the privilege to be a part of.

My deepest gratitude goes to Professor Tibor Tajti, who has been my supervisor through this research process. His direction, support, and mentorship have seen me through the program. I have thoroughly enjoyed our exchanges that extended beyond the law. Just words cannot express my heartfelt gratitude. I am truly grateful to the members of faculty and staff of the Legal Studies Department here at CEU, for their immense contributions. Professor Moschel, for his role as director of the doctoral program, who has been immensely supportive and kind. I am also grateful to Professors Karoly Bard, Renata Uitz, Catarina Sganga, Markus Petsche, and Jessica Lawrence. Also, Emeritus Professor Tibor Varady and Emerita Professor Csilla Kollonay-Lehoczky have played no small role and deserve special mention. Many thanks to the department staff, especially Tunde Szabo, Andrea Volgyes, and Nori Kovacs for their important role in making the academic and non-academic processes work well.

Also, I wish to thank the dedicated staff of the CEU Library who were ever willing to assist and for making the library conducive for research. Robin Beller of the Center for Academic Writing has been quite helpful with advice on writing. Thanks Robin.

I have also immensely benefited from the grants by CEU Budapest Foundation (CBF). Thanks to the generous grant from the CBF, I was able to take up visiting positions at both Cornell Law School and the Oxford Commercial Law Center. On this, I am also grateful to Professors Charles Whitehead of Cornell Law School and Professor Louis Gullifer of the Oxford University, for hosting me during my time researching in both prestigious institutions. Also, I am grateful to Professor Saule Omarova for her kind permission to audit her Corporate Finance course at Cornell and also to Professor Kristen van Zwieten for her permission to take part in the

Corporate Insolvency seminars at Oxford. During my research time at UNCITRAL, I had the privilege of having meaningful conversations with Spyridon Bazinas and Claudia M. Gross who shared their wealth of knowledge with me on such matters that pertain to superpriority for new financing. I am most grateful to Lucia Scheidl-Kornis, whose kind assistance and warm smile made my time enjoyable.

I have benefited from the warmth and friendship of my colleagues in the doctoral program at CEU. Although I unfortunately did not get to spend more time in the SJD lab, I have been blessed by our conversations and interactions. Especially Albana (a dear sister), Wasiq, Pins, Boris, Viktor, Berihun, Giulia, Dorothee, and others, thank you all for your friendship. Also, worthy of special mention are Michael, Debjyoti, and Rebecca who, although have recently defended, were equally part of the process and I am thankful for knowing them.

My family has been especially supportive. Thank you Ugoo, for ably holding the fort these years and for all the support. To Adeline K. Mba and Justina U. Nwachukwu, thank you for the prayers and for being inimitable models to your children. Also, Chief Alex Nwachukwu for all the kind words of encouragement. My siblings Cynthia, Ik, and Mary-Ann, for all the love and for coming through when it mattered the most. Kingsley Uzowulu is a study in benevolence. I still believe his selfnessness is the stuff of legend. I am eternally grateful. Franklin Maduko has been my flat mate for the last 3 years. I have learnt so much from him and we have argued through many things, from issues pertaining to our home country to economic assumptions in this book.

Professionally, I have benefited from friends and colleagues. I have enjoyed the mentorship of Dr. A.I. Layonu (SAN) from whom I developed a keen interest in Insolvency Law and practice. Ebimobowei Jikenghan has always provided me with the latest state of the Nigerian law, in terms of both reform efforts and practice insights. Dr. Chima W. Iheme has been a sounded board, given our common interest in the reform of Nigerian business laws. I have immensely benefited from Dr. Bolanle Adebola with whom I have also had meaningful exchanges on aspects of the research. I will not fail to thank Stephen Azubuike and Moriam Animashaun (HMCA Attorneys and Solicitors) for keeping me actively engaged in legal practice with quite challenging, yet interesting consultancy on transactions. Also, to my legal family at Layonu & Co. Thank you all.

I have been truly blessed by the friends at the CEU Christian Fellowship. For friends like Agatha, Deborah, Daniel, Andras, and all others, I am grateful. Finally, to all those who opened their hearts and doors to me in my sojourn around the world these 4 years, I am grateful. To the Mandalay International Church in Mandalay, the Bethel Groove (and the CCF) in Ithaca, MFM in Budapest, the Lawyers Christian Fellowship, London, as well as the Christ und Jurist in Germany, Stuttgart. Many blessings.

Budapest, Hungary
April 2019

Sanford U. Mba

Contents

Abbreviations

ABS	Asset Backed Securities
AIFMs	Alternative Investment Fund Managers
AMCON	Asset Management Corporation of Nigeria
BIA	Bankruptcy and Insolvency Act
CAMA	Companies and Allied Matters Act
CVA	Companies Voluntary Arrangement
CLO	Collateralized Loan Obligations
DIP	Debtor in Possession
DIP Financing	Debtor in Possession Financing
EHYA	European High Yield Association
EU	European Union
EEA	European Economic Area
ESUG	Gesetz zur weiteren Erleichterung der Sanierung von Unternehmen
GmbH	Gesellschaft mit beschränkter Haftung
GP	General Partner
LP	Limited Partner
IA	Insolvency Act
InsO	Insolvenzordnung
NPL	Non-Performing Loan
PAMC	Private Asset Management Company
PMSI	Purchase Money Security Interest
SMEs	Small and Medium-Sized Enterprises
SPV/E	Special Purpose Vehicle/Enterprise
ST Act	Secured Transactions Act
UK	United Kingdom
UCC	Uniform Commercial Code
UNCITRAL	United Nations Commission on International Trade Law
US	United States
USD	United States Dollars

Chapter 1
Introduction

In my school-days when I had lost one shaft,
I shot his fellow of the self-same flight
The self-same way, with more advised watch,
To find the other forth; and by advent'ring both
I oft found both: I urge this childhood proof,
Because what follows is pure innocence.
I owe you much; and, like a wilful youth,
That which I owe is lost: but if you please
To shoot another arrow that self-way
Which you did shoot the first, I do not doubt,
As I will watch the aim, or to find both
Or bring your latter hazard back again,
And thankfully rest debtor for the first.[1]

Financial distress is often an unnerving experience for business borrowers, their creditors, and the concerned stakeholders. In the most basic terms, absent a concerted effort at stemming the distress, it may well mean the death knell on the life of the company. Like the merchant Bassanio in the excerpts above, a distressed firm that wishes to forestall impending, (or work its way out of actual) insolvency, faces several challenges. One of the most pressing, is generating the required liquidity to tide itself over (thereby preserving its value), and in general terms, work its way out of its financial troubles.[2] If such finance is unavailable, the distressed firm, irrespective of its viability or the potential value it holds, may be unable to continue in operation,[3] while seeking to arrive at a possible consensual resolution of its financial distress.[4]

---

[1] Excerpt from Shakespeare (1874), Act 1 Scene 1, where Bassanio seeks distress finance from Antonio (a prior lender). This excerpt gives an apt, albeit basic, representation of financing of a distressed business debtor with an appreciation of the value of new financing.

[2] See generally Skeel and Ayotte (2013).

[3] See Westbrook and Gottlieb (2009) and Loubser (2014) ("Because rescuing a business requires that the business should continue trading, and that, in turn, requires working capital…").

[4] See Martin et al. (2009) (noting that without distress financing to maintain business operations during formal restructuring, companies may be forced to liquidate rather than restructure); See also

S. U. Mba, *New Financing for Distressed Businesses in the Context of Business Restructuring Law*, https://doi.org/10.1007/978-3-030-19749-0_1

International instruments bordering on corporate restructuring have corroborated the vital role of new financing for distressed businesses undergoing restructuring. The United Nations Commission on International Trade Law (UNCITRAL) is one of such institutions. UNCITRAL notes that for a distressed firm to continue in operation, it is vitally important that it has "access to funds to enable it to continue to pay for crucial supplies of goods and services, including labor costs, insurance, rent, maintenance of contracts and other operating expenses, as well as costs associated with maintaining the value of [its] assets."[5] This further points to the importance of "new money" in the panoply of device that facilitate the successful restructuring of distressed firms.[6]

More recently, on a regional level, the European Union, through its proposed Directive on Preventive Restructuring Frameworks has also hinted at the importance of new financing to the successful restructuring of a distressed business. The proposal notes that "[the] success of a restructuring plan may often depend on whether there are financial resources in place to support first the operation of the business during restructuring negotiations and second the implementation of the restructuring plan after its confirmation."[7] In addition to lending credence to the importance of new financing to the restructuring process, the EU proposed Directive brings to the fore, the critical stages where a distressed business desirous of turning around its fortunes may require the infusion of new financing: as restructuring negotiations are underway, and as the plan of restructuring is to be implemented.[8]

The importance of new financing and the value it may bring to a distressed business is not just intuitive. It is supported by empirical research. Empirical studies suggest that new financing is key for the distressed debtor especially because it can have value enhancing effects given that it plays an important role in getting the distressed debtor back on its feet again. In the US, for instance, researchers following empirical research generally have this to be true. Maria Carapeto following empirical investigation found that new financing for distressed corporate borrowers undergoing formal restructuring provided a greater chance of their successful restructuring.[9] On their part, Dahiya et al. found that firms which received new financing in the course of commencing their formal restructuring spent less time in resolving their filings, and in making a decision whether to restructure or alternatively, liquidate the firm.[10] For firms that go on to restructure, the authors found that they spent much less time restructuring than those that did not have access to new financing.[11]

Henoch (1991) ("... without financing to keep the debtor-in-possession (DIP) in business, the company will, in all probability, fail quickly.").

[5] UNCITRAL Legislative Guide on Insolvency Law (2005).

[6] See for instance, Triantis (1993) (noting that that in the US, debtor financing in the context of the Bankruptcy Code is one major motivation for formal restructuring in the US). See also Chap. 3, on the key requirements of a restructuring regime.

[7] See Proposal for a Directive on Preventive Restructuring Frameworks (2016).

[8] See Sect. 1.5.3 below.

[9] See also Carapeto (2003).

[10] Dahiya et al. (2003).

[11] Ibid.

1.1 The Aim of the Book: New Financing as Component of Restructuring Regimes, Lender Capture and the Distress Debt Market

In the light of the important place of new financing to the restructuring process, as well as the increased attention on the subject, this book addresses the interrelated questions of the place of new financing as a component of the restructuring regime. In general terms, it also addresses, how statutory interventions and the courts may create a balance in respect of contentious issues that arise from the provision of new financing whether through new financing agreements, or through distressed debt investors' participation in the restructuring process.

This research and the approach adopted is timely, for three cogent reasons. First, in the last two decades, there appears to be a resurgence in the need for reform of bankruptcy laws across several jurisdictions.[12] Law reform commissions, policy and lawmakers in countries and regional blocs have revived the discourse on improving on, or enacting bankruptcy legislations with restructuring designs that cater to the needs of financially distressed businesses and their stakeholders. This may be attributable to various reasons, chief amongst which may be regulatory competition,[13] what may be described as keeping up with international best practices,[14] or the fallout of global financial crises. Regarding the last, it has been argued and one may tend to agree, that times of widespread financial distress provide opportune moments for the reform of the restructuring component of bankruptcy laws.[15] Given the key

[12] This book adopts the term bankruptcy law to generally refer to the procedure otherwise known elsewhere as corporate insolvency law. Bankruptcy is here used as the American co-equivalent of (corporate) insolvency law in England and Wales and company insolvency also in German law. Presently and by virtue of legislation, the term "bankruptcy law" in the US properly covers both creditor and debtor relief of both the individual and corporate debtor and are governed by the US Bankruptcy Code, 1978. -Tabb (1997). In terms of statutory regulation, German law (*Insolvenzordnung, InsO*) provides for a uniform procedure applying to both companies and the individual and so corporate bankruptcy, when used in this book refers to German company insolvency. Historically, insolvency law in England and Wales has developed "parallel" systems in the regulation of individual and corporate insolvency. Thus, while the term "bankruptcy" is used for the insolvent individual, the insolvency of legal persons (companies) is generally termed corporate insolvency. See generally, Tolmie (2003) and Finch (2009).

[13] See for instance, Bork (2012) ("[t]he German reform debate in particular has been shaped by unfavorable comparison with foreign regulatory frameworks, especially because many states provide for separate restructuring procedures that either engage sooner than or can operate parallel to insolvency proceedings focused on liquidation").

[14] For instance, in the summary of World Bank's *Resolving Insolvency Reforms BY Economy from 2008–2018*, there appears to be an increase in the number of jurisdictions with reform of business restructuring regimes in their insolvency legislations. See World Bank Doing Business (2018).

[15] Westbrook (1999) (noting the growing connection between world concerns about restructuring and the awareness that globalization can lead to the distress of businesses that may be otherwise fundamentally sound). See also Cirmizi et al. (2012) (noting that in times of financial crises, "policymakers have responded in part by shifting their attention to the effectiveness of current bankruptcy laws and their role as a key mechanism in addressing widespread firm-level financial distress.").

importance of new financing to the process of restructuring, and a growing list of countries with legislation tying new financing to their formal restructuring regime,[16] a research that undertakes an analysis of the approaches to the question of incentivizing new financing as part of the restructuring regime remains critically important.

Secondly, as one considers the need (or otherwise) of creating incentives for new financing to support formal restructuring frameworks, it is also equally important that account is taken, of the phenomenon of lender capture. Today's market is ruled much more by the dictates of prudence, so that even in relationship lending, the relationship is underpinned by profit maximization. In addition, for the prudent lender, it is no doubt ordinarily counterintuitive to invest (or a prudent pre-distress lender to invest more) money in a distressed business. Investors and scholars appreciate the dangers of providing new money to distressed businesses. This is so especially if it comes on the heels of an initial failure.[17] Yet, the pertinent question is, how far, and to what extent will the law concede to the use of new financing to capture the restructuring process? One way of analyzing this question is by examining **lender capture** (especially by pre-distress lenders) through the terms of new financing agreements and how they may impact the restructuring of the distressed business and its other stakeholders.

Thirdly, one of the fallouts of the financial distress of businesses is that it is increasingly revealing the concerns that the current architecture of bank lending may no longer be suitable for the facilitation of new financing and the support of restructuring.[18] The constraints which traditional lenders now face, mean that policymakers who are desirous of advancing a policy that helps distressed businesses successfully restructure may also pay attention to the growth of the distressed debt market for two particularly cogent reasons. First, because of the globalization of the market.[19] Although the origin of the distressed debt market is traceable to the US, and the specific effects of the US formal restructuring regime, today their relevance and strategy transcend borders and appear to adapt to the legal environment in which they find themselves.[20] This means that as more distress opportunities exist, the more the distressed debt market players become relevant in countries where they operate. The second reason for which it makes sense to study the distressed debt market touches on its role as a source of new financing for restructuring distressed businesses through its strategy of providing financing (loan-to-own) and the rather conflicting signals which their involvement in distressed businesses gives, in terms of value for the stakeholders.[21]

---

[16] See Sect. 1.2.1 below.

[17] Moore (1991) ("After all, [the distressed debtors] have failed to meet their commitments to existing creditors."); Wolf (2016) (noting that creditors generally do not trust debtors who are often generally considered to have been responsible for the failure in the first place).

[18] Bank lending architecture here refers to the intermediation role for which traditional lenders are known. See Chap. 2, Sect. 2.6.2.1.

[19] Flood (2001).

[20] Harner (2008).

[21] See Sect. 1.2.3.

In the light of the foregoing, the book builds around literature that captures restructuring regimes and the key prerequisites for a restructuring regime, as well as the propriety or otherwise of a financing incentivizing component as part of that regime. It also examines the lender capture phenomenon, especially as it ties into the role of providers of new financing, through their financing agreements. Finally, the literature takes on the role of the distressed debt market as a source of new financing for distressed borrowers and the matters arising therefrom.

1.2 About the Literature: Approaches to Incentivizing New Financing, Lender Capture and the Role of the Distressed Debt Market

Given the growing awareness regarding what may be contained in the design of restructuring regimes, one may easily see a pattern that suggests certain key requirements for the facilitation of restructuring. It is thus required that the distressed business is provided a breathing spell from creditor enforcement, the preparation of a restructuring plan, a means of binding the creditors to the restructuring plan in a manner that does not unfairly prejudice them, and a determination on the management of the borrower during the period of restructuring.[22] Most jurisdictions agree and work around including these requirements in their restructuring regimes.[23] What appears to be more contentious is the financing component i.e. how facilitating new financing as part of the restructuring regime is to be provided for. The state of the literature on the new financing component, lender capture and the role of the distressed debt market is now examined below.

1.2.1 Approaches to Incentivizing New Lending

From the literature, one may broadly classify statutory incentivization of new financing as part of the formal restructuring regime into two. Some jurisdictions have opted for a statutory detailing of incentives to attract new money financers for the distressed business (addressed in this book as **a prescriptive approach**). In other jurisdictions, there has not been much enthusiasm in expressly spelling out in detail the terms of the incentives to attract new money financing in the course of a formal restructuring. The approach has been instead to leave the legislative regime that makes possible to either imply the incentive in some cases or leaves to the market players the decision to provide financing or allow new lenders incentives to

[22] These key elements are exhaustively examined in Chap. 3.

[23] This is also applicable to informal restructuring regimes. See also Chap. 3.

provide the financing in other cases (addressed in this book as **a market-based approach**).

The US presents an example of a jurisdiction with a statutorily prescribed super-priority framework, designed to incentivize new financing for the distressed business. The drafter of Chapter 11 of the US Bankruptcy Code has statutorily expressed new lending incentives, the nature of protections afforded pre-distress lenders in view of the disruption of pre-distress rights arising from the incentives, as well as the grounds on which the court may begin to consider a case for approving the incentives for this provider of new financing.[24] Put in other words (and as adopted in this book), the US takes a **prescriptive approach** to incentivizing new financing. Apart from the US, it is important to note that a growing number of countries are already adopting this path of a prescriptive approach to new financing, albeit with varying nuances in a bid to balance the competing stakeholder interests that arise from the design of this incentive structure.[25]

Scholars who appear to advocate the prescriptive approach and the use of incentives are predominantly from the US, given that the prescriptive approach has its origins in the US. For instance, **Charles J. Tabb** considers these incentives as inducements and points out what now appears to be common knowledge, that such inducements are considered "necessary to overcome the typical hesitancy of creditors to extend credit or loan money to debtors [undergoing restructuring]".[26] One may ask how effective the prescriptive approach and its heightened incentivizing component has been in truly incentivizing distressed lending. The answer is positive, as the literature suggest. For instance, **Marshall Heubner**, points to the logicality of such a prescriptive regime, noting further that by virtue of the prescriptive incentive structure epitomized by the US formal restructuring regime, new money financing to distressed debtors may well be the safest loans provided in a troubled industry.[27] On his part, **David Skeel, Jr**. notes that the prescribed "generous terms" offered to new financers is instrumental to the stimulating effect on lending to

---

[24] See for instance, Baiser and Epstein (1992) ("To counter the understandable reluctance of financial institutions to lend to Chapter 11 debtors, section 364 of the [Bankruptcy] Code provides incentives to lenders to provide financing to borrowers who are the subject of bankruptcy cases.").

[25] See for instance:

i. Canada: See generally, Sarra (2013).
ii. South Africa: See generally, Calitz and Freebody (2016).
iii. Brazil. See Benes and Filho (2009).
iv. Spain: Pallares (2012).
v. Italy: Gallagher and Lombardo (2013).
vi. Singapore: Rajah (2017).

[26] Tabb (1986). See also, Baiser and Epstein (1992) ("To counter the understandable reluctance of financial institutions to lend to Chapter 11 debtors, section 364 of the [Bankruptcy] Code provides incentives to lenders to provide financing to borrowers who are the subject of bankruptcy cases.").

[27] Heubner (2005).

"cash-starved debtors".[28] As a matter of fact, this legislative approach in the US saw the emergence of a dedicated market that lived off of the incentives created by the law in financing formal restructurings.[29]

All other jurisdictions which lie outside the prescriptive approach may be classified as market-based. This is the default approach to addressing new financing for distressed businesses. It therefore may explain why more countries are likely to fall into this category. In some national restructuring regimes, the approach appears to be to leave the question of new financing to be reviewed by transaction avoidance regimes. This, according to **Rolef de Weijs** and **Meren Baltjes** has been the prevailing approach in Europe.[30] This perhaps may explain the initial approach in the EU reflected in its Recommendation taken by which it sought to protect new financing through the same rules.[31] This approach that relies on transaction avoidance rules is criticized in this book, it is argued that new priorities better serve as incentives.[32]

The literature appears to recognize what may be considered as an **implied prescriptive approach**. Some authors imply the creation of new financing from the reading of the statute. In the UK for instance, **Gerard McCormack** notes that the UK Enterprise Act does not expressly address questions of incentivizing new money financing for the distressed corporate debtor.[33] He argues, however, that this fact notwithstanding, the administration procedure (restructuring mechanism[34]) addresses the incentive question impliedly. He situates this within the powers allowed the court (or party appointed) insolvency practitioner (administrator), akin to that exercisable by the directors of the distressed debtor. These powers will typically include the powers to borrow money and create security over the interests of the distressed debtor.[35] Germany presents another example. Reinhard Bork argues that under the German InsO, it is possible for a provider of a new line of credit to the distressed borrower in a formal restructuring to enjoy a level of priority in a

[28] Skeel (2004). See also Rizzi (1991) ("New postpetition lenders can earn attractive returns from relatively secure assets and participate in a growing market").

[29] AFME, Frontier Economics and Weil, Gotshal and Manges LLP (2016) ("A specialised market has evolved in the U.S. for this sort of rescue funding."); Darla D. Moore who was managing director in the corporate finance division's restructuring and reorganization group at Chemical Bank, where she was in charge of distressed financing in Chapter 11 noted as follows: "We at Chemical have worked in this business [distressed borrower financing] for more than five years, building a specialty in Chapter 11 financing as a third party. In other words, we approach the market as a new business opportunity and typically have no existing exposure to the debtor." See Moore (1991).

[30] Weijs and Baltjes (2018).

[31] See EU Recommendation on A New Approach to Business Failure and Insolvency (2014).

[32] See Chap. 4, Sect. 4.3.

[33] McCormack (2008).

[34] For a contrary opinion, see Goode (2011) (noting that an administration is not necessarily a restructuring procedure, and when a restructuring is to be facilitated in the UK, it is done through procedures such as a Company Voluntary Arrangement (CVA), or a Scheme of Arrangement).

[35] McCormack (2008).

subsequent insolvency proceeding.[36] This he notes however, will require the lender with priority to open the subsequent insolvency proceeding. He further notes that in practice, the protection does not account for much.[37] Leo Plank et al note the lack of clarity in the German formal restructuring framework on the status of new money financers.[38] Given that this implied prescriptive approach is not quite clear by way of being expressed in statute, the book will stick with the **prescriptive** and **market-based approaches**, treating the implied prescriptive approach as a market-based approach.

In defense of the market-based approach, there have been arguments which support the approach. There is a strand of the literature which show concern that the **prescriptive** vs. **market-based** approaches and the preference for one over the other, may be indicative of expectation of reform proponents that reform which tracks US formal restructuring will yield similar results as in the US. Thus for instance, on whether there is any need for any form of uniformity in the approaches to incentivizing new financing for distressed businesses, McCormack draws attention to what appears to be a systematic nudge by international institutions such as the World Bank (through its doing business reporting) in the direction of the prescriptive approach.[39] He points out that reforms touching on the approach to incentivizing new financing both in terms of the prescriptive vs. market-based approach, as well as the use of priorities must necessarily take into account, "the business culture and the economic environment" of the specific jurisdiction.[40] McCormack's arguments, is instructive as well, given that mere legal transplants shorn from the context of the law may not yield the expected results. However, somewhat curiously, McCormack gives an indication of his preference for the market-based approach, when he points out that: "[t]he decision whether or not to lend to a distressed business and on what terms, is a business judgment that maybe best left to the market."[41] One may even add that McCormack's position does not necessarily exclude the possibility of a market-based approach that is equally supported by prescriptive rules. Similarly, **Jennifer Payne & Janis Sarra** commenting on the UK also suggest that in practice, the market-based approach has worked well in the

---

[36] Bork (2012).

[37] Id ("This protection [of priority] … in practice … appears not to play any major role.").

[38] Plank et al. (2012).

[39] McCormack (2017a, b). To buttress the point, McCormack quotes the 2017 Doing Business Report as follows:

> Whether post-commencement finance receives priority over ordinary unsecured creditors during distribution of assets. A score of 1 is assigned if yes; 0.5 if post-commencement finance is granted superpriority over all creditors, secured and unsecured; 0 if no priority is granted to post-commencement finance or if the law contains no provisions on this subject.

See Doing Business 2017: Equal Opportunity for All (2017).

[40] Id.

[41] Id.

UK, as lenders (especially pre-distress lenders) who consider the distressed borrower viable will generally provide new financing for them.[42] Some other authors like **Weijs** and **Baltjes** have argued that if at all the prescriptive approach is with heightened priority for new lenders will be adopted, such priority ought to be limited to new security against new money.[43] However, this argument mirrors a much earlier argument made by Professor **George Triantis**, who making a law and economics argument proposed the limitation of new lender priority to the value created by the financing provided.[44] His proposal like that made by Weijs and Baltjes, seeks to tie new financing to the projects which they support, in terms of project financing.[45] However, it is not in every case that new financing is used to execute projects over which the new lender may take a security interest. The financing may serve more mundane purposes like meeting the expenses of the operating expenses of the business. Herein lies the limitation of that proposal.

If the market-based approach is considered to be appropriate as **McCormack** suggests, it appears that proponents of the market-based approach leave out the possibilities that in the cases of small and medium businesses (SMEs) faced with strategic behavior on the part of a pre-distress controlling lenders who already hold security interest over all of the assets of the distressed borrower. This book therefore extends the literature by arguing that market-based approaches may be limited by situations where a strong lender can decide the fate of a distressed borrower, absent prescriptive incentives that may encourage participation of new lenders. Also, in the specific context of Nigeria where there is scant literature on how new financing may be approached, the book makes a case for a prescriptive approach to new financing, with heightened priority for providers of new financing.

1.2.2 Lender Capture Through New Financing

On the lender capture phenomenon, new financing provides motivation for the providers of new financing to intervene with the restructuring process in ways that may advance their interest ahead of that of other stakeholders of the distressed borrower. This has been described by some authors as lender opportunism,[46] and as a highjack of the restructuring process.[47] The new financing agreement and its terms indicate this. In the first place, the literature identifies what may be considered as non-contentious terms.[48] There are however more contentious terms. These provisions in

---

[42] Payne and Sarra (2017).

[43] Weijs and Baltjes (2018).

[44] Triantis (1993).

[45] Id.

[46] Weijs and Baltjes (2018).

[47] See Kuney (2005).

[48] These include (1) increased interest margins chargeable on the loan to the distressed business; (2) affirmative covenants on periodic disclosure; (3) negative covenants which identifies and restricts

the financing agreement have the potential to interfere with the chances of other stakeholders to recover their claims and firmly placing the control of the distressed business seeking to restructure in the hands of the provider of new financing.

These other contentious clauses have become quite a feature in many a financing agreement especially in the US. Some authors have focused on those clauses that interfere with the recovery of other creditors, while others have reflected on the control of the restructuring process especially by pre-distress secured creditors. Regarding the first category, the earliest authors to critically analyze one of such clauses (cross-collateralization) is **Charles J. Tabb**, who, drawing on judicial opinions highlight the weaknesses of arguments supporting cross-collateralization.[49] **Mark Roe** and **Frederick Tung** have focused on how pre-distress lenders have convinced US courts to approve the use of another such clause (i.e. the roll-up) clause.[50] Beyond the cross-collateralization clause, other clauses have also been relied upon by providers of new financing.[51] This book provides a broader view which includes those other clauses in the critical analysis. Regarding the second category suggesting the use of financing agreement to gain control over the restructuring process, **David Skeel Jr**. specifically identifies how new lenders in the US exert control through new financing. **Miller & Waisman** also identify this control, decrying how it is changing the original purpose and design of the US formal restructuring regime.[52]

As the EU is looking to introduce new financing incentives, scholars have also raised concerns of possible capture of the restructuring process especially using such clauses.[53] One may also see such situations arising in other jurisdictions which

---

the use to which the loan is to be put; (4) elaborate covenants. See Squire (2016) (noting that the typical interest rate chargeable by distressed lenders is about 2 percentage points above the rate offered to non-distressed businesses.); Kuney (2005), p. 56 ("[t]he one feature that almost all forms of DIP financing share is an interest rate significantly higher than that of similar loans provided to non-debtors."); Kuney (2005), p. 52 (noting the use of affirmative covenants that require distressed borrower to "periodically disclose financial records and information so that the [new financer] can easily monitor the debtor's performance"). See also, Bussel and Klee (2009), p. 707 (the authors highlight some other conditions to which the new financing may be tied to include "releases, sale and reorganization timelines, use of collateral or priming, additional collateral grants, stipulated claims allowance, current payment of interest, … standard budgetary controls, and statutory adequate protection and priorities available to post-petition lenders"); see Chatterjee et al. (2004), p. 3111 ("…a majority of the loans have clauses clearly stating that the DIP loan cannot be used for investments in projects and is to be used primarily for working capital needs. Over 63% of the sample restricts the use of proceeds to working capital needs…"). Note that the use of such covenants is not only restricted to new lending in the US. For similar covenants and more, see Wood (2007), pp. 675–676.

[49] Tabb (1986).

[50] Roe and Tung (2013), p. 1238.

[51] Some of these clauses are examined in detail in Chap. 5 of this book.

[52] Miller and Waisman (2007), p. 175; Miller and Waisman (2004), p. 185.

[53] Weijs and Baltjes (2018), p. 228 (on the chances opportunistic use of new financing agreements by pre-distress lenders in Europe).

opt for the prescriptive approach to incentivizing new financing. However, given the differences between the restructuring regimes in the US and European jurisdictions like the UK and Germany, it makes sense to examine how new financing concerns (both in terms of clauses that overreach other creditors, as well as lender control clauses) are dealt with in these jurisdictions. **McCormack**,[54] and lately, **Weijs & Baltjes**[55] have helped shed light on these issues in the European context.

Given that the seeming statutory silence on the legality or otherwise of these clauses, the theoretical justifications which underpin reliance on them require critical examination. In the same vein, the enhanced control of lenders also requires balancing, to the extent that it results in value diversion from other stakeholders to the lender.

1.2.3 On the Role of the Distressed Debt Market in Financing and Restructuring

Given the focus of the book on distressed debt investors as providers of financing for the distressed business, the literature focused upon are those that situate distressed debt investors in this role. Authors have also shown their misgivings with the involvement of distressed debt investors in the restructuring of distressed businesses, focusing on their control and short-term approach. For instance, Harvey Miller expresses reservation on the involvement of distressed debt investors, in view of the effect of their control and its likely effect on both the debtor and its other stakeholders. For Miller, the formal restructuring process of the US appear to be "mortally wounded" by several factors which includes the rise of investors who are financially focused and have only a short-term objective.[56] Besides, given that distressed debt investors appear to be financially focused, their control of the restructuring process makes them less suited to "make optimal decision on behalf of the stakeholders."[57]

Consequently, Miller and Waisman advocate the imperatives of a formal restructuring regime that affords the borrower an opportunity for rehabilitation in the interest of all of its stakeholders, rather than for "a group of sophisticated, aggressive lenders and speculative investors."[58] By way of commentary, it would appear that Miller and Waisman's position is largely backed by anecdotal evidence, as the authors do not rely on much provide empirical support for this claim. On the other hand, Michelle M. Harner, Jamie Marincic Griffin and Jennifer Ivey-Crickenberger relying on empirical data provide at least some support for the position of Miller

[54] McCormack (2008), p. 205 ff.

[55] Weijs and Baltjes (2018).

[56] Miller (2007), p. 391.

[57] Miller and Waisman (2007), p. 175.

[58] Ibid, p. 180.

and Waisman by casting doubts on the value enhancing "credentials" of distressed debt investment in restructuring firms.[59] They concludes that it is not exactly easy to concretely determine whether the involvement of distressed debt investors in the restructuring process is positively or negatively associated with value.[60] In other words, as far as it pertains to the creation of value by distressed debt investors, perceptions differ along the lines of the position of stakeholders in the capital structure of the distressed business.

Early on, Harner identified distressed debt investors as comparable to the corporate raiders who ruled the US corporate space in the 1980s only that this time, they do so with debt rather than equity and in the context of distressed businesses desirous of restructuring and in need of new financing.[61] Their involvement she notes, may result in "a restructuring that undervalues the company to the direct detriment of junior creditors and shareholders,"[62] as these investors seek to generate returns not through the interest or principal on the debt which they hold, but through eventual ownership of the distressed business.[63] Instructively, Harner does not however discountenance the key contribution of these investors which are capable of enriching the governance of the distressed businesses as they emerge from distress. Indeed, the dilemma now becomes how to balance the "liquidity, discipline, and accountability attributes" for which these investors are reputed, against the potential downsides that may result from their presence in the capital structure of the distressed business.[64]

For many other authors, distressed debt investors are considered to provide value for restructuring distressed debtors. One of the earliest research endeavors on the role of distressed debt investors in the restructuring of financially distressed firms was carried out by Edith Hotchkiss and Robert Mooradian, investigating the influence of distressed debt investors on the operations performance of selected US distressed firms that emerged from formal restructuring.[65] The result of their data showed that following emergence from the restructuring process, about 60% of the firms which had distressed debt investors in their capital structure either as debtholders or equity financers emerged with higher operations performance, compared to the period when the investors gained control.[66] In sum, the authors found that distressed debt investors can play value-enhancing role for the distressed business "through their activity in management of the restructured firm."[67]

[59] See Harner et al. (2014), pp. 167–194.

[60] Ibid, p. 193.

[61] Harner (2011), p. 160 (noting that these investors are borrowing tactics from the corporate raiders of the 1980s).

[62] Ibid, p. 163.

[63] Ibid, p. 165.

[64] Ibid, p. 163.

[65] See Hotchkiss and Mooradian (1997), pp. 401–432.

[66] Ibid, p. 403.

[67] Ibid, p. 427.

With a focus on the provision of new financing for distressed business undergoing a restructuring, authors have also identified their critical role as providers of new financing and the benefits that arise from the alignment of the interests of the investors with that of profit maximization of the distressed business. On this point, Paul Goldschmid links the control of the distressed business and the provision of new financing by the distressed debt investor, to the maximization of long-run profit for the distressed business. This, the author argues, is because the investors are "efficiently motivated to deploy DIP loans to maximize firm wealth."[68] As proof of this assertion, Goldschmid points to the willingness of distressed debt investors to convert the restructuring financing provided to the debtor to an equity stake in the distressed business post-restructuring.[69] The result is an alignment of the interest of the investor with the maximization of profit in the distressed business. Daniel Kamensky also suggests that distressed debt investors play an important role in the provision of new financing for the distressed business, especially in times of volatility, while also "creating efficiencies" in the process of restructuring, and "improv[ing] active, productive negotiations that are critical to maximizing value" in the distressed business.[70]

Despite these divergent positions, it does appear that distressed debt investors may well have a salutary effect on the distressed business or may cause the diversion or even the destruction of value in the distressed business. Authors like Richard D. Thomas suggest that it is important for the US formal restructuring regime to be reworked so that "predatory" investor behavior is nipped, while the positive aspect of distressed investor involvement can be preserved.[71] While reform efforts are still being considered and the influence of distressed debt investment continues to expand beyond the shores of the US, the critical question becomes whether to exclude distressed debt investors from a borrower's capital structure, for fear of the possible negative effects of their participation as some private borrowers tend to do contractually. The consequence of such exclusion may well deprive the distressed business of a potential source of new financing which can be provided by the investor. In the light of the foregoing, this book explores what critical role the courts can play in balancing distress debt investor self-interest against the state policy on restructuring of financially distressed businesses.

One will readily see that most of the academic work on the distressed debt market have been written by US scholars, often about the US market. This ought not be very surprising as again; the market has its origins in the US. However, the reader might be mistaken to think of the market as purely a US problem as there continues to be a growing presence of the market outside of the US, with investors seeking

[68] Goldschmid (2005), p. 225.

[69] Id.

[70] Kamensky (2014), pp. 236–237.

[71] Thomas (2010), p. 244 ("Creditors have evolved, becoming more sophisticated and more adept at finding ways to minimize risk and maximize profit from corporate failures; meanwhile, the forum and tools available to the debtor remained unchanged.").

opportunities farther afield even into frontier markets.[72] As Harner points out, although the market has its origins in the US and grew under the Chapter 11 of the US Bankruptcy Code, being the formal restructuring regime in the US, what we see today is a market that is developing outside of that restructuring regime.[73] Harner came to this conclusion following her investigation of the role distressed debt investors in the UK and the US, noting that in spite of the differences in the restructuring regimes of both countries, they are beginning to play an important role in restructuring in both jurisdictions.[74] Sarah Paterson has also highlighted the involvement of distressed debt investors in the UK, highlighting their frontline role in financing and participating the restructuring.[75]

At least as the book will show, English courts have been faced with formal restructuring proceedings in which distressed debt investors have been active participants. This points inexorably to the fact that the regulatory framework in formal restructuring may well not have been designed to expressly manage the possible value destructive tendencies that may be orchestrated by distressed debt investors. As its contribution to knowledge, the book proposes a rule that may be applied by courts when faced with the task of balancing between the financing and ancillary value enhancement role of distressed debt investors against the value destructive tendencies that may result from their involvement.

1.3 Choice of Jurisdictions: Rationale

The primary jurisdictions analysed in this book are the US, UK, and Germany. Lessons are however drawn for jurisdictions in the frontier market that are similar to Nigeria. In the recent past, many developed economies which were hitherto characterised as 'creditor-friendly' have taken incremental steps towards business restructuring (where feasible) by way of changes to their bankruptcy legislation. These changes follow the broad contours of the US Chapter 11 framework. Chapter 11 of the US Bankruptcy Code provides the framework within which distressed firms restructure.[76] As a piece of legislation, it has influenced reform of commercial laws around the world where lawmakers are desirous of promoting restructuring of distressed businesses.[77] As has been pointed out, a rationale for these changes is to

---

[72] See for instance, Beverini and Cova (2006), p. 12 (But as hedge funds increase their positions [in the US], the returns are diminishing. So, several funds have opened European offices, mainly in London, Paris and Frankfurt, or started looking for investment opportunities in Europe directly from their US headquarters").

[73] See Flood (2001) and Harner (2008).

[74] Id.

[75] Paterson (2015), p. 708.

[76] Weiss and Wruck (1998), p. 57 ("Chapter 11 of the U.S. bankruptcy code defines the rules by which a distressed firm's stakeholders renegotiate their claims.").

[77] Warren and Westbrook (2009), p. 604 ("So powerful is the idea of [restructuring] that Chapter 11 has heavily influenced commercial law reform throughout the world.").

allow for ease in the implementation of formal corporate restructuring loans, by introducing elements such as superpriority financing.[78] Specifically, on the issue of new financing for the distressed business, it bears restating that developments in the US, both statutorily and in terms practical changes in the financing market continue to shape and influence statutory changes (or deliberations for statutory changes) and financing practices elsewhere in the world.

The choice of UK law is informed by a two-fold consideration. The first is that UK law affords one of the leading systems of transactional law, especially as it hosts one of the world's leading financial centers and arguably the most-restructuring-friendly jurisdiction in Europe. The flexibility of English common law and the commercial pragmatism of the English courts has seen the migration of several distressed businesses in the direction of the UK for the purpose of effecting debt restructuring.[79] In the course of this research, the UK voted to exit from the European Union (EU).[80] Since then, the government has commenced, and is negotiating exit procedures from the EU.[81] While it is not clear how much role English courts will continue to play in the restructuring of European companies,[82] it can be argued that at least so far as financing agreements continue to be governed by English law, and the reputation of the UK remains as a tested and trusted "financial restructuring destination", we may well continue to see its dominance.

The second reason is that as will be seen in this book, the UK presents a well-debated contrast to the US in terms of incentivizing new financing through priority creation. In addition, the UK, when compared to other jurisdictions, presents a menu of corporate restructuring options, from which distressed debtors may choose to pursue a financial restructuring. Although corporate bankruptcy law serves as the

---

78 Gudgeon and Joshi (2013), p. 8.

79 Mallon and Waisman (2011). The "restructuring-friendly" nature of the English jurisdiction has seen the migration of several EU companies to that jurisdiction, to take advantage of the restructuring regime. In some cases, the distressed companies changed their Center of Main Interest (COMI), e.g. the German companies Deutsche Nickel and Schefenacker to restructure using an English Company Voluntary Agreement (CVA). In some other cases, the English courts have assumed jurisdiction based on the governing law of the financing facility agreement. See for instance *Apcoa Parking Holdings GmbH & Ors* [2014] EWHC 1867 (Ch). Still, in some other cases, companies have changed their COMI as well as the governing law of the financing agreement, in order to benefit from the "restructuring friendly" UK regime. See for instance, *In re DTEK Finance BV* [2015] EWHC 1164 (Ch). See also, McCormack (2009), p. 180 (citing the difficulty in the use of debt-equity swaps under the extant German law, author notes that "[a] debt for equity swap under German law encounters "holdout" problems which can be overcome in the UK restructuring environment through making use of a CVA which allows a 75% majority of creditors to bind the minority.") Although German law has since been reformed, the UK remains an important restructuring jurisdiction.

80 The Brexit referendum held on 23 Jun 2016.

81 The government started this process by triggering Article 50 of the Lisbon Treaty. The UK is expected to leave the EU after March 2019, whether or not there is an agreement between the UK and the EU. See generally, Brexit: Article 50 has been triggered—what now? (29 Mar. 2017). In: BBC News. Available at https://www.bbc.com/news/uk-politics-39143978. Accessed 27 Jun 2018.

82 See generally, Fletcher (2017), p. 1032 (noting that "the outcome of the relationship between the UK and the EU after March 2019, is likely to remain unclear for a considerable time.").

cornerstone of many a restructuring procedure, the UK, in addition to options afforded under Insolvency Act (IA) 1986, provides for other non-comprehensive regimes that enable the successful restructuring of the distressed debtor. Examining the financing component of these regimes is particularly important for jurisdictions which desire to model their restructuring regime in such a way that provides multiple pathways to financial restructuring.

Germany, on the other hand, is a leading and developed market economy with a civil law orientation. Apart from being Europe's number one economy, it is also a model civil law jurisdiction. Although it belongs to a different legal family (i.e. civil law), its approach to distressed debtor financing may well provide useful insights, given the progress it has made with its formal restructuring efforts. The jurisdiction has been variously characterized as being very "creditor friendly" and its reputation for bankruptcy stigmatization is a reality with which many other jurisdictions can very well relate.[83] First its approach to the reform of its business bankruptcy regime combined with the bankruptcy stigma can provide useful lessons for jurisdictions which equally show high bankruptcy stigma and desire to provide for restructuring through their bankruptcy regimes. Secondly, being a largely bank-based system, its approach to the provision of new lending will provide some lessons, especially given its progressive and deliberate adaptation of bits and pieces of re-organization ingredients—for which the US Bankruptcy law is known—into her insolvency legislation.

Many frontier markets are characterized by their low liquidity, immature capital market,[84] as well as their low market capitalization,[85] and unpredictable restructuring regimes.[86] This has implications for distressed businesses operating within such markets. When businesses undergo strain, they have limited options when sourcing new financing. In addition, whether the distressed business survives through the distress is a function of the disposition of the lender towards the restructuring of the debtor, coupled with the regulatory constraints such lenders face. The traditional lenders who typically provide financing in this market may not be able to provide

[83] This is not to say that this stigma may not play a role in common law countries, compared to them, Germany is often considered "a paradigm". Tajti (2018) (on bankruptcy stigma and its negative impact on the restructuring policy); Bork (2012) at para 2.12, 24.

[84] The "frontier market" classification of certain developing economies is a somewhat recent classification applicable to certain countries with certain features which include high economic growth rates, but with small and relatively illiquid stock markets. They represent developing countries with high rates of economic growth but small and relatively illiquid stock markets. These markets are often at an early stage of development and have attracted attention due to their diversification opportunities and growth potential. Frontier Market securities tend to be more thinly traded than their Developed and even Emerging Market counterparts. Currently, about 26 countries fall within this categorization. See the Financial Times Stock Exchange (FTSE) Russel (Sept 2014).

[85] See FT, Definition of Frontier Market. Available at <http://lexicon.ft.com/Term?term=frontier-markets> accessed 18 Aug 2015 ("a frontier market is considered to have lower market capitalization and less liquidity than many emerging markets.").

[86] This is a problem not just for frontier markets but also for many emerging markets. See Wielebinski (2017) ("The one single factor that presents the most difficult challenge in addressing workouts and insolvencies in emerging markets is the lack of predictability.").

the financing required by the debtor to steer itself away from troubled waters, especially in situations where the lenders themselves are struggling with huge non-performing loans of their own.

Nigeria is used as a representation of frontier markets. Prior to its economic recession in 2016 and afterwards, businesses operating in Nigeria have faced multiple challenges. As a result, otherwise viable businesses face dire financial distress, leaving many in need of financing.[87] As businesses groan under this difficult business environment, investors continue to search for stable markets in which they can invest capital. This initial decision to invest is largely determined by the predictability of the law of the host country on issues like the enforcement of debt and an orderly distribution of assets in the event of default by the debtor.[88] As has been pointed out elsewhere, these sophisticated lenders will first consider countries with reformed insolvency legislations, which meet their desire of certainty and predictability.[89] Presently, the absence of a coherent and elaborate corporate restructuring framework with a robust debtor-financing component has bothered investors who are intent on investing in Nigerian distressed businesses.[90]

Nigeria's corporate bankruptcy law presently runs on the steam of the Companies and Allied Matters Act (CAMA).[91] In spite of efforts made in the revision of this flagship company legislation, two points may be made. The first is that the statute—as the name suggests—is a company law legislation and at the time of the enactment of the statute, the brief of the drafters did not specifically include corporate rescue. Given that the statute is essentially creditor and liquidation oriented, the rescue devices in the statute have only been adapted to serve such purposes.[92] Secondly, as much as the drafters tried to take Nigeria's peculiar circumstances into account,[93] there was a deliberate attempt by the draftsmen to retain the structural and conceptual framework of the extant British law at the time of the enactment. To this extent, it is understood that the legislation still substantially bears the relics of Nigeria's historic attachment to English law, which has since moved along.[94] The stunted

[87] Raval (2016); Cirmizi et al. (2012), p. 188.

[88] Lubben (2008).

[89] Uttamchandi (2004), p. 9.

[90] See Mundy (2010).

[91] This statute is contained in Cap C20, Laws of the Federation of Nigeria (LFN), 2004. It is available online at <http://www.nigeria-law.org/CompaniesAndAlliedMattersAct.htm> (accessed 7 Sept 2015).

[92] For an overview characterizing the receivership in CAMA as rescue oriented, see Adebola (2013).

[93] The Companies and Allied Matters Act Decree of 1990 was the result of a comprehensive review of Nigeria's company law by the Nigerian Law Reform Commission. A subsequent amendment was made in 2004 to facilitate the enactment of the Investment and Securities Decree. For a historical perspective on the enactment of this statute, see Id.

[94] Adeniran (2003), p. 293 ("the current [Nigerian] law on corporate reorganization … still smacks of antiquated nineteenth century British experimentation gone sore [sic].").

legislative advancement also means that the country has not taken part in the growing convergence in global restructuring.[95]

Presently, there are ongoing attempts to enact a corporate bankruptcy law legislation with a restructuring components.[96] In the same vein, attempts to amend CAMA to provide for a more "restructuring-friendly" regime is underway.[97] One of the tasks of this book is to examine the existing restructuring framework as well as the proposed reforms, to see how they meet the key requirements of restructuring, their failings, whilst drawing lessons and recommendations for the approach to the provision and incentivizing of new financing as a part of the restructuring regime.

1.4 Methodology: Choices and Limitations

Primarily, the book in the main employ comparative and analytical methods. Comparative in view of the number of jurisdictions whose approaches are examined and analytical, in view of the detailed study and critical evaluation of statutes, case law pertaining to subject areas of the book. Vital to the research is the predominantly qualitative methodology employed in the book. The qualitative method takes on a doctrinal analysis of these statutes, judicial pronouncements and decisions that have informed and shaped the jurisdictional disposition to the matters with which the book deals. Furthermore, as part of the doctrinal qualitative method, the book adopts a socio-legal approach in the examination of existing legal patterns touching on the subject area. In this sense, the book not only examines the law on the books,[98] but as much as possible, it considers the underlying debates, law reform documents and opinion of practitioners found both in law reform consultation materials and from expert publications on the subject areas including rationales that have informed changes in—and resistance to changes in—the law. In addition, the qualitative method of the book embraces theories in law and economics. Just to mention two examples, in the analysis that support the superpriority approach to new financing, the book relies on the debt overhang theory.[99] Also, in making a case for a prescriptive approach to new financing for distressed SMEs or single lender businesses, the book makes its argument relying on strategic illiquidity.[100] Both debt overhang and the strategic illiquidity are borrowed from the law and economics literature.

---

[95] Halliday and Carruthers (2007), p. 1136 (the authors in their seminal work suggest that the growing convergence in fields like corporate bankruptcy law is the result of the work of global institutions, supported by the US, who "are building an international financial architecture with law as a principal foundation.").

[96] Idigbe and Kalu (2015).

[97] See analysis in Chap. 3, Sect. 3.8.

[98] See Morris and Murphy (2011).

[99] See Chap. 4, Sect. 4.6.1.

[100] See Chap. 4, Sect 4.6.4.2.

To a very limited extent, the research incorporates some empirical elements. This essentially comprises unstructured interviews.[101] Although some of these informal interviews were made with academics and practitioners in Europe,[102] the more relevant interviews were with respondents from Nigeria.[103] For the Nigerian respondents that range from business owners, legal practitioners involved in corporate restructuring and some bank lenders, the purpose of the interviews were essentially to support information publicly available.[104] Furthermore, the interviews were undertaken to provide support for the analysis and proposal, especially relating to the argument supporting a prescriptive approach to incentivizing new financing, as part of the Nigerian formal restructuring regime. Furthermore, generally, the book relies on court cases and decisions as a source of empirical support.

A practical challenge encountered during the research touches on the differences in the three dominant legal systems analyzed in the book. Given the differences in the levels of advancement in restructuring and the exposition of black-letter law by the courts on the subject. It will appear that US court decisions dominate the discourse, and from the other end, less judicial decisions from Germany is discussed. This disparity owes not only to the fact that when compared to the other jurisdictions, restructuring in German law is still relatively recent, but also to the availability of quite few English language materials on German law restructuring. Also, as one will readily see from the sources (and as inevitably reflected in the book), German law is largely positivistic, in the sense of attachment to the text of statutes. There are however only few academic expositions and empirical research about new financing in the English language. Hence, the reader will typically find detailed analysis of US and sometimes UK decisions, but less of German empirical evidence and court decisions in the book.

One of the consequences arising from the comparative approach and interdisciplinary nature of the book, are certain terminologies that require clarification. The clarification is needed either because of jurisdictional nuances owing to the design of the relevant legal structures in the jurisdictions, or due to the technical nature of the book's subject area. Some key terms are now discussed below. The terms clarified in the next section do not exhaustively address all the terms used in the book. For the most part, an explanation of terms and their usage is provided where those terms are used in the book.

[101] Fontana and Frey (2005).

[102] For the practitioners, the interviews broadly related to how informal restructuring is carried out in practice, especially with dissenting financial lenders; how German companies in formal restructuring obtain financing and why new financing is not considered topical especially amongst professionals. For the academics, questions generally revolved around UK Insolvency Law Reform efforts, the scope of reform of the moratorium in the administration and the seeming general lack of enthusiasm for a prescriptive financing regime in the UK.

[103] Apart from the telephone conversations, most of the physical interviews were conducted from December 2017 to January 2018.

[104] This essentially included questions on access to financing, the challenges with the lending market, sale of loans to the Asset Management Corporation of Nigeria (AMCON), and other related issues.

1.5 Terminology Issues

1.5.1 Financial Distress and Restructuring

In this book, new financing for a financially distressed debtor is examined within the context of restructuring. Financial distress in this book refers specifically to the inability of the business to meet up with its current obligations, because of cashflow difficulties.[105] The cash flow difficulty in turn may well be because of the inappropriateness of the capital structure of the firm for its balance sheet. The rationale for this adjustment is the understanding that although the business has hit a rough patch, it still has viable operations, hence the need for intervention to save it from the impending fate of a liquidation.[106] A liquidation may result in the destruction of the going concern value of the business.[107] In turn, the destruction of the going concern value of the business will typically have detrimental consequences for not only the creditors of the financially distressed business, but also other interests such as "communities or purchasers" that benefit from the continuing existence of the distressed business.[108] Thus, a restructuring for such business may be the best option.

Theory and policy of restructuring have tended towards the consensus that when businesses are undergoing financial distress, the appropriate course to follow is the restructuring of the business, the alternative being an insolvent liquidation of the assets of the distressed entity or its business.[109] To be clear, this is not to suggest that

---

[105] Wruck (1990), p. 421; Roe and Tung (2016), p. 92 (suggesting that financial distress "can arise from the firm having borrowed too much. It does less well than expected, and it can't pay back its debts"). Such cash flow difficulty is sometimes considered as cash flow insolvency. Payne (2014), p. 188.

[106] Roe and Tung (2016), p. 92 (stating that some distressed "firms are economically worth continuing in business and should be saved from closing up because their operations are viable.").

[107] On the meaning of going concern value, see Levitin (2012), p. 1434 ("...the value of an enterprise above liquidation value or difference between the value of the whole enterprise and the sum of its parts.").

[108] Ibid. See also, Korobkin (1993), p. 554 ("[The] problem of financial distress affects virtually all persons in society... As a result, all persons in society should have representation in the choice of [insolvency law] principles.").

[109] Legislative policies tend in this direction. For instance, in the US, the legislative history of the Bankruptcy Code indicates that:

> The purpose of a business reorganization case, unlike a liquidation case, is to restructure a business's finances so that it may continue to operate, provide its employees with jobs, pay its creditors, and produce a return for its stockholders. ... It is more economically efficient to reorganize than to liquidate, because it preserves jobs and assets.

H.R. REP.NO. 95-595, at 220 (1977), reprinted in 1977 U.S.C.C.A.N. 5963, 6179.

See also Warren (1993), p. 355 (on the social and economic costs of liquidation authors argue that liquidation "affect employees who will lose jobs, taxing authorities that will lose ratable property, suppliers that will lose customers, nearby property owners who will lose beneficial neighbors, and current customers who must go elsewhere."); Lipson (2009), p. 1651 ("Chapter 11 negotiations are thus premised on the complex proposition that value can be maximized for all stakeholders in a debtor if the debtor is given reasonable opportunity to restructure its affairs.").

all distressed businesses deserve to, or indeed ought to be saved.[110] This explains the need to distinguish businesses that are deserving of being saved (or at least, an attempt at saving), from those, in which attempts at saving is tantamount to an exercise in futility. Remarkably, even making this distinction itself is not a precise science. However, there are telltale signs that may indicate financial distress from which further diagnosis can proceed.[111] These signs manifest in broken promises by the business borrower to their creditors, or when those promises are honored, they are honored with visible difficulties on the part of the distressed debtor.[112] In other cases, the difficulties of the distressed borrower could be something greater. It could be an indication of a more ominous sign that the corporate is not itself worthy of efforts at restructuring, and an orderly liquidation of its affairs would be more

---

Also, in the UK, similar sentiments have been echoed in the First Commission Report on Insolvency Law 1985. See generally, Hunter (1999) (on the rescue culture in the UK and what it entails). The same can be said for Germany, although it appears that liquidation and restructuring are somewhat considered co-equal in the resolution of financial distress. See Erster Bericht der Kommission für Insolvenzrecht 1985, Sentence 2.1.1, para. 1, 162 ("The aim of the restructuring is to ensure the survival of the debtor company and ensure sustainable profitability.") See also § 1 Abs. 1 InsO ("The insolvency proceedings shall serve the purpose of collective satisfaction of a debtor's creditors by liquidation of the debtor's assets and by distribution of the proceeds, or by reaching an arrangement in an insolvency plan, *particularly in order to maintain the enterprise*" [Emphasis supplied]).

[110] Gross (1994), p. 1033 (pointing out that rescuing the debtor does not imply attempting to rescue any and every business which have exceeded their useful life, making such attempt a sheer waste of time); Franks and Sussman (2005), p. 93 (noting that an assumption that liquidation is a bad outcome is "a strong and unrealistic assumption that biases the evaluation of a bankruptcy system … against procedure[s] like that of the UK which does not put a restriction on exercising contractual liquidation rights."); Eidenmuller (2013), p. 136 ("A business in financial distress should be kept alive only if it is economically viable"); McCormack (2017a, b), p. 173 ("Certainly not all 'business' that be saved.").

[111] On the major warning signs of financial distress, see Anderson and Fuhr (Oct 1994) cited in Harner et al., at 211 (fn 11). The signs are said to include:

> Declining net income; decreasing or inadequate margins; creditors unwilling to advance credit; loss of a major supplier with special credit terms; reduction in lines of credit; excessive receivables over 90 days; default on payment by a major customer; excessive payables unpaid over 90 days; inability to make timely deposits of trust funds such as employee withholding taxes; inability to service long-term debt requirements; excessive re-negotiation of broken loan covenants; unusual or extraordinary litigation and events not customarily encountered in the industry; loss of key financial officers or key personnel; cash management becoming a primary activity at the expense of traditional management functions; new long-term financing proceeds applied to pay off debts rather than acquisition of assets; poor record keeping or inadequate financial records, lack of basic controls, such as perpetual inventory record keeping; significant discrepancies between actual and projected results over the prior three years.

[112] Brealy et al. (2011), p. 447. Such visible difficulties may be in the nature of "technical defaults" manifested in the breach of debt covenants apart from those specifying the payment of interests and the principal debts. Such technical defaults may include defaults of tangible net worth ratios, default of interest cover (operating profit ratio to borrowing costs), etc. Wruck (1990), p. 421.

appropriate.[113] Those situations—aptly described as economic distress[114]—are cases where an orderly liquidation of the affairs of the corporate is particularly advocated.[115] Those situations are outside the remit of this book.

1.5.2 Choice of Restructuring Among Similar Terms

It is necessary that the readers understand the usage of the term restructuring in this book and the rationale for it. The choice of restructuring as against other similar terms such as "rescue" and "reorganization" is informed by two reasons. Firstly, the book settles for restructuring, given the uncertain nuances that attend the concept of "rescue", as understood in the UK for instance, and the concept of "reorganization" as provided for in the US, especially as it pertains to their expected outcomes.[116] As designed, the US reorganization regime sets out to not only rehabilitate the business of the distressed corporate, but in addition, help the corporate entity itself survive, and continue as a going concern.[117] Whether this dual goal is always achieved in practice is a different matter.[118]

In the same vein, the rescue concept started out in the UK as a concept focused on the rescue of the business of the distressed debtor. In this sense, the hiving-off of the viable portion of the distressed business and the transfer of that portion to another corporate entity, may well qualify as a rescue.[119] With the passage of the Enterprise Act, 2002, it would appear that the notion of rescue has transitioned to one where the default model is to see to the rescue of the entity. Instructively, however, it is arguable that this approach seems to be only reflected in formal restructuring procedures that are provided for in bankruptcy law. As will be shown, English

---

[113] See Baird (1998), pp. 581–582 (distinguishing financial distress from economic distress, the latter being candidates for a liquidation); Frisby (2004), p. 248 (noting that rescues need not be as of right hence the appropriate procedure for the "genuinely doomed" corporate is an immediate liquidation).

[114] When a business is economically distressed, it is an indication that its business plan is not working and has a flawed economic model. See McCormack (2008), p. 9.

[115] Payne (2014), p. 93 ("Where the company is economically distressed (so the net present worth of the business as a going concern is less than the total value of its assets, were they to be broken up and sold separately) then liquidation may be the only sensible option.").

[116] See Adebola (2014) (noting that traditionally, the anticipated outcome of Chapter 11 reorganization is the preservation of the distressed entity).

[117] LoPucki and Whitford describe these goals as "business survival" and "entity survival" respectively. See Lopucki and Whitford (1993), p. 599; see also Bork (2012), at para 1.28, 13 (noting that the process of corporate reorganization "achieves its goals when not only the business itself but also its holders are either restored to productivity or have averted their likely insolvency such that they can carry on at the head of the reorganized business.").

[118] Lopucki and Whitford (1993), p. 621 (in cases of large US corporates, the authors found that "… [s]ometimes the survival was in the same entity; sometimes it was as part of a sale to another company.").

[119] See generally, Frisby (2004).

law provides multiple restructuring pathways—some albeit formal, but outside of the confines of bankruptcy law—through which distressed corporates may resolve financial distress with their borrowers.[120] In those procedures, the focus is more on the negotiation and resolution of financial distress in ways that maximize value in the business, with less emphasis on the ownership of the business upon its emergence from distress.

In the case of Germany, not much is made of such idiosyncratic debates on the consequence of restructuring, i.e. whether the distressed entity continues to exist. Given the existing bankruptcy culture, the debate still largely turns on the choice between a liquidation and restructuring of distressed businesses. For this reason, it appears that a liquidation was considered to be as valuable as a restructuring, so that too much emphasis was not placed on restructuring.[121] In sum, the book as much as possible avoids an emphasis on the theoretical debates pertaining to the sale or otherwise of the business, as much as it is concerned with the financial restructuring of the business itself.

Secondly, restructuring is used as against reorganization. Reorganization is the term by which formal restructuring in the US is known. The danger of relying on reorganization may give the impression that informal restructuring regimes are excluded from the scope of the book. This may be misleading when we bear in mind that a restructuring may well be pursued through a formal restructuring procedure,[122] or through a consensual arrangement between the debtor and its relevant creditors out of court (informal procedure).[123] Therefore, the term restructuring represents a more neutral term than a reorganization which is mostly associated with Chapter 11 of the US Bankruptcy Code. Even more importantly, the expected outcome of the reorganization procedure in the US, is the restructuring of the distressed business,[124] further strengthening the case for the use of the term restructuring as against reorganization.

In the light of the foregoing, restructuring is used to mean a procedure (formal or informal)[125] that affords the reform of a financially distressed business, by taking care of its cash flow and balance sheet difficulties, thereby restoring its productivity and competitiveness, whether or not this is done in contemplation of a subsequent

[120] See generally, Chap. 3.

[121] See Wolf (2016), p. 8 ("Restructuring of an insolvent company is ranked equally for both realization and liquidation").

[122] This will include both collective proceedings under bankruptcy, as well as other procedures found in other legislations such as the company law regime in the UK. The usage of bankruptcy/insolvency law is further explained in Chap. 3 of the book.

[123] Also see Chap. 3 of the book.

[124] See for instance, *See* H.R. REP. NO. 595, 95th Cong., 1st Sess. 125 (1977), *reprinted in* 1978 U.S.C.C.A.N, 5963 at 6179 ("The purpose of a business reorganization case, unlike a liquidation case, is to *restructure* a business's finances so that it may continue to operate, provide its employees with jobs, pay its creditors, and produce a return for its shareholders" [emphasis supplied]).

[125] For an understanding of the use of formal and informal restructuring, see Chap. 3, Sect. 3.2.

sale of the business.[126] Incidental to this meaning, restructuring as used in this book, is the existence of a dual regime of policy goals. One is directed towards the maximization of the value in the business. The other towards the rehabilitation of the distressed business. Thus, a successful restructuring regime will be one that balances between these policy goals.[127]

1.5.3 Connotation of "New Financing"

Given that the book addresses new financing provided to a distressed business, it is necessary to define or clarify the terms used in describing this new financing. Generally, new financing for the restructuring distressed business is addressed using different terminology. In the US for instance, new financing provided in the context formal restructuring in Chapter 11 of the US Bankruptcy Code is referred to in the literature as debtor-in-possession (DIP) Financing.[128] In the UK, it is more common to find the use of the term rescue finance in reference to new financing.[129] In the European Union, two terms are used which seek to adequately define the timing of the new financing. On the one hand, the borrower may need new financing on a temporary basis, to enable it to meet up with pressing cash flow demands. This is termed in the EU as interim financing.[130] On the other hand the borrower may require new financing to enable it to implement the restructuring plan of the distressed business, in its quest to emerge from its distress. This is termed new

[126] This working definition of restructuring is consistent with the definitions of restructuring in art. 5(b) of the EU Recommendation on Business Failure, which defines restructuring as "changing the composition, conditions, or structure of assets and liabilities of debtors, or a combination of those elements, with the objective of enabling the continuation, in whole or in part, of the debtors' activity".; see also Payne (2014), p. 187 ("Debt restructuring is a process that allows a company facing cash flow problems and financial distress to reduce and renegotiate its delinquent debts, in order to improve or restore liquidity and rehabilitate it so that it can continue its operations, possibly with a view to selling the company or its business."); See also, Bork (2012), at para 1.28, 13.

[127] See, Harner and Griffin (2014), p. 214 (noting that an optimal restructuring is one that strikes a balance between value maximization and rehabilitation). For instance, the going concern sale of a business although may take the entity out of the ownership of pre-distress owners, but may still achieve the maximization of the value of the business for the creditors, as "a living business-with established customers, knowledgeable employees, and so forth-may well bring a higher price as a unit than would the sale of each asset separately…." See Westbrook (2004), p. 811.

[128] Some authors refer to this as DIP lending. See for example Ayer et al. (2004).

[129] This term is used by the UK Insolvency Services. See for instance, The Insolvency Service (2016).

[130] See for instance, Art. 2(12) Proposal for a Directive on Preventive Restructuring Frameworks (2016), which defines interim financing as "… any funds, whether provided by an existing or new creditor, that is reasonably and immediately necessary for the debtor's business to continue operating or to survive, or to preserve or enhance the value of that business pending the confirmation of a restructuring plan."

financing.[131] Any of these terms when used should be understood by the reader as referring to new funds extended to the distressed borrower, for facilitating the restructuring.

In the analysis pertaining to the use of priority as incentive for new financing, there is the possibility that new financing is afforded priority as part of the costs of administering the estate of the debtor during the restructuring. This priority is otherwise known as an administrative expense priority in many bankruptcy laws. In some other jurisdictions, while the expression administrative expense priority may not be used, one may find such expressions suggesting that certain expenses are considered the liability of the estate of the debtor. for instance, In Germany for instance, the costs of the insolvency proceedings, as well as liabilities traceable to the activities of the insolvency administrator, are typically considered to be liabilities of the estate of the debtor (*Masserverbindlichkeiten*).[132] This is itself the equivalent of the cost of administering the estate of the debtor and as such, the book treats this priority position as such.

1.6 Delimitation of This Book: Focus on "New Money" and Non-bank Distressed Borrowers

Another recurring term in the book is the provision of new financing for the distressed debtor. New financing essentially refers to the injection of new money, by way of cash, into the business. This focus on new money essentially limits the scope of the book to financial creditors providing new financing. Notably, a distressed business may obtain new financing on a temporary basis, to enable it to meet up with pressing cash flow demands. In the same vein, it may also require new financing to enable it to finance the implementation of the plan of the distressed business, in its quest to emerge from its distress. In this book, reference to new financing refers to both interim financing, as well as financing meant for the implementation of the restructuring plan of the distressed business. Where the distinction between both types of new financing is required in the book, this distinction will be made.

It is also important to note that the borrowers envisaged in this book are non-bank and non-financial institution businesses. Typically, the regime for resolving the distress of banks and other financial institutions involve more than that provided for in the case of ordinary businesses dealt with in this book.[133] The analysis on the role of the distressed debt market in the purchase of loans from the secondary

[131] Article 2(11) of the proposed directive recognizes this as new financing, defining it as "new funds, whether provided by an existing or a new creditor, that are necessary to implement a restructuring plan that are agreed upon in that restructuring plan and confirmed subsequently by a judicial or administrative authority."

[132] See s. 55(2) InsO. See also, Spahlinger and Kortz (2015), at para 10.59, 216.

[133] For instance, in the EU, see the BRRD Directive (2014).

market should not cause any confusions as the loans in any case are purchased off the books of the banks. The obligor is still the non-financial institution borrower with which the book is concerned.

1.7 Roadmap of the Book

For the sake of emphasis, the book addresses issues pertaining to the provision of "new money" to the distressed business. It does this by examining the essential requirements of the restructuring regime and how the rules provide for liquidity for distressed borrowers. It also examines how the statutory regimes for restructuring approach the provision new lending incentivizing through priority, as a part of the restructuring regime. It further examines lender capture through financing agreements, their implication for other stakeholders, rebutting theoretical justifications for such provisions and examining legal rules that countermand such overreach. Finally, given the place of the distressed debt market as a source of new financing, the book examines how the courts may balance the interests of such investors against that of the set goals of restructuring. To address these issues, the book is divided into five chapters.

In Chap. 2, the book lays a background by examining the sources of new financing for the distressed borrower. It pays attention to how new financing may be sourced, following the corporate finance classification particularly accounting for nuances, given that the businesses in question are distressed. As part of the debt-equity mix, the chapter devotes some attention to the somewhat tricky question of debt financing by shareholders of distressed businesses and the bankruptcy implications, focusing on the US common law approach versus the German statutory regime on the subject. Given the pre-eminent role which commercial banks will typically play in the restructuring of distressed businesses, the chapter finally examines how this role is changing, the factors underlying this change and importantly, the new players with strategies more attuned distressed lending. This last part sets a background to the focus of Chap. 5 on the distressed debt market.

Given the context of the research, Chap. 3 is devoted to a comparative analysis of the restructuring regimes in the major jurisdictions. Against what is considered the key requirements for a restructuring regime the book examines how and to what extent these jurisdictions meet these criteria. A tangential consideration in the chapter is to see how these key requirements inure to facilitating liquidity preservation for the distressed business. Although informal restructurings do not necessarily have the binding force of formal restructuring regimes, the chapter also examines the practical ways by which informal restructurings are carried on. The second part of the chapter is devoted to Nigeria its quest for a working restructuring regime. These efforts are examined against the standards set out in part of the book. The chapter concludes with the question of the need for the enactment of a bespoke restructuring regime that meets the analyzed key restructuring requirements, first given the multiplicity of regimes in a country like the UK and second given a country with a single regime but a bankruptcy stigmatization concern like Germany.

One issue is left unresolved in Chap. 2. It is the question of the financing of the distressed business, although as already canvassed from the early parts of this book, this requirement is often key to a successful restructuring. Chapter 4 focuses on this requirement. The chapter starts by analyzing the use of law as an incentive for behavior, delving into the issue of extrinsic and intrinsic motivation and how they apply to providers of new financing. The chapter examine two methods of incentivizing new financing i.e. the use of negative protections as in the EU Recommendation and the use of heightened priority, arguing that that the latter represents a better approach. The chapter further highlights divergent approaches i.e. the market-based and prescriptive approaches as represented by the UK and Germany on the one hand and the US on the other respectively. Following the analysis on the justifications for a prescriptive approach, the chapter highlights the place of SMEs or single lender borrowers and how a market-based approach may work against their interest. All these form part 1 of the chapter. In part two, distressed financing is analyzed in the context of Nigeria's extant defective regime, and in the light of ongoing reform efforts which also suggests that a market-based approach is taken. A case is however made for a prescriptive approach, given the realities of new financing in the Nigerian lending market.

Chapter 5 focuses on the lender capture phenomenon. The chapter examines what is the trend (typically in the US), by which providers of new financing (especially pre-distress lenders) employing new financing agreements in ways that interfere with the interests of other stakeholder constituencies. The chapter on the one hand examines the use of clauses that enhance pre-distress facilities and that which places control in the hands of the lender. Particularly regarding the former clauses, given that the clauses are not statutorily prohibited or expressly approved, the chapter examines the judicial treatment of the clauses and critically examines the theoretical justifications which appear to form the backbone of their use. Given what seems to be a convergence between the US and Europe (UK and Germany) in terms of lender control of the restructuring process, the chapter examines how the latter have statutorily (in principle) balanced lender interest against that of other stakeholders. In conclusion, the chapter reflects on the possible correlation between the statutory policy to leave the management of the distressed borrower in place and the use of financing contracts to defeat this end. Lessons are drawn from this for jurisdictions interested in reform.

Chapter 6 fully revisits a point briefly touched upon in Chap. 1. It is dedicated to the role of the distressed debt market in the financing of the distressed borrower and the restructuring process. Part 1 examines the market as an alternative to traditional lenders to distressed businesses, the players in the market, and the strategies. It further explores the nature of the players in the market as self-interested actors and how this self-interest is channeled to value creation. Given the equally valid concerns that players in the distressed debt market can equally pursue strategies that may be value destructive and possibly derail the restructure, the chapter proposes a principle to balance between their involvement and restructuring goals. This done through reliance on English and US case law. Part 2 is devoted to the exploration of the distressed debt market in a frontier market, using Nigeria as an example. It highlights the most defining feature of the market as one that is dominated by the state-owned AMCON. The book advocates a liberalization of the market, arguing that recent efforts at encouraging participation by distressed debt investors ignore their role as providers of new financing for distressed businesses which may in dire need of new money. The chapter concludes amongst other things, by highlighting the limitations of the proposal.

Finally, the book draws a conclusion which reflects on findings in the chapters as well as providing recommendations and lessons for policy and law reform for Nigeria.

References

Adebola B (2013) The Nigerian business rescue model: an introduction. http://papers.ssrn.com/sol3/papers.cfm?abstract_id=2297824. Accessed 10 Oct 2014

Adebola B (2014) A few shades of rescue: a critical assessment of the rescue concept. SSRN Electron J

Adeniran A (2003) A mediation-based approach to corporate reorganizations in Nigeria. NCJ Int Law Com Reg 29:291–350

Ayer JD, Friedland JP, Bernstein ML (2004) Obtaining DIP financing and using cash collateral. Am Bankr Inst J 23:16

Baird DG (1998) Bankruptcy's uncontested axioms. Yale Law J 10:573–599

Baiser PM, Epstein DG (1992) Postpetition lending under section 364: issues regarding the gap period and financing for prepackaged plans. Wake Forest Law Rev 27:103–122

Benes TF, Filho PFC (2009) Corporate bankruptcy and reorganization in Brazil: national and cross-border perspectives. In: Norton annual review of international insolvency. https://www.iiiglobal.org/sites/default/files/Felsberg%2C%20Thomas%20B.%20and%20Filho%2C%20Paulo%20Fernando%20Campana.pdf. Accessed 10 Aug 2017

Beverini I, Cova B (2006) How hedge funds are changing distressed debt. Int Financ Law Rev 25:12

Bork R (2012) Rescuing companies in England and Germany. Oxford University Press, Oxford

Brealy RA, Myers SC, Allen F (2011) Principles of corporate finance, 10th edn. McGraw-Hill/Irwin, New York

Bussel D, Klee KN (2009) Recalibrating consent in bankruptcy. Am Bankr Law J 83:663–748

Calitz J, Freebody G (2016) Is post-commencement finance proving to be the thorn in the side of business rescue proceedings under the 2008 Companies Act? De Jure 49(2):265–287

Carapeto M (2003) Does debtor-in-possession financing add value? http://citeseerx.ist.psu.edu/viewdoc/download?doi=10.1.1.197.6324&rep=rep1&type=pdf. Accessed 10 May 2016

Chatterjee S, Dhillon US, Ramírez GG (2004) Debtor in possession financing. J Bank Financ 28:3097–3111

Cirmizi E, Klapper L, Uttamchamdani M (2012) The challenges of bankruptcy reform. World Bank Res Obs 27(2):185–203

Dahiya S, John K, Puri M (2003) Debtor-in-possession financing and bankruptcy resolution: empirical evidence. J Financ Econ 69:259–280

Eidenmuller H (2013) A new framework for business restructuring in Europe: the EU commission's proposals for a reform of the European insolvency regulation and beyond legal developments. Maastricht J Eur Comp Law 20:133–161

Finch V (2009) Corporate insolvency law. Cambridge University Press, Cambridge

Fletcher I (2017) The law of insolvency, 5th edn. Sweet and Maxwell, London

Flood J (2001) The vultures fly east: the creation and globalisation of the distressed debt market. In: Nelken D, Feest J (eds) Adapting legal cultures. Hart Publishing, Oxford, pp 257–278
Fontana A, Frey JH (2005) The interview: from neutral stance to political involvement. In: Denzin NK, Lincoln YS (eds) The Sage handbook of qualitative research, 3rd edn. Sage, Thousand Oaks, pp 695–728
Franks J, Sussman O (2005) Financial distress and bank restructuring of small to medium-sized UK companies. Rev Financ 9:65–96
Frisby S (2004) In search of a rescue regime: the enterprise act 2002. MLR 67:247–272
Gallagher A, Lombardo F (2013) New rules on DIP financing in Italian restructurings. Am Bankr Inst J 32:48–49
Goldschmid P (2005) More phoenix than vulture: the case for distressed investor presence in the bankruptcy reorganization process. Colum Bus Law Rev 2019:191–267
Goode R (2011) Principles of corporate insolvency law, 4th edn. Sweet and Maxwell, London
Gross K (1994) Taking community interest into account in bankruptcy. Wash Univ Law Q 72:1031–1046
Gudgeon MR, Joshi SA (2013) The restructuring and workout environment in Europe. In: Larkin B (ed) Restructuring and workout strategies for maximizing value, 2nd edn. Globe, Law and Business, UK, pp 7–14
Halliday T, Carruthers B (2007) The recursivity of law: global norm making and national lawmaking in the globalization of corporate insolvency regimes. Am J Sociol 112(4):1135–1202
Harner MM (2008) The corporate governance and public policy implications of activist distressed debt investing. Fordham Law Rev 77:703–772
Harner MM (2011) Activist distressed debtholders: the New Barbarians at the gate? Wash Univ Law Rev 89:155–206
Harner MM, Griffin JM (2014) Facilitating successful failures. Fla Law Rev 66:205–253
Harner MM, Griffin JM, Ivey-Crickenberger J (2014) Activist investors, distressed companies, and value uncertainty. Am Bankr Inst Law Rev 22:167–194
Henoch BA (1991) Post-petition financing: is there life after debt? Bankr Dev J 8:575
Heubner M (2005) Debtor-in-possession financing. RMA J:30–33
Hotchkiss ES, Mooradian RM (1997) Vulture investors and the market for control of distressed firms. J Financ Econ 43:401–432
Hunter M (1999) The nature and functions of a rescue culture. Com Law J 104:426–463
Idigbe A, Kalu O (2015) Nigeria: recent strides in Nigerian insolvency law – banking insolvency & AMCON act. Mondaq. http://www.mondaq.com/Nigeria/x/431946/Insolvency+Bankruptcy/Recent+Strides+In+Nigerian+Insolvency+Law+Banking+Insolvency+AMCON+Act. Accessed 7 Oct 2015
Kamensky DB (2014) Furthering the goals of chapter 11: considering the positive role of hedge funds in the reorganization process. Am Bankr Inst Law Rev 22:235–246
Korobkin D (1993) Contractarianism and the normative foundations of bankruptcy law. Texas Law Rev 71:541–632
Kuney GW (2005) Hijacking Chapter 11. Emory Bankr Dev J 21:19–112
Levitin A (2012) Bankrupt politics and the politics of bankruptcy. Cornell Law Rev 97:1399–1458
Lipson JC (2009) The shadow bankruptcy system. Boston Univ Law Rev 89:1609–1669
Lopucki LM, Whitford WC (1993) Patterns in bankruptcy reorganization in large publicly held companies. Cornell Law Rev 78:597–618
Loubser A (2014) Post-commencement financing and the ranking of claims – a South African perspective. In: Perry R (ed) European insolvency law: current issues and prospects for reform, pp 29–37
Lubben SJ (2008) Financial distress and emerging markets. http://ssrn.com/abstract=1282355. Accessed 8 Sept 2015
Mallon C, Waisman SY (2011) Introduction. In: Mallon C, Waisman SY (eds) The law and practice of restructuring in the UK and US. Oxford University Press, Oxford

Martin JB, Kristofor WN, Rudenberg E, Squires J (2009) Freefalling with parachute that may not open: debtor-in-possession financing in the wake of the great recession. Univ Miami Law Rev 63(4):1205–1232
McCormack G (2008) Corporate rescue law: an Anglo-American perspective. Edward Elgar, Cheltenham
McCormack G (2009) Jurisdictional competition and forum shopping in insolvency proceedings. Camb Law J 68(1):169–197
McCormack G (2017a) Business restructuring law in Europe: making a fresh start. J Corp Law Stud 17(1):167–202
McCormack G (2017b) Corporate restructuring law – a second chance for Europe? Eur Law Rev 42(4):532–561
Miller H (2007) Chapter 11 in transition - from boom to bust and into the future. Am Bankr Law J 81:375–403
Miller HR, Waisman SY (2004) Does chapter 11 reorganization remain a viable option for distressed businesses for the twenty-first century? Am Bankr Law J 78:153–200
Miller HR, Waisman SY (2007) Is chapter 11 bankrupt? Boston Coll Law Rev 47:129–181
Moore DD (1991) How to finance a debtor in possession. Com Lend Rev 6:3–12
Morris C, Murphy C (2011) Getting a PhD in law, vol 35. Hart Publishing, Oxford
Mundy S (2010) Distressed assets: brothers go for broke. Financial Times. http://www.ft.com/cms/s/0/5488f652-ca97-11df-a860-00144feab49a.html#axzz3l2uTtvLB. Accessed 18 Aug 2015
Pallares I (2012) Spanish act changes. In: Global turnaround. https://m.lw.com/thoughtLeadership/spanish-insolvency-act-changes-january-amendments. Accessed 10 Aug 2017
Paterson S (2015) Rethinking corporate bankruptcy theory in the twenty-first-century. OJLS 36(4):697–723
Payne J (2014) Schemes of arrangement: theory, structure and operation. Cambridge University Press, Cambridge
Payne J, Sarra J (2017) Tripping the light fantastic: a comparative analysis of the European commission's proposals for new and interim financing of insolvent businesses. Oxford legal studies research paper no. 41/2017. https://ssrn.com/abstract=2976446. Accessed 10 Oct 2017
Plank L, Meyer-Löwy B, Pickerill C (2012) The new German insolvency code: decoding improvements and remaining risks. Am Bankr Inst J 46
Raval A (2016) Domestic oil companies hit hardest by funding crisis. Financial Times. https://www.ft.com/content/56793724-923c-11e6-a72e-b428cb934b78. Accessed 10 Mar 2017
Rajah I (2017) Enhancing Singapore as an international debt restructuring centre for Asia and beyond. In: Singapore Ministry of Law. https://www.mlaw.gov.sg/content/dam/minlaw/corp/News/Note%20on%20Debt%20Restructuring.pdf. Accessed 10 Dec 2017
Rizzi JV (1991) Opportunities in DIP financing. Bankers Mag 43–49
Roe MJ, Tung F (2013) Breaking bankruptcy priority: how rent-seeking upends the creditors' bargain. Va Law Rev 99:1235–1287
Roe MJ, Tung F (2016) Bankruptcy and corporate reorganization: legal and financial material, 4th edn. Foundation Press, St. Paul
Sarra J (2013) Rescue! The companies' creditors arrangement act, 2nd edn. Carswell, Toronto
Skeel D, Ayotte KA (2013) Bankruptcy law as a liquidity provider. Univ Chic Law Rev 80:1559–1560
Skeel DA Jr (2004) The past present and future of debtor in possession financing. Cardozo Law Rev 25:1905–1934
Spahlinger A, Kortz H (2015) Germany. In: Baer G, O'Flynn K (eds) Financing company group restructurings. Oxford University Press, Oxford
Squire R (2016) Corporate bankruptcy and financial reorganization. Wolters Kluwer, New York
Tabb CJ (1986) A critical reappraisal of cross-collateralization in bankruptcy. S Cal Law Rev 60:109–175
Tabb CJ (1997) The law of bankruptcy. Foundation Press, New York

Tajti T (2018) Bankruptcy stigma and the second chance policy: the impact of bankruptcy stigma on business restructurings in China Europe and the United States. China-EU Law J 6:1–31
Thomas RD (2010) Tipping the scales in chapter 11: how distressed debt investors decrease debtor leverage and the efficacy of business reorganization. Emory Bankr Dev J 27:213–253
Tolmie F (2003) Corporate and personal insolvency law. Taylor and Francis, London
Triantis GG (1993) A theory of the regulation of debtor-in-possession financing. Vand Law Rev 46:901–935
Uttamchandi M (2004) The case for debtor-in-possession financing in early transition countries: taking a DIP in the distressed debt pool. In: Law in transition online. 1–10, p 9. https://www.ebrd.com/downloads/research/law/lit042.pdf. Accessed 18 Aug 2015
Warren E (1993) Bankruptcy policymaking in an imperfect world. Mich Law Rev 92:336–387
Warren E, Westbrook JL (2009) The success of chapter 11: a challenge to the critics. Mich Law Rev 107:603–634
Wielebinski JJ (2017) Financial restructuring and insolvency challenges in emerging markets. Financier Worldwide. Available at: https://www.financierworldwide.com/financial-restructuring-and-insolvency-challenges-in-emerging-markets/#.XO1bvYhKg2x. Accessed 10 Aug 2017
Weijs R, Baltjes M (2018) Opening the door for the opportunistic use of interim financing: a critical assessment of the EU draft directive on preventive restructuring frameworks. Int Insol Rev 27:223–254
Weiss LA, Wruck KH (1998) Information problems, conflicts of interest, and asset stripping: chapter 11's failure in the case of Eastern Airlines. J Financ Econ 48:55–97
Westbrook JL (1999) The globalisation of insolvency reform. N Z Law Rev 401:403
Westbrook JL (2004) The control of wealth in bankruptcy. Texas Law Rev 82:795–861
Westbrook JL, Gottlieb LC (2009) Reorganizations, exemption of financial assets. Am Bankr Inst J 27:10
Wolf A (2016) Sense of modesty: Germany's progress towards corporate rescue. NIBLeJ 8 4(2)
Wood PR (2007) Law and practice of international finance: principles of international insolvency, 2nd edn. Sweet and Maxwell, London, pp 675–676
Wruck KH (1990) Financial distress, reorganization and organizational efficiency. J Financ Econ 21:419–444

Chapter 2
New Money for Distressed Businesses: Sources, Options and the Changing Financing Landscape

2.1 Overview

In analyzing distressed debtor financing in restructuring regimes, it is important to understand the commercial environment within which new financing is provided. It requires answers to practical questions such as: what financing options are open to a distressed borrower? What motivates the provision of financing for distressed businesses? How do the applicable rules affect the class of financing a potential lender may provide? Given that commercial banks have played (and in some countries) still play the lead role of traditional lenders, how suited are traditional lenders to financing distressed businesses and if they are not, what bespoke options exist? To understand the issues surrounding the financing of distressed businesses, it is fitting to start against a background which answers the questions above. It is of importance that the reader keeps in mind that the focus is on financially distressed businesses, which have already been defined as businesses unable to meet their debt obligations as they arise.[1] Bearing this mind, the categorization of financing options for distressed businesses may take at least two forms. The first classification follows the well-known path of corporate financing with a nuance to account for the distress of the business. The second follows the way the financing is sourced by the management of the distressed borrower.

In general terms, businesses when they are healthy, may finance themselves through a variety of options. Generally, corporate financing follows the classification of debt, equity and retained earnings.[2] In other words, financing may be obtained in any of these ways, or a combination of them.[3] However, the fact of distress may introduce nuances that may require the expansion of the financing options or the

[1] See Chap. 1, Sect. 1.1.3.

[2] See generally, Chiappineli (2006), p. 152.

[3] See Gullifer and Payne (2015), p. 59 ("… companies can finance their operations via share issues, debt, retained profits or, more likely, a combination of these options.").

S. U. Mba, *New Financing for Distressed Businesses in the Context of Business Restructuring Law*, https://doi.org/10.1007/978-3-030-19749-0_2

possible exclusion of particular options of financing. As for retained earnings, it may even be preferred as a source of financing for healthy businesses.[4] However, this may not always be applicable when businesses are financially distressed.[5] The fact of distress presupposes that the business is at least illiquid, and thus may not have enough internal funding in terms of retained earnings, being itself in need of cash. As a result, one is likely to find asset disposal or divestment as a replacement for retained earnings.

Another way to classify lending options to distressed businesses will be to consider where the management of the distressed business looks for new financing. In this sense, new financing may be sourced internally or externally. Internal sources of new financing may come from capital contribution by existing equity lenders, asset disposal or divestments, shareholder loans or even through money contributed in a cash pooling system by companies within a group. Externally, distressed borrowers may issue equity, obtain loans, issue bonds, or other forms of debt instrument. There might in some cases be intervention by the state in the form of bailouts to the distressed business.

Regarding the identity of the providers of new financing, the fact of distress also means that certain financers who will typically finance healthy businesses may be less inclined to do so, or those who may well have been so inclined previously, may be more hesitant. Also, new lenders seemingly suited, or willing to take their chance as lenders to distressed businesses are emerging on the horizon. It is for this reason that this chapter not only identifies the likely financers but also outlines possible motives that can be ascribed to their decision to provide financing for the distressed businesses.

As between the corporate finance (albeit altered) and the source-based financing classifications highlighted above, the chapter will adopt the former, given that the latter still follows one or a combination of the options highlighted above. Thus, for instance, debt financing by way of loans can be provided either externally or internally, the same for equity.[6] Also, the choice of the corporate finance classification is to allow for a simultaneous discussion of the possible actors and their motivation. This simultaneous discussion sometimes presents quite interesting jurisdictional conflicts as in the case of shareholder loans and the different jurisdictional approaches ranging from non-regulation in bankruptcy law (like in the UK) to largely uncertain rules (as in the US) to precise "no-fault" approach in Germany. The complexity in the treatment of shareholder loans attracts detailed analysis in the chapter.

---

[4] See Meyer (1984); see also Watson and Wilson (2002) (showing that for SMEs in the UK, retained earnings may be the most preferred source of financing, followed by debt, and then new shares to outsiders).

[5] Wood (2007), p. 718 ("… free cash resources of the debtor [is] usually nil ….").

[6] Although this might not be applicable to asset sales and divestitures, it reinforces the reason for the choice of classification. Consistent with the classification, asset-sales and divestitures are discussed as a separate head.

In the light of the forgoing, the chapter proceeds as follows. The chapter analyses distress financing options through debt, equity, the theoretical and statutory considerations that arise debt financing (loan) is provided by equity holders when the debtor is distressed and the consequences that follow in bankruptcy. **Thereafter, asset disposal and divestment as a financing option for a distressed business is examined**. The chapter then goes on to examine bank lending (as a traditional lending form) and the changes in global financing markets that calls to question the capacity of banks to serve distressed borrowers, bringing to the fore, the need for bespoke strategies that meet new financing needs of distressed but viable businesses. This is followed by a conclusion. Finally, although the financing actors and options of financing are not necessarily peculiar to any one jurisdiction, it is possible to find that certain jurisdictions disclose advanced options not available or well advanced in others. Also, business size may determine the type of lender. Thus, as much as is possible and necessary, jurisdiction-specific analysis will be provided.

2.2 Financing the Distressed Debtor Through Debt: Identifying Lenders and Motivation

In broad terms, businesses may be more inclined to finance their operations through debt, if the cost of debt is lower than having to raise capital through equity.[7] Debt financing providers, or better still lenders, to a distressed business may be classified along the lines of lenders with pre-distress relationship with the borrower (**prior lenders**) and lenders with no prior lending relationship with the borrower (**new lenders**). In addition, new financing may be provided to a distressed borrower on the basis of collateral provided by the distressed debtor, making the lender a **secured lender** or possibly on an unsecured basis, making the lender an **unsecured lender**. This classification is relevant, given that what follows is an explication on the underlying the motivation that inform the practical choices of providing debt financing to the distressed business. More importantly, the motivation analysis helps provide backgrounds to the interest of new money providers in the restructuring process, an issue which pre- occupies most of the subsequent chapters.

It bears restating that the focus of the book is on the availability of cash for the distressed business to tide itself over as it puts its plan of restructuring in place, and also, cash to effectuate the plan of restructuring. This is exactly why the focus is on lenders and exclude trade creditors as well as lease financing for instance, which may undoubtedly aid the process of restructuring, but do not provide cash for the borrower.

[7] Levmore (1982), p. 67. On the purchase of the stock of distressed businesses, see Sect. 2.3 below.

2.2.1 Prior Lenders Versus New Lender

A pre-existing lender may be willing to provide financing to enable the restructuring process of the distressed debtor.[8] In fact, this lender is often the natural choice of refinancing for the debtor, depending on how much liquidity pressure it is faced with. As is often the case, the debtor may have little time to source for credit from new sources,[9] and even where a new source exists, interest rates may be much higher.[10] Hence, a pre-distress lender with which the debtor has a relationship is often the first option.[11] At least two incentives for the advancement of new financing by a prior lender may be identified. Providing new financing may, in a broader sense, improve the chances of a successful restructuring and by implication, the value of returns to the prior lender providing new financing. Secondly, in a narrow sense, it may also improve the chances of recovering both the pre-distress loan alongside the new restructuring loan.

In the broader sense, the new financing provided may prevent the liquidation of the distressed business, so that as the value in the estate of the debtor is preserved, the interest of the pre-distress lender is also protected. This is even more important for a secured pre-distress lender. Further financing may be a means of avoiding diminution in the value of the asset(s) by which the lender secures its interest. This is especially so, as the value creditors receive in a liquidation is usually lower, compared to what creditors may receive, had the debtor continued as a going concern.[12] Financing by a prior lender may also be a kind of protective advance to the estate of the borrower, with the intention that such advance is used to preserve the collateral of that lender.

---

[8] For instance, empirical evidence from the US show that when financing is provided by pre-existing lenders, the debtor spends less time in Chapter 11. This evidence supports the idea that the level of exposure to the debtor, and the information at the disposal of such lenders may help their lending decision and facilitate the emergence of the debtor from Chapter 11, when compared to financing by new lenders. See Dahiya et al. (2003), p. 276.

[9] Henoch (1991) ("Often the need for an influx of cash is so acute that the bankruptcy court may not have time to issue a written decision, as "the time necessary to [produce] an opinion could effectively doom any chance of reorganization.").

[10] Adler (2007), p. 479.

[11] Id.

[12] This is particularly so when there is a general downturn in the market for such an asset. In the US, see Prager (1990), p. 2131 ("… [t]he extension of credit aids preservation of the prepetition collateral's value as a corollary to preserving the debtor-in-possession's ongoing enterprise since liquidation values are traditionally a fraction of those attendant to going concern.") Commenting on the motivation for new financing in Germany, Schultz and Braun note that:

> Under insolvency, [new] financing is often provided by German banks which already have exposure to the debtor. Banks are often prepared to finance the [distressed management], because they do not want to risk the administrator closing down the business… German banks consider the [new] financing more as a necessary evil….

See Schultze & Braun, German Insolvency Law in a Nutshell. Available at: https://www.schubra.de/downloads/broschueren/0027_en.pdf accessed 10 May 2017.

Depending on the jurisdiction, the new lending may be relied upon to further improve the chances of recovery on its prior loan.[13] A prior lender with an unsecured exposure to the distressed business may provide new financing with the intention that the collateral provided in respect of the new loan will cover both the new and old loan.[14] Such a lender may also provide new financing, building into it, the pre-distress loan, especially as the new loan enjoys priority repayment. These practices are however still subject of debate, especially on their statutory validity and effect.[15] In the same vein, as a strategy, a pre-distress lender keen on maintaining its priority position may provide new financing, to ensure that a claim of a new lender who provides new financing does not rank ahead of its own pre-distress claim,[16] and their claim is not thereby undermined.[17]

Although it is the case that many distressed businesses receive financing from pre-distress lenders for reasons set already,[18] it is also very likely that distressed businesses may obtain financing from lenders with whom they have no previous financing relationship. One consideration that may influence lending to a distressed debtor by a new lender is the availability of liquid assets, which may be easily used as collateral.[19] This makes sense as the availability of such an asset means that the lender can secure its interest over such liquid collateral. Furthermore, lending to a distressed business with good fundamentals and less credit risks, which successfully emerges from the formal restructuring process may well mean a new customer for the new lender. In addition, the availability of heightened priority position in the repayment of the new lender whether statutorily provided or negotiated between the lender, on the one hand, and the borrower and its stakeholders on the other hand, may create an incentive on the part of the lender to provide new funds for the cash-strapped business.[20] Aside from the foregoing, such lending appears to be very lucrative for a

[13] See Heubner (2005), p. 30 ("In common bankruptcy parlance, [new financing] provided by the existing secured lenders is referred to as a defensive DIP…").

[14] See for instance, Qi (2008), p. 164 (noting that unsecured creditors may be inspired by "[t]he desire to cross-collateralize their debts or the unsecured portion of their debts.").

[15] The use of new financing to gain such advantages is exhaustively examined in Chap. 4 below.

[16] For instance, in an investigation of firms that received financing under the formal restructuring framework between 1996 and 2013 in the US, Kai Li and Wei Wang find that such financing "is primarily used by pre-petition lenders to enforce their seniority in the claims structure, in addition to meeting the financing needs of the debtor." See Li and Wang (2016), p. 129.

[17] Sarra (2011) ("Even where their claims are already covered by their secured charge on the debtor's assets, pre-filing secured creditors may agree to provide DIP financing where they want to ensure that their position is not compromised during the workout process; that the debtor restructures in a manner that maximizes protection of their interests; or to maintain some control over the debtor during the proceedings.").

[18] See discussion above.

[19] This of course also applies to pre-filing lenders. See Dahiya et al. (2003), p. 269 ("… [Lenders in formal restructuring] prefer to lend against liquid collateral). Most asset-based lenders providing facilities to distressed businesses will equally fall within this category. See for instance, Nash (2007).

[20] For further analysis of the use of heightened priority positions to incentivize lending across jurisdictions, see Chap. 4, Sect. 4.5.

lender in terms of the higher interest rates and fees chargeable, when compared to normal lending to businesses that are not distressed and undergoing restructuring.[21] Lenders with no pre-distress lending relationship may also provide financing to the distressed business, with the intention of becoming invested in the business of the debtor, owning a controlling equity stake in the distressed business.[22]

2.2.2 *Secured Versus Unsecured Lenders*

Another classification that describes providers of new lending to the distressed borrower is the secured and unsecured lending class. The motivation for providing new financing on a secured basis to a distressed firm is essentially the same reason for which a lender will provide secured lending for healthy businesses. Security interests essentially serve to assure the lender of payment priority in respect of particular assets of the debtor over that of other creditors.[23] Although scholars have sought to find theoretical justification for security interests in property[24] and contract law,[25] the

[21] Qi (2008), p. 164. ("...the interest rate that banks charge on [formal restructuring financing] usually are 2–5% point higher than ordinary loans and transactional fees to administer the loans are also very lucrative.").

[22] This investment strategy by new lenders is subsumed in the distressed debt market and the distressed debt market as a source of new financing for distressed borrowers is extensively analyzed in Chap. 6 below.

[23] Baird and Jackson (1984).

[24] See for instance, Steven L. Harris and Charles W. Mooney, Jr., who conclude that:

> It seems clear enough that security interests, under ... are interests in property. The legal regime for security interests reflects property law functionally as well as doctrinally. We believe it follows that the law should honor the transfer or retention of security interests on the same normative grounds on which it respects the alienation of property generally.

Harris and Mooney (1994), p. 2051. For a critique of this property (proprietary) theoretical justification and the challenges that arise from the theory, see LoPucki et al. (2013), p. 1788 ff.

[25] See Leebron, who opined that:

> ...the priority of a secured creditor over other financial creditors can be justified on the grounds that non-secured creditors grant a loan knowing that some assets are subject to security interests or could be subjected to security interests without their permission. If particular creditors will not tolerate other creditors having security interests in the borrower's assets, they can refuse to make a loan or make it only if the borrower agrees not to subject its assets to any security interests.

Leebron (1991), p. 1646. More apt on the contractual theory is the opinion of McCormack who states thus:

> The question arises why the law should permit the taking of security. Three justifications are usually offered. The first reason is based on freedom of contract: security is seen as representing a fair exchange for the loan. In other words, the secured creditor has bargained for rights of a proprietary nature over the debtor's property whereas the general creditors have not.

bottom line is that the true test of the value of a security interest is in the event of the inability of the debtor to make good its obligation to repay the debt which the asset serves as its collateral i.e. in the context of insolvency.[26] A secured lender both in the context of healthy and also distressed businesses is in some sense, considered to have "bought" the right to enjoy the privilege of their ranking position in the event of a bankruptcy proceeding. The rationale for the acquired right is to reduce ex-ante the risk of default, at the expense of the risk premiums which they may well have otherwise demanded from the debtor.[27] In the light of the above, a lender to the distressed business on a secured basis may be counting on the right which the security affords in the event that the restructuring efforts fail and the borrower is unable to meet its repayment obligations. The secured lender may be inclined to lend on a secured basis to the distressed business, whether on the basis of unencumbered assets or as a claim subordinated to an already existing secured claim, where there is sufficient cushion in the asset to accommodate the security interest of the new lender.[28]

The challenge however is that at the time of distress, the distressed business may have no free assets available over which security interest may be created in favor of a new lender. This is not uncommon where the borrower is overleveraged. When there is no available asset over which the borrower may offer secured lending to new lenders, a new lender may still be motivated to provide financing as a result of the higher interest rates that may be received from such lending. Such lending appears to be very lucrative for a lender in terms of the higher interest rates and fees chargeable, when compared to normal lending to businesses that are not distressed.[29] In many cases also, depending on restructuring regime, or the agreement of the parties concerned in an informal restructuring, the new financing provided in the interim basis may be paid in priority as an expense of administering the estate of the debtor. In this case, the investment may well be a low-risk but high-yield venture for the investor.[30] Furthermore, a lender on an unsecured basis may be drawn to such lending as a result of its desire to take up an equity stake in the course of the restructuring of the distressed business. This may be mainly achieved by the exchange of debt for equity and is a major strategy that may be employed by a distressed debt investor to increase its chances of gaining control of the distressed business following the emergence of the debtor from the restructuring.[31]

Mccormack (2004), p. 12. For a critique of the contract theoretical justification, see Warren (1993), p. 354.

[26] See Drobnig (2010), p. 449.

[27] See generally, Benmelech (2009) (suggesting that lenders are willing to make larger loans with longer duration when the borrower provides collateral with higher liquidation value).

[28] Schwartz (1989), p. 217 (noting that pre-distress secured creditors always restrict the creation of security interest unless there is sufficient cushion).

[29] Qi (2008), p. 164 ("…the interest rate that banks charge on [formal restructuring financing] usually are 2–5% point higher than ordinary loans and transactional fees to administer the loans are also very lucrative.

[30] Id.

[31] The distressed debt market, its role in financing distressed businesses and the strategy of the players is examined in Chap. 6.

2.3 Equity Financing for Distressed Businesses

As often provided for in many jurisdictions, stock or share corporations are entitled to issue shares of stock.[32] The infusion of new equity financing into a distressed business can provide the much-needed funds required by a distressed business. New equity has an important advantage as a source of financing for a distressed business. New money which enters the capital structure of a distressed business as equity does not attract the payment of interest as it is the case with debt.[33] Consequently, the borrower is not obligated to make periodic payment as may be the case when debt instrument is issued. Especially where the borrower is distressed, the interest rate against which debt will be provided will be typically higher to reflect the lending risk, a situation which could make the borrower the more prone to bankruptcy.[34] Again, in the context of distressed businesses, new shares may be issued, or there may be an exchange of debt for equity. While it is the former that ordinarily allows for the infusion of new capital in the distressed businesses, the latter plays a vital role in the reduction of the debt burden of the distressed business, allowing for the capitalization of the debt.[35]

When new equity is issued by the distressed business, the newly issued equity may be purchased by pre-distress equity holders,[36] prior debt holders[37] or by entirely

---

[32] A share refers to that unit of residual ownership in the assets or earnings (stock) of a corporate entity. This difference is hardly made out today, hence it is typical to find the use of "stock" (as in the US) to mean "share" (as in the UK). Both terms are used interchangeably to mean equity.

[33] Collard (1994), p. 1 ("The advantage of equity funding is that funds are provided without interest cost and thus enhance cash flow.").

[34] Cusmano (2015) ("... loans to companies that already have considerable amounts of debt tend to have higher interest rates, and increase the risk of financial distress and bankruptcy.").

[35] Applicable jurisdictional rules may affect the use of debt-equity swaps. For instance, prior to the coming into effect of the ESUG in Germany, a creditor will be wary to take up equity in exchange for debt for fear of possible liability arising from an overvaluation of claims at the time of initial contribution by the shareholders, thereby offending the legal capital rules. The consequence of such liability is that in an insolvency proceeding, the creditor may be obligated to provide the difference between the value of the contribution and the initial contribution. However, ESUG does away with such liability in the context of formal restructuring (see Section 254 paragraph 4 second sentence ESUG), so that a creditor may freely exchange debt for equity in formal restructuring. See generally, Schafer and Frischemeier (2012) (on the practical implications of the debt-equity swap regime).

[36] For instance, pursuant to an English scheme of arrangement which was approved by the court, Ladbrokes Coral Group proposed the issuance of new equity to previous equity holders at 32. 7 pence per share in a bid to raise financing for its restructuring. See Re Ladbrokes Coral Group Plc. [2018] EWHC 1382 (Ch). Also, in the second Chapter 11 restructuring of the US footwear company, The Walking Company, controlling shareholders provided $10 Million in equity financing as part of exit financing for the distressed borrower. See Rizzo and Fitzgerald (2018).

[37] For instance, in the restructuring of Tele Columbus, existing lenders acquired the equity of the company from its holding company. See Takacs A, European Restructuring Report, Defaults, Restructuring and Recoveries 2008–2010. In: Debt Wire, 33. Available at http://www.debtwire.com/pdf/Restructuring_Report_2008_2010.pdf accessed 2 Jan 2017.

new investors. The purchase of equity by pre-distress equity holders is considered as the provision of new value, and it is the basis on which equity—which ordinarily occupies the lowest position of priority in bankruptcy—may be entitled to continue to hold equity in the restructured business.[38] It is also of importance that the new value which a pre-distress equity holder wishes to invest meets a market valuation of the equity, to ascertain that the capital infusion is truly valuable, commensurate to the value which the pre-distress equity holder seeks to retain and is actually useful for the restructuring.[39] In a distressed business, this procedure is undertaken by the restructuring management and typically under the supervision of the courts.[40] The management of the distressed business may decide to shelve payment of dividend, unlike in the case of debts where the failure to keep up with payment schedule may trigger bankruptcy proceedings.

New equity financing may also be provided by new investors who hold no pre-distress equity in the distressed business. The pattern of such new financing may either be as direct equity purchase or may be as some kind of structured financing. In the former case, an investor may be interested in owning equity stakes in the distressed business by providing new financing for funding the restructuring of the business, of course in exchange for equity in the business as it emerges from distress.[41] In the latter case, structured equity investing straddles between debt and equity. Here, the investor originates the financing as a loan, structuring it as a subordinated debt. In addition to its debt position and its attractive interest rate, the investor attaches equity kickers as part of the financing package. The equity kicker comes in form of warrants, stock options, convertible debt or preferred stock,[42] which essentially entitles (but does not obligate) the investor to purchase a specified number of equities at an exercise price prior to a specified expiry date.[43] Such equity

[38] In the US for instance, retention of equity by equity holders in a formal restructuring generally offends the absolute priority rule, where creditors will not receive the full value of their claims. See Lewis (2004), p. 67 ("the absolute priority rule seriously calls into doubt the chance of old equity of a company whose assets truly cannot meet its liabilities ever participating in the reorganized debtor absent creditor agreement"). For a further analysis on the role of absolute priority in the preparation of a restructuring plan in the US, see Chap. 3, Sect. 3.6.

[39] See the US case of *In re General Teamsters, Warehousemen and Helpers Union,* Local 890265 F.3d 869 (9th Cir. 2001). To ensure that value is given in return for the issued shares, in jurisdictions like the UK, it is a requirement of the law that the shares in a limited liability company that has a share capital must have a fixed nominal value. This can be relevant for determining the value of new investment by a pre-distress shareholder. See generally, Gullifer and Payne (2015), p. 153.

[40] For an analysis of the management prong of the procedural aspect for the restructuring of distressed businesses, see Chap. 3, Sect. 3.7.

[41] Gilson (2010), p. 194 (noting the example of the corporate restructuring of Continental Airlines (now United Airlines) which saw the investment of about $ 450 million from outside investors, in exchange for the common stock and other debt instruments of the debtor).

[42] Ibid ("These kinds of investments are structured in the form of private subordinated debt or private equity transactions in which hedge/private equity fund managers would provide financing in the form of newly issued subordinated debt with attached warrants or stock options...").

[43] Historically, preferred equity has been largely used as the choice equity issued by distressed railroads and is arguably a precursor to the structured equity in use by equity investors in distressed

kickers play the useful role of bringing the investors interested in equity ownership an inch closer to owning equity in the debtor.[44]

The possibilities of equity financing by new investors notwithstanding, the option might be considered a costly one for the pre-distress and equity holders, when compared to debt financing. This, in some cases may determine the willingness of management or prior equity holders to accede to the infusion of new financing by way of equity. For one, the issuance of new equity in distressed businesses is the unwillingness of shareholders to have their franchise further diluted and may mean the ceding of control rights over the business. On the flip side, there may well be unwillingness or lack of interest in the securities of the business, especially in the light of its distress.

2.4 The Shareholder as Lender: To Lend or Not to Lend?

As the debtor flounders under the strains of distress and possibly impending insolvency, one of the means by which the debtor may more easily obtain liquidity is through the extension of loans by the shareholder(s) (or their family members or friends) to the debtor. Especially for closed corporations, the shareholders are first to perceive the impending crisis and there may well be the need to move swiftly.[45] Speaking generally, this loan is provided with optimism on the part of the shareholder-lender that it will facilitate a successful restructuring.[46] It is elementary, but worth mentioning, that a shareholder has what may be regarded as an equity stake in the distressed debtor. Rather than have the debtor slide into insolvent liquidation, it may be willing to provide the debtor with financing, but this time not as share capital (equity) but as a loan (debt) repayable by the distressed business.[47] Apart from the fact that shareholders may provide the easiest means of sourcing quicker financing for the debtor in distress, some of the arguments in support of shareholder loans are grounded both in corporate governance and economics.

Speaking in corporate governance terms, the loan extended by shareholders may prove valuable in reining in the "risk appetite" of shareholders who have control over the distressed debtor. The maximization of the claim of a creditor squarely

businesses today. See Evans (1989) (noting that the earliest use of preferred equity in the US is traceable to the recapitalization of failed railroads in the late 1840–50s). See also, Tufano (1997), p. 23 ("By aggressively using innovative securities like preferred equity… reorganized railroads substantially reduced their fixed financial charges.").

[44] See Schlunk (2002), p. 884 ("Economically, convertible debt is like equity when equity performs well (because the debt will be converted) but is like debt when equity performs badly (and the conversion feature is not exercised).").

[45] Skeel and Kraus-Vilmar (2006), p. 268.

[46] Gelter (2006).

[47] The reader may have to be reminded that the essence of this book is not just about creditor protection, but distressed debtor financing, hence the relevance of this analysis.

rests on the higher likelihood of the payment of that claim.[48] In other words, creditors generally prefer lower risk.[49] However, shareholders in a firm with higher leverage may be positioned to reap from the upside that may result from a risky venture that promises a higher payoff. The availability of limited liability further increases the risk appetite of the shareholders who can create wealth for themselves but also potentially take away wealth from creditors. This sums up the classic asset-substitution and risk shifting theory.[50] All of this is at the expense of the creditors. In the light of this, one may see some sense in having the shareholder not only as an equity investor, but also as a creditor. The argument is therefore that as a loan provider (creditor) of the business, the shareholders may well have a reason to be more circumspect with regard to the risk they take.[51]

From a welfare economics perspective, the maximization of the interest of all stakeholders of the distressed debtor may well mean that the rescue attempt that a shareholder loan may occasion in certain cases may lead to an increased pool from which all stakeholders of the debtor may draw from in the event of a liquidation.[52] It is however germane to point out that unlike the cases of transaction avoidance, the claim or interest of a subordinated shareholder does not border on disallowing the claims or interest but the re-prioritization of the claim. This explains why the analysis will consider the impact the rules may have on financing emanating from shareholders as loan to the distressed business.

2.4.1 The Problem with Shareholder Loans

While it is true that shareholder loans may be useful as a source of distress financing, it is one problematic source of financing, consequently, it is viewed with suspicion and attracts a predominantly negative treatment. One of the arguments that has been canvassed against shareholder loans is that it may just be a means by which shareholders delay an inescapable liquidation and in the course of the delay, the value of the distressed debtor is deflected away from the creditors. An already over indebted business may choose to pursue projects with net negative values.[53] As has been argued, the loan by the shareholder is essentially borne out of the self-interest of the shareholder-lender, to ensure that its equity interest in the business remains

48 Miglo (2016), p. 71 ("Usually, a creditor's claim is maximized when the probability of the claim being honored is maximized.").

49 Id.

50 The effect of asset substitution and risk shifting was first introduced by Jensen and Meckling. See Jensen and Meckling (1976).

51 This argument, although made in the context of German law may be considered as valid for shareholder lending to a distressed business. See Engert (2004), p. 820.

52 Gelter (2006), pp. 483–484.

53 Skeel and Kraus-Vilmar (2006), p. 270.

alive.[54] However, if the financing is provided by outsiders operating at an arm's length with the debtor, these difficulties may not arise.

Furthermore, the situation is even more complicated where the shareholder loan is backed by security interest obtained over the assets of the distressed debtor. Recall the argument made in the preceding subhead on the possibility of reining the "risk appetite" of shareholders with shareholder lending. Where the shareholder loan is secured, it reduces the risk of default, meaning that the shareholders' loan does not achieve this "reining in" effect.[55] In distressed corporations where the shareholders exercise direct control over the management of the business, they may seek to shore up the assets over which the debtor has created the security interest, a practice commonly described as "feeding the lien".[56]

Again, as between shareholders as insiders and creditors, information asymmetry may mean that creditors may be unaware of the true state of affairs of the distressed debtor, hence the need to protect the creditors from such situation through rules that ensure that the loan advanced by shareholders take a "back seat" as against the claims of the creditors.[57] This however is not to say that an outside creditor who diligently scrutinizes the books of the debtor will not be able to avail itself of such information and therefore make informed lending decisions, absent fraud on the part of the debtor.[58]

There is another argument that the financing provided by the shareholder as a loan may well have been a contribution to the capitalization of the distressed debtor and as such should be subordinated to loans of the same class (subordination), or worse, still be considered as an equity interest and not even a credit claim (recharacterization). The rationale will be that if the distressed business is undercapitalized, it is the duty of the shareholders to see to its capitalization rather than having their eye on better treatments (as creditors) in the event of filing formal insolvency proceedings. As such, the courts, whether deriving their powers from statutes, or in the exercise of their equitable powers, prevent those who "own"[59] the business from transferring the inherent risks in the business to unsuspecting creditors. In this sense, subordination will be justified on the failure of shareholders to adequately capitalize the newly formed corporate entity in the light of the scale of business to be undertaken by that entity.[60]

The jurisprudence on the treatment of shareholder loans is quite nuanced. For instance, while UK law does not specifically single out shareholder loans for special treatment, it is arguable that this is covered under the preference avoidance rules pertaining to persons connected to the business.[61] This is especially so, given the

---

[54] Ibid, pp. 270–275.

[55] Ibid, p. 283. See also Engert (2004), p. 831.

[56] Skeel and Kraus-Vilmar (2006), p. 272–275.

[57] This is an argument canvassed in Germany, to support the case for the equity substitution principle discussed below. See Gelter (2006), p. 494.

[58] See *In re Lifschultz Fast Freight* 132 F. 3d 339, 346.

[59] Ownership is used here to mean control over the business.

[60] See Macey (1980), p. 45.

[61] See s.239 (6) IA, 1986.

fact that connected persons who receive payments or property of the debtor for loans provided in times of distress when liquidation follows, may have benefited from a "breach of the canons of commercial morality"[62] unless there is proof to the contrary. However, at least, one authority shows that English law may not have any outright misgivings against shareholder loans extended to the debtor.[63]

The underlying basis for the shareholder subordination rule may be generally summed up as the presumption of fraudulent or at least the inequitable behavior of the shareholder-lender in choosing to provide loans instead of equity to the distressed debtor. The examination of the jurisdictions below will highlight the nuances; track the development of the jurisprudence; and the approaches adopted by the US and German laws in the regulation of shareholder loans. It is important to keep in mind that the goal is to see how the jurisdictions approach the question of protection for loans when they originate from shareholders.

2.4.2 *Subordination of Shareholder Loans: US and Germany*

2.4.2.1 United States

Shareholder loan subordination in US jurisprudence evolved from case law[64] to the equitable principle now codified in s.510(c) of the Bankruptcy Code.[65] This equitable principle is grounded on the jurisdiction of bankruptcy courts as courts of

[62] See generally, Finch (2009), p. 681.

[63] In *re Matthew Ellis & Co. Ltd.* [1933] 458 in that case, the lender (Chairman of the debtor) had granted a loan to the debtor for the purchase of goods and took a floating charge over the assets of the debtor. The English court in this case did not find anything wrong with the loan given and also held that the security interest held by the Chairman was not defective. Note that although this question was recognized as an area for reform by the Cork Committee, it however refrained from making any recommendations given the complexity of the subject and the several other issues embedded in shareholder loans. IA, 1986. See generally, Cork (1982), at para. 1933 ff. p. 435 ff.

[64] See the case of *Taylor v. Standard Gas v. Electric Co. (Deep Rock)* 306 US 307. (The court in this case developed the equitable doctrine which became known as the "Deep Rock Doctrine". This doctrine in sum entails the subordination of credit advanced by a controlling shareholder of the debtor, where the insolvency of the debtor arises from the undercapitalization and mismanagement of such controlling shareholder). Also, see *Pepper v. Litton* 308 U.S. 295. (The Supreme Court in the same year as the earlier case expounded on the basis for subordination, stating that even in the absence of fraud, shareholder/creditor control or undercapitalization, the claim of the shareholder may be subordinated if such shareholder breached the fiduciary duty owed to other shareholders and creditors). In *Comstock v. Group of Institutional Investors,* 335 U.S. 211,229 (the Supreme Court introduced unconscionableness or bad faith on the part of the controlling shareholder as a prerequisite for the subordination of the claim of such shareholder/creditor).

[65] S.510(c) of the Bankruptcy Code provides that after a notice or a hearing, the court may:

(1) under principles of equitable subordination, subordinate for purposes of distribution, all or part of an allowed claim to all or part of another allowed claim or all or part of an allowed interest to all or part of another allowed interest; or
(2) order that any lien securing such a subordinated claim be transferred to the estate.

equity[66] and this may well explain why Congress left to the courts the development of the principles underlying the subordination of shareholder loans.[67] It is in exercise of this jurisdiction that bankruptcy courts alter existing priorities amongst claimants of the debtor if such claimants have acted in a manner considered inequitable.[68] In *Benjamin v. Diamond (In re Mobile Steel Co.)*[69] decided just a year before the inclusion of equitable subordination in the US Bankruptcy Code of 1978, the court set forth the grounds on which the claim or interest of a shareholder or creditor may be equitably subordinated. It also set forth the basis for a proper implementation of the equitable subordination principle. Given the importance of these grounds, a quick look at these grounds and then the basis for the implementation of the principle will be undertaken.

2.4.2.2 Grounds for Equitable Subordination

The equitable subordination of claims or interest are based on court-developed principles. The court set forth three grounds on which a claim or interest may be equitably subordinated. Although court-developed, the rules were predictable and straightforward. To be subjected to equitable subordination, the lender must have engaged in an "inequitable conduct" which must have either resulted in the conferral of an unjustified advantage on the lender (now defendant) or has resulted in injury to the creditors of the distressed business. Furthermore, the equitable subordination of the claim must be consistent with the provisions of the Bankruptcy Code.[70]

While the conferral of unjustified advantage on the defendant and consistency with the Code do not pose any serious difficulties,[71] the issue of the inequitable conduct of the defendant-claimant has been analyzed and expounded by the courts. The action that is complained about need not necessarily be unlawful. It suffices that such action fails the test of "equity and good conscience". The court also identified three cases in which the conduct of the defendant-claimant may be regarded as falling short of the "equity and good conscience" test. The first case involves the initial undercapitalization of the debtor, so that the "so-called loans or advances by the dominant or controlling [shareholder] will be subordinated to claims of other credi-

[66] *Bank of Marin v. England*, 385 U.S. 99, 103 (1966) (the court emphatically points out that "there is an overriding consideration that equitable principles govern the exercise of bankruptcy jurisdiction.").

[67] See 124 Cong.Rec.H 11095, H 11113 (Sept. 28, 1978).

[68] *Prudence Realization Corp. v. Geist*, 316 U.S. 89, 93 (1942).

[69] 563 F.2d 692 (5th Cir. 1977).

[70] *Benjamin v. Diamond (In re Mobile Steel Co.)* 563 F.2d 692 at 700.

[71] Particularly on the inconsistency with the Code, it has been suggested that it may well be redundant now given that the s.510(c) of the Bankruptcy Code expressly provides for and authorizes the remedy of equitable subordination. See *80 Nassau Assocs. v. Crossland Fed. Sav. Bank (In re 80 Nassau Assocs.)*, 169 B.R. 832, 841(Bankr.S.D.N.Y.1994).

tors and thus treated in effect as capital contributions by the shareholder."[72] This case does point to the inequitable situation that arises from a dominant or controlling shareholder with knowledge of the erosion of the capital of the business, puts itself ahead of non-insiders. Obviously, the motivation will be to ensure that it protects its chances of recovery, while creditors with less information and control over the business bear the brunt of bankruptcy.

The second case in which the conduct of the lender will be regarded as falling short of the equity and good conscience test will arise from mismanagement, breach of fiduciary duties, and abuse of its fiduciary position. Thirdly, the control or use of the debtor as an alter ego for the benefit of the defendant fails the equitable and good conscience test.[73] The facts and the decision of the court in *In re Herby's Foods Inc.*[74] provide a simple illustration of the application of the grounds on which the loan of shareholders may be subordinated by a bankruptcy court. The corporate structure of the debtor showed that it was owned and controlled by the insiders (S, because the debtor was wholly owned by S and D because all of the voting securities of S were owned by D). At different times, the insiders provided loans to the debtor, both to partly finance the purchase of the debtor from its previous owner and as working capital. For these loans, the insiders obtained security interests covering nearly all of the debtor's assets. The security agreements were not perfected until very much later in the life of the debtor. The reason advanced for the delay was to explore the possibility of obtaining secured financing from an outside lender. As at the time the debtor decided to file bankruptcy petition, two remarkable incidents had occurred. First, the debt to the unsecured creditors of the debtor had grown over five times more than what it was at the time of the acquisition of the debtor. Secondly, another insider had made further unsecured advances to the debtor. Following the commencement of bankruptcy proceedings, the insiders filed claims as unsecured creditors, which were challenged by the unsecured creditors committee.

In affirming the decision of the bankruptcy and the district courts to subordinate the claims of the insider shareholders, the Court of Appeals of the fifth circuit considered and applied the three grounds on which the debt owed to shareholders may be subordinated. First, the court had to consider whether the conduct of S and D as insiders were inequitable. The closest point on which this could have been determined was whether the debtor was under-capitalized from the start. Relying on the testimony of a financial expert witness as well as a former finance officer of the debtor prior to the sale of the debtor, the court found that the debtor was already insolvent as at the time of its acquisition and lenders were generally unwilling to lend to the debtor in that state. Now, instead of providing equity, the insiders opted to provide loans.[75] Furthermore, this strategy of "loan instead of equity" and the

---

[72] *Pepper v. Litton* 308 U.S. 295, 309–310. Note however, that the courts have held that undercapitalization by itself is not enough to justify the subordination of shareholder loan.

[73] See *Granite Partners*, 210 B.R. at 514; 80 *Nassau Assocs.*, 169 B.R. 832 at 838.

[74] 2 F.3d 128 (5th Cir. 1993).

[75] Other inequitable conducts of the insiders identified by the court include (a) with full knowledge of the debtor's undercapitalization, the debtor continued to provide debt capital instead of equity

hiding of the shareholder loans from the books of the debtor led external creditors to continue lending to the debtor and without a subordination by the courts, the insiders would have enjoyed priority over those creditors. On the question of harm to external creditors, the court reasoned that the structuring of the capital of insiders as loans and keeping the debt away from the books of the debtor led to a significant increase in the trade credit exposure of the external creditors thereby "... reducing their ultimate dividend in the liquidation."[76]

In view of the dangers against which the equitable doctrine is designed to protect, and the need to provide financing when appropriate, it is important to assess the capacity of the inequitable conduct rule as providing a predictable yardstick.

2.4.2.3 Inequitable Conduct: A Predictable Yardstick for Shareholder Lending

Bearing in mind the important role played by shareholder financing and the importance of stemming the likelihood of abuse by shareholders, it makes sense that the inequitable conduct of the controlling shareholder is made central to the decision of the court to subordinate the debt. There exists a line of cases suggesting, however, that a creditor need not have engaged in inequitable conduct for its claim to be subordinated to that of unsecured creditors. While the US Supreme Court is yet to make a definite statement on this, it is gratifying that such cases although involve the creditors of the debtor, such creditors are not shareholders or even distressed lenders, but tax authorities.[77]

It is submitted here that the policy considerations that inform such decisions should not apply to cases of financing of the distressed business by shareholders. In those tax cases involving tax penalty for non-pecuniary losses, the basis for the subordination is to avoid the reduction in value for unsecured creditors where the debtor is liquidating.[78] Where a financing shareholder has done no wrong by acting

---

capital (b) the insiders tried to keep the facts of the loans away from creditors by keeping them out of the books of the debtor and even when it did, it listed that particular debt as unsecured (c) the loans were meant to yield minimal or in one case no interest and only when interest payments stopped on the first two loans did S and D perfect their security interests.

[76] Ibid, p.134.

[77] *Schultz Broadway Inn v. United States*, 912 F.2d 230, 234 (8th Cir.1990) (subordination of non-pecuniary loss tax penalty); *In re Virtual Network Services Corp.*, 902 F.2d 1246, 1250 (7th Cir.1990) (inequitable conduct on the part of a creditor is not always required for subordination under s.510(c) (1)). *In re Cassis Bistro, Inc.* 188 B.R. 472 (Florida 1995) (Bankruptcy court approved the subordination of tax penalty claims without proving misconduct on the part of the tax creditors).

[78] *Schultz Broadway Inn v. United States*, 912 F.2d 230, 234 (8th Cir.1990). It appears that the subordination of such tax creditor claims rest on whether the debtor is liquidating (under Chap. 7 or reorganizing (under Chapter 11). In the case of the former, the reasoning is that such penalty will result in a reduction of the claims of the unsecured creditors and thus should be discouraged. On the other hand, since a reorganizing debtor is likely to continue in business and possibly become

inequitably, it will certainly be misplaced to subordinate the claim of such a shareholder. Chances are that shareholders may shy away from extending rescue financing to distressed debtors, instead preferring the slide into bankruptcy proceedings and possibly defeating the chances of a timeous out-of-court restructuring.

2.4.2.4 From Shareholder Equitable Subordination to Recharacterization

Instead of the now familiar s.510(c) equitable subordination of shareholder loans, some courts in the US have taken a related but somewhat different approach, which entails the outright recast of the loan from a debt to equity. This is known as the recharacterization of the transaction as a capital contribution (equity).[79] When the debt of a shareholder is so recharacterized, the shareholder is precluded from claiming the repayment of the funds advanced as a corporate debt whether on a secured or unsecured basis.[80] It is important to note that unlike the express provision in the Bankruptcy Code empowering courts to equitably subordinate shareholder loans, the principle of recharacterization of shareholder loans is nowhere expressly provided for in the Code. However, courts that have adopted this approach have drawn their enablement to do so from the general equitable powers of the courts.[81] It is submitted that, unless in cases of subordination of the claim of secured creditors (such as second lien financers), the practical effect of the subordination of a shareholder unsecured loan and the recharacterization of the same as equity comes to one and the same thing. The effect of the subordination is that the claimant whose claim is subordinated takes what is left only after the unsecured creditors have been paid.[82]

---

viable, then such penalty has to be borne by the debtor. See *In re Sheldon Transfer & Storage Co., Inc.* Bankr. L. Rep. P 74, 949. (Mass., 1992).

[79] Skeel and Kraus-Vilmar (2006), p. 264 (Recharacterization is said to differ from ordinary subordination in two respects: it does not require a showing that the shareholder acted inequitably; and rather than being subordinated to other creditor claims, the shareholder's contribution is treated as equity).

[80] *United States v. Colorado Invesco, Inc.* 902 F. Supp. 1339 (Colo. 1995).

[81] For a critique of this, see *Unsecured Creditors' Comms. Of Pac. Express, Inc. v. Pioneer Commercial Funding Corp. (In re Pacific Express, Inc.)*, 69 B.R. 112, 115 (B.A.P. 9th Cir. 1986) (the court pointed out that "[w]here there is specific provision governing these determinations, it is inconsistent with the Bankruptcy Code to allow such determination to be made under different standards through the use of courts equitable powers. See also *In re Pinetree Partners Ltd.* 87 BR 481, 491 (Bankr. N.D. Ohio 1988);

In re Dornier Aviation (North America), Incorporated 453 F.3d 225, 233 (4th Cir. 2007) (recharacterization power is integral to the consistent application of the Bankruptcy Code. In the more recent case of *In re Fitness Holdings International, Inc.* 714 F.3d 1141 (9th Cir. 2013), the 9th circuit more or less refused to follow its earlier decision in *In re Pacific Express*, stating instead that the Code gives the court the power to recharacterize debt claims as equity. See also Nozemack (1999), p. 707.

[82] As will be seen very shortly, while the difference between both concepts is certainly not in the result, it may be in the means of reaching that result. See Wheaton (2015), p. 788. ("Equitable subordination serves to punish creditors that act inequitably, while debt recharacterization corrects 'sham' loans by properly reclassifying as equity contributions.").

This is essentially the same fate an equity holder is faced with and like the claimant whose claim is subordinated, there may be nothing left to satisfy their claims.

2.4.2.5 Court Developed Tests for Recharacterization: A Doctrinal Bedlam

The recharacterization of shareholder loans largely rests on the notion that the so-called loan was actually meant to capitalize the distressed business, which is considered as under-capitalized. Although the result of the application of the principle is the same as the equitable subordination of shareholder loans (at least in cases of unsecured shareholder loans), as earlier canvassed, it is conceded that it serves a somewhat different purpose by determining whether a loan was made at all in the first place.[83] It is necessary to keep in mind the reason for this analysis. Lending by shareholders may serve as an important source of new financing for the distressed business. Understanding the risks inherent in this type of financing may well be determinative of the willingness of shareholders to come forward with such financing. More so, the clearer the applicable legal principles, the better potential lenders are able to determine the character of the financing to be provided and to manage their expectations.

As has been earlier stated, the Bankruptcy Code does not expressly provide for the recharacterization of shareholder claims. The courts have tried to work out the grounds on which the debt of shareholders may be recast as equity and as we shall see, the state of the law appears to be in a flux and courts have overtime developed a host of criteria to be considered in reaching a decision to recharacterize or not. Regarding these criteria, the courts have strived to make three points as the backdrop against which these tests are to be applied. First, the circumstances of each case determine the applicability of the tests or criteria. The tests do not strictly carry equal weight; neither is any one test preponderant. Finally, the more a transaction appears to have been conducted at arm's length, the more the proclivity of the courts to regard the transaction as debt rather than equity.[84] The sixth Circuit in *In re Autostyle Plastics Inc.*[85] listed the recharacterization tests as follows:

---

[83] Ibid.

[84] These points were made *In re Cold Harbor*, 204 B.R.904 at 915.

[85] 269 F.3d 726 (6th Cir. 2001). Note that the tests applied in this case were originally applied in respect of a tax law case (*Roth Steel Tube Co. v. CIR* 800 F.2d 625 (6th Cir. 1986)). The court in *Re Autostyle Plastics Inc.* however was of the opinion that the factors listed in that case "provide a general framework for assessing recharacterization claims that is also appropriate in the bankruptcy context." For a contrasting opinion, see *In re Rego Crescent Corp.* 23 B.R. 958, 962 (In refusing to follow the tests laid down in the context of taxation, the court stated that "the legal questions and policy considerations underlying [the tests in the tax contexts] are so removed from determining whether money advanced should be considered capital contributions or loans for bankruptcy purposes.").

> (1) the names given to the instruments, if any, evidencing the indebtedness; (2) the presence or absence of a fixed maturity date and schedule of payments; (3) the presence or absence of a fixed rate of interest and interest payments; (4) the source of repayments; (5) the adequacy or inadequacy of capitalization; (6) the identity of interest between the creditor and the stockholder; (7) the security, if any, for the advances; (8) the corporation's ability to obtain financing from outside lending institutions; (9) the extent to which the advances were subordinated to the claims of outside creditors; (10) the extent to which the advances were used to acquire capital assets; and (11) the presence or absence of a sinking fund to provide repayments.[86]

The proliferation of tests as shown above is suggestive of one thing: the difficulty in deciphering the true nature or character of funds provided by a shareholder, for the purpose of tiding it over, when in distress and insolvency is imminent. Again, this raises the question of the impact of a somewhat complicated doctrine of recharacterization versus the more predictable equitable subordination and their impact of distress financing.

2.4.3 *Between Equitable Subordination and Recharacterization: Impact on Distress Financing*

In the build up to the analysis of shareholder loans in the US, the point had been constantly made that the difference between the principles of equitable subordination and recharacterization do not go as far as the results that each yield. While it has been recently argued that the principle of recharacterization deserves to be retained,[87] the similarity in outcome has not been faulted or challenged. If the relevance of the inquiry is to alter the bankruptcy law priority of the shareholder lender, the question that arises is why retain the recharacterization principle?

In answering the above question, the principles of equitable subordination by the various courts in the US yields some predictability more than that of recharacterization. Even though what amounts to inequitable conduct (the chief consideration in equitable subordination) is largely left for the court to decipher in most of the cases, the signposts for such a determination have been largely set out. This means that a shareholder who wishes to finance a distressed business may do so, so far as it can prove that his conduct is without fault. The same may not be said for a recharacterization, as it has been even argued that many of the several tests itemized are "either unhelpful or used precisely in the wrong way".[88]

Closely connected to the point made above is that equitable subordination properly mirrors the fault element on the part of the shareholder who is also a lender. The fault element, it is submitted, sits well with a policy aimed at facilitating the provision of financing for the distressed debtor while it needs it. It must be remembered

---

[86] *Re Autostyle Plastics Inc.* case at 750.

[87] Wheaton (2015), p. 769.

[88] Skeel and Kraus-Vilmar (2006), p. 278.

that like every other lender, shareholders are also aware of the fact that equity investment in the distressed debtor may leave them at the lowest rung of the bankruptcy "pecking order". At that position, a shareholder investing in the equity of the distressed debtor may only be setting itself up for completely losing out of its investment.[89] The decision to protect itself from the risks associated with the financing of the debtor in this situation through a loan does not, and should not warrant the imposition of a rule, which without any wrongful conduct on the part of the debtor results in the recasting of the loan. A *per se* prohibition of shareholders lending may have a chilling effect on an increasingly important source of distressed debtor financing and may be detrimental to restructuring. The view of the tenth Circuit in *In re Mid-Town Produce Terminal Inc.*[90] is instructive in this regard and will be quoted here:

> We are unwilling to find a dominant shareholder may not loan money to a corporation in which he is the principal owner and himself become a secured creditor. To hold the debt may be subordinated on that basis alone would discourage owners from trying to salvage a business, and require all contributions to be made in the form of equity capital. We do not think that is desirable as social policy, nor required by the cases.[91]

It is submitted that the desire to penalize the shareholders for merely providing the loans misses the point. What is in fact reprehensible is the unconscionable use of the position of control by the shareholder in control to cause injury to the distressed debtor and the creditors who have dealt with the business prior to the commencement of insolvency proceedings. Being able to determine this will depend on the facts of the case. Unlike the case law approach of the US Bankruptcy Code, German law statutorily regulates shareholder loans. It is to this that attention is now turned.

2.4.4 Germany

2.4.4.1 Equity Substitution Law (*Eigenkapitalersatzrecht*)

German law, like the US law, provides for shareholder loan treatments when bankruptcy proceedings commence. In fact, scholars situate the development of the law in Germany at the same time with that of the US.[92] Also like the US law on the treatment of shareholder loans, the courts were at the vanguard of developing the rules that applied to such means of financing.[93] Like the subordination of unsecured shareholder loans or the recharacterization of such loans in the US, the key result of

[89] Stadler (1997), p. 3.

[90] 599 F.2d 389, 392 (10th Cir. 1979).

[91] Ibid.

[92] Skeel and Kraus-Vilmar (2006), p. 279.

[93] See Verse (2008), p. 1114.

the German equity substitution law is the recasting of loans granted by shareholders pre-insolvency proceedings as equity.[94] Deeply entrenched in German law is the principle that loans (i.e. non-equity funding) provided by shareholders of the business are subordinated to the claims of third party unsecured creditors. Unlike in the US, however, the regulation of shareholder loans is statutory. It is important to bear in mind that the aim here is to track incentives for financing provided in the context of informal restructuring by way of negative protection.

2.4.4.2 Statutory Codification of the Equity Substitution Rules

A shareholder who provides a loan to a business may have its claim substituted for equity, if at the time he advances or recoups the loan, the debtor is in crisis. In the case of a loan advanced pre-distress by the shareholder, if it is not immediately recouped as the business enters into crisis, such loans are also caught by the equity substitution rule. As has been pointed out, a business is considered to be in crisis if "it is either insolvent (illiquid or over-indebted) or at least unworthy of credit".[95] Clearly, shareholders lending to distressed businesses are caught by the equity substitution rule. It is important to note that the equity substitution, although it initially applied to private limited liability companies (GmbH), company law reforms made the rule applicable to all companies with limited liability.[96] It need be pointed out here also as will be seen below, further reforms now mean that the applicable rule is now housed in bankruptcy law.[97]

The reasoning grounding the equity substitution rule is that when shareholders opt for the continued survival of a distressed business, the risks attendant with that decision ought not to be borne by outside creditors.[98] Consequently, money advanced to the debtor cannot be taken out until the business navigates its way out of the crisis and money provided in the course of the crisis will be substituted for equity when insolvency proceedings are opened.[99] A close look at the statutory provision enabling this substitution, will reveal that it is grounded on the supposition that the shareholder ought to have provided capital rather than a loan if acting as a competent business person.[100] Authors have described the German equity substitution rule as a

[94] Gelter (2006), p. 480.

[95] Verse (2008), p. 1114.

[96] This will include private limited liability companies (GmbH), stock corporations (*AG*), limited partnerships which do not have an individual as their general partner (GmbH & Co. KG).

[97] See Sect. 2.4.4.3 below.

[98] Verse (2008), p. 1114.

[99] Id.

[100] Para 32(a) 1 Gesetz betreffend die Gesellschaften mit beschränkter Haftung (GmbHG). See also para 39(1) 5 which, subject to the provisions of para 39(4) and (5), provides that claims for repayment of loans which replace equity (or such similar loans) shall be satisfied after all the claims of other creditors have been satisfied.

remote equivalent of the US recharacterization[101] or equitable subordination[102] principles. Again, as earlier pointed out above in respect of the US, whether this rule is described as a recharacterization or subordination, the practical effect of the rule is that such a shareholder queues behind all the creditors, making its claim residual.

The rule was quite extensive in its reach as it also extended to financing provided by third parties (for which guarantee or security is provided by a shareholder) when capital contribution, rather than loans should have provided to the debtor. In this circumstance, the third party loan provider may only have recourse to the debtor in insolvency on the sum outstanding after such third party has recovered on the security or guarantee provided by the shareholder.[103] The rule further extended to all other similar legal transactions which in their effect, compare economically to loan by either the shareholder or third parties to the debtor as already described.[104] The consequence of the equity substitution rule when the loan to third parties has been repaid within one year of the commencement of insolvency proceedings is that the shareholder who has provided guarantees or security had to reimburse the distressed debtor.

2.4.4.3 A New Regime Under Insolvency Law: Changes to German Equity Substitution Rule

Following amendments to the German Insolvency Act, the regime on equity substitution previously provided for in German corporate law has now been relocated to the insolvency statute.[105] An important provision of the amended legislation that touches on the fate of loans by shareholders is the removal of the distinction between loans provided during distress and at any other time in the life of the business. In other words, lending by shareholders, are without distinction subject to being substituted for equity, doing away with the need for the determination of whether the business was distressed at the time of advancing the loan.

The new regime of the equity substitution rule of German law makes somewhat radical changes to how shareholder loans are construed. Under this regime, it is now

---

[101] Andenæs and Wooldridge (2009), p. 209.

[102] Verse (2008), p. 1111.

[103] Para 32(a) 2 GmbHG.

[104] One of the situations considered by the Federal Supreme Court (Bundesgerichtshof) (BGH) as being economically comparable to be treated as shareholder loans are cases where third party lenders exert control on the management of the debtor. The court reasoned that such a lender will be made liable to the capital maintenance rules which shareholders are subject. (July 13 1992, II ZR 251/91). Until recently, lease of assets by shareholders to their subsidiaries were treated as comparable transactions and as such subjected to the equity substitution rule. The recent decision of the BGH (January 29 2015, IX ZR 279/13) has clearly pointed out that in this regard, the claim of shareholders are not subject to the equity substitution rule. The court reasoned that leases do not compare economically to loans by shareholders and does not lie within the reach of rules applying to shareholder loans and comparable transactions.

[105] See s. 39(1) n 5, (4)-(5) InsO.

irrelevant that the loan was granted by a shareholder at a time when the debtor is in crisis, as all loans originating from shareholders are subject to being substituted for equity.[106] This is understandable, given the difficulty of proving when the debtor became distressed. In a recent case decided by the *Bundesgerichtshof*,[107] the central question before the court was whether the distress of the debtor was a prerequisite for the application of equity substitution rules and a consequent claw back of payment made by the distressed business on debt guaranteed by a former shareholder. The court in its opinion stated that under the relevant legislation,[108] the relevance of the fact of distress has been done away with. It stated that the intention of the legislature as deduced from the plain wordings of the statute is that all loans originating from shareholders be substituted as equity. As will be shortly shown, this decision may now be limited by reason of the safe harbor introduced by legislation.[109]

Remarkably, this rule does away with the difficult question of determining the financial health of the debtor at the time of the shareholder lending. Commendably, the rule immensely gains on certainty in that shareholders providing loans may not have to second-guess the implication of providing loan financing at any point in the life of the business.[110] However, if this still represents the state of the law, it would appear that the law does not countenance the need to support the superstructure on which informal distress financing rests, one of which is the provision of restructuring financing and an increasingly important source of this financing being insider/shareholder financing. The new rule, may have promoted the virtue of certainty at the expense of creating a chill in loan financing by shareholders. For the purpose of financing a distressed business and in the context of informal restructuring, it is submitted that the rule on equity substitution should strive to avoid overreaching by insiders. A *per se* equity substitution of all shareholder loans suggests an irrefutable presumption that shareholder loans are all unconscionable. As long as shareholder loans have been excluded from the financing option of distressed lenders, it means one less option for distress debtor financing. This should tell particularly on informal restructuring as an option for distressed business.

One proposal that bears consideration is shareholders providing financing in distress make full disclosure of the health situation of the business to its creditors, and proposing its intention to make loan investments. Creditors will usually be loath to agree to shareholders providing investment as debt rather than equity, especially where the odds are stacked against a controlling shareholder who fails to commence insolvency proceedings in the face of distress. However, the demise of the debtor may mean a loss of a customer and if the business ever gets to survive, there

[106] Id. Certain exceptions exist and are discussed in Sect. 2.4.4.4.

[107] (April 30, 2015 IX ZR 196/13).

[108] Gesetz zur Modernisierung des GmbH-Rechts und zur Bekäa¨mpfung von Misbra¨uchen [Law for the Modernisation of the Private Limited Companies Act and to Combat its Abuse] (Germany) 1 November 2008, BGBI I, 2026 (MoMiG).

[109] See Sect. 2.4.4.4.

[110] See Naruisch (2011), p. 158 (noting that "... all [shareholder] loans, irrespective of when they were granted, will now be subordinated to claims of other creditors in case of insolvency.").

continues a productive relationship between the borrower and the creditors. This notwithstanding there appears to be a clear delineation of a safe harbor for shareholders who provide debt, in place of equity. This recognition in German law is addressed now.

2.4.4.4 Safe Harbors for Shareholder/Insider Loans[111]

As stringent as the rules on equity substitution appear, German bankruptcy law allows two important safe harbors pertaining to shareholder loans relevant to distressed debtor financing. To be exempt from the blanket rule on the substitution of shareholder loans for equity, the insolvency legislation provides two grounds. The first of these grounds pertains to the degree of control such a shareholder has over the business. Hence, a loan provided to a corporate debtor by a shareholder with not more than 10% of the registered capital, as well as no directing role in the business, is exempt from the reach of the equity substitution rule.[112] What this provision seems to suggest is that compared to a director or holder of more than 10% with control over the distressed debtor (as in the context of this research), the exempted class will not be in a position to make financing decisions on behalf of the distressed debtor and as such should be free of blame.

The other safe harbor pertains to investors with the intent to rescue the business i.e. distress financers. This exception covers investors without prior equity stake in the debtor or a holder of not more than 10% equity stake (as already provided for and discussed above). Investment by this category of financers is spared from the equity substitution rule if the rational for the investment is to save the debtor from distress. As such, "existing or newly granted loans or … claims from legal transactions which correspond in economic terms to such a loan" will not be substituted for equity.[113] Again, this safe harbor is characteristic of the precision of the German law on this subject. This approach on the one hand recognizes the need for financing the process of restructuring. On the other hand, it at least seeks to exclude the chance that a controlling shareholder will exploit the creditors.

However, the exclusion of the controlling shareholders first suggests that they cannot be guiltless in the incidents leading up to the distress of the corporate debtor. It also suggests another way around. A shareholder and lender who wishes to finance the distressed debtor by debt other than equity, may do so by setting up a separate business vehicle or a third-party business entity to provide a loan to a distressed business. This is given that third party lenders are not constrained by the equity substitution rule by its connection to the debtor. If this is the case, perhaps, the lending by this third-party entity may not be subjected to the rule on equity substitution.

[111] These safe harbors were previously contained in Para 32(a) 3 GmbHG now reflected in the amended insolvency statute.

[112] S. 39(5) InsO.

[113] S. 39(4) InsO.

2.4.5 *Shareholder Loans: A Case for Disclosure in Place of a "No-Fault" Rule*

Two jurisdictions that provide for specific treatment of shareholder loans in the context of bankruptcy proceedings have been examined above. Both jurisdictions provide different approaches as shown above. The German approach automatically views loans provided by shareholders as improper, while providing important safe harbors. This approach relies on the fault of the shareholder/lender advancing financing when the business is distressed. If at all it does, the fault lies in the provision of the loan when equity contribution should have been appropriate.[114] The approach of the US, on the other hand, provides for fluidity and pays attention to the intention of the shareholder lender. In other words, one may think of the German rules as relying on an objective criterion, while the court made rules in the US is subjective, looking to the intent of the shareholder, hence the seeming absence of well-defined criteria.

In contrast to the fluidity of the recharacterization rule espoused in the US, the German rule does not countenance the intentions behind the provision of the financing to the debtor by the shareholders, deducible from the formality and absence of uncertainties on the nature of the transaction.[115] The undercapitalization of the debtor and the fact that the debtor was in distress at the time when the loan financing was provided such that a prudent lender will not have provided the debtor a loan, appear to be the only material facts that may need to have been proved. Implicit in this requirement is a similarity with the US recharacterization rule that gives the appearance of shareholder loans as something "morally reprehensible".

In the light of the foregoing, a prescriptive approach to the protection of shareholder lending may be designed along the lines of the imposition of disclosure requirements on the part of the lender at the time of lending. Such statutory prescription may create exemptions based on the fulfilment of board-level procedural steps at the time of the provision of the loan. The problems typically arise because the details of the loan and whatever protection granted to the shareholder, especially one that is controlling, is because the details of the loans are unknown to the other creditors whose interests ought to be protected by the shareholder/lender. Hence, it may be helpful that the loan transaction is negotiated at an arm's length. Even where directors appointed by the shareholder/lender are represented on the board, it may make sense to create a special committee of the board to decide on the loan. Such precaution by the lender at the time of granting the loans may be necessary to prevent a subsequent challenge.

---

[114] See Verse (2008), p. 1112.

[115] Ibid.

2.5 New Financing Through Asset Sales/Divestiture

Asset sale or divestiture in this sense need be distinguished from the use of asset-based financing. Both may appear similar in that they both serve as a means through which the distressed debtor is able to raise financing to support its operations as it tries to overcome its financial distress.[116] However, the most fitting distinction will be that while asset-based lending entails the use of assets of the business as security for the loan, asset sale is an outright disposal of the particular asset as a means of generating income to drive the operations of the business.[117] As part of its restructuring plan, a distressed debtor may choose to dispose of assets, especially its non-core assets. This sale may be of "a division, segment, subsidiary, or product line" of the distressed business.[118] It may even involve the sale of intangible assets such as one or more brands owned by the financially distressed borrower.[119] Apart from helping the debtor shed off the weight of unprofitable (or marginally profit-generating) assets, it also serves the purpose of injecting some liquidity into the distressed business. This way operating expenses and ancillary costs which gulp liquidity may have been taken care of and new financing injected into the distressed business.

It is noteworthy that this option may not always be certain to provide the financing required by the debtor, even if it does, it might not provide immediate financing. Where the assets are already encumbered, unless the sum realizable from the sale meets the value of the interest held by the secured creditor, such sale may not have much of an impact as a source of financing for the financially distressed borrower. Also, when asset sale is to be undertaken, it is often expected that valuation and marketing is undertaken in advance before the sale is negotiated.[120] In this sense, when compared to debt financing, it may not provide an immediate source of cash for the debtor.[121] Furthermore, when sales are driven by the need to generate quick revenue, such sales may result in discounted prices because of possible illiquidity in the market for the assets to be disposed of. This is more so where there is an industry or economy-wide distress and debt financing capacity in the industry is low.[122] Asset

[116] Lasfer et al. (1996) (noting that apart from achieving the transformation of the portfolio of a business, asset sales can be used to "steer the company out of potential bankruptcy").

[117] See generally, John (1993), p. 66 (noting that one way to deal with financial distress is to generate sufficient cash through asset sales to meet debt obligations).

[118] Eckbo and Thorburn (2008), p. 427.

[119] See for instance, CFI, Divestitures. Available at: https://corporatefinanceinstitute.com/resources/knowledge/finance/divestiture-overview/ accessed 10 Aug 2016.

[120] Parkinson (2016), p. 498.

[121] Id.

[122] Shleifer and Vishny aptly describes this as follows:

> The principal reason for asset illiquidity … is the general equilibrium aspect of asset sales. When firms have trouble meeting debt payments and sell assets or are liquidated, the highest valuation potential buyers of these assets are likely to be other firms in the industry. *But these firms are themselves likely to have trouble meeting their debt payments at the time assets are put up for sale as long as the shock that causes the seller's distress is industry- or*

sale in situations described above may result in the sale of the assets at an undervalue. In addition to the likely undervaluation arising from an industry or economy-wide depression, the distressed business may incur huge tax liabilities from asset disposal. This is especially so in view of the typical treatment of asset sales as a capital gain, taxable at the corporate rate.[123]

In the US, there exists a statutory basis for a court-supervised disposition of an asset of a debtor.[124] This disposition is carried out in the course of the formal restructuring of the business, pursuant to the approval of the court. One of the advantages of a sale carried out through this statutory provision is that the purchaser of the asset does so free of any lien which may have attached to the asset, which is now transferred to the proceeds received by the financially distressed debtor.[125] it does appear that businesses and their lenders do not just consider asset sales under the statute as a means of raising financing to continue to support the business. Rather, it has now served as a means of effecting the disposal of large businesses in Chapter 11.[126]

2.6 The Changing Landscape for Distressed Financing: From Commercial Banks to Niche Markets

The provision of financing for businesses has experienced changes. Understanding the rationale for these changes ties into the considerations that inform the provision of new financing for distressed borrowers and sometimes, the willingness of traditional pre-distress financers to participate or continue to remain financially invested in distressed businesses undergoing restructuring. This section therefore examines the pre-eminent role which commercial banks[127] play, given their traditional

---

economy-wide. When they themselves are hurting, these industry buyers are unlikely to be able to raise funds to be buy the distressed firms' assets. [Emphasis supplied].

Shleifer and Vishny (1992); see also Pulvino (1998), p. 939 ("Immediate cash liquidation of distressed firms' assets via [...] could result in suboptimal outcomes"); Bernardo et al. (2016), pp. 395–432 (noting the impact of asset sales on the price of the assets of the bankrupt firms).

[123] It is worth noting that following tax reforms in Germany, there exists a capital gains exemption, which could benefit firms disposing of assets. See for instance, Shackelford et al. (2001) (authors use "Germany as a natural experiment to provide evidence on the extent to which taxes present a barrier to the efficient acquisition and divestiture of stakes in other firms.").

[124] See 11 USC §363. Note that Canada also provides for a statutory sale of assets by a debtor that is in financial distress. for a comparative analysis of the US and Canadian approaches to asset sales, see Ben-Ishai and Lubben (2011).

[125] On the advantages of a s. 363 sale, see Gilson (2010), p. 24.

[126] For an analysis of the use of for the sale of distressed businesses, see Baird and Rasmussen (2002); see also Lubben (2005).

[127] "Commercial bank" is stressed to distinguish between the investment bank in the US (or merchant banks in the UK) and commercial banks which can be distinguished on the basis of the scope of their operations. The former is concerned with the provision of specialist services for large companies and investors, such as underwriting and Mergers and Acquisitions, while the latter is

function as lenders. It proceeds to examine how and why commercial banks are becoming less suited as the choice providers of financing to distressed borrowers. Finally, the section looks at new players being thrown up in the quest to fill the niche in the distressed lending space.

2.6.1 Commercial Bank and Private Lending

Commercial banks have played the traditional role of private lenders to businesses.[128] As traditional lenders, banks were considered better placed to play this role for several reasons. Since private lending rests on the relationship existing between the lender and the borrower, there is the possibility of negotiating, and when the borrower is financially challenged, renegotiating the terms of the loan and new financing.[129] Also, this existing relationship also means that they are better seized of information on the debtor.[130] In addition, compared to disperse lenders, as in bonds for instance, traditional bank lenders are considered better equipped to monitor and protect their interests through the use of covenants, collateral control, and monitoring.[131] This holds true when the businesses are healthy and more so when they are in distress. In the case of the latter, it has been argued that the banks, compared to non-bank lenders are better placed to speedily renegotiate and contain financial losses in the case of borrower's distress.[132] However, the ability to do so notwithstanding, whether banks are often disposed to exercise this option in the light of the evolution in the market is becoming increasingly doubtful.[133]

When businesses are healthy, lenders may provide financing on a secured or even unsecured basis.[134] When distressed, the bank lenders are in position to make a

---

chiefly concerned with deposit taking and lending to businesses of different sizes. It is the latter that is focused upon here. On the differences between commercial and investment (or merchant) banks, see FT Lexicon, *Definition of Investment Bank* available at http://lexicon.ft.com/Term?term=investment-bank accessed 10 June 2017.

[128] See generally, Becker and Josephson (2016) (noting that in most countries, corporate debt is in the form of bank loans).

[129] See Morris (2014) (Quoting the then managing director of the Loan Market Association Claire Dawson: "[l]oans are very flexible instruments and the market tends to remain open during times of stress, and offers borrowers that have established relationships with banks the opportunity to have a conversation about their funding requirements.").

[130] Black (1975), p. 323–324 (pointing out that that banks have the advantage of being able to access information at comparatively lower cost compared to other financial intermediaries).

[131] See generally, Whitehead (2009), p. 651 ("[traditional bank lenders] rely on relationship to monitor and enforce covenants to address credit risk, typically at lower cost than public debt holders.") Also, in the US, such monitoring services were largely achieved through the help of collateral certification or management industry. For an analysis of this industry, see generally, Tajti (2014).

[132] See Arena (2011), p. 394.

[133] See Sect. 2.6.2 below.

[134] Mann (1997), p. 629 (arguing that that the strongest companies in the US would not ordinarily secure their debts).

decision on whether to provide financing for the distressed business on the basis of the information at its disposal.[135] Also importantly, loans usually occupy higher positions in the capital structure of business and combined with the quality of collateral provided to the debtor[136] banks may be in a position to provide new financing for distressed borrowers.

Bank lending may also be distinguished on the basis of the nature of the line of credit made available by the lender. Hence, a distinction can be made between a term loan facility and a revolving facility. When a bank provides financing based on a term loan, it essentially commits to provide financing to the borrower—through one lump sum, or spread through tranches—over a period.[137] In repaying the loan facility, the borrower may do so through a single repayment (also known as a non-amortizing or bullet repayment), or pursuant to a scheduled or installment repayment (also known as an amortizing repayment). On the other hand, a borrower and bank lender may agree that financing is provided to the borrower for an extended period, allowing the borrower to draw down on the facility, repay what is borrowed, and redraw all or part of the facility again until the end date of the facility.[138]

Unlike term loans, the maturity for revolving facilities are shorter, and depending on borrower's compliance with the typically strict cash flow targets, the loan may be rolled over for the debtor.[139] In the context of lending to a distressed business, in meeting the interim financing needs of the distressed businesses, bank lenders are considered to do so on the basis of a revolving facility.[140] The shorter term means that the bank is able to impose strict cash flow target on the borrower and is able to better manage disbursement and limit exposure, in addition to higher interest rates.[141] On the other hand, a term loan facility may follow after the parties have agreed upon the restructuring plan and a new loan for the debtor is agreed upon.

Bank lending may be undertaken by a single lender, or by two or more banks. When two or more banks do so in a coordinated manner, it is a syndicated lending. Syndicated lending involves an arrangement where two or more lenders provide credit facility to a borrower through a single credit document. This is in contrast to

[135] This may depend in many cases on the level of exposure to that borrower. Prudential rules in different countries set limits on exposure to any one borrower. See Core Principle 19 in The Core Principles for Effective Banking Supervision, published by the Committee in September 2012. Available at www.bis.org/publ/bcbs230.pdf. accessed 19 Mar 2018.

[136] Lumpkin (2003), p. 54.

[137] The period of term is typically between 1 and 5 years. See generally, Loan Market Association (Oct 2013) Guide to Syndicated Loans & Leveraged Finance Transactions. Available at: http://www.lma.eu.com/application/files/1614/7749/3386/LMA_Guide_to_Syndicated_Loans.pdf accessed 14 June 2017.

[138] See 29 (noting the similarity of a revolver to an overdraft).

[139] Mcknight (2008), p. 94 (The arrangement is also structured in a way that the total unpaid amount does not exceed the value of the limit that has been set by the agreement).

[140] Gullifer and Payne (2015), p. 29 (noting that such financing can be sued to meet working capital needs).

[141] In the US for instance, see Baird and Rasmussen (2002), p. 784 ("[i]n the typical case, there is a revolving credit facility put in place when financial distress appears on the horizon.").

situations where one lender provides all of the financing and then "participates out" to other lenders, so that each participation is governed by different agreements.[142] Especially as it pertains to lending to distressed businesses, syndicated lending may reflect the risk inherent in financing a distressed business, hence the need to distribute such risk across several lenders.[143] At the helm of the syndicate is a lead arranger bank ("lead lender") whose role is to underwrite the facility and the other lenders ("participants"), who purchase stakes in the financing arrangement from the lead arranger are assigned stakes in the loan. The outcome of this arrangement has been that the participants are only entitled to repayment by the obligor but cannot seek to enforce a default by obligor on the assets by which the obligor has secured the facility.[144]

Amongst the reasons for which banks may resort to syndicated lending will be the size of the loan and importantly, the risk involved in lending to the debtor. In the case of the latter, a consideration to be considered by lenders is that syndicated lending will help to spread the risk of providing the facility. It has been pointed out that when the debtor is distressed, it is the more difficult for it to resist such lending, as it may be unable to (through bargain), object to the syndication or say no to the assignment fee which it now has to bear.[145] The forgoing notwithstanding, concerns have been raised regarding the seeming decline in the role of banks as lenders in situations of distress, where borrowers seek to embark on a restructuring.

2.6.2 *Banks as Distressed Lenders: The Decline and Emergence of Non-bank Lenders*

Although commercial banks still provide lending services,[146] the trend in current times is suggestive of a decline in their provision of new financing to distressed business borrowers or even playing an active part in their restructuring.[147] A number

---

[142] See Wood (2008).

[143] See Foglia et al. (1998), p. 1448. See also, Ajibo (2015), p. 478 ("... syndicated arrangement helps to spread the risks among various lenders thereby reducing the exposure of one bank.").

[144] See generally, Hilson and Sepinuck (2012).

[145] Goldschmid (2005), p. 229.

[146] Commercial bank is stressed to distinguish between the investment bank in the US (or merchant banks in the UK) and commercial banks which can be distinguished on the basis of the scope of their operations. The former is concerned with the provision of specialist services for large companies and investors, such as underwriting and Mergers and Acquisitions, while the latter is chiefly concerned with deposit taking and lending to businesses of different sizes. It is the latter that is focused upon here. On the differences between commercial and investment (or merchant) banks, see FT Lexicon, Definition of Investment Bank. Available at: http://lexicon.ft.com/Term?term=investment-bank accessed 10 June 2017.

[147] See generally, The European Federation of Financial Analysts Societies, Non-Bank Financing of European Non-Financial Firms, Study Report July 2016. Available at: https://effas.net/pdf/Nova_SBE_EFFAs_Non_Bank_Financing_EU_12102016.pdf accessed 13 May 2017. (Research showing that following the financial crises, most European banks have found it difficult to finance themselves and more so, to lend to businesses).

of identifiable factors account for this.[148] These factors include **the effect of regulatory constraints faced by commercial banks, the opportunity of risk shifting**, and **the growth of dis-intermediation**, have played roles either in reducing the involvement of commercial banks with the borrowers in the first place or negatively impact their willingness to further finance the distressed borrower in a restructuring. These factors have also show the emergence of other non-bank actors who serve as providers of financing to distressed borrowers.

2.6.2.1 Effect of Bank Regulation on Distressed Lending

Another factor which determines the willingness of commercial banks to provide new financing to distressed borrowers is the existence of regulatory constraints that impact their ability to do so. To properly contextualize this constraint, it may be worthwhile to understand the traditional role which commercial banks as deposit-taking and loan providing institutions play. Traditionally, they take money from their depositors, lenders and other investors, and use the money received to provide loans to their borrowers.[149] This is the process of intermediation, a classical attribute of these banks.[150] For the purpose of avoiding the possibility that the borrowers of the banks are unable to pay their debt to the banks, and the banks in turn are unable to pay its own creditors (especially its depositors), at least three supervisory requirements are imposed on banks. First, the banks are required to maintain a certain amount of cash reserve (capital), which should ostensibly protect the fund of depositors.[151] Secondly, commercial banks are required to set aside a certain amount to serve as a cushion where it is expected that there will be losses on loans.[152] Thirdly, the exposure of banks to any one borrower is also limited, so that there is no concentration of exposure to any single borrower.[153]

---

[148] Apart from the factors noted above, it is instructive to note that after 2007, there appeared to be a tightening of lending policy, especially to distressed business as "political, public and regulatory attention" appeared to focus on their role in contributing to the financial crisis. See Vriesendorp and Gramatikov (2010).

[149] Bell and Dawson (2002), p. 541 ("The difference between what it is required to pay to [their depositors, lenders, and other investors] and that received from [their borrowers], post expenses, represents the bank's profits.").

[150] Matthews and Thompson (2005) ("[F]inancial intermediation is a process which involves surplus units depositing funds with financial institutions who in turn lend to deficit units.").

[151] Bell and Dawson (2002), p. 543. Basel III requires a capital to risk weighted asset of 8%.

[152] This is known as loan loss provisioning (LLP). See generally, Ozili and Outa (2017). Basel III advocates and actively supports the approach of the International Accounting Standards Board (IASB) to provisioning known as the "Expected Credit Loss" (ECL) approach, as against the prevalent Incurred Loss Approach. See Basel Committee on Banking Supervision, Basel III: A Global Regulatory Framework for More Resilient Banks and Banking Systems, Para 43. Available at: http://www.bis.org/publ/bcbs189.pdf accessed 10 Oct 2017.

[153] See Core Principle 19 in The Core Principles for Effective Banking Supervision, published by the Committee in September 2012. Available at www.bis.org/publ/bcbs230.pdf. accessed 19 Mar 2018.

One may wonder why this analysis is at all necessary to understand the effect of regulatory constraints on bank lending to distressed businesses. Although there is not much in terms of data to show the correlation between increased cash reserve requirement and lower enthusiasm on the part of banks to participate in restructuring, economists have theoretically argued that increased capital requirements can increase bank credit rationing and the availability of credit.[154] Consequently, rather than provide lending on the margins for private borrowers, commercial banks may be disposed to investing in government securities.[155] In addition, although there is no empirical evidence on the effect of provisioning on a restructuring, one may make an intuitive argument that where these banks are required to make provision for expected credit loss, rather than for incurred loss,[156] it is likely that banks may refrain from throwing good money after bad. Instead they may opt for disposing the debt on the secondary loan market. The same applies to the restrictions on the amount of exposure which the bank may have in respect of one borrower. Providing restructuring financing may well mean that the bank may exceed this limit. This in turn may further dampen any enthusiasm to further lend to a defaulted borrower.

From the foregoing, one may see that the regulatory constraints of commercial banks may mean that they may well not be suited to serve the role of distressed financers. The search for new financing may require more lenders with bespoke strategies that can fit into the specific contexts of distressed lending. While this issue will be addressed in a different section. For now, one may consider another factor that support the changing role of commercial bank as possible lenders to distressed borrowers. The ability to shift lending risks is now considered.

2.6.2.2 Availability of Risk-Shifting

The existence of innovative derivative products in the financing market, as well as the ability of bank lenders to mitigate their exposure by spreading the default risk may have an impact on the willingness to provide new financing or take part in the

---

[154] Thakor (1996), p. 282.

[155] Id. This is also applicable to frontier markets like Nigeria, where there appears to be an increased preference for government issued securities, in preference to lending to private sector borrowers. One newspaper recently reported as follows:

> "Banks in Nigeria have a reduced incentive to lend to the private sector because of the favourable interest on government securities," Akintunde Majekodunmi, a banking analyst at Moody's Investors Service, said by phone from London on Wednesday. "They have increased appetite for government securities, which may cannibalise private-sector credit.

See Nigerian banks tie money in government bonds, cut bank (sic) on loans (7 April 2017). In: The Guardian. Available at: https://guardian.ng/business-services/nigerian-banks-tie-money-in-government-bonds-cut-bank-on-loans/ accessed 11 Aug 2017.

[156] See Basel Committee on Banking Supervision, Basel III: A Global Regulatory Framework for More Resilient Banks and Banking Systems, Para 43. Available at: http://www.bis.org/publ/bcbs189.pdf accessed 10 Oct 2017.

restructuring efforts of the borrower who is in financially distressed. Traditional lenders who have taken advantage of the opportunity to shift or hedge the default risk of their borrowers may well be less inclined to provide further financing when such a borrower is distressed. A derivative product which has been considered to have greatly impacted debtor-creditor relationship is the credit default swap (CDS).[157] For instance, a bank lender may have, prior to the default by the distressed borrower, entered a CDS with a third party. Although the default on the part of the debtor translates to a loss on the loan, that loss can be recouped through the swap agreement between the bank and the third party. On the other hand, if the debtor is able to keep up payments in line with the loan agreement, the bank may be obligated to make a payment to the third party pursuant to the CDS agreement, meaning a reduction in the profit of the bank lender on the loan.[158] A lender who has protected itself against the possible default of the debtor may very well care less about the fate of the debtor and its business.[159] In this case, new lending to protect its prior exposure may be unnecessary.[160] One may quickly point out that the use of CDS in this way by banks may be applicable where there is a developed credit derivatives market.

Another possible disincentive to providing new financing or participating in the borrower's restructuring is the spreading out of the risk of default and the limitation of individual exposure. A bank (or a consortium of them) may provide new financing to a distressed business, with the loan participated out, so that their actual credit exposure is limited.[161] In this situation, unless of course the lenders have other reasons to cooperate, there may well be not much incentive on the part of a lender to restructure or provide additional lending, in the face of negligible prior exposure.

Indeed, the issues discussed in this subsection readily apply to large borrowers and to markets with developed derivative markets. Notwithstanding this, as the derivative markets begin to take root in emerging and frontier markets, these developments will increasingly become the reality in the borrower-lender relationship, adding to the list of factors that is hitherto leading to a decline in bank lending to distressed business. Another factor that impacts the relevance of commercial banks

[157] See generally, Bolton and Oehmke (2011) (on the effect of credit insurance on creditor willingness to restructure).

[158] See Partnoy and Skeel (2007), pp. 1021–1022. See also Whitehead (2009), p. 643 (pointing out that for over twenty years, there has been changes to the relationship of banks and their customers. Banks now tend to manage default risks by buying and selling loans and other exposures to borrowers, by which they now generate better returns on the loan portfolios).

[159] See Goldschmid (2005), p. 222 (noting that through such credit insurance, the bank lender may have transferred the willingness to restructure to the third party).

[160] Hu and Black address this issue as the "uncoupling" of the creditor and company interest, so that the creditor who holds a CDS has no incentive to support the restructuring of the distressed borrower. See Hu and Black (2008), p. 728.

[161] Goldschmid (2005), p. 222 ('... senior debtors typically off-load these loans to others through syndications, collateralized loan obligations (CLOs), and collateralized bond obligations (CBOs), often leaving them with "little money" in true credit exposure.').

to restructuring is the increasing intermediation that is becoming a characteristic of lending in general. This is considered below.

2.6.2.3 Disintermediation: Bespoke Distress Lending Options?

As already noted, commercial banks thrive on their role as intermediaries between depositors and investors on the one hand, and borrowers on the other.[162] There however appears to be a growing disintermediation, so that the investors increasingly bypass the banks to directly invest in businesses. For example, big and mid-cap companies now have an array of options for sourcing financing whether within their home countries or outside, using different types of financial instruments.[163] For large and mid-cap companies, **institutional lenders** like hedge funds and Collateralized Loan Obligation (CLO) funds whose strategy include providing direct lending to borrowers in need of financing are taking center-stage.[164] For these institutional lenders, their motivation as distress lenders is essentially tied to the yield from the investment. In the US where, institutional lenders are known to provide distress lending, unlike traditional bank lenders who may provide revolving loans to the borrower, they typically provide new financing as term loans, given the longer spread of interest payments.[165] Driven by the yield, it is argued that accessing new financing through term loans provided by institutional investors tend to be more expensive, compared to the revolver of traditional bank lenders.[166] The above suggests that commercial banks may not even be in the capital structure of the business in the first place.

It is not only the bigger corporations who experienced these changes that impacted the relevance of traditional bank lending. SMEs may well have also experienced changes in their capital structure which have replaced bank lending as a major source of lending. The implication therefore is that even when the businesses are healthy, the changes in the capital structure indicate that the role of banks as financers may be declining. If in distress, such funding may be minimal or even non-existent. Be that as it may, SMEs in certain jurisdictions largely meet their financing needs through options such as asset-based financing. Asset-based financing is itself a type of debt financing characterized by the availability of revolving

---

[162] See Sect. 2.6.2.1.

[163] These instruments range from commercial papers, bonds, and even convertible preference shares. See City of London Law Society (1996) "Corporate Restructuring and the London Approach", 1.16-1.18 (unpublished paper cited in Flood (2001), p. 273. More recently, banks could repackage the debts of large corporates and sell them off under securitization arrangements similar to that used in mortgage transactions. In addition are the use of credit default swaps which serve more as insurance against default on loan obligation by borrowers. See generally, Armour (2012), p. 54.

[164] Mariathasan (2018) (on how institutional investors are replacing banks through direct lending).

[165] Apart from the yield arising from the longer spread, institutional investors also take advantage of the portfolio interest exemption in the US income tax that allows them to avoid payment of income tax on income derived from investment in funded assets. See generally, Zumbro (2016), p. 8.

[166] Id.

loan to a borrower by reference to the value of the assets on the balance sheet of the borrower.[167]

It ought not to be surprising that the ABL industry is associated with the provision financing for distressed businesses. Its historical origin in the US point to association with cash-strapped businesses who approach the industry as lenders of last resort.[168] The goal of the borrowers was to obtain interim financing to enable the business to keep its head above water, until when they can obtain facilities from traditional lenders.[169] Today, although the industry may not be regarded as exclusively providing financing for distressed businesses,[170] or for SMEs, it still plays a strong role in the financing of distressed businesses seeking new financing to support their restructuring especially in the US where it originated.[171] In the same vein, it has been pointed out that asset-based lending has also accounted for the change in the capital structure of SMEs of UK firms. Armour points out, behind this change in the capital structure of SMEs in the UK is the growth of asset-based financing, altering the situation where there was one "main bank" providing the relevant financing. What we see now is that private or closely held corporations now "have a multiplicity of financing creditors, each providing funding for particular assets or asset classes."[172] Again, we see that the bulk of the financing for these businesses are not necessarily routed through the commercial banks but directly made available to the businesses. Hence, for some SMEs, traditional lenders may play little or no role in their financing either prior to or during their distress.[173]

Also, the distressed debt market may be considered a key source of the change in the way distressed businesses are financed and in the pattern of restructuring. The role of the distressed debt market as lender and its role in the changing face of business restructuring is the subject of Chap. 6.[174] It however bears stating here, as will be discussed in that chapter, that while bank lenders increasingly turn to the market to dispose of their own defaulted loans, it has been argued that borrowers are 'increasingly likely to turn ... to [distressed debt investors] or to other sources of "alternative capital."'[175]

Finally, one option which is not often talked about is the bailout option for distressed businesses. A bailout entails state intervention in otherwise private

---

[167] See Comptroller's Handbook (2017).

[168] Rutberg (1994) (noting that this association with cash-strapped businesses posed an image problem for the industry).

[169] Ibid, p. 5.

[170] Id.

[171] Recent research by the Turnaround Management Association (TMA) indicate that new financing provided in the Chapter 11 restructuring of 8 large retail companies, were all provided by ABL lenders. See Myers (2018).

[172] Armour (2012), p. 54.

[173] On the growing influence of asset-based lending for German medium-sized companies (*Mittlestand*), see Visintin (2004), p. 65.

[174] See Chap. 6, Sect. 6.2.

[175] See Finch (2008), p. 762. The distressed debt market, its players and its role in the financing of distressed businesses is extensively explored in Chap. 6 below.

businesses faced with financial difficulties with a view to preventing the collapse of such businesses. It typically involves public financing for distressed businesses, such public financing justified on the socio-economic implications that may result if the state idly sits by and allow the business to go under.[176] State intervention—in the form of new financing, guarantees, asset reliefs—became a prominent option employed by states, following the aftermaths of the global financial crisis, to stem the effects of the crisis.[177] Although financial institutions (which are outside the scope of this research were the major beneficiaries), non-financial businesses, were also beneficiaries.[178] The reason for this is that both financial and non-financial firms became susceptible to the same kinds of "systemic risks",[179] for which state intervention was required.[180] There are however, mixed reactions on the use of bailout as means for providing financing to distressed businesses.

State intervention by way of bailout is faulted on several grounds. Much of the criticisms of bailouts stem from the use of taxpayers' monies to save private businesses, the absence of a statutory basis on which rescue choices are made, and the moral hazard that it may bring about. For instance, bailouts seem to create the impression that in good times, the profits arising from the business is privatized for the benefit of shareholders, whereas when things go wrong, taxpayers are called upon to pick upon to salvage the same business.[181] Furthermore, state intervention in this way has often been considered problematic both for intra-community trade, as well as for rival businesses, especially in the light of its effects on competition.[182] For this reason, state intervention is provided as sparingly as possible.

---

[176] Azgad-Tromer (2017), p. 174 ("It is not the firm-specific risks of corporate failure that justify rescue funding from the public, but rather the implications outside the firm … that make the public particularly vulnerable to a too-big-to-fail firm's potential failure and thereby merits rescue funding.").

[177] While most of the bailout packages went to financial institutions, the focus in this book is not very much on financial institutions but on businesses that are not financial institutions.

[178] Take Germany for instance, in 2009, the German federal government and four federal states granted bridge facility of Euros 1.5 billion to car manufacturer Opel, holding out prospects of additional guarantees of Euros 4.5 billion. Also, container shipping company Hapag-Llyod Ag was granted guarantees up to the tune of Euros 1.2 billion with the bulk of it coming from the Federal and state government of Hamburg. See Robert Wright (8 Oct 2009) Germany steps in with aid for Hapag-Lloyd. In: FT.

[179] See Schwarcz (2008), p. 231 (on the various meanings of systemic risks).

[180] Levitin (2011), p. 452 (on the systemic risks for which bailout may be required by both financial and non-financial troubled firms).

[181] Commenting on the recent insolvency and suggestions for bailout of Carillion, one of the largest British construction companies until its demise, David Lammy, a labor politician tweeted as follows: "Carillion becoming another tragic case study in what happens when we privatise profits when things go well and nationalise risks so the taxpayer picks up the bill when things go wrong [emphasis supplied]." Available at https://twitter.com/DavidLammy/status/952641674186035200 accessed 10 Feb 2018). See also Freytas-Tamura (15 Jan 2018) Collapse of U.K. Construction Giant Rattles the Government. In: NYTimes. Available at https://www.nytimes.com/2018/01/15/world/europe/carillion-bankruptcy-outsourcing-britain.html accessed 10 Feb 2018.

[182] Take the European Union (EU) for instance, Consolidated Version of the Treaty on the Functioning of the European Union art. 107(1), 2008 O.J. C 115/47. Provides that "save as other-

On the other hand, other arguments have been advanced to justify its use, given the socio-economic considerations that necessitates it. A hallmark of market economies is the limited intervention of the state in the market. It is exactly for this reason that laws are prescribed, so that parties can bargain within the framework of the law, or at best against the backdrop of the law in the resolution of distress. However, not all situations can readily fit into the design of the law, given the socio-economic ramification, hence requiring state intervention by way of public financing. Certain businesses fall within the category for which their financing may not be left to the restructuring regime especially because of the socio-economic implications of their failure, to warrant public financing.[183]

Allowing the business to fail may come at an economic cost in the nature of its possible impact on connected firms, such as its suppliers, purchasers, and possibly its own competitors. A major manufacturer who is allowed to fail may be indebted to its suppliers, who in turn may be indebted to their own suppliers. Where suppliers have to struggle to meet their own obligations, it may have an adverse effect on the competitors of the manufacturer, as they may be unable access credit lines to which the supplier may readily provide before the distress of the initial distressed manufacturer.[184] Moreover, following the 2008 financial crisis, weighed against the losses to bondholders, massive job cuts that may follow and the likely panic systemic crisis may bring about, government financing was thought a better option.[185]

Finally, although bailouts may be a political decision and typically available to big businesses, one may well consider this as an option that may be an option that may be considered states, to help salvage distressed businesses.

2.7 Conclusion: Making Distressed Financing Available in Frontier Markets Like Nigeria: What Lessons Can Be Learnt?

So far, this chapter has outlined the sources of financing for distressed businesses. A closer look will show that the focus has been on cash financing for the distressed business and has not addressed title financing such as leasing as well as trade financing which as indicated has been left outside of the scope of this book. It bears restating that distressed lending, unlike lending to financially stable businesses indicate nuances which distinguish it from financing to businesses which are healthy and

wise provided in the Treaties, any aid granted by any Member state or through State resources in any form whatsoever which distorts or threatens to distort competition by favoring certain undertakings or the production of certain goods, shall in so far as it affects trade between Member States, be incompatible with the internal market."

[183] See Azgad-Tromer (2017), p. 159 (on why in spite formal restructuring regimes, public financing may be necessary for certain businesses).

[184] Levitin (2011), p. 456 (for examples on obligor and counterparty contagion can result in systemic risk, requiring state intervention).

[185] Samuelson (2015).

outside of the region of distress and requiring a restructuring. While this chapter modestly aims to do no more than provide an overview of financing options and an identification of the actors in a distressed context, it has provided some analysis on the challenges which particular financing options may face in the context of distressed businesses. To enable distressed businesses restructure, it is important that they have access to a variety of options through which financing may be raised.

One source of financing that appears to be prevalent across board is that which comes from within the distressed business itself i.e. from the shareholders. Indeed, this is one option that may well cut across all jurisdictions. The chief difficulty with such financing in some jurisdictions is exactly with the desire of the shareholders to structure that financing as a loan, to increase their chances of recovery in a formal bankruptcy proceeding. In jurisdictions that frown at such structuring of the new financing, clarity in the applicable rules is key and the German statutory intervention and its explicit rendition of the rules may provide some useful guidance for jurisdictions that object to such structuring. Nevertheless, it is equally of great importance that shareholders as possible first interveners are not disincentivized from doing so. A clear system of disclosure and approval by shareholder-lenders at the time of financing and some court flexibility may better create the needed balance.

As reform efforts of restructuring regimes continue, it is important to appreciate the peculiarities that influence the access to financing for distressed businesses, as this is without doubt critical to the success of the restructuring itself. One thing that must be borne in mind is that providing new money to a distressed borrower brings up the need to reflect on considerations that determine how new money is provided, who provides it, what motivation drives the providers of new financing and what changes are decipherable from the changes in the market for new financing. In the same vein, the sources of financing and the implication of the new financing has been shown to matter in certain jurisdictions, showing the difficulty in regulating such situations. This chapter has tried to cover all of these considerations.

From the chapter, one may readily see that in developed jurisdictions, apart from banks providing new financing, distressed businesses are already able to tap into the capital market as a means of obtaining financing. in developing economies, it is more likely to find that financing still come from traditional lenders. Also, both for developed and developing ones, when it is politically expedient, bailouts may be used to rescue so-called systemically important businesses. Most of the other financing techniques are typically in their early stages of development or not even in existence in developing economies. It is expected that as efforts are directed towards making their legal systems more efficient, there is likely to be a growth in financing options especially for distressed businesses within those economies.

One conclusion that can be drawn from the role of banks as providers of financing, is that newer lenders or products that meet the financing needs of distressed borrowers are becoming the more relevant and in demand. Irrespective of the market-based and bank-based divide, the recognition of the importance of distressed lending should mean that more non-bank sources or better still, products suited for the particular situation of distressed lending will become the more relevant as the lending market continues to evolve. Against this background, the book now examines the key requirements for a restructuring regime, how liquidity is facilitated through these requirements.

References

Adler BE (2007) Bankruptcy cases, problems and materials, 4th edn. Foundation Press, New York
Ajibo CC (2015) Syndicated lending: re-conceptualising the role of the managing bank and agent bank. JIBLR 30(9):476–486
Andenæs MT, Wooldridge F (2009) European comparative company law. Cambridge University Press, Cambridge
Arena M (2011) The corporate choice between public debt, bank loans, traditional private debt placements, and 144A debt issues. Rev Quant Financ Acct 36(3):391–416
Armour J (2012) The rise of the 'pre-pack': corporate restructuring in the UK and proposals for reform. In: Austin RP, Aoun FJG (eds) Restructuring companies in troubled times: director and creditor perspectives. Ross Parson Center for Commercial, Corporate and Taxation Law, Sydney, pp 43–78
Azgad-Tromer S (2017) Too important to fail: bankruptcy versus bailout of socially important non-financial institutions. Harv Bus Law Rev 7:159–187
Baird DG, Jackson TH (1984) Corporate reorganizations and the treatment of diverse ownership interests: a comment on adequate protection of secured creditors in bankruptcy. Univ Chic Law Rev 51(1):112–130
Baird DG, Rasmussen RK (2002) The end of bankruptcy. Stan Law Rev 55(3):751–781
Becker B, Josephson J (2016) Insolvency resolution and the missing high-yield bond markets. Rev Financ Stud 29(10):2814–2849
Bell I, Dawson P (2002) Synthetic securitization: use of derivative technology for credit transfer. Duke J Comp Int Law 12(2):541–562
Ben-Ishai S, Lubben SJ (2011) Sales or plans: a comparative account of the "new" corporate reorganization. McGill Law J 56(3):591–627
Benmelech E (2009) Asset salability and debt maturity: evidence from 19th century American Railroads. Rev Financ Stud 22:1545–1584
Bernardo AE, Schwartz A, Welch I (2016) Contracting externalities and mandatory menus in the U.S. bankruptcy code. J Law Econ Org 32:395–432
Black F (1975) Bank funds management in an efficient market. J Financ Econ 2(4):323–339
Bolton P, Oehmke M (2011) Credit default swaps and the empty creditor problem. Rev Financ Stud 24(8):2617–2655
Chiappineli EA (2006) Cases and materials on business entities. Aspen Publishers, New York
Collard JM (1994) Businesses in distress: turnaround financing for distressed companies. J Work Cap Manag:1–4
Comptroller's Handbook (2017) Asset based lending. https://www.occ.treas.gv/publications/publications-by-type/comptrollers-handbook/asset-based-lending/pub-ch-asset-based-lending.pdf. Accessed 1 Aug 2018
Cork K (1982) Insolvency law and practice: report of the review committee. HMSO, London
Cusmano L (2015) New approaches to SME and entrepreneurship financing: broadening the range of instruments para 36, 11. https://www.oecd.org/cfe/smes/New-Approaches-SME-full-report.pdf. Accessed 12 Jan 2016
Dahiya S, John K, Puri M (2003) Debtor-in-possession financing and bankruptcy resolution: empirical evidence. J Financ Econ 69:259–280

Drobnig U (2010) Basic issues of European rules on security in movables. In: de Lacy J (ed) The reform of UK personal property security law: comparative perspectives. Routledge, London, pp 444–455
Eckbo BE, Thorburn KS (2008) Corporate restructuring, breakups and LBOs. In: Eckbo BE (ed) Handbook of corporate finance: empirical corporate finance, vol 2. Elsevier, Amsterdam, pp 432–486
Engert A (2004) Die Ökonomische Begründung der Grundsätze Ordnungsgemäßer Unternehmensbewertung [The Economic Justification of the Principles of proper Business Financing]. Zeitschrift für Unternehmens- und Gesellschaftsrecht, 813
Evans GH Jr (1989) The early history of preferred stock in the United States. Am Econ Rev 19(1):43–58
Finch V (2008) Corporate rescue in a world of debt. J Bus Law 8:756–777
Finch V (2009) Corporate insolvency law. Cambridge University Press, Cambridge
Foglia A, Laviola S, Marullo Reedtz P (1998) Multiple banking relationships and the fragility of corporate borrowers. J Bank Financ 22:1441–1456
Flood J (2001) The vultures fly east: the creation and globalisation of the distressed debt market. In: Nelken D, Feest J (eds) Adapting legal cultures. Hart Publishing, Oxford, pp 257–278
Gelter M (2006) The subordination of shareholder loans in bankruptcy. Int Rev Law Econ 26:478–502
Gilson S (2010) Creating value through corporate restructuring: case studies in bankruptcies, buyouts, and breakups, 2nd edn. Wiley, Hoboken
Goldschmid P (2005) More phoenix than vulture: the case for distressed investor presence in the bankruptcy reorganization process. Colum Bus Law Rev:191–267
Gullifer L, Payne J (2015) Corporate finance law principles and policy. Hart, Oxford
Harris SL, Mooney CW Jr (1994) A property-based theory of security interests: taking debtors' choices seriously. Va Law Rev 80:2021–2072
Henoch BA (1991) Post-petition financing: is there life after debt? Bankr Dev J 8:575
Heubner M (2005) Debtor-in-possession financing. RMA J:30–33
Hilson JF, Sepinuck SP (2012) The perils of participations (and secrets to successful subordinations). Trans Lawyer 2:1–7
Hu HTC, Black B (2008) Equity and debt decoupling and empty voting ii: importance and extensions. Univ Penn Law Rev 156:625–739, at 728
Jensen MC, Meckling WH (1976) Theory of the firm: managerial behavior, agency costs and ownership structure. J Financ Econ 3:305–360
John K (1993) Managing financial distress and valuing distressed securities: a survey and a research agenda. Financ Manag 22(3):60–78
Lasfer MA, Sundarsanam PS, Taffler RJ (1996) Financial distress, asset sales, and lender monitoring. Financ Manag 25(3):576
Leebron DW (1991) Limited liability, tort victims, and creditors. Columbia Law Rev 91:1565–1650
Levitin AJ (2011) In defense of bailouts. Georgetown Law J 99:435–513
Levmore S (1982) Monitors and freeriders in commercial and corporate settings. Yale Law J 92:49–83
Lewis PB (2004) 203 N. LaSalle five years later: answers to the open questions. J Marshall Law Rev 38:61–96
Li K, Wang W (2016) Debtor-in-possession financing, loan to-loan, and loan to own. J Corp Financ 39:121–138
LoPucki LM, Abraham AI, Delahaye BP (2013) Optimizing English and American security interests. Notre Dame Law Rev 88:1785–1864
Lumpkin S (2003) The integration of the corporate bond and commercial loan markets. OECD Financ Mark Trends 85:51–86
Lubben SJ (2005) The 'new and improved' chapter 11. Ky Law J 93(4):839
Macey MW (1980) No fault subordination of loans in bankruptcy. Comm Law J 85:44
Mann RJ (1997) Explaining the pattern of secured credit. Harv Law Rev 110:625–683

Mariathasan J (2018) Direct lending: becoming a banker. In: IPE. https://www.ipe.com/investment/direct-lending-becoming-bankers/www.ipe.com/investment/direct-lending-becoming-bankers/10024461.fullarticle. Accessed 30 May 2018
Matthews K, Thompson J (2005) The economics of banking. Wiley, Queensland
Mccormack G (2004) Secured credit under English and American Law. Cambridge University Press, Cambridge
Mcknight A (2008) Law of international finance. Oxford University Press, Oxford
Meyer SC (1984) The capital structure puzzle. J Financ 39:575–592
Miglo A (2016) Capital structure in the modern world. Springer, Cham
Morris S (2014) Billionaire Dangote leads record Nigerian syndicated loan surge, 20 Feb 2014. https://www.bloomberg.com/news/articles/2014-02-20/billionaire-dangote-leads-record-nigerian-syndicated-loan-surge. Accessed 10 Mar 2015
Myers J (2018) Market trends, recent deal terms in retail Dip financing. https://turnaround.org/jcr/2018/06/market-trends-recent-deal-terms-retail-dip-financing. Accessed 18 Oct 2018
Naruisch T (2011) Corporate finance and share transfers in Germany: the reform of private limited companies in practice. Comp Law 32(5):156
Nash D (2007) ABL and distressed companies. Corp Resc Insol 1(3):104
Nozemack M (1999) Making sense out of bankruptcy courts' recharacterization of claims: why not use § 510(c) equitable subordination. Wash & Lee Law Rev 56:689–720
Ozili PK, Outa E (2017) Bank loan loss provisions research: a review. Borsa Istanbul Rev 17(3):144–163
Parkinson MM (2016) Corporate governance during financial distress - an empirical analysis. Int J Law Manag 58:486–506
Partnoy F, Skeel DA (2007) The promise and perils of credit derivatives. Univ Cin Law Rev 75:1019–1051
Prager ML (1990) Financing the chapter 11 debtor: the Lenders' perspective. Bus Lawyer 45(4):2127–2150
Pulvino TC (1998) Do asset fire sales exist? An empirical investigation of commercial aircraft transactions. J Financ 53(3):939–978
Qi L (2008) Availability of continuing financing in corporate reorganizations: the UK and the US perspective. Company Lawyer 29(6):162–167
Rizzo L, Fitzgerald P (2018) Footwear retailer the walking company files 'Chapter 22' bankruptcy. In: WSJ. https://www.wsj.com/articles/footwear-retailer-the-walking-company-files-chapter-22-bankruptcy-1520348024. Accessed 12 Mar 2018
Rutberg S (1994) The history of asset-based lending. CFA, New York
Samuelson RJ (2015) Celebrating the auto bailout's success. In: Washington Post. https://www.washingtonpost.com/opinions/celebrating-the-auto-bailouts-success/2015/04/01/67f3f208-d881-11e4-8103-fa84725dbf9d_story.html?noredirect=on&utm_term=.a9d25d3ab37a. Accessed 16 May 2015
Sarra J (2010–2011) Financing insolvency restructurings in the wake of the financial crisis: stalking horses, rogue white knights and circling vultures. Penn St Int Law Rev 29:581–612
Schafer P, Frischemeier A (2012) Corporate finance by way of debt equity swaps in light of new amendments to the German insolvency statute. J Int Bank Law Regul 27(5):195
Schlunk HJ (2002) Little boxes: can optimal commodity tax methodology save the debt equity distinction? Texas Law Rev 80:859–891
Schwarcz SL (2008) Systemic risk. Georgetown Law J 97:193–249
Schwartz A (1989) A theory of loan priorities. J Legal Stud 18(2):209–261
Shleifer A, Vishny RW (1992) Liquidation values and debt capacity: a market equilibrium approach. J Financ 47(1):1344–1366
Shackelford DA, Lang MH, Maydew EL (2001) Bringing down the other Berlin wall: Germany's repeal of the corporate capital gains tax. SSRN Electron J
Skeel DA, Kraus-Vilmar G (2006) Recharacterization and the nonhinderance of creditor. Eur Bus Org Law Rev 7:259–279

Stadler MC (1997) Treatment of shareholder loans to undercapitalized corporations in bankruptcy proceedings. J Law & Comm 17:1

Tajti T (2014) The resurrection of field warehousing – the booming hungarian field warehousing sector, the incomplete English narrative and the unexplored field warehousing law of the United States. Acta Juridica Hungarica 55(3):185–235

Takacs A. European restructuring report, defaults, restructuring and recoveries 2008–2010. In: Debt wire, 33. http://www.debtwire.com/pdf/Restructuring_Report_2008_2010.pdf. Accessed 2 Jan 2017

Thakor AV (1996) Capital requirements, monetary policy, and aggregate bank lending: theory and empirical evidence. J Financ 51(1):279–324

Tufano P (1997) Business failure, judicial intervention, and financial innovation: restructuring U.S. railroads in the nineteenth century. Bus Hist Rev 71(1):1–40

Verse DA (2008) Shareholder loans in corporate insolvency- a new approach to an old problem. German Law J 9(9):1109–1124

Visintin A (2004) Receivables financing - the drive to Germany. Eur Law 44

Vriesendorp RD, Gramatikov MA (2010) Insol International Academics' Group, impact of the financial crisis survey, 12. https://www.debrauw.com/wp-content/uploads/NEWS%20-%20PUBLICATIONS/INSOL-Survey-2009-final-version-23-3-2010.pdf. Accessed 10 Oct 2016

Warren E (1993) Bankruptcy policymaking in an imperfect world. Mich Law Rev 92:336–387

Watson R, Wilson N (2002) Small and medium size enterprise financing: a note on some of the empirical implications of a pecking order. J Bus Financ Acc 29(3–4):557–578

Wheaton C (2015) Clearing a minefield of insolvency law: toward debt recharacterization as a supplement to the bankruptcy code. Santa Clara Law Rev 55:769–798

Whitehead CK (2009) The evolution of debt: covenants, the credit market, and corporate governance. J Corp Law 34:641–677

Wood PR (2007) Law and practice of international finance: principles of international insolvency, 2nd edn. Sweet and Maxwell, London

Wood PR (2008) Law and practice of international finance. Sweet & Maxwell, London

Zumbro PH (2016) DIP and exit financing trends and strategies in a changing marketplace. Aspatore, Boston

Chapter 3
Restructuring: Key Elements and the Financing Component

3.1 Overview

Chapter 1 has provided a primer on the identity of new financing and the various modes of financing the distressed debtor. While it is one thing to identify the financing options, it is another thing to situate those options within the extant frameworks which support the restructuring of a financially distressed business. On the one hand, although debt restructuring is essentially a private matter between the distressed debtor and the relevant creditors, it is also commonly agreed that the state has a role in facilitating the functioning of the economy.[1] Without doubt, restructuring frameworks—whether found embedded in formal restructuring or ensconced in workout structures—play an important role in the functioning of market economies. Hence, through a comparative statutory, case law and normative analysis, the preoccupation of this chapter is to identify the key components (toolkit) that have been suggested to facilitate successful debt restructurings. Setting forth the ideal toolkit of a business restructuring, the chapter seeks to identify which (if any) of the components play any role in supporting liquidity or new financing for the financially distressed business.

Relieving a business of distress presupposes agreement between the debtor and the various counterparties to its hard contracts,[2] such that restructured obligations regarding pre-distress property rights and obligations are respected by the parties. This agreement can be reached within a formal or an informal restructuring framework. Most jurisdictions provide both options and both options have their upsides and downsides especially in the way they cater for new financing as a part of the

[1] Stiglitz (2001), pp. 3–4.

[2] Hard contract generally refers to financial contracts where the parties have specified the terms and conditions of their association with each other. This is in contrast to soft contracts which do not specify what is to be delivered to either party. See generally, Heery and Noon (2008). In the particular context used above, financial contracts such as a bank loan or bond will qualify as a hard contract, while common or preferred stock will qualify as soft contracts.

S. U. Mba, *New Financing for Distressed Businesses in the Context of Business Restructuring Law*, https://doi.org/10.1007/978-3-030-19749-0_3

restructuring toolkit. As many jurisdictions pursue the possibility of formal restructuring through favorable legislations, it even becomes more likely that firms which need liquidity to be restored to profitability may be willing to take advantage of the statutory architecture which enables the businesses to restructure, while maintaining liquidity as the restructuring is underway. Thus, this chapter will consider both formal and informal restructuring.

This chapter is approached in two ways. Firstly, it provides a primer on the informal and formal restructuring frameworks. While the former is applicable nearly in every jurisdiction and has its benefits. The latter comprises restructuring designs which are the subject of formal regimes. The section proceeds to highlight the known regimes in the chosen jurisdictions. Section 3.2 focuses on the toolkit for restructuring. Following the analysis of these tools is the examination, on the one hand of how they are reflected in workout regimes, and on the other, how they are reflected in formal restructuring regimes in the jurisdictions. Secondly, given that Nigeria is used to represent frontier markets, the rest of the chapter deals with its approach to formal restructuring. This approach is examined in view of its ongoing efforts to reform its formal restructuring framework.

3.2 Between Formal and Informal Restructuring Regimes

3.2.1 Informal Restructuring: Typical First Choice

Informal debt restructuring embraces all efforts at debt restructuring, which build on a consensual agreement between the debtor and its creditors, or a class of them, outside of a statutorily prescribed framework.[3] It is not unusual that when a borrower begins to feel the strains of liquidity pressures bordering on financial distress, it will first resort to its creditors to work things out. It is after this process has failed that formal restructuring comes on the table.[4] This informal restructuring is also known as a workout. The choice of an informal restructuring over a formal restructuring could be informed by the benefits it confers on the relevant parties, especially in terms of its tendency to be expeditious and economic.

It is expeditious because relative to the procedures afforded by formal restructuring regimes, it affords a greater measure of flexibility that allows for speedy resolution, which is especially beneficial to the debtor as well as the relevant creditors who in principle are better off with a quicker resolution of the financial distress. Especially in Europe, formal restructuring does not yield the same level of

---

[3] An out of court workout will qualify as an informal restructuring framework.

[4] Finch (2009), p. 294 ("noting that for most troubled companies, entering into formal insolvency procedures is a course of last resort only to be pursued when informal strategies have been exhausted"); Jostarndt and Sautner (2010), p. 624 (noting that in Germany, "… most firms first try to restructure their debt out of court.").

flexibility.[5] The success of a workout presupposes that interested parties take part in the process in good faith and with a genuine desire to achieve amicable resolution. Hence, flexibility by way of compromises is key. More so, given the value of time to the relevant creditors, they may well reach a compromise faster than the process of formal restructuring proceedings will allow.[6]

Informal restructuring is also economic. This is because compared to formal procedures; it does away with costs which results from delay and the superstructure of a formal restructuring process.[7] These costs may be manifested by way of the loss of going concern value for the business, especially where a going concern asset sale is contemplated.[8] Another manifestation of this cost is in the likely loss of confidence within the debtor's business community (especially vendors, customers and creditors), and the attendant interruption of the operations of the business following the commencement of formal restructuring.[9] This is more so where the restructuring procedure is one provided for in bankruptcy law. It is true that the chosen jurisdictions differ in terms of their response to bankruptcy stigmatization[10]; this is perhaps a bit more than stigmatization. It is more about the asymmetry of information. Given that, some customers and creditors will be uncertain of the extent of the troubles of the debtor and its capacity to survive it, this incomplete information may trigger a crisis of confidence. Vendors and customers may for instance, avoid credit transactions, preferring upfront cash payments or delivery before payment respectively. In other words, the signal of formal restructuring may negatively impact the

[5] See Tilley (2005), p. 102 (arguing that European restructuring is still best achieved outside of formal restructuring "and with the exception of the UK, among the major economies, is still inflexible, bureaucratic and value destructive.").

[6] One may argue that pre-packaged bankruptcies (as in the US) take a shorter time. However, a counter-argument will be that the relevant negotiations have already been carried out informally and this is what makes the shorter time in bankruptcy possible.

[7] See Gilson et al. (1990), p. 319 ("When debt is restructured privately, legal costs are reduced because such decisions can be made more quickly.") See also Adler (1993), pp. 316–317 (arguing for a contractual resolution of distress (in legal systems that tolerate such types of contracts) as opposed to formal bankruptcy law-based restructuring; he identifies different costs associated with the latter. He identifies amongst others, the substantial costs arising from claimants' maneuverings in order to gain strategic advantages as well as the distraction for management that arises therefrom. Other costs he mentions are the monitoring costs that may arise on the part of high priority creditors for fear of deprivation of contractual priorities already bargained for *ex ante* upon formal bankruptcy proceedings).

For a summary of empirical studies showing the direct cost of formal restructuring in the US, see Armour and Deakin (2001), p. 25; Also see Branch (2002); Larkin and Smolinsky (2015).

[8] Gilson et al. (1990), p. 319.

[9] Id.

[10] See for instance, Tajti (2018), p. 1 (on bankruptcy stigma and its negative impact on the restructuring policy); Bork (2012), at para 2.12, 24–25 (in the case of Germany for instance, author notes the effect of the emotional inhibition of bankruptcy in the German society and its implication for formal restructuring through bankruptcy law). See also McCormack (2009), p. 114. ("On the 'stigma' point, it is very difficult to find hard empirical evidence but within Europe as a whole, including the UK, there is certainly the opinion that stigma exists and that this works as a deterrent to entrepreneurial initiative.").

customer base of the business, as well as its brand perception. All of these may be disruptive of the business of the debtor.[11]

In sum, informal restructuring saves the distressed firm transaction costs, while averting interference with the operations of the business and consequently saving resources for and preserving value in the distressed business.[12] This however is not to say that informal restructuring is without difficulties, neither does it suggest that formal restructuring has no value.[13]

3.3 Specific Formal Restructuring Regimes in the Jurisdictions: A Typology

Formal restructuring can be regarded as a statute-based system which embodies tools by which states can (and do) facilitate the restructuring process.[14] Facilitation in this sense would mean providing a legal regime that ensures the successful restructuring of the debtor in distress.[15] In mapping formal restructuring regimes available in the different jurisdictions under review, one may think in terms of two typologies: **targeted** and **collective** restructuring regimes. **Targeted** regimes are not necessarily addressed to all the stakeholders of the distressed business; hence the participation of the stakeholders not addressed is not required. Such regimes are mostly popular in the UK and include the English schemes of arrangement,[16] company voluntary arrangement (CVA),[17] as well as the administrative receivership,[18] will all fall within the class of targeted formal restructuring regimes. On the other hand, are the procedures, which are by their nature **collective**. These procedures are collective because they are by design addressed to all the creditors. They also generally designed to bind all the parties to the restructuring. Another feature of collective restructuring regime is that that they are typically provided for in bankruptcy statutes although insolvency of the debtor is not generally a criterion for entry.

[11] See Erhemjamts and Raman (2011), p. 411 (suggesting that assets of this nature may erode in a formal restructuring).

[12] See White (1994), p. 267; also, McCormack (2009), p. 132.

[13] See Sect. 3.5.1 below.

[14] See generally, Seidman and Seidman (1994), pp. 75–84.

[15] Pottow (2014), p. 222.

[16] Note that when targeted formal restructuring regimes (like the schemes of arrangement) exclude creditors, the excluded creditors reserve the right to attend court during sanctioning of the hearing by the schemes court, where the court will address the question of whether such a creditor has an economic interest in the distressed business, and thus should have been involved. See the scheme confirmation cases of *Re MyTravel Group plc* [2004] EWCA Civ 1734; *Re Bluebrook Ltd* [2009] EWHC 2114 9 Ch. This notwithstanding, the procedure is by design targeted at certain stakeholders.

[17] As a targeted restructuring regime, the CVA is analyzed in this chapter in terms of how it meets the key requirements of restructuring.

[18] See Sect. 3.3.2.2 below.

Procedures like the UK administration, reorganization of Chapter 11 of the US Bankruptcy Code, as well as the insolvency procedure (including umbrella proceedings) of the German Insolvency Act belong to the class of collective restructuring regimes.

Although the main benefits of informal restructuring have been canvassed early on, formal restructuring regimes are not without their own benefits either. A key feature of informal restructuring which will continue to play out in this chapter, is its recourse to voluntariness. In other words, renegotiating hard contracts will largely depend on the whim of the holders of those contracts. Formal restructuring provides a framework within which the state is able to drive policy goals, such as the restructuring of distressed businesses. Formal restructuring therefore has the advantage of binding all relevant stakeholders to the restructured contractual obligations.

3.3.1 Collective Regimes

3.3.1.1 Chapter 11 of the US Bankruptcy Code

Financially distressed companies in the US which are faced with the prospect of bankruptcy may opt to restructure through Chapter 11 of the US Bankruptcy Code[19] which essentially provides a collective framework that offers businesses the opportunity to restructure their debt, emerge and continue to operate as a going concern.[20] At the heart of this Chapter, is the policy goal aimed at the preservation of the going concern value of the debtor, with the attendant saving of jobs and continued operation of the business.[21] Although there has been intense criticism of the legislation,[22]

---

[19] 11 U.S.C. §§1101-1174.

[20] Note that apart from businesses, individuals are allowed to restructure their debt under Chapter 11. See *Toibb v. Radlof* 111 S.Ct. 2197 (1991), where the Supreme Court resolved that a consumer debtor was eligible to file under Chapter 11 of the Bankruptcy Code.

[21] See *NLRB v Bildisco* 465 US513 at528 (1983) where the Supreme Court opined that: "The fundamental purpose of reorganization is to prevent a debtor from going into liquidation, with an attendant loss of jobs and possible misuse of economic resources."

See also Kerkman, who commenting on the rationale for chapter 11, says:

> Congress envisioned the objectives of Chapter 11 reorganization to allow a debtor, usually a business, "to restructure a business' finances so that it may continue to operate, provide its employees with jobs, pay its creditors, and produce a return for its stockholders."'... Creditors, employees and equity holders all benefit by allowing the business to operate and reorganize. The end result sought in a reorganization is a confirmed plan and a profitable business.

Kerkman (1987), p. 161.

[22] See for instance, Bebchuck (1988), pp. 780–781 (describing the numerous costs and inefficiencies in the current Chapter 11 scheme); Jones (1992), at p. 1089 ("... for all practical purposes, Chapter 11 is not facilitating reorganizations."); Jensen (1989) (arguing that too often, financially distressed businesses end up in cumbersome court-supervised bankruptcy process that diverts

it still largely serves as a framework within which formal restructuring is carried out in the US. In addition, it continues to help US distressed companies emerge from distress by providing a framework that enables the debtor to compromise debts, thereby allowing it to "free itself from large legacy costs or obsolete business models."[23] Chapter 11 of the US Bankruptcy Code has served as a benchmark legislation so that many a reform endeavor is shaped around its contours.

3.3.1.2 The UK Administration Procedure

The administration procedure may be regarded as the lead formal rescue procedure in the UK law.[24] Following reforms of the UK insolvency law in 1986, it became an important part of the corporate rescue framework of English law.[25] The administration procedure is aimed at the promotion of the culture of rescue, by handing management of the debtor to an insolvency office holder (known as an administrator). The goals of this procedure as articulated in the statute give priority to the restructuring of the company as a going concern over other possible outcomes.[26] Where this is not practicable, then the goal will be to achieve better results for the general body of creditors, better than a liquidation will yield. If it is the case that neither of the already mentioned goals are attainable, then, the objective of the administration will be the realization of the property of the debtor to make a distribution to one or more of the secured or preferential creditors.[27]

Notwithstanding the priority of corporate rescue as the goal of this procedure, it is argued that the administration procedure is not so much a restructuring procedure in comparison to the US reorganization procedure.[28] Its attraction as will be seen is its provision of a moratorium for the debtor for the benefit of unsecured creditors.[29]

---

management time and attention away from managing the enterprise"). Baird and Rasmussen (2002), p. 752 (noting that traditional formal restructuring under Chapter 11 has become irrelevant for most financially distressed firms); Dickerson (2003), p. 3 (arguing that US bankruptcy laws does not do enough to "encourage directors of [distressed firms] to seek protection afforded before the firm becomes is insolvent....").

[23] Ball (2013).

[24] Finch (2012), p. 194 (stressing that the administration procedure is "the main, formal, procedure for effecting corporate rescue" in the UK).

[25] See generally, Cork (1982).

[26] See Sch B1 para 3, IA, 1986. See also the speech of Lord McIntosh of Haringey in support of the Enterprise Bill, 2003, where he noted that Parliament intend that the new administration procedure would serve as a means to rescue companies. See House of Lord's Debate, Jul. 29, 2002, vol. 638, para 766.

[27] Schedule B1, para 3, IA, 1986.

[28] See Walters (2015), p. 563 (noting that the administration procedure "has always functioned principally as a procedure designed to facilitate a better (i.e. going-concern) realization of business assets than could be achieved through a piecemeal liquidation); see also, Paterson (2015), p. 705 ("... administration was reserved for a sale of the business and assets, or just the assets, to a third party if the banks decided that they were no longer willing to support the business").

[29] See generally, Goode (2011), at para 11–17, 393.

It is not a procedure that provides for the restructuring of the claims and interest of creditors as it does not provide the facility to enforce a restructuring proposal. This means that it has to be combined with another procedure such as the CVA or the scheme of arrangement to bring about a restructuring.[30] Also in practice, the goal of corporate rescue notwithstanding, the administration procedure has also been adapted as a procedure by which the assets of the company is realized through winding up and a going concern sale of the business.[31] Used in this way, an administration can result in a going concern sale of the business, which yields better value for the creditors. It is thus arguable that such meets the goal of restructuring. Most restructurings in the UK have been achieved through the administration procedure, either in combination with other procedures, or as a standalone procedure as in a prepackaged administration.[32]

3.3.1.3 The German Insolvency Statute and the ESUG

The German 1999 Insolvency Act (InsO) represented a shift in paradigm of German insolvency law from one that was liquidation-oriented to one that recognized and made provision for the restructuring of distressed businesses.[33] However, the legislation turned out to have several defects which as it turned out, did not encourage restructuring.[34] Not only was it considered a lengthy and cumbersome process,[35]

---

[30] Payne (2014a, b), p. 293.

[31] Ibid. Winding up is used as equivalent to a liquidation and both terms refer to "a collective insolvency process leading to the end of the existence of the company…." See Goode (2011), at para 1–39, 36. Both terms will be used interchangeably.

[32] See Bork (2012), at para 6-30, 67 (relying on statistics from 2005 to 2010). It is also very possible that many of the cases involve the negotiated sale of all or part of the company as a going concern before the administrator is appointed, and the company or parts of it, is sold off as a going concern following the commencement of the administration procedure. This is known as "pre-packaged administration (or pre-pack). See Payne (2014a, b) (provides a detailed discussion of the pre-pack administration in English law).

[33] The objective of the reform was to facilitate bankruptcy procedures with a focus on the enforcement of the right of creditors rather than what became of the insolvent business. See Amtliche Begrundung [Official Explanation of the Government Draft], reprinted in 1/92 BR-DS 75 (March 1, 1991). See also, Kamlah (1996), p. 423.

[34] See generally, Bork (2012), at para 1.08, 4–5 (listing these defects to include a mandatory insolvency application, the inflexibility of the procedure, inadequacy in the law which governed the insolvency plan, the difficulty of effecting a debt-equity swap under the law).

[35] For instance, the delay arose as a result of the ability of a dissenting creditor to delay the implementation of an insolvency plan. Bork explains this as follows:

> … [I]f a creditor makes out a *prima facie* case, the court is bound to gather evidence to render a decision on it. The drafting and submission of the necessary expert advice takes a great deal of time and will generally condemn the restructuring to failure since the plan agreed by the majority cannot be put into effect.

Id, at para 17. 61, 262.

there was no mechanism by which single creditors could be made to consent to the insolvency plan.[36] These challenges necessitated a reform of the regime, to better facilitate the restructuring of German companies.[37]

The purport of the amendment of the InsO, as embodied in the Act for the Further Facilitation of the Restructuring of Companies ("ESUG") was essentially geared towards encouraging debtors to file for restructuring early enough, and to ensure the preservation of financially distressed businesses as a going concern. Prior to the reform of the German InsO, German businesses in need of restructuring had opted for other jurisdictions in order to restructure, given the inadequacies of the InsO.[38] Hence, one of the very significant reasons for the reform of the InsO was the need to make German law on restructuring as competitive as other formal restructuring regimes.[39] The reform introduced, amongst other things, allow the conversion of debt held by creditors to equity, in a less cumbersome manner.[40]

To promote preemptive restructuring, German bankruptcy law creates three categories, relevant for the commencement of designated proceedings: illiquidity, imminent illiquidity and over-indebtedness. A company is considered illiquid when, as a result of want of funds, it is unable to fulfil its financial obligations to its creditor as at when due.[41] A debtor is over-indebted when the total assets of the debtor are less than its total liabilities based on liquidation value, such that there is no positive going concern prognosis.[42] The third class however involves companies which may very likely become unable to pay their debts (imminent illiquidity).[43] Imminent

[36] See Westpfahl (2010) (on the difficulty of binding dissenting creditors).

[37] The Act came into force on 12 March, 2012.

[38] See Bork (2012), at para 1.08, 4-5. See also, Global Turnaround (2007). Also, but for the 99% approval of the restructuring plan by Monier, the German roofing tiles company, plans were already underway to relocate the COMI. See Attila Takacs, European Restructuring Report, Defaults, Restructuring and Recoveries in 2008–2010, 27. Available at http://www.debtwire.com/pdf/Restructuring_Report_2008_2010.pdf. Accessed 1 Feb 2017.

[39] It was indeed clear from the reform document that this forum shopping by companies in need of restructuring informed the need for reform. See Bundesregierung, 2011. *Dokumentations und Informationssystem Deutscher Bundestag* [Documentation and Information System German Bundestag]. Available at: http://dipbt.bundestag.de/dip21/btd/17/057/1705712.pdf. Accessed 1 Feb 2017.

[40] Prior to the reform, the conversion of debt to equity was achieved in two ways: first, by decreasing the share capital of the debtor and then an increase in the share capital, with the debt claims of the creditor recharacterized as a contribution in kind. The alternative was to transfer shares of the debtor to the creditors who go on to waive their claim against the debtor. The challenge was that for either of these transfers to occur, the consent of the extant shareholders was required, and shareholders were often unwilling to give this consent, resulting in the collapse of the restructuring effort. See generally, Kann and Redeker (2012), p. 439.

[41] S. 17 para 2 InsO.

[42] This is the so-called *Forthestehensprognose* and the prognosis period is generally considered to run from the current, to the following business year of the company. Other factors such as the sector or nature of the business may be taken into account to extend the period. See Westpfahl and Schonen (2015), pp. 334–335.

[43] S. 18 para 2 InsO.

illiquidity presupposes that although the business is not already illiquid, it may soon become so. In a case of imminent illiquidity, only the debtor can file the petition before the bankruptcy court and the specific prerequisite for filing the petition is that the business is more likely to continue, than cease operation.[44] Decipherable from this is the intention of the German policymakers to encourage commencement of restructuring efforts as early as management of the distressed business perceive that the business is entering into distress.

While German law—at the risk of criminal and civil liability for directors—mandates the debtor to file for insolvency when illiquid and over-indebted, within 3 weeks of becoming illiquid or over-indebted,[45] no such obligation is imposed on the debtor when there is impending illiquidity.[46] The consequence of the civil and criminal liability imposed by the law is the obligation on the part of the culpable directors to provide compensation to not only the company, but also to the creditors who have incurred losses as a result of the delay in commencing bankruptcy.[47]

Generally, German law may be said to provide for three collective proceedings, the commencement of which may depend on the financial situation of the distressed business. The first is the **regular bankruptcy proceeding** which less frequently facilitated restructuring, especially as the business is already insolvent (over-indebted or illiquid) at the time of the commencement of the procedure.[48] The second is the **self-administration** which as will be shown later in this chapter, allows distressed borrowers who may imminently become illiquid to remain in place and pursue a restructuring, with the supervision of a court-appointed official.[49] It is

---

[44] Bärenz and Bach (2017), p. 148.

[45] S. 15a para 1 InsO.

[46] On the criminal liability imposed, see 2. 15(a)(4) InsO. Regarding the civil liability imposed, see s. 823 Abs 2 BGB. The practice of imposing liability on directors for failing to petition for insolvency also applies in the UK, see s. 214 IA, 1986; See also See also Finch (2009), p. 300. The US presents a sharp contrast. The nearest to liability directors may come is based is based on their fiduciary duty. Attempts to rely on the theory of "deepening insolvency" have been consistently refused by the court as grounding a cause of action against the directors of a distressed and now insolvent debtor. See *In re Hydrogen LLC* 431 BR 337, 357. A powerful statement of the law rebutting deepening insolvency as a cause of action was proffered by Delaware Court of Chancery in *Trenwick Am. Litig. Trust v. Ernst & Young, L.L.P.*, 906 A.2d 168, 205 (Del.Ch.2006) as follows:

> [T]he fact of insolvency does not render the concept of "deepening insolvency" a more logical one than the concept of "shallowing profitability." That is, the mere fact that a business in the red gets redder when a business decision goes wrong and a business in the black gets paler does not explain why the law should recognize an independent cause of action based on the decline in enterprise value in the crimson setting and not in the darker one. If in either setting the directors remain responsible to exercise their business judgment considering the company's business context, then the appropriate tool to examine the conduct of the directors is the traditional fiduciary duty ruler....

[47] Bärenz and Bach (2017), p. 153.

[48] See Bork (2012), at para 5.10, 48.

[49] See Sect. 3.7.3 below.

noteworthy that reforms in 2012 introduced a protective restructuring regime ("**the umbrella proceedings**"), it may be considered a variant of the self-administration given that bears the features of a self-administration, providing also for features that better meet the requirements of a preemptive restructuring regime. The third is the insolvency plan procedure, which may well not necessarily be considered a standalone restructuring regime, as it is designed to facilitate voting on a plan of restructuring, hence can be combined with either a self-administration. Indeed, being a means by which a plan is made binding, it is discussed as the German version of one of the key elements for effecting a restructuring.[50]

3.3.2 *Targeted Regimes*

3.3.2.1 The Schemes of Arrangement

The scheme of arrangement is an English company law procedure of notable significance. It is first notable because it is not a procedure that is triggered by the insolvency of the company. The implication is that it is available to a distressed borrower to use before it becomes insolvent.[51] Secondly, it lacks the collectivity required of bankruptcy proceedings.[52] Hence, as a debt restructuring device, it is targeted at specific stakeholders or a class of them. This is somewhat consistent with its original design, by which it was specifically made applicable to arrangements proposed by a company with its creditors as it wound up.[53] Thirdly, the scheme of arrangement does not provide for specific contents for which they may be used. Hence, it could prove useful in bringing about the modification of the rights or claims of the targeted class and can be combined with other procedures in order to achieve the corporate purpose of the company.[54] It is however important that the scheme receives

[50] See Sect. 3.6.3 below.

[51] Payne (2013), p. 567 (Given that it is not a bankruptcy procedure, it "allows the company's financial problems to be tackled at an earlier stage than might otherwise be possible.").

[52] While the scheme may easily serve as a restructuring device in the UK, it is not clear how courts in other jurisdictions perceive the schemes sanctioned by the English courts, in terms of their recognition. See for instance the case of *Equitable Life*, where the German Federal Supreme Court (*Bundesgerichtshof*), like the Celle Higher Regional Court re-emphasized the point that the scheme of arrangement does not qualify as an insolvency proceeding in the EU Regulation. This decision has been reinforced by the recast Insolvency Regulation 2015/848 where in Recital 16, it is pointed out that proceedings which are rooted in "general company law not designed exclusively for insolvency situations should not be considered to be based on laws relating to insolvency."

[53] See Payne (2014a, b), p. 175 ("When schemes of arrangement were first introduced in 1870, they applied only to arrangements between a company and its creditors ….").

[54] Ibid, at 176 (pointing out that absent this statutory content, the scheme can be used to "… remove or modify all aspects of the creditor–debtor relationship, including security rights [and] can also be used to swap debt for equity, and to reorganize corporate groups.").

the support of the creditors who hold 75% of the value and majority in number, in order to be presented to the court for sanctioning.[55]

The English schemes of arrangement has its own shortcomings. Without going into the specifics of how it measures up against the key requirements of restructuring highlighted in this chapter,[56] the procedure is considered to be complex and quite an onerous one.[57] Its complexity stems largely from the procedural requirements of the preparation of "extensive and detailed explanatory statement" which must be provided by the distressed corporate debtor.[58] In addition, it provides for three stages, with a minimum of two distinct court applications. All these will involve professionals such as lawyers and accountants. This in turn implicates huge fees which smaller companies may be unable to afford. In spite of these, the schemes of arrangement has seen extensive use by large companies to facilitate arrangement with their creditors and have combined the procedure with the administration procedure, in what is now termed a "twinning" of procedures.[59] This twinning itself can prove an unwieldy and generally gives rise to questions that border on the valuation of the distressed company.[60] Nonetheless, as a standalone procedure, the English schemes of arrangement has served as a tool for restructuring distressed groups across European borders.[61]

3.3.2.2 Administrative Receivership

Although the administrative receivership procedure may qualify as a restructuring regime, it is not focused upon in this book. This is because it presently has limited use following its restricted availability to holders of floating charges. Nonetheless, it bears highlighting its relevance, given that it serves as a precursor to other procedures and a building block of some sort for the other procedures that have now been

---

[55] In *re Hawk Insurance Co. Ltd* [2001] BCLC 480, Chadwick LJ had pointed out that at the sanctioning of the scheme, the court is interested in ascertaining that (1) the meeting convened was in line with the initial order made by the court (2) the approval was secured by the statutorily mandated number of those who are present at the meeting(s) and (3) that the views and interests of those who have not voted in support of the proposal are properly taken into account. See para. 12.

[56] On the key requirements, see Sect. 3.4. below.

[57] See McCormack (2008), p. 276 ("Schemes of arrangement … [are] complex and difficult to organize, demanding of expensive legal resources and generally the preserve of larger companies.").

[58] Payne (2014a, b), pp. 33–36 (on the level of detail and complexity of the explanatory statement).

[59] The twinning of the schemes and administration (especially the pre-pack administration) procedure entails the combining of both procedures. The result is that once the scheme is confirmed by the court, all or part of the assets and business of the distressed company are transferred to a new company. The claim of junior claimants is however left in the old company. See Payne (2014a, b), p. 247.

[60] Ibid, at 254 (proposing reform that streamlines debt restructuring regime).

[61] See generally, Payne (2013).

put in place. Originally, the receivership in English law served the purpose of security enforcement for the holder of the security. When the borrower defaulted, the lender may by itself (pursuant to its contractual rights) or through the courts, have appointed, a receiver whose role was essentially to do what is necessary for the repayment of the lender out of the assets over which the debt owed to the lender is secured.[62] Receivership evolved over time from the appointment of a person who merely facilitated the receipt of income for the repayment of a lender, to one who was also appointed statutorily, or pursuant to a debenture deed, to receive income and manage the business.[63]

What links this device to our discussion is that for some administrative receivership had the capacity to facilitate the successful restructuring of distressed businesses. The plank of this argument was that when appointed, the administrative receiver could swing into action, immediately take steps to halt the downward spiral of the business of the debtor and effect a going concern sale of the business.[64] On the other hand, there was the concern that the administrative receivership regime was problematic. The concerns stemmed from the cost implications for unsecured creditors who were at the receiving end of the hasty disposal of the assets of the debtor.[65] More so, with the powers at its disposal, the lender hardly had the incentive to effectively maximize the value of the business for the creditors as a whole.

---

[62] Jessel MR defined a receiver as follows:

> a person who receives rents or other income paying ascertained outgoing, but who does not … manage the property in the sense of buying or selling or anything of that kind. We were most familiar with the distinction in the case of partnership. If a receiver was appointed of partnership assets, the trade stopped immediately. He collected debts, sold the stock-in-trade and other assets, and then under the order of the court the debts of the concern were liquidated and the balance divided. If it was desired to continue the trade at all it was necessary to appoint a manager, or a receiver and manager as it was generally called. He could buy and sell and carry on the trade.

See *re Manchester & Milford Railway Company* (1880) 14 Ch. D 645, at 653.

[63] This was introduced by Schedule 1 to the IA, 1986. See Goode (2011), at para 10–01-02, 315-6 (on the evolution of the role of the receiver).

[64] For instance, the Cork Report had this to say of the administrative receivership procedure:

> There is … one aspect of the floating charge which we believe to have been of outstanding benefit to the general public and to society as a whole; we refer to the power to appoint a receiver and manager of the whole property and undertaking of a company. … Such receivers and managers are normally given extensive powers to manage and carry on the business of the company. In some cases they have been able to restore an ailing enterprise to profitability, and return it to its former owners. In others, they have been able to dispose of the whole or part of the business as a going concern. In either case, the preservation of the profitable parts of the enterprise has been of advantage to the employees, the commercial community and the general public.

See Cork (1982), at para.495 p. 17.

[65] Goode (2011), at para 10–05 ("banks that were over-secured had little incentive to ensure that receivers they appointed kept costs and fees down.").

Prior to the changes made to the UK IA in 2001, the holder of a floating charge could appoint an administrative receiver over the whole, or substantially the whole of the property of the debtor. The administrative receivership fell out of favor in view of what was considered the seemingly unfettered powers it gave to the holder of the floating charge to choose between a sale of the assets of the debtor or a restructuring. To this extent, the enforcement of floating charges became restricted to the administration procedure, so that subject to certain exceptions, the use of the administrative receivership procedure to enforce floating charges has been narrowed down to particular transactions.[66]

3.3.2.3 The German Bond Act

Targeted restructuring by its design is addressed to a certain class of stakeholders. In this sense, it becomes possible to think of the German Bond Act (*Schuldverschreibungsgesetz*, SchVG) as capable of facilitating restructuring amongst bondholders. While the initial version of the legislation did not envisage the possibility to alter the rights of bondholders,[67] the subsequent reforms in 2009 now allow that.[68] Under the dispensation of the reformed law, a given percentage of bondholders may bind others where questions pertaining to the terms of bonds are concerned, provided the bond is governed by German law, and the terms of the bond provide for such alteration by the consent of the majority.[69] The regime of the Bond Act as a restructuring legislation is limited to its ability to bind dissenting bondholder creditors. Hence, it is not designed to restructure the distressed debtor as a whole, as other restructuring regimes are wont to do.

So far, the formal restructuring regimes of the US, UK and Germany have been examined. A general analysis has also been provided for informal restructuring, which applies to all of these jurisdictions. This analysis is necessary to help unpack the tools of restructuring, how the legal regimes provide for these tools, and what purpose these tools serve in terms of liquidity provision. These issues are now analyzed in the next section.

---

[66] On the prohibition of floating charge holders to appoint the administrative receiver, see s. 72A, IA, 1986. The exempted transactions on which the floating charge holder may be allowed to appoint an administrative receiver relate to capital markets; public private partnerships, utilities, project finance; certain financial markets; and registered social landlords and housing authorities. See ss. 72B-72G, IA, 1986.

[67] The German Bond Act was first passed in 1899. See generally, Tschauner and Wolfram (2010) (on the original legislation and its overhaul).

[68] Bork (2012), at para 1.13, 6 (noting that the amendment of the Act allows for the "suppression of dissenting creditors against decision taken by majority of creditors.").

[69] See s. 5 of the German Bond Act. But see also the decision of the German Federal Court of Justice 9 BGH, 01.07.2014 – II ZR 381/13 = BGHZ 202, 7 = NZG 2014 1102 para. 11 (deciding that even in the absence of a provision prescribing the majority that may alter the terms and conditions, such a provision may be inserted by a creditors' meeting, where an super majority of the creditors (75%) vote in favor of it).

3.4 Key Requirements for an Effective Debt Restructuring Regime

Facilitating the successful restructuring of distressed borrowers continues to inspire reform efforts. While it cannot be said with certainty that an existing regime will always guarantee successful restructuring of financially distressed businesses, regimes are converging around, or are at least having conversations on what requirements can enable successful restructuring. For instance, faced with financial distress, a borrower should be able to continue in the use of its assets or as much of its assets as is necessary to facilitate the restructuring. It also should be able to get a breather from claim enforcements that may result from breaches of financial covenants triggered by distress. It may require this for some time, within which its pre-distress secured creditors may not remove assets which may be necessary for the continued operation of the business, while management come up with a proposal or plan for the restructuring and implements same. The proposal or plan of restructuring lies at the heart of the restructuring regime. Hence the framework must be able to facilitate its acceptance and implementation. This is even against the objection of some creditors, to the extent that such creditors are not treated unfairly. Also significant is the identity of the management of the business during this period of restructuring. Although as shall be shown, this issue is quite nuanced and dependent on certain variables. The last but by no means least, is the need for funding the restructuring process.

The restructuring of distressed businesses whether in the informal or formal context are impacted by all of these elements and thus requiring a restructuring regime with the necessary elements. Put together, all of the highlighted elements will require firstly, that the debtor should be able to have an interim stay (moratorium) on enforcement of actions or claims against its assets. Secondly, it should be able to prepare a restructuring plan with a fair enforcement mechanism. Thirdly, it is necessary that a capable management is in place to drive the process of restructuring. Fourthly, financing is important. Each of these elements will be analyzed in turn with the jurisdictional nuances.

3.4.1 The Stay of Creditors' Action and Enforcement

In the quest to facilitate the restructuring of the distressed business, it is critically important that the borrower can hold together the operations of the business. By this, it is meant that it can continue to operate the firm, and meet pressing financial obligations which if not met, may impair the chances of a successful restructuring. Essential to the chances of the business continuing is business is the provision of a breathing spell for the borrower from creditor enforcement of their claims. This breathing spell typically gives the borrower a temporary reprieve from creditor action and enforcement, allowing it focus on the most appropriate plan of effecting the restructuring. This applies both in formal and informal restructuring.

A theoretical justification which has gained much acceptance as underlying bankruptcy law is the role it plays in solving the "common pool" problem. The common pool problem is the result of creditors acting in their individual self-interest, when the corporate is distressed. When creditors race to the court-house to enforce their credit claims, they do so because—although they may presumably know that suspending their collection rights may mean increased collective value for creditors—pursuing their claim against the debtor individually presents the prospects of the full satisfaction of their claim.[70] However, the result of the pursuit of self-interest by the creditors in this manner may be a piecemeal liquidation of a firm which has the potential to survive its liquidity crisis.[71] This, "common pool" problem gives rise to the need for collective proceedings in Professor Jackson's "Creditor's Bargain Theory",[72] and as a typical feature of many bankruptcy legislations, serves the purpose of protecting the estate of the debtor from the adverse effects of the "common pool problem".[73]

This theoretical justification for a stay in creditor enforcement during bankruptcy proceedings bears semblance to the stay of proceedings typically imposed in many jurisdictions in the course of liquidation proceedings and is reflected in legislations in different forms.[74] To a large extent, it has been accepted as somewhat key to the process of debt restructuring.[75] Apart from serving the now already recognized role

---

[70] Skeel and Ayotte (2013), p. 1564.

[71] Id (In the individual pursuit of their claims in "a self-interested way, creditors can dismantle a firm that is worth more together than in pieces.").

[72] The creditor bargain theory is a normative theory justifying the existence of corporate bankruptcy law. Its proponents are Professors Thomas Jackson and Douglas. G. Baird. For the most part, the theory emphasizes the valuable role corporate bankruptcy plays in ensuring a collective action for creditors thereby preventing the inefficiency that may arise from individual enforcement by multiple, uncoordinated creditors of a financially distressed corporate. See Jackson (1982), pp. 861–868 (author developed the Creditors Bargain Theory); Baird and Jackson (1984), pp. 116–125 (authors suggested that the role of bankruptcy law ought to be designed in such a way that it prevents individual actions against the assets of the debtor, so that it does not interfere with the use of the assets favored by the investors as a group); see also Jackson (1986), pp. 11–12.

[73] See Jackson (1986), pp. 157–172; see also Skeel and Ayotte (2013), p. 1564 (suggesting that the stay of creditor enforcement is the most familiar tool for nipping the common pool problem).

[74] This stay is automatic in the US, as it comes into effect by operation of law, upon the filing of the bankruptcy petition and unless one of the limited exceptions provided for under the law arises, or the court varies the stay, it continues until the end of the bankruptcy case. See 11 USC 362. In UK company law, the stay of creditor actions and claims come into effect only after the making of a winding up order by the court and commencing or continuing proceedings against the debtor may be continued with the leave of court and subject to the limitations the court imposes. See s. 130 of the IA, 1986. The stay does not however apply to secured creditors by preventing them from enforcing their claims. (See *In re David Lloyd & Co* (1877) 6 Ch D 339, 343–6). German law on its part affords the insolvency court the discretion to stay or forbid the execution of claims against the debtor upon the commencement of insolvency proceedings. See s.21 InsO.

[75] See The Insolvency Service (2016) (On the need for a pre-insolvency restructuring procedure, two-thirds of the respondents agreed to the introduction of a stay of creditor enforcement action

of solving the common pool problem and consequently, preserving the assets of the debtor for the creditors, the stay of proceedings does play a role in ensuring the availability of financing for the debtor.

The stay imposed by the restructuring framework has the effect of freeing up cash (albeit temporarily) and allows for liquidity at the disposal of the debtor. Indeed, in some cases, there may be adequate liquidity at the disposal of the debtor to enable it take care of the expenses of the business as it wishes to restructure,[76] in other cases—which is more likely—the debtor may be in short supply of liquidity. In these other cases, the distressed debtors may have cash flow which is tied to servicing pre-commencement liabilities, hence unavailable for pursuing the business expenses of the debtor. Depending on the extent and the quality of stay afforded in the restructuring framework, the restructuring regime can halt payments (if you like the "servicing") of pre-commencement obligations, enabling the debtor to access liquidity that will enable it to continue its business operations, pending the negotiation of a restructuring plan.[77]

Jurisdictions that have extensive stay provisions (as in the US, as will be shown below) afford the distressed debtor the opportunity to widen its financing base. One example of the value of an extensive stay is with regard to negative pledges. Negative pledges are clauses that form part of loan agreements between the debtor and a lender, essentially prohibiting the grant of security interests over particular assets of the debtor to a later creditor, without first obtaining the consent of the initial lender.[78] The underlying consideration for the initial lender (whether secured or not) is to avoid a situation where the debtor could grant security interest over its assets, to a new lender, so that the new lender enjoys a claim which ranks ahead of the initial lender's.[79] It is important to note that a breach of a negative pledge has consequences

---

(temporary moratorium). See Articles 5(c), 6(c) and 10 of the EU Recommendation on Business Failure (recommending the design of a court-ordered stay in the context of corporate restructuring enabling the preservation of the assets of the distressed debtor and avoiding a piecemeal liquidation by the creditors).

[76] UNCITRAL Legislative Guide on Insolvency Law (2005).

[77] See COMMENTARY TEXT on post-commencement finance as it appeared in WP. 70, the draft before Working Group V (Insolvency) at the session in New York from March 29, 2004 through April 2, 2004, 241. Available at: https://www.iiiglobal.org/sites/default/files/media/Post-Commencement%20Finance%20Excerpts.pdf (last accessed 20 Nov 2016). The Working Group recognizes that the automatic stay as well as (temporary) cessation of payment on pre-commencement obligation of the debtor which is provided for in formal restructuring legislations may provide a means through which the debtor may finance its business.

[78] See Finch and Milman (2017), p. 338 (on the negative pledge being an impediment to new financing); Wood (2007), at para 8-031 – 8-033, 136–137 (on the scope and efficacy of the negative pledge); Ali (2002).

[79] Benjamin (2007), at para 8.38, 166. As Cranston points out, this consideration by lenders captures the essence of the negative pledge when it originated in the US early in the twentieth century. He states that:

> In its basic form, it is simply a promise by a borrower that it will not grant security to a third party (the "basic negative pledge"). In another form, there may be a promise on the part of

for the debtor.[80] For the most part however, the nature of the consequence resulting from the breach is contractual and against the person, rather than against property.[81] Concretely, a negative pledge presupposes litigation so that even after a judgment is obtained, the claimant remains an unsecured creditor and does not enjoy any priority. Nonetheless, the threat of the consequences that follow from the breach of a negative pledge clause may stand in the way of the debtor in accessing financing, and the automatic stay (depending on its scope), may effectively deal with that threat.[82] Furthermore, a wide stay of action ensures that secured creditors are included within its scope. This is especially where the assets of the secured creditor are necessary to achieve the ends of restructuring. Below is the jurisdictional approach to the stay of creditor action, and how they serve to ease liquidity constraints.

3.4.2 *Informal Restructuring: Standstill and Waiver Default Agreements*

In view of the challenges of the business, as a first step to attending to the challenge, is the introduction of a standstill and waiver agreement. In the case of informal restructuring this is normally only a contractual agreement, voluntarily entered into by the parties, in a bid to ensure that—"during a defined and usually short period"—no one party commences any adverse action.[83] As already noted, such action will be at the expense of other creditors and to the detriment of the restructuring.[84]

> the borrower to grant equal and rateable security in the same asset to the [lender], or matching security in other assets, if it does grant security to a third party (the "equivalent security" negative pledge). Some negative pledge clauses go further and provide that the [lender] shares in any security the borrower grants in breach of the clause, or that security is automatically conferred in the same asset should breach occur (the "automatic security" negative pledge).

Cranston (2002), p. 315.

[80] Cranston goes on to list the cause of actions open to the initial lender when a negative pledge is violated:

> … The first, is that it can obtain an injunction to prevent breach of the basic negative pledge clause, not to give security; the second is that it can obtain specific performance of an "equivalent security" negative pledge; and the third is that, if an "automatic security" negative pledge is in place, this will give it security which trumps any security taken by the third party.

Ibid, 317.

[81] Bjerre (1999), p. 306 ("… a negative pledgee's remedies are purely contractual; the covenant confers no rights in the property.").

[82] Skeel and Ayotte (2013), p. 1591.

[83] See Garrido (2012).

[84] See Sect. 3.4.1 above.

Concretely, when any one party commences an adverse action, it interferes with ongoing negotiations and can negatively impact the pace of restructuring. It may also not be sufficient that the borrower is afforded a standstill on the enforcement of claims. Even with a standstill, an initial default by the distressed debtor may be considered continuing by a creditor, even after the cure of the default, hence entitling the creditor to an acceleration and payment of interests.[85] In view of such possibilities, it may therefore be necessary that in addition to the standstill agreement, a waiver of default is negotiated between the debtor and its creditors. The combined effect will therefore be that within the defined period, the creditors will not exercise their acceleration rights against the distressed debtor.

The voluntary nature of the standstill represents its shortcoming. A creditor may decide to opt out of it and pursue enforcement.[86] Furthermore, compared to a statutorily imposed stay, the creditors are at liberty to choose which particular events of default for which their acceleration rights may be suspended.[87] In the restructuring of large distressed businesses, with complex capital structures, the process of negotiating the standstill agreement may be quite long-drawn-out and time consuming. The result will be that even when there is a standstill agreement prepared, it may be left unsigned, and the restructuring carried on pursuant to an informal understanding amongst the relevant creditors to stay action.[88] This is unlike most formal restructuring regimes which halts any, or most enforcement rights which creditors to a standstill agreement can choose to retain.

3.4.3 Stay in Formal Restructuring

3.4.3.1 The US: Comprehensive Automatic Stay and Liquidity Facilitation

The US automatic stay is designed to prevent the commencement or continuation of any form of action, which may ordinarily have been instituted against the debtor prior to the filing of the petition, and in respect of claims that that arose prior to the filing of the bankruptcy petition.[89] It also prevents the enforcement acts, possessory acts, as well as acts directed towards the creation or perfection of property rights over the estate of the debtor, where such rights arose before the commencement of

[85] Shutter and McLaughlin (2011), at para 6.4, 150 (on the need to seek waivers).

[86] Garrido (2012) at para 60 ("[S]ome creditors may be tempted to enforce their claims against the debtor while other creditors grant the debtor a grace period before enforcing their claims.").

[87] Shutter and McLaughlin (2011), at para 6.09, 151 (on the effect of a standstill on creditor's right to accelerate their loans).

[88] Goode (2011), at para 12-06, 479 ("There may, indeed, be no standstill agreement at all, merely a general understanding among creditors to refrain from enforcement action for a given period.").

[89] 11 U.S.C. § 362 (a) (1).

the bankruptcy case.[90] Commenting on the rationale for the automatic stay in the Bankruptcy Code, the drafters pointed out that:

> the automatic stay is one of the fundamental debtor protections provided by the bankruptcy laws. It gives the debtor a breathing spell from his creditors. It stops all collection efforts, all harassment, and all foreclosure actions. It permits the debtor to attempt a repayment or reorganization plan, or simply to be relieved of the financial pressures that drove him into bankruptcy.[91]

It may well be that the draftsmen did not directly allude to the role the automatic stay may play in the financing that may be afforded the Debtor-in-Possession (DIP), however, implicit in the above statement is the protection of the DIP from the possible creditor harassment that may result from creditor enforcement action. These creditor actions have the capacity to interfere with the ability of the distressed borrower to maintain liquidity and access new financing.

The effect of the automatic stay on negative pledges point to the value of the US automatic stay as not only extensive, but liquidity providing. Outside of the formal restructuring regime, a distressed borrower will worry about the consequences that flow from the breach of the negative pledge clause. This is essentially because such a breach gives rise to a default, giving the prior creditor a basis to seek state-law enforcement remedies.[92] The case is different when the debtor files a Chapter 11, which automatically kicks into effect, the automatic stay. The automatic stay applies to the negative pledge clause, so that a prior lender is prevented from commencing an action to challenge the violation of that clause. With this challenge out of the way, the distressed debtor can grant heightened priority position to distress financers as provided for in the Code.[93]

The automatic stay of the US Bankruptcy Code has a reputation to be much wider in its scope and reach to allow the debtor to continue to have the advantage of contracts which are designed to be terminated upon the commencement of bankruptcy proceedings. Furthermore, during the period of the automatic stay, obligation to pay accruing interest on unsecured loans is suspended.[94] Regarding secured debt, the distressed borrower is permitted to continue to use the asset for the purpose of

---

[90] See generally 11 U.S.C. § 362(a) (2)-(6).

[91] H.R. REP. No. 95-595, at 340 (1977).

[92] Skeel and Ayotte (2013), p. 1591.

[93] Id, authors stated as follows:

> Inside bankruptcy, by contrast, any threat of suit that would come from violating the negative pledge clause would be nullified by bankruptcy's automatic stay. And no court, to our knowledge, has limited or conditioned [DIP financing], or granted a lien to a pre-bankruptcy lender, based on a negative covenant violation by a [DIP financing] or granted a lien to a prebankruptcy lender, based on a negative-covenant violation by a DIP loan. Emphasis supplied.

[94] See U.S.C. § 502 (b). See *In re Energy Future Holdings Corp.*, 540 B.R. 109, 111 (Bankr. Del. 2015) ("It is well-established that when a debtor files for bankruptcy, the accrual of interest on its loans is suspended, and any subsequent claims brought by unsecured creditors for the amount of this "unmatured interest" is prohibited ….").

the restructuring, provided that certain safeguards are granted to the secured creditor and other relevant factor are taken into consideration.[95] It is important to note that the ability of the distressed borrower to continue to use the asset stems largely from how US bankruptcy law interferes with the enforcement rights of the secured creditor. In bankruptcy, the secured creditor is essentially entitled only to the value of its secured claim, and cannot enforce the rights which may have been open to it outside of bankruptcy, which simply entails the seizure and disposal of the asset.[96] To be able to take any of such enforcement measures, the secured creditor will require the court to lift the automatic stay.[97]

Whether the secured creditor is entitled to the payment of interest on the loan depends on whether the value of the collateral exceeds the amount of the claim of the secured creditor.[98] If the value of the collateral exceeds the amount of the claim, the secured creditor is entitled to interest.[99] Otherwise, the distressed borrower need not pay interest. This rule can help an overleveraged distressed borrower save much-needed funds.[100]

3.4.3.2 UK: Multiple Restructuring Regimes But Limited Moratorium?

English law as noted already provides multiple restructuring procedures that can be used by financially distressed businesses. However, in all of these procedures, the stay of creditor action (moratorium[101]) is statutorily provided for in only two of

[95] In terms of safeguards, the court will lift a stay where there is no adequate protection afforded the secured creditor. The other factors to be considered by the court will be whether the distressed debtor has an equity in the asset which is the subject of the stay, as well as whether the asset is necessary for the restructuring effort. See 11 U.S.C. § 362(d).

[96] Baird (2010), p. 199. Segal succinctly captures the three policies that capture the treatment of the secured creditor in a Chapter 11 restructuring as follows:

> … first, they are entitled to either the collateral or its full value. Second, for the benefit of their debtor or other creditors who might be injured by the repossession of their collateral, they may be required to wait for that to which they are entitled. Third, if secured creditors are required to wait they may be "adequately protected" against loss during their wait. There remains a fundamental policy difference between the English and the U.S. systems. The secured creditor's interest in the collateral is commandeered by the bankruptcy system primarily to prevent two kinds of losses.

See Segal (2007), p. 928.

[97] Id.

[98] See 11 U.S.C. § 506(b).

[99] Ibid. It is often a contentious issue in practice to determine the secured creditor's entitlement to interest, as well as the applicable rate of interest. For an analysis of the issues surrounding these determinations, see t*he Prudential Insurance Co. of America v. SW Boston Hotel Venture LLC (In re SW Boston Hotel Venture, LLC)*, 748 F. 3d 393 (1st Cir. 2014).

[100] Gilson (2012), p. 27.

[101] Moratorium is used here in the sense of a statutory stay as envisaged in Sch. B1 paras 42-43, and Sch. A1 Part III, IA, 1986 and not in the more general sense of a period when debt is considered not due and payable.

these procedures: in an administration as well as in a CVA (albeit in a limited sense). Based on the criteria on which businesses may be entitled to a moratorium,[102] it is safe to assume that only smaller businesses were within the contemplation of the drafters, while larger businesses undertaking a CVA are not entitled to a moratorium. This means that the moratorium in a CVA is limited in its applicability, on the basis of the size of the businesses to which it applies. On the one hand, compared to the CVA, the administration procedure provides for a wider moratorium in the sense that it applies in respect of administration commenced through a court order or out of court, without discrimination based on the size of the debtor. On the other hand, compared to the automatic stay of the US Bankruptcy Code, the administration moratorium is not as far reaching. Yet, it nevertheless plays a critical role in supporting the restructuring process.

When in administration, a company cannot be proceeded against for the purpose of winding it up, whether by way of a resolution or an order to that effect.[103] The more relevant provision which impacts the chances of funding the restructuring process is that which restrains the holders of security interest from enforcing their security interests without the permission of the court or that of the administrator.[104] Further, those with proprietary interests such as owner of a hire purchase assets, as well as property owners are prevented from taking steps that may well be open to them outside of the restructuring framework, without the consent of the court or the administrator.[105]

This moratorium comes into effect upon the appointment of the administrator.[106] Ordinarily, this may be considered a difference between the US automatic stay, which is activated upon the filing of the bankruptcy petition by the debtor. In other words, while the US automatic stay comes into effect upon the filing of the bankruptcy petition, the moratorium in an administration comes into effect upon the appointment of the administrator.[107] English law however accounts for the gap in the

[102] To be qualified for a moratorium, the company needs to meet at least one three criteria: (1) have a turnover of £6.5m; (2) asset balance sheet below £3.26m; (3) employees not exceeding 50. See para 3(2)(a) of Sch A1, IA 1986 and s. 382 (3) English Companies Act, 2006.

[103] Para 42, Schedule B1, IA, 1986. The same applies to CVAs for small companies. See Sch.A1 paras 12–23 IA 1986.

[104] Para 43, Schedule B1, IA, 1986.

[105] Ibid. see *Re Paramount Airways Ltd, Bristol Airport plc v. Powdrill* [1990] BCC 130, where the court held that the assertion of a statutory lien (considered a proprietary interest) over the airplane of the debtor was caught by the moratorium provision of the IA, 1986. See also *Re Sabre International Products Ltd* [1991] BCC 694, where the court also held that the goods in the possession of a haulage contractor over which it had a lien, was caught by the moratorium. For a discussion on the now expansive scope of security interest under the IA, 1986 and how it interacts with the moratorium in administration proceedings, see De Lacy (2010), pp. 37–42.

[106] Recall that the administrator may be appointed by the directors of the company or the company itself (para. 31, Schedule B1, IA, 1986), the holder of a floating charge (paras 14 and 19, Schedule B1, IA, 1986), or by the court (para 13(2), Schedule B1, IA, 1986).

[107] Ibid, for the UK position. In the US, see 11 U.S.C. § 362(a).

time from when the court may for instance issue the order appointing the administrator or the notification of the holder of the floating charge, which qualifies to appoint the administrator and the actual appointment. An interim stay comes into effect for the period from which the application for a moratorium is made to the court or a notice is issued to the holder of a qualifying floating charge for the appointment of an administrator.[108] Essentially, the same result achieved by the US automatic stay, which is to prevent overreaching on the part of creditors and the enforcement of claims, is reached in the UK administration.[109] The moratorium continues for the life of the administration, which the law generally sets at 1 year.[110] While it is possible for a creditor to seek leave from moratorium, the court has the discretion to grant or deny same, if the administrator is able to show that granting the leave could defeat the purpose of the administration, thereby negatively affecting all the creditors.[111] The moratorium is however limited in some respects. Two concrete examples include its non-applicability to negative pledge clauses and to the rights of contractual termination.

As seen already, while the automatic stay catches the negative pledge clause in a Chapter 11 filing, the same is not true of the UK law moratorium, whether in an administration, or a small business CVA. The negative pledge in English law, just like in the US, is a contractual provision. It still enjoys vitality in contracts by both secured and unsecured creditors.[112] Given that it does not lose its efficacy following the commencement of restructuring, a subsequent creditor who for instance takes a security interest over an asset subject of the charge opens itself up to an action at the instance of the prior lender. In essence, the subsequent lender may be liable for encouraging the debtor to breach its lawful obligation to the prior lender.[113] Absent any specific provision protecting the charges created by an administrator from action by a negative pledgee, one would assume that the administrator ought not to breach such covenant. It therefore would follow that such restrictions place a constraint on the chances of the administrator to receive new finance based on the creation of priority above a negative pledgee.[114]

---

[108] Para 44, Schedule B1, IA, 1986.

[109] See Keay and Walton (2008), p. 106. It is however worthy of note that the interim moratorium does not prevent the holder of a qualifying floating charge from appointing an administrator over the debtor or (in appropriate situations), appointing an administrative receiver, who is also not prevented by the interim moratorium from carrying out its functions.

[110] See Para 71, Schedule B1, IA, 1986.

[111] See *Re Atlantic Computer Systems plc* [1990] B.C.C.859.

[112] See Yeowart (2009), p. 527.

[113] *Astor Chemical Ltd v Synthetic Technology Ltd* [1990] B.C.C. 97.

[114] But see Yeowart (2009), p. 523 ("Negative pledges commonly exclude charges arising by operation of law. Even if a negative pledge is silent on this question, a court might construe it to exclude charges arising by operation of law through no act on the part of the company, depending of course on the terms of the contract containing the negative pledge construed as a whole.").

Regarding contractual termination rights, the UK moratorium does not prevent counterparties of distressed businesses from exercising that right.[115] While specified providers of utility as well as IT may be made to continue providing their services,[116] this is tied to the willingness of the administrator to give personal guarantee for such supplies. Giving personal guarantees provide the supplier with the required comfort that it will receive payments for future supplies. There will often be other creditors not included within the specified classes to which the moratorium applies who are yet important for the facilitation of the restructuring. The implication of this is that such suppliers are put in a position to hold the administrator to ransom, resulting in payments of pre-filing claims of such creditors.[117] This in itself has the tendency to negatively affect the liquidity at the disposal of the administrator, when such resources may have been deployed in better ways.

For larger UK companies seeking to restructure through a CVA, as well as companies opting for the Companies Act's schemes of arrangement, there presently exists no provision for a moratorium. Scholars have noted that the absence of a moratorium in these procedures disadvantages the restructuring effort.[118] Consequently, proposals geared at reforming the UK debt restructuring have touched on the necessity of introducing a moratorium to these procedures. However, it did appear that the responses to the proposal did not disclose an urgent need for amendment.[119] The arguments have been that with the available framework, the parties are coping.

For those who argue that the UK system copes well without the moratorium, the reference point is the consensual contractual regimes. Through this regime, the distressed debtors have been able to reach agreements with their lenders in the course of such restructuring, the effect being a moratorium. The case of *Primacom Holding GmbH v A Group of the Senior Lenders & Credit Agricole*[120] is illustrative of the point. The creditors in the scheme of arrangement had entered into financing agreements with the scheme company prior to its proposed restructuring. Because of a decline in its financial performance, the scheme sought to restructure its debt. More pertinently, the company was concerned that two interest payments on its borrow-

---

[115] See *re Olympia & York Canary Wharf Ltd* [1993] BCC 154, 158 (holding that a notice for termination following a repudiatory breach does not require the consent of an administrator or the leave of court).

[116] See generally, The Insolvency (Protection of Essential Supplies) Order 2015.

[117] Such creditor takes advantage of the powers of the administrator to make payments outside of the ordinary distribution order if "he thinks it is likely to assist the achievement of the purpose of the administration" and to make "any payment which is necessary or incidental to the performance of his functions." See IA 1986, Sch. B1, para. 66 and Sch. 1, para. 13.

[118] Finch (2009), p. 485 (noting that between the period of formulating the scheme and the approval of same by the court, each creditor may take steps to enforce their rights and remedies against the company).

[119] Insolvency Service (May 2011), at para 4, 5. ("It is generally felt that the existing UK insolvency framework is coping and adapting well to the challenges that the current round of restructurings are posing, and the urgency of the case for introducing a new moratorium is not fully made out.").

[120] [2012] EWHC 164, 209 (Ch).

ings were due. The directors of the scheme company faced even a more precarious situation regarding the second loan, should the interest payment on that loan become due before the completion of the proposed restructuring absent a further forbearance by the lender.[121]

Furthermore, with a restructuring in view, an English court has exercised its discretion to stay a creditor enforcement action, to give the distressed borrower the chance to pursue a restructuring that appeared feasible.[122] The court took into consideration the right of a creditor to have its claim enforced weighed against the prejudice that will result to the general body of creditors, following enforcement. Attaching more weight to the latter consideration, the court exercised its discretion in favor of a stay.[123]

3.4.3.3 German "Moratorium": A Case of a Functional Equivalent?

Although the German restructuring framework does not expressly provide for a moratorium, it does however recognize the need to protect the estate of the debtor from further decline, as soon as an application has been made. Instructively, the rationale for this preservation of the estate of the debtor is focused on the creditors, unlike the general notion of a moratorium, in the context of corporate restructuring, where the recovery of the debtor is the focus. This creditor focus notwithstanding, the courts are empowered to make orders to ensure that there is no decline in the economic position of a debtor that has filed an insolvency application.[124] The orders made by the court run from the time when the court receives the application for insolvency and when the decision is taken by the court to open the proceedings, or otherwise.[125] The orders may be directed either at the debtor itself or its creditors, so far as such orders are not detrimental to the interests of the creditors, in the form of reduction of the value of the assets.[126]

Furthermore, through a string of statutory measures that also circumscribe certain pre-restructuring rights of the debtor,[127] some of the benefits of a moratorium are achieved. A typical example will be with regard to insolvency rules, which prevent the enforcement of creditor claims[128] and (with limited exceptions), the disposal of movables by creditors[129] during the insolvency proceedings. These are

[121] The company would have become illiquid by German law standards, imposing an obligation on the directors to open insolvency proceedings.

[122] *Bluecrest Mercantile BV v. Vietnam Shipbuilding Industry Group* [2013] EWHC 1146 (Comm.).

[123] See ibid at para 41.

[124] S.21 (1) InsO.

[125] Bork (2012), at para 10.15, 135.

[126] Ibid, 10.16, 136.

[127] See for instance s. 80 InsO, which takes from the debtor the right to dispose of assets in the estate of the debtor. Any transfer from the estate by the debtor is legally invalid, by s. 81 InsO.

[128] S. 89 InsO.

[129] S.166 InsO.

described as security measures. Unlike the other jurisdictions dealt with above, the German security measure which deals with secured creditor claims, does not appear in principle, to play the liquidity providing role for the restructuring debtor. Thus, although in most cases, the security measure provided for may functionally operate as a moratorium, it may not serve the same use of freeing up cash or assets to enable the debtor create priority interest or positions to incentivize new lending.

Having said the foregoing, preliminary insolvency proceedings introduced by the amendments through the ESUG regime does provide some semblance of protection for the debtor for the 3-month period of the preliminary proceedings. During this period, a competent insolvency court may order interim protective measures, which include an order restraining secured creditors or holders of a right of asset segregation from doing so, for the purpose of employing the assets in the continued operation of the business of the debtor.[130] For this 3-month period, the debtor need not pay for the use of the asset but is liable for loss in value, which arises from the use of the asset.[131]

It is doubtful if the above fits into the mainstream understanding of a moratorium as a stay. The moratorium is only good as far as the debtor is able to pay its debt and so far as an interim creditors committee or a creditor has not applied to the court for its discontinuance. In addition, it does not offer an automatic protection for the debtor as restructuring proper commences, the protection being subject to a grant of protective measures by the court where necessary.[132] However, it cannot be ruled out that the interim provision does satisfy the purposes of a moratorium and does in fact achieve this aim in many cases. Think, for instance, about a logistics company whose assets are largely made up of trucks over which the plaintiff has security interests. The enforcement of the claim of the secured creditor in this case will mean an immediate termination of the business of the debtor. An interim protective measure by the court means that the debtor can indeed not only have a breathing room (albeit for a short period of time), but also continue its business operations with the hope of successfully restructuring when the main proceedings commence.

In sum, even if one does agree that the 3-month protection of the preliminary proceedings is not a moratorium as provided in the US or UK, it does serve some purpose in providing the debtor breathing room, within which it can generate further liquidity not tied to offsetting pre-filing obligations, but also increase the chances of a successful restructuring.

---

[130] S. 21(2) (5) of the InsO. See also s. 172 InsO.

[131] Ibid. This is known as compensation for use. The German Federal Court of Justice ((September 8 2016, IX ZR 52/15) has had to decide on whether the insolvency administer need pay compensation for the use of the property subject to segregation within the first 3 months of the order of the court. Holding in the affirmative, the court clarified that the provision of the law only pertained to the free use of the asset and not for use without the compensation of the secured creditor (or its successor in title) for the deterioration of the asset whether arising from standard or excessive use of same. See also, Bork (2018). In: McCormack (2018), at para 191, 227 (emphasizing the ability of a secured creditor to claim for compensation from the insolvency estate for loss of value that affects the collateral).

[132] Bork (2012), at para 10.24, 139. See also S. 21(1) InsO.

3.5 Restructuring Plan Approval Mechanism

The restructuring plan is an important component of any restructuring. It is the blueprint of what the formulator (the debtor, the insolvency office holder or any other restructuring stakeholder) wishes to achieve from the restructuring and the modalities for achieving the same. Therefore, the plan often provides for alterations of the financial and business structure of the debtor.[133] While the debtor might require immediate cash before a plan is formulated to keep the business operational; the restructuring financing, any incentives for the restructuring lender, and the compromises which the stakeholders will have to make, in order to accommodate the financing by the restructuring lender, are often an integral part of the restructuring plan.[134] Although the formulation of the plan in many cases is generally left to the management of the debtor in distress,[135] the stakeholders will necessarily have an input, for the plan to be binding.

By default, to be enforceable, the plan will require the unanimous consent of all whose rights or claims are implicated in the restructuring plan. To insist on this unanimity of consent is not only wishful but may amount to imposing an impossible condition for the enforceability of the restructuring plan. This is because not every creditor will particularly be satisfied with the provision of the plan to meet their claims. In other cases, creditors driven by their self-interest may strategically seek to derail the restructuring process with the intention of asserting their nuisance value in a bid to extract value from other creditors. In addition, some creditors may have no interest in the restructuring efforts and thus have no desire to compromise their pre-distress claims or rights.

Critically important too is the need to avoid the possibility of the tyranny of the majority. If a plan is to be imposed against the will of dissenting creditors, it is important that the dissenting creditor is not unjustly schemed out of what it ought to be entitled to, in terms of its claims. It does matter that the dissenting stakeholder is not unduly shortchanged and value transferred from it to the majority as a result of the imposition of the will of the majority on it.[136] In this wise, it may also be important too that there is a mechanism by which the entitlement of the dissenting creditor

---

[133] Ayer et al. (2003).

("Such changes [in the financial and business structure of the debtor] may include sales of assets, cancellation or refinancing of debt(or conversion of debt to equity), curing or waiving of defaults, satisfaction or modification of liens, amendment of the debtor's corporate charter, or changes in the amount, interest rate or maturity of outstanding debt.").

[134] Dhillon et al. (2007), p. 241 (Pointing out that the restructuring plan determines whether the distressed debtor seeks the infusion of cash to continue operations and how the firm reorganizes its capital structure).

[135] The management of the debtor in distress may be the pre-distress management (as in a debtor-in-possession), a new management as in a trustee or administrator appointed by the court, or a kind of supervised management. See Sect. 3.7 below.

[136] Payne (2018), p. 130 ("the ability of the restructuring to be imposed on a dissenting group leads to the possibility of abuse of that group by the majority, and of wealth transfers between creditors as a result of the restructuring process.").

may be ascertained, at least for the purpose of determining what (if any) value such a dissenting creditor has at stake.

The above speaks to the imperatives of the existence of a mechanism by which a plan is made compulsory and binding on stakeholders. Equally imperative is the need to balance the compulsoriness of the plan against the interest of dissenting relevant stakeholders. In other words, there is the need for a means to ensure the protection of the minority from the "tyranny" of the majority. As this section will show, unlike informal restructuring regimes, formal regimes achieve this approval through a system of voting and approval by the courts. Informal restructuring regimes on the other hand achieve the same ends through normative and contractual routes.

3.5.1 *Informal Restructuring*

3.5.1.1 Achieving Binding Resolutions: The "London Approach" Model

The "London Rules", which have now come to be known as the "London Approach" was once a popular normative tool with which lenders were constrained to constructively participate in the restructuring of the debt of a distressed debtor. It embodies a set of rules that evolved from the role of the Bank of England in the rescue of financial institutions in the course of the banking crisis of the 1970s.[137] In the course of time following its success, the Bank directed its usage not just at financial institutions, but also to companies faced with hard times and in need of financial restructuring.[138] In the case of non-financial corporates, the popularity of the London Approach is attributed to the growth of syndicated loan markets, which became popular with corporates pursuing expansion of their concerns through acquisitions, coupled with the market instability brought about by the recession, which continued into the 1980s.[139] Faced with temporary illiquidity crisis, there was the need to coordinate the response of lenders, to ensure that they are able to reach a consensus directed towards supporting the corporates out of the crisis.[140] The Bank of England through a set of prescribed rules encouraged lenders to undertake this process.

At the core of the London Approach are a set rules which encouraged the bank lenders and creditors to exercise some restraints in the face of default, that they provide relevant information as workout is explored, sharing in the benefits and

---

[137] Paterson (2014), p. 335. The British Bankers Association has also described the London Approach in quite similar terms. It describes the London Approach as 'a non-statutory and informal framework introduced with the support of the Bank of England for dealing with temporary support operations mounted by banks and other lenders to a company or group in financial difficulties, pending a possible restructuring'. Quoted in Armour and Deakin (2001), p. 31.

[138] Armour and Deakin (2001), p. 33 ("The Bank [of England] was able to transfer the expertise it had developed in dealing with the banking crisis to the orchestration of support operations for non-financial firms.").

[139] Westbrook et al. (2010), p. 177.

[140] Ibid.

burden of the rescue on a pro rata basis. Also important to this discourse is that the principles encourage the lenders to reach consensus on whether the distressed corporate will be provided financing and how such financing would be provided.[141] As part of the process of negotiating the informal restructuring, work closely to provide the debtor with required financing to achieve the workout plan.[142]

On achieving compliance through the London Approach, two considerations did play significant roles in supporting the restructuring process as well as the resolutions reached by the parties. The looming shadow of the Bank of England as well as the existence of market norms embedded in the restructuring process. Regarding the role of the Bank, while it may not have been actively "policing" the restructuring process,[143] its capacity to "quietly" oversee the parties through its regulatory role at the time, may have counted. On the other hand, the existence of self-enforcing market norms counted for much.[144] In other words, these compliance solutions demonstrated a deregulated approach to coordinating the lenders. It must be kept in view that lending at the time were done by just a handful of bank lenders and hence it was easier to manage deviance. So, for instance, a member of the lending syndicate that is overly absorbed with maximizing its own utility even at the expense of the other lenders and the successful restructuring of the distressed business may just have put itself in a position to be censured by the other lenders through the imposition of informal sanctions. One may ask, what were these sanctions?

Armour and Deakin[145]—from their findings on the type of sanctions that may apply to a deviant lender—pointed out two specific sanctions that may be applied especially where for instance a "standstill" norm is violated. First is the unwillingness of other lender(s) to co-operate with the deviant in subsequent restructuring exercise(s). The authors find this form of sanction less effective for good reason. It is true that this group of lenders will likely be repeat players in the course of lending. It is however also true that the decision to be subsequently non-co-operative may not only hurt the previous deviant but also the present deviant and possibly result in losses for the syndicate. Adopting such norm enforcement mechanism imposes costs, which may prove unsustainable.[146] The second and more pragmatic sanction is the exclusion of the deviant lender from subsequent syndicate lending arrangements whether on a temporary or permanent basis. In this case, the deviant lender is left out of the opportunity to partake in or profit from gainful lending contracts at minimal costs to the other lenders, syndicate or the distressed borrower.[147]

The framework of the London Approach has largely influenced the practice in informal restructuring. It has largely set the tone for informal restructuring

[141] Finch (2008), p. 771.

[142] Gudgeon and Joshi (2013), p. 11.

[143] Armour and Deakin (2001), p. 31 (noting that they did not find evidence of such policing).

[144] Paterson (2014), p. 336.

[145] Armour and Deakin (2001), p. 21.

[146] Ibid 46.

[147] Ibid. See also Paterson (2014), p. 336.

practices.[148] However, a closer look at its foundations and application would reveal that it envisaged some form of benign regulatory presence, but more importantly, the existence of a handful of lenders, who were repeat players, hence the incentive to participate in the resolution of the distress of the borrower. In concrete terms, this entails lenders making concessions, compromises, and arriving at a restructuring plan. The absence of such conditions as envisaged by the London Approach may well mean that key financial stakeholders resolve compliance questions contractually. Besides, following changes in the lending markets, its popularity has waned, possibly making its existence of little or no consequence. But exactly is this achieved?

3.5.1.2 Achieving a Binding Resolution: The Contractual Model

Informal restructuring necessarily depends on the willingness of the relevant creditors to shift grounds and agree to the alteration of their pre-distress rights. Absent this willing and consensual agreement, it may be difficult to justify such changes in a restructuring plan. Examples drawn from Germany and the UK can be used to buttress this point. Take the example of Germany for instance, as a distressed borrower attempts to informally restructure its debt, it will find that there is no provision of the law, which compels a pre-distress insolvency lender to compromise its debt. In spite of arguments to the contrary, German case law has resolutely maintained an unshaken stance on the alteration of creditors' claims.[149] German scholars in canvassing for the ability to bind a dissenting creditor in an informal restructuring have argued that holdout creditors have often made the borrower elect between the repayment of the claim of the holdout creditor and the failure of its restructuring effort.[150] The holdout creditor obviously overlooks the forbearance of the other creditors in the interest of the successful restructuring of the distressed borrower, and poses a threat to the restructuring of the borrower.[151]

In the case of the UK, the applicable principles to changes to pre-distress agreement reached by creditors is quite settled. Mere forbearance does not suffice to effect a compromise of contracts. A party which seeks such forbearance must furnish sufficient consideration for it.[152] In situations where the pre-distress creditors are lenders in a syndicate for instance, all the lenders need to agree to changes to their individual pre-distress rights, in exchange for new ones as provided for in the

---

[148] See for instance, INSOL International, Statement of principles for a Global Approach to Multi-Creditor Workouts (October 2000).

[149] See BGHZ 116, 319, 321 (The Budesgerichtsof restated that a creditor is not obliged to take part in an agreement which requires it to compromise its debt).

[150] See Bork (2012), at para 5.03, 46.

[151] Bitter (2010), p. 172 (arguing that there exists a duty of care between creditors even though they are not connected, in view of the intensity of the power to affect the legal and financial position of others and a corresponding duty to sacrifice one's legal position ("Aufopferungspflicht")).

[152] See *Brikom Investments Ltd. v Carr* [1979] Q.B. 467, at 484-485per Lord Denning MR.

plan.[153] It is this unanimous consent that now constitutes the consideration, which is sufficient to facilitate a binding agreement.[154]

The foregoing notwithstanding, to forestall the difficulty that may arise as a result of the inability to reach agreement with all the relevant creditors,[155] pre-distress loan agreements or an inter-creditor agreement may provide for a mechanism to bind the minority. One example of such a mechanism is to provide for specified binding majority and buy out clauses. In concrete terms, either of those documents may provide for a specified majority that may be required to vary the terms of the lending arrangement of the borrower, as well as the right of the majority to buy out a dissenting financial creditor.[156] What this means therefore is that in the event of a restructuring, the stated majority will be able to have its way, as far as the terms of the loan is concerned.

In this context of informal restructuring, although the majority may so bind the minority, legal principles may be called in aid to protect the interest of minority creditors who may dissent. These protections may be in the nature good faith requirement and proper purpose.[157] Another pragmatic approach may be to have provisions within either of the agreements, which entitles a majority lender, or any other lender for that matter to purchase the claim off a dissenting lender pursuant to an already agreed mechanism.[158]

What has been analyzed above applies in the context of the restructuring of large distressed debtors with multiple lenders, where the restructuring is essentially focused on getting the lenders to agree to a restructuring. In the case of small and medium-sized enterprises, a contractual model can still operate, so that binding resolutions are achieved, especially where the business has just one bank lender and trade creditors. This much has been argued by Frank and Sussman.[159] They debunk the hypothesis that as the bank lender begins to make efforts to restructure the debt of the distressed borrower, it may be faced with repayment demands from the trade creditors, which likely results in placing the business in bankruptcy. Based on their

---

[153] See Moss et al. (2011), p. 165 (on the importance of consideration for forbearance).

[154] Id ("The mutual release of rights by the lenders and the debtor company is sufficient consideration for both the compromise and the new rights created.").

[155] Creditor here refers specifically to providers of loan i.e. lenders.

[156] Moss et al. (2011), p. 166.

[157] For instance, English case law imposes a duty on the majority in a syndicated lending to exercise good faith and ensure that it has exercised its powers for the purpose for which it was conferred. On improper use of power, see *British America Nickel Corporation v. O'Brien* [1927] AC 369. See also *Redwood Master Fund Ltd. v. TD Bank Europe Ltd* [2002] EWHC 2703 (Ch).

[158] Ibid. This approach is not unusual, even when the loan is not provided pursuant to a syndicated loan and even when there is no prior inter-creditors agreement. Responding to an unstructured interview, an insolvency and restructuring lawyer familiar with restructuring by German lenders noted that many times, the pre-distress financing is not provided by a syndicate. In restructuring the distressed borrower, the dissenting lender may be a senior creditor but with a low exposure and basically wants out. Another senior lender will have not much of an option but to buy out the lender to enable the restructuring process to go on unhindered.

[159] See Franks and Sussman (2005), p. 65.

findings on a study conducted in the UK, they note that in fact, there exists "contractual solution by which the debtor and creditors can resolve [coordination problems] on their own, in a decentralized manner, and without active court involvement."[160] This presupposes that dissenting creditors can still be locked into the restructuring spearheaded by the bank lender.

This contractual solution is achieved through the position of the bank lender as a secured creditor, which gives it priority to reclaim its secured property out of the estate of the distressed business. By this, the secured creditor is already placed ahead of the pack of creditors. This existing liquidation priority means that even where for instance, a dissenting trade creditor proceeds to bring recovery action and a winding up ensues, then such a trade creditor is not necessarily better off than the other trade creditors as whatever is left will be shared pro rata by the trade creditor. This is of course after the claims of other higher-ranking creditors have been settled. Hence, the Frank and Sussman suggest that a trade creditor does not necessarily have a "first mover advantage", which distorts the restructuring efforts of the bank lender.[161] Hence, disrupting the informal restructuring effort may have no concrete benefit for such trade creditor.

Modelling bankruptcy law in ways that show protection of the secured creditors may be advantageous in preventing dissent. Yet, such an arrangement does not countenance the possible overreach by such bank lenders. Besides, it appears that binding dissatisfied creditors through this contractual model may yield mixed results. Speaking of the UK—which formed the basis of the assertion of the authors—it is doubtful how the above position of the authors, measure up to the changes in the law which provides a ring-fenced portion of the assets of the debtor for the satisfaction of the claims of unsecured creditors.[162] The question that needs to be resolved will be how unsecured creditors will react to debt restructuring, in the face of the prospects of such prescribed part.

3.6 Formal Restructuring Regimes

3.6.1 US Chapter 11: A "Cram Down" of Dissenting Creditors

At the heart of every Chapter 11 restructuring is the confirmation of the plan. For this purpose, the stakeholders are put in classes that reflect their claims and interests. The US Bankruptcy Code grants to the debtor, the exclusive right to propose the plan within a specified time frame, after which creditors may proceed to propose a plan.[163] However, before the plan becomes confirmable, it must meet either of two

[160] Ibid at 90–91.

[161] Ibid at 89.

[162] Section 176A (2) IA, 1986.

[163] 11 U.S.C. § 1121.

criteria.[164] The first criteria set forth in the Code requires that the plan is accepted by all the claims and the interests,[165] or in the alternative, all such claims and interests do not suffer any impairment.[166] When the claims do not suffer any impairment, it is irrefutably presumed that the plan has been accepted, obviating the need for the solicitation of acceptance from the holders of the interest or claim.[167] Furthermore, the plan will be deemed to have been accepted based on its acceptance by a minimum of creditors who hold two-thirds of the amount, and one-half of the claims allowed within the voting class.[168] For the holders of allowed interests, the approval of the plan by two-thirds of them suffices for the plan to be deemed accepted.[169] However, this is the best case situation. It is possible that creditors within a class may not be agreeable to the plan. How then does the plan become enforceable? This brings us to the second criteria for the enforceability of the restructuring plan.

The binding mechanism of the US formal restructuring regime is seen in the second criteria for the enforceability of the plan, prescribed in Chapter 11 of the US Bankruptcy Code. This is often described as the "cram down" of the plan.[170] The cram down mechanism operates in such a way that the proposed plan can be enforced by the court when one or more classes of impaired claimants accept the plan by voting in its favor.[171] This without more, will appear to be a recipe for possible prejudice and discrimination against dissenting classes. How then does the US Bankruptcy Code protect the interest of dissentients?

One will readily see how much of work is put in by the drafters to protect the interest of claimants who are unwilling to go with the plan. Apart from the raft of general requirements which the plan must meet, the Code imposes two key provisos against which the plan will be tested, before it may be imposed on dissenting classes.

[164] Either of the criteria yet need to meet an additional layer of requirements. Amongst others, the Bankruptcy Code imposes the good faith requirement (11 U.S.C. § 1129(a)(3)); the disclosure of identities, and affiliations of post confirmation directors, officers and voting trustees, including those with insider status and that such participation is consistent with public policy and the interests of the creditors and equity security holder (11 U.S.C. § 1129(a)(5)(A)(i) & (ii), (5)(B); and that the plan meets a feasibility test (11 U.S.C. § 1129(a)(11).

[165] Although the Bankruptcy Code does not define "interest", it is argued that it could be read to mean the right of an equity holder. See Riesenfeld (1987), p. 391(fn5) ("The right of an equity security holder is an interest, as can be seen from § 501(a) and § 101(15), but the legislative history supports the conclusion that any ownership interest is an interest for purposes of Chapter 11.").

[166] 11 U.S.C. § 1129(a) (8). What amounts to an impairment is covered in 11 U.S.C. § 1124.

[167] 11 U.S.C. § 1126(f).

[168] 11 U.S.C. § 1126(c).

[169] 11 U.S.C. § 1126(d).

[170] "Cram down" is not expressly used in the US Bankruptcy Code. It is the name by which the plan binding mechanism provided for in the Code was called in the cause of legislative development. See H.R. Rep. No. 595, 95th Cong., 1st Sess. 411, 413 (1977). See also *Bonner I*, 2 F.3d at 906 (The confirmation of the plan in this manner is called a cram down because "the plan is crammed down the throats of the objecting class(es) of creditors.").

[171] 11 U.S.C. § 1129(b).

First is the unfair discrimination test, and the other is the fair and equitable test.[172] On the one hand, the unfair discrimination prohibition ensures that a dissenting class receives essentially the same treatment which similarly situated classes receive.[173] On the other hand, the fair and equitable test sets forth considerations that may apply to such classes of secured creditors, as well as that which may apply to classes of unsecured creditors and interest holders.[174] Regarding the fair and equitable standard, although the US Bankruptcy Code does not spell out the meaning of what is fair and equitable, at least such a plan must respect the "absolute priority rule". The absolute priority rule requires that any plan of reorganization must recognize the right of creditors to receive full payment in respect of their claims before lower ranking creditors or even shareholders receive any distribution.[175]

3.6.2 *UK Restructuring Regimes: Binding Dissenting Stakeholders to the Plan*

The restructuring regimes of UK law all recognize the importance of the plan, not all however provide for tool by which the plan may bind dissenting creditors to them. Take the administration procedure for instance, upon appointment, the administrator prepares a proposal which details how it intends to achieve the aim of the administration. This proposal is lodged with the Registrar of Companies and made available to the members and creditors of the company alike.[176] Since time is of the essence, the administrator is required to do this as soon as is reasonably practicable, with a time limit of 8 weeks from when the company enters administration.[177] The administrator thereafter calls the first creditors meeting where the creditors deliberate and take a stand on the proposal, whether to go with the proposal as it is or a

[172] Ibid.

[173] 5 Collier on Bankruptcy ¶ 129.03(3)(b) (15th ed. 1989) ("… a dissident class must … also receive treatment which allocates value to the class in a manner consistent with the treatment afforded to other classes with similar legal claims against the debtor").

[174] Given that 11 U.S.C. § 1129(b) (2) states that the concept of fair and equitable "includes the following requirements .... [Emphasis supplied]", it is suggestive that the provisions that follow are not exhaustive of what may be considered as fair and equitable.

[175] This rule is a legislative requirement for the purpose of confirming a plan in the face creditor objection, requiring that creditors be fully paid the value of their claim before equity claimants receive anything. See generally, s. 1129(b)(2)(i)(B)(ii). On the possible rationale for designing this rule, see Watson (2000), p. 1197 ("Congress apparently designed the absolute priority rule so that the only way a class of unsecured creditors could be excluded unwillingly from receiving full compensation is if the reorganization value of the debtor, when distributed in order of seniority, runs out prior to the unsecured claims being fully paid.").

[176] Sch B1 para 12(1) (c) IA, 1986.

[177] Sch B1 para 49(5)(a) and (b). The rules on timing have been tightened from the 3 months previously provided for to 8 weeks. The idea is to accelerate the process of administration. See Goode, at para 11–109, 467.

modified version of the proposal. Yet, there is no means by which the plan may be imposed over the objection or dissent of claimants unwilling to go ahead with it. This further supports the claim that the administration procedure is not very much a restructuring procedure.[178]

Unlike the administration procedure, the scheme of arrangement procedure, as well as the CVA provide a formula by which an arrangement plan may become binding. In this regard, an arrangement becomes binding on creditors, if three-quarters of the creditors in a creditors' meeting vote in support of the arrangement.[179] The plan also requires the support of one-half of the shareholders, although even when the shareholders object to the plan, such objection is material only if there has been an unfair treatment of the shareholders.[180] When the scheme receives the support of the required number of creditors and shareholders, the scheme may be effectively made binding over the other dissenting members of the class.[181] While it appears that dissenting individual creditors may be bound to follow through with a plan, a CVA or scheme of arrangement does not provide for a cram down in the sense of the US Chapter 11, where a whole class of creditors may be prevented from derailing the restructuring plan, subject to provisos designed to protect such dissenting classes. The regime of both restructuring procedures of schemes of arrangement and CVA only create a binding mechanism in respect of minority members within the class. In essence, each separate class of creditors will have to vote in favor of the plan as statutorily prescribed, before its approval may be sought from the court.[182] This may indeed be limiting of the efficacy of the plan. Where all of the members of a class agree to vote down the plan, the result will be that the plan cannot pass muster. It may well be the end of the restructuring efforts. Besides, with particular regard to secured creditors in a CVA, their interests are excluded from the proceedings.

It is in view of this structural limitations highlighted above that English lawyers have adopted an innovative approach to achieving the ends of whole class cram downs, by combining especially the scheme of arrangement with an administration procedure.[183] This approach still leaves much to be desired in terms of its fairness on the creditors who have been left out of the voting and therefore had no say in the plan of restructuring.[184]

Unlike in the US, the administration procedure does not provide a means by which secured creditors may be compelled to agree to the proposal of the adminis-

[178] See Goode (2011), at para 11–17, 393.

[179] See Rule 1. 19, IR 1986.

[180] See Rule 1. 20, IR 1986.

[181] See *re Wisepark* [1994] B.C.C. 221 at 223 ("The effect of an approval of a scheme of arrangement by creditors in the normal case is effectively to subsume the claims of creditors in the arrangement where there is a contractual release of those claims against provisions in the scheme to pay a dividend on those claims from assets which have been placed in the scheme").

[182] English Companies Act 2006, s. 899(1).

[183] See also Payne (2014a, b), pp. 300–301.

[184] See generally, Paterson (2017), pp. 611–15 (on the notions of fairness that arise with the use of twinning schemes and pre-pack administration).

trator as touching the enforcement of its security interest, neither can the proposal alter the priority position of a preferential claim nor can it result in the lower payout of a preferential creditor, compared to another similarly situated creditor.[185] This invariably means that in raising restructuring financing, the administrator is limited in its ability to bind parties to the proposal. Also, the proposal of the administrator, if it provides for restructuring financing that impacts pre-commencement secured and preferential creditors, must be as expressed or implied by the statute, otherwise, it must be consensual, to be approved by the court. It is important to bear this in mind as such limitation has implication for the ability of a lender to create incentives for new lending.

3.6.3 Approving the German Restructuring Plan

The insolvency plan is an integral plan of the restructuring framework of German insolvency law. As pointed out in the statute, one of the objectives of the plan is to pursue the restructuring of the company and help it survive distress.[186] The intent of the drafter, it is argued, is to enable the parties (debtors and creditors) come up with the most workable solution on a case-by-case basis, and to enable them reach a compromise.[187] When a group of claimants refuse to give their approval to a plan, the court has the prerogative to allow the plan if it finds that the plan does not leave the group of claimants worse than it would have been, without the insolvency plan and also if the share distributable to the group of claimants is economically reasonable. It would therefore appear that the court has the discretion to enforce the plan if it believes that the relevant criteria has been satisfied.

Although the plan procedure is provided for in the statute books, the procedure had hardly been greeted with enthusiasm by practitioners.[188] This is so because in a bid to balance the interest of dissenting creditors against the majority creditors voting on the plan, dissenting minority creditors still have wider powers deprive the plan of coming into effect.[189] What this means in effect is that for restructuring plans to become effective, stakeholders may have to somehow reach consensus among all of the relevant stakeholders.

---

[185] Sch. B1 para. 73(1).

[186] See s. 1 InsO, which in providing for the objectives of insolvency proceedings states that they "shall serve the purpose of collective satisfaction of the of a debtor's creditors by liquidation of the debtor's assets and by distribution of the proceeds, or *by reaching an arrangement in an insolvency plan, particularly in order to maintain the enterprise* [emphasis supplied]."

[187] See Klein (2012), p. 303.

[188] Dimmling (2017), p. 86 (noting that although the insolvency plan procedure has been in place since 1999, between 1999 and 2012, it had been used only in approximately 1% of corporate bankruptcies).

[189] See ss. 245 (1)(1) and 251(1)(2) InsO on the ways in which the minority dissenting creditors can sidestep the majority decision and derail the plan procedure.

3.7 Managing the Distressed Business

Another equally critical tool in the restructuring effort is the determination of the management of the distressed business through the restructuring process. This is important because the management of the business will be largely responsible for driving the process of restructuring. It has been argued that the emphasis on who manages the business in distress reflects "a tendency to simplify "scenarios and exaggerate the extent" to which any person controls all of the events that make for a successful restructuring of the business.[190] This point is undoubtedly a valid one, as invariably, successful restructuring requires broader participation and the exertion of control over the restructuring process by different actors including the directors, creditors, shareholders, investors, courts as well as regulators.[191] However, the determination of who manages the process has its own implications that do not necessarily derogate from the participation of other stakeholders in the restructuring process. Such a determination for instance, may lean into how and when a restructuring will commence, it may signal a "vote of no confidence" on management, such management may enjoy specific powers that enable the restructuring process, and the management may determine the willingness of a lender to provide funding.

In the light of the above, three distress management patterns are discernible. The first pattern is one that allows the management of the distressed business in place, to manage and negotiate the restructuring (retained management). The second pattern stands at the other extreme, displacing the management and replacing it with a new management which begins to exercise the management powers (management displacement). The third pattern stands in-between the first and the second. While the management is retained in place, an external person is appointed to supervise the management of the distressed business as the restructuring is negotiated, and a restructuring plan is put in place (supervised management).

3.7.1 Retained Management

The management of the business may be left in place to see to the restructuring of the distressed business. One of the strongest arguments in support of retaining the distressed management as the business commences restructuring, is the experience and knowledge which the management of the debtor provide. This experience and knowledge may be lost with the immediate displacement of the management of the debtor upon the commencement of formal restructuring. The US formal restructuring regime through its debtor-in-possession (DIP) is the pioneer of this retained management regime and this is understandable, given the philosophical

[190] Finch (2005), p. 375.

[191] Id.

underpinning of the regime as one that seeks to give to the debtor another shot at survival.[192] Also, the English schemes of arrangement as a debt restructuring regime has this feature. However, given the robust legislative framework as a management retaining regime, it is used to exemplify management retention.

Formal restructuring in the US is generally designed, so that the management of the distressed business remains in control of its property and its estate as the process of restructuring is underway.[193] This is known as the debtor-in-possession concept. As mentioned above, justifying the debtor in possession largely rests on the ability of the extant management to bring to bear its knowledge and experience at the helm of affairs of the business to bear, in order to facilitate the restructuring.[194] A demonstration of this experience and knowledge is the role which the DIP plays in maintaining relationships with the stakeholders of the firm and to make the relevant judgment calls to steer the business from the commencement of Chapter 11 proceedings, to confirmation of the re-organization plan. Indeed, pre-petition management can play a valuable role in the success of the process of reorganization. An important part of this role is the sourcing and facilitation of the financing of the re-organization of the debtor.

In addition to the knowledge and experience which is brought to bear, retaining the management of the distressed business may be a critical step to ensuring that the restructuring of the distressed business starts as early as the signs of distress become evident. This is because retaining at the early stage of its distress, the debtor presumably still has valuable operations and setting restructuring in motion can yield better chances of ensuring that the distressed debtor emerges successfully.[195] A statutory regime that allows such lenders to remain in charge of the restructuring may be advantageous in that it may induce early commencement of the restructuring.

The privilege of having the management in place is not an absolute one. Otherwise, if a management that has defrauded, or has been dishonest in its dealings will be afforded the leeway to continue in its fraud, at the expense of the creditors of the business. It is for this reason that the DIP not just remains in possession, but assumes certain responsibilities of a trustee, which invariably means that the DIP is duty bound to protect the interest of the creditors as well.[196] More importantly, the

---

[192] See 5 Collier on Bankruptcy 10, 1104.01, at 1104-21 ("The philosophy of Chapter 11 is to give the debtor a 'second chance'...."). Whether the retained management is still the norm in practice is analyzed in Chap. 5.

[193] 11 U.S.C. § 1107.

[194] See Butler Jr. et al. (2010), p. 338 ("A debtor's incumbent directors and officers bring to bear experience and institutional knowledge, which would be squandered if they were automatically replaced at the commencement of each chapter 11 proceedings ….").

[195] See generally, Westbrook et al. (2010), p. 133.

[196] See *Louisiana World Exposition v. Fed. Ins. Co., Inc.*, 858 F.2d 233 (5th Cir. 1988) (a DIP "both enjoys the rights and must fulfill the duties of a trustee.") *In re Devers*, 759 F.2d 751, 754 (9th Cir.1985) where the court pointed out that the DIP "has a duty to preserve and conserve property in his possession for the benefit of creditors." There has been some debate on whether the DIP is a separate entity separate and distinct from the distressed management. See for instance, Kelch (1992), p. 1331 (highlighting the increasing resistance to the "new entity" theory); also, Schwarcz

US Bankruptcy Code provides for a mechanism by which the debtor is replaced by the court, with a trustee, as a result of "fraud, dishonesty, incompetence, or gross mismanagement of the affairs of the debtor" by the management of the debtor.[197] However, even in light of this, the courts have noted that it is not enough to show "mismanagement, imprudent decision making,"[198] and the absence of the "exemplary business acumen" on the part of the management.[199] Accordingly, it might not be enough to displace management because it had made poor business planning.[200]

The management retention has faced stiff criticisms both from scholars in the US[201] and on the other side of the Atlantic.[202] More so in practice, it would appear that the management of distressed firms in the US is increasingly moving in the direction of displaced management or a supervised management as a result of private arrangements between lenders and the distressed business.[203]

3.7.2 Displacing Pre-distress Management

Another pattern applicable to the management of the distressed business is that which displaces the management of the distressed business, replacing extant management with an officeholder. This officeholder takes over the management functions in the distressed business and possess wide discretionary decision-making powers at its disposal. The preference for a management displacing pattern rests largely on the way policymakers perceive the extant management, especially as it

(1999), p. 527 (noting cases where the courts have held that the "new entity" theory in refusing waivers in bankruptcy).

[197] See 11 U.S.C. § 1104.

[198] Berdan and Arnold (1984), p. 471.

[199] *In re Sea Queen Kontaratos Lines, Ltd.*, 10 Bankr. 609, 610 (Bankr. D. Me. 1981).

[200] Berdan and Arnold (1984), p. 471 ("... merely establishing that the debtor exercised poor business planning will not suffice to overcome the presumption that the debtor shall remain in possession.").

[201] See for instance, Frost (1992), p. 118 (highlighting the conflict of interest of the pre-distress management in relation to its new role as fiduciary for creditors); Dickerson (2004), p. 135 (arguing that the pre-petition directors of the debtor ought to be presumed unfit to serve on boards and should be disqualified from taking up future roles as board members); Rotem (2008) (proposing the appointment of a monitor by the bankruptcy judge who supervises the business activities of the debtor, in conjunction with the pre-commencement management of the debtor, as it is the case in Canada).

[202] See for instance, Goode (2005). (noting that insolvency is the result of management failure and the last people to leave in control of the business are those who have caused the failure); Moss (1998), pp. 18–19 (arguing that leaving the management of a distressed business in place is tantamount to leaving an alcoholic in a pub); Schiessl (1988), p. 247 (noting the doubts of the German Law Reform Commission of the value of the management skills and the creditors' reliance on the old management).

[203] See Chap. 5 for more on this.

pertains to their perceived role in leading the business into distress in the first place.[204]

An observation on the restructuring regimes that adopt this management displacement pattern is that they are bankruptcy procedures. In other words, these procedures commence after the debtor has "hit rock-bottom". This makes less of trusting the skills of the management to help the business chart its course out of distress in the insolvency proceedings.[205] Leaving such management in place may therefore only encourage a management with nothing to lose, to pursue high-risk strategies in future investments which may be detrimental to the interest of the creditors.[206] The UK law administration procedure and its German main proceedings counterpart can be used to exemplify this.[207]

The UK administration procedure introduced the office of the administrator as an insolvency office holder.[208] The commencement of restructuring under this procedure, is marked by the appointment of this insolvency office holder, whether through the courts[209] or out of court.[210] The appointment of an administrator displaces the pre-filing management of the company,[211] hence all decisions regarding the management of the debtor rest with the administrator upon appointment, with a statutory mandate to take all necessary and pragmatic steps in the course of the management

[204] See Goode (2005) and Moss (1998).

[205] Schiessl (1988), p. 247.

[206] McCormack (2007), p. 524 ("... the management personnel who originally precipitated the company's financial difficulties have not only an incentive but also the power and authority to initiate high-risk strategies.").

[207] McCormack (2018), at para 113, 348 (noting that administration proceedings involve the appointment of an insolvency practitioner and the displacement of the existing board of the company from their management functions). See also Bork (2012) at para 5.08, 48 ("Restructuring is usually the job of a neutral, court-appointed insolvency administrator....").

[208] The provisions of this restructuring regime largely adopted the recommendations of the Cork Committee Report of 1982. See Cork (1982). The Committee did recommend the introduction of the formal corporate restructuring procedure known as the administration procedure. See McCormack (2007), p. 518 ("Cork recommended the introduction of a wholly new corporate insolvency mechanism primarily designed to facilitate the restructuring and rehabilitation of the viable parts of the company in financial difficulties—the administration order procedure"); note that the Enterprise Act 2002 further introduced new changes to the administration procedure, to better serve the goals of rescue. For a detailed analysis of these changes, see Finch (2009), p. 380 ff.

[209] This will follow from the application of the company, its directors, one or more of the creditors of the company, or a combination of these parties. See Sch. B1, para 11-13 IA 1986.

[210] This is the case where the holder of a qualifying floating charge exercises its right to appoint the administrator (see Sch. B1, para 14-21 IA 1986) or the company or directors choose to do so (see Sch. B1, para 22-34 IA. 1986). On the chances of non-recognition of out-of-court-appointed administrators beyond the UK, see Moss (2004).

[211] On the assumption underlying the administration as a management displacing procedure, see Goode (2011), at para 11–18, 394 ("Administration ... is predicated on the assumption that where a company becomes insolvent, this is usually due to a failure of management and the last people to leave in control are those who were responsible for the company's plight in the first place.").

of the distressed business.[212] This mandate necessarily includes the power to take financing initiatives, such as borrowing money and in principle, granting security to lenders during the period of restructuring.[213]

It is clear that a strategy employed by the UK law is to grant to the administrator wide discretion regarding its role in the management of the debtor and to possibly restore it to "financial health".[214] Secondly, and closely connected to the first is that in the exercise of its duties, the administrator, where he believes that financing is necessary to achieve a successful restructuring of the debtor, may incur debt for that purpose and may provide security to lenders.[215] It is important to note here, as will be emphasized further, that the administrator has at his disposal the assets of the debtor and may deal with it in any way which includes a sale. In the case where there exists a floating charge over the asset, the administrator can deal with the property in spite of the charge.[216] Where the security interest is not a floating charge, the administrator requires the approval of the court to deal with the secured property and upon the disposal of the property, the sum realized has to be first used to pay up the secured creditor.[217]

On the other hand, German law also provides for a management displacing regime for restructuring conducted through regular bankruptcy proceedings. In regular bankruptcy proceedings geared towards the restructuring of the debtor, the management of the debtor shifts to an insolvency practitioner. This insolvency practitioner is also appointed by the courts. However, unlike in the case of the special pre-insolvency proceedings, the creditors are much more involved with regard to who is appointed. As the manager of the estate of the debtor, the practitioner has a responsibility to preserve assets of the debtor, dispose of the assets of the debtor, enter contractual relations on behalf of the debtor and in general, maximize returns for the creditors as a whole.[218] Transactions which were undertaken by the management of the now distressed business which the administrator considers to have been disadvantageous to the body of creditors are challenged before the courts requiring that they be clawed back into the estate of the debtor. Again, this might be a way to raise financing for the debtor. However, it need be noted that these cases are very unlikely to yield immediate financing for the debtor and there are no certain guarantees that all pre-commencement transactions challenged will be decided in favor of the estate of the debtor.

In contrast to the management retention pattern characteristic of the US DIP, it would appear that the management displacing pattern thrives on the skepticism of

---

[212] See para 59(1) of schedule B1, *IA*, 1986: "The administrator of a company may do anything necessary or expedient for the management of the affairs, business and property of the company."

[213] See generally paras. 14 and 15 Schedule 1, *IA* 1986.

[214] Sch. B1 para 59(1), IA, 1986; Sch. B1, para 3(1) (a), IA, 1986.

[215] Sch. B1, para 3, IA, 1986.

[216] Para 70(1) Schedule B1, IA, 1986.

[217] Para 71 Schedule B1, 1986.

[218] See generally, s. 80 InsO on the administrative powers of the insolvency practitioner.

the capacity of extant management. Hence, while in the face of some indiscretion on the part of the pre-distress management, the tendency of the courts is to retain the DIP, management displacement regimes as in the UK administration and German main proceedings respond to this management indiscretion by removing management and replacing it with an insolvency practitioner. In doing this, while the latter regimes tend to miss out on whatever value that extant management may afford, particularly—especially the timely restructuring of the business—the former is hardly ever the case in recent practice. Hence, the third pattern represents something of a mid-way course.

3.7.3 A Supervised Management

The supervised management represents a pattern that balances the concerns of management retention and the prevention of opportunism on the part of the management. Consequently, a third party is introduced, whose job is essentially to align the interest of the management with the policy goals of restructuring. One noticeable feature of procedures that adopt this pattern of management as will be seen, is that the distressed borrower need not be already insolvent. Thus, although the procedures are contained in insolvency laws, they may be used before insolvency sets in. UK and German restructuring regimes provide examples.

The UK CVA is designed to leave the management of the distressed debtor in place, as it seeks to restructure its debt. The management it is, which initiates the proposal to the company and its creditors. This proposal is delivered to a person who the creditors intend to nominate as a supervisor. This nominee is also required to fulfil certain responsibilities, which are in the nature of preparing and submitting a report to the court, which is essentially its opinion on the feasibility of the restructuring plan of the distressed borrower. In addition, the supervisor stands in between the management and the creditors. For instance, where the CVA is one in which the company continues to trade, payments from the trading assets are made to the supervisor who in turn makes the payments to the relevant creditors in accordance with the proposal.

In Germany, the management of a distressed debtor will depend on the stage of distress of the debtor and as a consequence of this, the nature of the proceedings opened by the debtor. Faced with imminent illiquidity or over indebtedness, German law provides for two possible alternatives which the distressed business may opt for and which both leaves the extant management substantially in charge of the distressed business. The debtor may file for a self-administration proceeding, or it may file an umbrella proceeding.

The self-administration proceeding is a special pre-insolvency proceeding, which is subject to the approval of the courts. Under this procedure, the debtor may agree with its creditors on a pre-packaged plan of insolvency within a timeframe of about 3 months.[219] In that case, the extant management may continue to run the affairs of the debtor (*Eigenverwaltung*).[220] However, the management is supervised by a supervisor (*Sachwalter*), who may be generally chosen by the debtor.[221] Hence, this hybrid procedure allows the pre-distress management to administer itself but with the assistance of this official, who plays a supervisory role over the self-administration process. As a prerequisite to granting authorization, the court will have to be sure that such appointment is not prejudicial to the interest of the creditor. In this case, management does retain the power to carry on transactions, albeit in the ordinary course of business. The consent of the supervisor will be required before the management may incur liabilities outside of the ordinary course of business. With all these checks in place, it is argued that it is unlikely for a debtor to abuse the process, thus protecting the interests of the creditors.[222]

The umbrella proceedings of the ESUG is a bespoke regime in the formal restructuring framework of German bankruptcy law, whose set objective is the encouragement of the timeous restructuring of distressed businesses within the framework of bankruptcy law.[223] It is instructive to note that although the procedure is in itself a first step in opening insolvency proceedings, it provides a protective shelter within which the debtor can take steps to sort out its affairs in a more formal restructuring proceeding.[224] The process, which is administered by the debtor itself is supervised by an insolvency office holder who may be generally chosen by the debtor.[225]

As may be seen, both self-administration and umbrella proceedings similarly address the retention of management. For a system skeptical of retaining the management that has led the debtor into distress, but also wishes to encourage the debtor to take proactive steps to prevent the total failure of the business, it does make sense that the debtor may be required to enlist the services of a supervisor through a process closely monitored by the courts and is time-bound. This, it is argued, helps to keep in check the tendency of the debtor to abuse the process, and to protect the interests of the creditors.[226]

---

[219] Bork (2012), at para 10.25, 140.

[220] Consistent with the ideas justifying the retention of the pre-filing management, German practitioners have opined that the continuation of the pre-distress management "allows the debtor's management to widely maintain control over the process of insolvency, it provides for continuity of business administration, and thus might help to retain the confidence of business partners". See Westpfahl and Schonen (2015), at 13.72, 350.

[221] S.270b para 2 sentence 2 InsO.

[222] Bork (2012), at para 10.26, 140.

[223] See Kann and Redeker (2012).

[224] German scholars have referred to this as restructuring preparation proceedings. See Westpfahl and Schonen (2015), p. 338; Bork (2012), at para 10.23, 138.

[225] S.270b para 2 sentence 2 InsO.

[226] Bork (2012), p. 140.

3.8 Restructuring Regimes in Nigeria: The Present and the Future[227]

3.8.1 Restructuring Regimes in Nigeria: The Companies Act Regime and Its Deficiencies

As already noted in the introduction of this book, Nigeria lacks a dedicated corporate bankruptcy regime. To put the examination of the state of the law in Nigeria in proper context, and to understand the restructuring regime provided for or envisaged in Nigeria, a bit of a background may be necessary. Despite the absence of a corporate bankruptcy legislation in Nigeria, CAMA chiefly filled in the void. The receivership, and arrangement and compromise provisions provided for in the legislation served or at least, ought to have served restructuring purposes.[228] The question that arises is: how well were these procedures suited to achieving this restructuring end?

CAMA provides for the offices of a receiver or receiver/manager, who may be appointed by the court, upon the application of an interested party, where the debtor has defaulted in the payment of interest or principal, or where it is perceived that the property or the security of the corporate debtor is in jeopardy.[229] The legislation distinguishes between a mere receiver and a receiver-manager. The former essentially has the responsibility to (without prejudice to the rights of prior encumbrancers), possess and protect the assets, receive rents and in general terms, do all which a common-law receiver may do.[230] The latter could in addition to playing the role of a common-law receiver, carry on the business of the debtor in respect of the particular asset over which (s)he has been appointed receive.[231]

The legal regime is designed in such a way that the office of the receiver/manager can facilitate restructuring. This is in view of the duties imposed on any person appointed as such. Herein lies the possibility of the receiver to achieve the restructuring of the financially distressed debtor. The legislation imposes the duty of a fiduciary on the receiver/manager,[232] requiring that (s)he:

---

[227] Some sections in this part have been addressed in Mba S U, Preventive Debt Restructuring and the Nigerian Draft Insolvency Legislation: Lessons from a Comparatists Perspective (forthcoming: (2019) AJICL) (on file with author).

[228] For a thorough analysis of both procedures, see Adebola (2013).

[229] S. 389(1)(a)-(b) CAMA.

[230] See s. 393(1) CAMA.

[231] Ibid. The Nigerian Court of Appeal in The Court of Appeal in *Ponson Enterprises Nigeria Ltd and ors v. Njigha* (2001) F.W. L.R (pt. 61) 1685 at 1699 clarified the difference between a mere receiver and a receiver/manager. The court pointed out that while a receiver halts the business of the debtor, calls in debts and realize on assets of the debtor, the receiver who is also a manager may continue to run the business of the debtor.

[232] S. 390(1) CAMA.

> … act at all times in what [s]he believes to be the best interests of the company as a whole so as to preserve its assets, further its business, and promote the purposes for which it was formed, and in such manner as a faithful, diligent, careful and ordinarily skilful manager would act in the circumstances.[233]

The difficulty posed by such a fiduciary duty is that it only comes into effect *ex post*, and never *ex ante*. Thus, misdeeds on the part of the receiver/manager can only be dealt with after the act: when the misdeeds of such a receiver-manager has worsened the situation of the debtor.

What is more, it requires the receiver/manager to consider, in addition to the interests of its appointing secured creditor, the interests of other stakeholders of the business.[234] Attempting to decipher the intendment of the draftsman, it has been pointed out that these duties imposed on the receiver-manager "suggest that the aim [of the provision] was to protect investors and the Nation as a whole by keep[ing] potentially profitable companies running; while also protecting the interest and right of the secured creditor to repayment."[235]

This aim of the drafter of the legislation mirrors a very important consideration, which is that pursuant to the *ex-ante* bargain of secured creditors, they may well have no real incentive to restructure the insolvent business, given that they will presumably be paid in full by the appointed receiver/manager after all.[236] Put in another way, even if the value of the assets of the debtor may well be more than the secured debt owed to the secured creditor, there will be hardly any incentive on the part of the receiver/manager to maximise value.[237] The unsecured creditors and other stakeholders of the company may thus be left at the mercy of the secured creditor(s) who appoint the receiver-manager. In spite of this recognition and statutory duty of the receiver/manager, it does appear that debtors are often deeply distressed by the time when the secured creditors seek the appointment of a receiver-manager. As such, there is hardly sufficient value left to satisfy the claims of unsecured creditors or to facilitate the restructuring of the business of the debtor. The result being a fire sale disposal of the assets of the debtor.

---

[233] S. 390 (2)(a) CAMA.

[234] S. 390(2(b) CAMA.

[235] Adebola (2011), p. 248.

[236] See LoPucki (2004), p. 1342. On the criticism that led to reform of the English receivership and the consequent reform under the Enterprise Act, 2002, see Armour et al. (2008), p. 158 ("…receivership led to excessive piecemeal liquidations and inflated costs on the theory that secured creditors (and, by extension, the receivers that they appointed) lacked the correct incentives to encourage them to maximise recoveries by favouring "going concern" outcomes and minimise the costs of their interventions.") A somewhat related problem, albeit on a larger scale, is faced by unsecured creditors in the case of big businesses that file under Chapter 11 (on corporate reorganization) of the US Bankruptcy Code. It has been argued that the consequence of the control exerted by secured creditors and their actions in exercising this control often results in the lack of incentive for those with power to recover any value for claims with lower priority. See Kuney (2005), p. 28.

[237] Armour (2012), p. 105 ("Where the value of the firm's assets was greater than the amount of secured debt owed, then the secured creditor was not the residual claimant and hence the receiver did not have strong incentives to maximize value.").

Furthermore, depending on the level of monitoring by the lender, and the asymmetry of information,[238] the lender with the right to appoint a receiver-manager may only become aware of the financial troubles of the debtor at a point a little too late, to undertake the rescue of the business effectively and successfully. Hence, the appointment of the receiver/manager is done to prepare the company for a liquidation.

On the other hand, the arrangement and compromise provision under CAMA—which is largely modelled on the English scheme of arrangement—provides a procedure that leaves management in place to negotiate the restructuring of the distressed company. Like its English counterpart (the schemes of arrangement), which has been described as composite and difficult to organise,[239] the point has also been made of its unsuitability in successfully facilitating the rescue of failing Nigerian companies and as such, unattractive as a rescue option.[240] One defect often hinted at is the absence of a moratorium on the claims of creditors as the negotiation process is underway.[241]

In the light of the foregoing, it would appear that the Nigerian restructuring regime is deficient and very much lacking in the relevant tools for successfully facilitating restructuring. The closest extant formal restructuring regime that come close to meeting the outlined criteria is that provided for under the AMCON regime.

3.8.2 *The AMCON Receivership: A Regulatory Approach to Corporate Restructuring*

Any analysis of distressed restructuring in Nigeria without a specific consideration of the role of AMCON in that regard will be an incomplete representation of the Nigerian corporate restructuring law and practice. This is particularly in view of what may be considered its pro-restructuring stance.[242] The Asset Management Corporation of Nigeria ("AMCON") was established under the AMCON Act.[243] Its mandate was essentially to mop up NPLs of Nigerian financial institutions that had been rescued by the Nigerian Central Bank, as well as the relatively stable financial

---

[238] Monitoring is a means by which lenders are able to check their exposure to the risk that a debtor will be unable to keep up with its obligations under a loan agreement, especially as it pertains to keeping up with the payment of the principal or interest thereon. It is generally the case that the more the monitoring by the lender, the lesser 'the degree of information asymmetries about the firm and with the nature of its assets.' See Rajan and Winton (1995), p. 1115.

[239] See McCormack (2008), p. 66 ("[...] schemes of arrangement under the Companies legislation [are] complex and difficult to organize, demanding of expensive legal resources and generally the preserve of larger companies.").

[240] See Adebola (2013). See also Idigbe (2011).

[241] Adebola (2015), p. 9.

[242] See Idigbe and Kalu (2015).

[243] See AMCON Act 2010. The Act was amended in 2015.

institutions that had huge NPLs as a result of margin loans.[244] The expectation was that through its intervention, stability would be restored to the banking and financial sectors of the country.[245] Upon purchasing debt claims from the qualified bank lender,[246] AMCON generally assumes all the rights of the lender, to the exclusion of all others who may be interested in the debt claim and any asset securing the claim.[247] Consequently, it steps into the shoes of the bank lender. Like the original bank lender, AMCON is empowered to by itself act as, or appoint a receiver/manager over the assets of the business. This power derives not necessarily from the prior financing agreement, but pursuant to the enabling statute of AMCON.[248] This is exactly where the law exerts itself in balancing the interest of recovering debt and as well facilitating the restructuring of the borrower.

Similar to the powers of the receiver/manager in CAMA, the AMCON receiver facilitates a management displacement regime, which effectively places the manager in charge of the affairs of the distressed business. As envisaged under the enabling statute, the receiver upon notification becomes responsible for the management of the business. This management displacing regime appears justifiable given the peculiar circumstance that give rise to the involvement of AMCON. In the first place, apart from cases where there is a legitimate dispute, the debt transferred to AMCON is owed because the borrower is unable to repay a loan which has becoming nonperforming, for which the lenders have had to make provision. It is therefore safe to assume at least that the borrower is distressed and in need of restructuring.

The management-displacing regime in Nigeria is necessitated by the need to curtail corporate governance failures and moral hazards on the part of management. The problem in most of the cases involving AMCON have been linked to poor corporate governance practices within the borrower. Indeed, AMCON's first recourse is not to show pre-distress management the door, even when it provides new financing for the business. The appointment of the receiver only becomes necessary when pre-distress management failed to successfully turnaround the fortunes of the distressed debtor.[249] Injecting new financing to a management that has already

[244] Margin loans are loans collateralized by the stock of the borrower trading on the Nigerian stock exchange. This was particularly a major cause of the spike in NPLs during the period leading up to the creation of AMCON. See Transcript: Interview with Nigeria's new central bank governor FT (21 Jun 2009). Available at: https://www.ft.com/content/9b5955c4-5e5d-11de-91ad-00144feabdc0. Last accessed 8 Oct 2016.

[245] See Igbokwe M, Receivership under the AMCON Act: Scope and Application. Text of paper presented at the 6th AMCON interaction with Federal High Court, Court of Appeal, and Supreme Court Justices held on March 27–28 at the National Judicial Institute, Abuja.

[246] See s. 61 of the AMCON Act for the definition of the Eligible Financial Institution.

[247] See s.34 (1) AMCON Act. The earlier legislation required AMCON to also assume the obligations of the lenders, however any reference to obligations have been deleted in the amended legislation.

[248] See generally s.48 AMCON Act.

[249] Prior to the reliance on the management displacing regime under AMCON, in 2012, the Nigerian Central Bank (CBN) directed the prohibition of new lending to defaulted borrowers. See CBN Circular, Prohibition of New Credit Facilities the Debtors of Asset Management Corporation of

incurred debt which it is unable to pay may encourage such defaulters to recklessly undertake risky investments, knowing that they do not bear the risk of failure. This point is very important given the fact that the contemporary trend is for providers of financing to seek to exert control over the distressed borrower.[250] In a sense, it is arguable that the displacement of the management of distressed borrower by the intervention of the AMCON receiver is appropriate especially if done in a timely manner.

In addition to preventing the dissipation of the assets in the debtor's estate, it is also important for the AMCON receiver to preserve liquidity as it restructures the business. In recognition of this, the AMCON Act imposes an automatic stay. The stay is automatic because it comes into effect upon the publication of notice of the appointment of the AMCON receiver. This stay is designed to suspend "judgments, claims, debt enforcement procedures existing or being pursued by against the borrower" for the lesser of the period of 1 year from the notice publication, or the period of management by the AMCON receiver.[251] The automatic stay provision, though terse and hardly elaborate, appears to be skewed in favor of the AMCON receiver without providing any protection for any other pre-distress lenders whose claim may be at stake.[252]

Although the AMCON Act provides for a plan procedure, the absence of a specific term of reference, and an orderly regime to bind other pre-distress lenders may affect the efficacy of the plan. When the appointed receiver is to manage the company over which (s)he is appointed, the AMCON Act imposes a strict obligation on the receiver to draw up a restructuring plan which is "detailed and comprehensive" within 30 days of appointment.[253] Two things are however curious about this provision and its enforceability. The first is that there is no clarity on what detail or comprehensiveness entails. For instance, is it enough that the plan provides for projections on profit and loss? Should it also provide for how the AMCON receiver intends to manage the business of the distressed debtor in order to lead to the growth

---

Nigeria (BSD/DIR/GEN/AMC/05/048) 17 Sept 2012 (on file with author). Such funding came through AMCON where necessary, yet the challenges persisted. The AMCON Chairman summarizes this point as follows:

To place the companies in a position to recover and generate adequate cash flow, we gave additional on-lending facilities (in collaboration with Central Bank of Nigeria and Bank of Industry) of almost N40bn on very good terms.

Unfortunately, notwithstanding this support, the companies could neither pay the old nor new loans. We have, therefore, been compelled to appoint receiver managers over a lot of the companies....

See Dada (2018).

[250] See Chap. 5 on how this control is exerted.

[251] See s. 48(7) AMCON Act.

[252] For instance, it is possible that the claim of some pre-distress lenders has not been taken over by AMCON. Also, there may be lessors, trade creditors, as well as creditors who have retained title to goods. The Act makes no mention of balancing the interests of these creditors against the imposition of the automatic stay.

[253] See s. 48(8) AMCON Act.

of the business? Should it make any forecasts on liquidation and the value of the liquidation, compared to what the growth potentials of the business may be? Also, does the AMCON receiver intend to write down claims of other creditors? It is this last point that gives rise to the second cause for concern.

The second concern regarding this restructuring plan provision is that it assumes that the borrower is only indebted to AMCON. Otherwise, if there are other pre-distress lenders, it appears the regime of the Act denies them any input to the plan, while imposing the automatic stay of enforcement of claims. In the absence of a mechanism that allows other pre-distress lenders to make an input to the plan, it is likely that the imposition of such plans over pre-distress lenders may not go down well with other lenders, can give rise to litigation and may derail the restructuring effort.[254] It is not enough that the automatic stay is lost if the AMCON receiver fails to prepare the plan within 30 days.[255] For other pre-distress lenders to be able to weigh in on the plan especially where it proposes the restructuring of the debt of the borrower. Furthermore, it is necessary that the law provides a mechanism that allows for input by other lenders, and a means to bind other creditors to the said plan.

The limitation of the AMCON Act restructuring regime lies in the fact that only businesses whose debt have been bought off the books of the bank lender will qualify for this type of restructuring under the framework of the law. This means that all other businesses seeking to be restructured may not be availed provisions that provide the restructuring toolkits which support restructuring. In view of the critical need for a restructuring law regime open to all distressed debtors, the restructuring framework of the draft Bankruptcy and Insolvency Act (BIA) as well as the draft CAMA (amendment) are examined below.

3.8.3 The Draft Bankruptcy and Insolvency Act

The present draft legislation is in very many respects an improvement on the extant regime under which financially distressed debtors may seek to reorganise their businesses.[256] In addition to the liquidation provisions that existed under CAMA, it now properly provides a formal pathway for the restructuring of insolvent debtors—an important feature that has characterised the insolvency systems of many developed

---

[254] See for instance, Dada (2018) (Noting the challenges faced by AMCON arising from lack of support especially by foreign lenders and trade creditors).

[255] See s. 48 (9) AMCON Act.

[256] The Draft Bankruptcy and Insolvency Act (BIA) has been passed by the Nigerian Senate but still awaits passage by the Nigerian House of Representatives. Generally, under Nigeria's written constitution, a draft legislation (bill) only becomes a law following the passage of the bill by its bicameral legislature and the assent of the President. For this, see s. 58 of the Constitution of the Federal Republic of Nigeria (CFRN) 1999 (as amended).

and developing countries.[257] The draft provides—to some extent—for key structural features that aid the formal restructuring of a distressed business. For instance, it may be deduced from the provisions of the draft legislation that it countenances the possibility of a debtor in possession as the management of the debtor may propose a restructuring.[258]

To facilitate the reorganization of the distressed debtor, the draft provides for a proposal, which is essentially in the nature of a request for 'a composition or an extension of time or a scheme or an arrangement.'[259] The insolvent debtor, its receiver or liquidator may make this proposal.[260] The draft legislation provides an elaborate structure for the classification of claims and voting on the proposal,[261] the treatment of secured creditors' claims,[262] for an absolute priority rule,[263] and vests enormous powers in the courts, so that even when the proposal is accepted by the creditors, approval may be denied by the courts if it fails a reasonability test, or does not benefit the general body of creditors.[264] Although like the AMCON plan proposal, there is not specific guidance on what is to be contained therein, at least it envisages the protection of creditors by the court.

The draft legislation also proposes an automatic stay that generally runs from the approval of the restructuring proposal, until the trustee appointed in respect of the restructuring is discharged.[265] In the same vein, it goes on to do away with ipso facto clauses that may impair the opportunity of a successful restructuring of the distressed debtor[266] and given the international trend, it creates a safe harbour for financial contracts.[267]

---

[257] Westbrook et al. (2010), p. 121 (identifying the two distinct pathways (liquidation and rehabilitation) which characterize the insolvency systems of many developed countries and an increasing number of developing countries).

[258] See s. 26(1)(a) of the draft legislation.

[259] See s. 3 of the draft legislation. While it is easy to tell what an extension of time is, it does appear that the draft legislation takes for granted, the meanings of 'a composition, a scheme, or an arrangement'. An arrangement is however defined in CAMA (s. 537) as 'any change in the rights or liabilities of members, debenture holders or creditors of a company or any class of them or in the regulation of a company, other than a change effected under any other provision of [the] Act or by the unanimous agreement of all parties affected thereby.' An arrangement in English law (on which Nigerian corporate law derives), is said to cover a broad range of schemes employed for the purpose of restructuring. These schemes include "conversion of debt into equity, subordination of secured or unsecured debt, conversion of secured into unsecured claims and vice versa, increase or reduction of share capital …." See Goode (2011), at para 1–46, 40.

[260] See s. 26(1).

[261] S. 35 of the draft legislation.

[262] S. 26(4) of the draft legislation.

[263] S. 42 of the draft legislation.

[264] S. 41(2) of the draft legislation.

[265] See generally, s. 55 of the draft legislation.

[266] S.49 of the draft legislation.

[267] See s. 49(7), (8), (9) and (10) of the draft legislation.

3.8.4 Proposed Restructuring Framework in CAMA

In view of the inadequacies of the adapted restructuring regime provided for in the present legal regime of CAMA, efforts to reform the restructuring framework (amongst other reasons) have led to changes to that piece of legislation.[268] The proposed reform takes a somewhat different approach that is suggestive of a preventive restructuring approach designed to enable the management of a borrower take initiative early enough. Under the proposed reform, the board of a distressed company (by a majority of its directors) may make a resolution that the company is distressed and that there are prospects of effecting a restructuring of the debt of the business.[269] However, merely making such a resolution is not enough as building a formal restructuring regime merely on the strength of management resolution may be subject to abuse by borrowers. Hence, to be effective, such a resolution has to be supported by a statement of the assets and liabilities of the distressed business and a creditor must not have commenced liquidation proceedings against the business.

Embodied in the restructuring framework is a supervised management regime, where a supervisor is appointed over the management of the business. It also imposes a temporary moratorium in favour of the company for the period of the moratorium, against the rights of claimants, as well as against the property of the business in the possession of such creditors. It also allows the debtor to develop and implement a plan to restructure the affairs of the business, property, debt and other liabilities and equity in a manner that results in its going concern or that maximizes value for the creditors and shareholders.[270]

The provision is largely skeletal, as it does not provide for a detailed regime, especially on the criteria for facilitating a plan that will be binding on the creditors, neither does it specify the duration of the moratorium, or what is covered in the moratorium. It leaves the working out of such and other details to the administrative institution of CAMA i.e. the Corporate Affairs Commission (CAC).[271]

3.8.5 Ongoing Law Reform Efforts and Implication for Corporate Restructuring

If the BIA and the proposed CAMA become law, in addition to the AMCON regime, three different statutes will regulate formal restructuring in Nigeria. Laudable as these reform efforts may be, it appears that the next phase will be how to deal with

[268] The Long title of the proposed legislation is the A Bill for An Act to Repeal the Companies and Allied Matters Act 1990 (CAP C20, LFN 2004) and Enact the Companies and Allied Matters Act, 2016. (Hereinafter "proposed CAMA"). The text is available at http://new.cac.gov.ng/home/wp-content/uploads/2016/07/Draft-Bill-for-the-Repeal-of-CAMA-and-Enactment-of-New-Act.pdf (last accessed April 10, 2018).

[269] See s. 402(2) proposed CAMA.

[270] See generally, s. 402(5) proposed CAMA.

[271] S. 402 (6) proposed CAMA.

an unnecessary and uncoordinated duplication of laws and administrative institutions. This has the tendency to result in confusion on the details. For instance, while the BIA regime envisages the appointment of a trustee over the distressed debtor for the period of the restructuring, CAMA proposes a temporary supervision of the management of the business as it undertakes the restructuring. While the CAMA envisages the Corporate Affairs Commission to be the administrative institution, the BIA creates new institutions to administer the law.

It may be argued that the three legal regimes serve somewhat different purposes: while the proposed CAMA regime envisages a prophylactic restructuring regime, the BIA envisages an insolvency restructuring and AMCON restructuring pertains to AMCON administered companies. This argument notwithstanding, each of the statutes essentially make similar restructuring provisions, which can be conveniently accommodated in one statute. More so, for ease of administration, it may be easier to have all the regimes administered under one legislation and through the same administrative institutions. Instructively, none of the restructuring regimes countenances new financing and its place in the proposed restructuring regime. This also informs the discourse on the incentivizing of new financing in Chap. 3.

3.9 Conclusion: What Has Been Learnt and What Is Unaccounted For?

This chapter has dealt with the key components of restructuring regimes and which make for successful restructuring of distressed businesses. This is so, regardless of whether the restructuring is conducted in a formal or informal restructuring. **A stay of creditor action and enforcement powers or moratorium, a plan and a means of enforcing the plan and the requisite management to see to the implementation of the restructuring** are all vital. For the purpose of ensuring liquidity for the business, depending on how wide the scope of it is, it would appear that the stay or moratorium can play a very crucial role.

In terms of formal restructuring, one thing that is also clear is that other than the US, no other jurisdiction analyzed above seems to have a complete set of the identified requirements facilitative of a successful restructuring of financially distressed businesses. In the UK for instance, there exists multiple regimes, yet no one provides a stand-alone regime that encompasses all of these toolkits. Consequently, there is the tendency that distressed borrowers undertaking a restructuring may have to combine procedures in other to get the best of "both worlds."[272] While this may

[272] For instance, an administration may be adopted for the sake of the moratorium provided therein, and a scheme of arrangement in order to take advantage of its voting procedure. Note that this may not always be the case especially where the scheme is combined with a pre-pack administration, where goal is to effect a sale of the distressed business following the restructuring. See generally, Payne (2016) The Future of UK Debt Restructuring. Available at: https://doi.org/10.2139/ssrn.2848160. Accessed 14 Mar 2017.

confer its own advantages, the cost of combining the procedures gives rise to other concerns, prompting calls for the introduction of a single all-encompassing restructuring framework that caters to formal restructuring.

On its part, one could argue that German law provides for a single-entry point that starts the process of a collective restructuring. Although this entry point is the same for already insolvent and liquidating borrowers, it creates what is in the nature of an early restructuring regime, providing hope that distressed borrowers will take early steps to effect restructuring. However, in the light of the unflattering perception of bankruptcy for which Germany appears to have a reputation, a stand-alone regime with built-in restructuring components may also be ideal. Emerging markets like Nigeria seem to be taking a cue from developments in these key jurisdictions and are being pragmatic with changes to their legal regime. The concern raised with the ongoing reform efforts in Nigeria rests on the need to ensure that the restructuring toolkit is manageable and considering the circumstances of the country, harmonized formal restructuring regime will be most beneficial.

No doubt, informal restructuring has its own key advantages, which sometimes see to the successful restructuring of distressed businesses, its entire reliance on the volition of its creditors is a limitation to the operability of the identified toolkits. One will therefore readily agree that informal restructuring best functions where the body of creditors are either few or share a homogenous goal of seeing the restructuring through.[273] With particular reference to the provisions of bankruptcy law which provide for the restructuring process, it does appear that statutes reflect their interest in providing support for firms when, amongst other things, coordination problems associated with private contracting may hamper the chances of successful restructuring.[274] A formal restructuring framework is ultimately supportive of the financing decision of lenders, chiefly because of the compromises and the modification of the capital structure of the debtor, which may accommodate the interest of the distress lender, and the legal certainty that attends the process. Importantly, apart from allowing the debtor a breathing spell, the stay can be co-opted as tool of ensuring that the debtor is able to maintain liquidity necessary for running the distressed business. This however depends on how wide and far-reaching the stay is.

There is wide acceptance of the key requirements of a restructuring regime, save for one equally vital component, which is not necessarily replicated with the same enthusiasm in statutorily prescribed restructuring regimes. This is the new financing component of the regime. As has been constantly emphasized, new financing plays a critical role in the success of the restructuring. Note that the financially distressed debtor is typically undergoing a shortfall on liquidity, hence the need for new financ-

---

[273] See Payne (2018), p. 127 ("contractual workouts … operate best when the lenders comprise a small group of like-minded individuals or organizations.").

[274] See Paterson (2014), p. 339 (the author points out that this interest of the state is borne out of its interest in promoting and stimulating economic growth). See also Bork (2012), p. 47 (pointing out that even though the text of German insolvency law does not express this forcefully, it can be gleaned from the provisions of the Insolvency Act that restructuring is a goal of the insolvency process and the parties are required to explore restructuring possibilities and to take advantage of the possibilities).

ing both in the interim, and for the purpose of effecting its restructuring plan. One needs to also note that facilitating this financing brings to fore quite weighty issues pertaining to incentives which in turn triggers other considerations. The approaches to these issues are varied and quite nuanced. Chapter 3 focuses on these issues.

References

Adebola BA (2011) The duty of the Nigerian Receiver to 'Manage' the company. Int Corp Rescue 8(4):248–254

Adebola A (2013) The Nigerian business rescue model: an introduction. NJIALS 1:35–64. Available at: http://papers.ssrn.com/sol3/papers.cfm?abstract_id=2297824

Adebola B (2015) Conflated arrangement: a comment on the company voluntary arrangements in the Proposed Nigerian Insolvency Act 2014. NIBLeJ 2:3

Adler BE (1993) Financial and political theories of American Corporate Bankruptcy. Stanford Law Rev 45(2):311–346

Ali P (2002) The law of secured finance. Oxford University Press, Oxford

Armour J, Deakin S (2001) Norms in private insolvency: the 'London Approach' to the resolution of financial distress. J Corp Law Stud 1:21–51

Armour J, Hsu A, Walters A (2008) Corporate insolvency in the United Kingdom: the impact of the Enterprise Act 2002. Eur Company Financ Law Rev 2:149–171

Armour J (2012) The rise of the 'pre-pack': corporate restructuring in the UK and proposals for reform. In: Austin RP, Aoun FJG (eds) Restructuring companies in troubled times: director and creditor perspectives. Ross Parsons Centre of Commercial, Corporate and Taxation Law, Sydney, pp 43–78

Ayer JD, Friedland JP, Bernstein ML (2003) The life cycle of a Chapter 11 Debtor through the Debtor's Eyes (pt. II). Am Bankr Inst J 183:1–18

Baird DG, Jackson TH (1984) Corporate reorganizations and the treatment of diverse ownership interests: a comment on adequate protection of secured creditors in bankruptcy. Univ Chicago Law Rev 51(1):112–130

Baird DG, Rasmussen RK (2002) The end of bankruptcy. Stanford Law Rev 55(3):751–781

Baird DG (2010) The elements of bankruptcy, 5th edn. Thomson Reuters/Foundation Press, New York

Ball D (5 April 2013) Europe builds own Chapter 11. In: The Wall St. J. Available at: http://www.wsj.com/articles/SB10001424127887323296504578398612178796882. Accessed 1 Mar 2017

Bärenz C, Bach A (2017) Germany. In: Mallon C (ed) Restructuring review, 10th edn. Business Research Ltd, London, pp 145–157

Bebchuck LA (1988) A new approach to corporate reorganization. Harv Law Rev 101:775–804

Benjamin J (2007) Financial law. Oxford University Press, Oxford

Berdan R, Arnold BG (1984) Displacing the debtor in possession: the requisites for and advantages of the appointment of a trustee in Chapter 11 proceedings. Marquette Law Rev 67(3):457–490

Bitter G (2010) Sanierung in der Insolvenz – Der Beitrag von Treue- und Aufopferungspflichten zum Sanierungserfolg [Restructuring in Insolvency – The Contribution of Loyalty and Sacrifice to the Success of the Recovery]. Zeitschrift für Unternehmens-und Gesellschaftsrecht 39(2–3):147–200

Bjerre CS (1999) Secured transactions inside out: negative pledge covenants property and perfection. Cornell Law Rev 84(2):305–393

Bork R (2012) Rescuing companies in England and Germany. Oxford University Press, Oxford

Bork R (2018) Security rights and insolvency law in the Germanic legal system. In: McCormack G, Bork R (eds) Security right and The European insolvency regulation. Intersentia, Cambridge, pp 173–312

Branch B (2002) The cost of bankruptcy: a review. Int Rev Financ Anal 11:39–57
Butler JW Jr, Dickerson CL, Neuman SS (2010) Preserving state corporate Governance Law in Chapter 11: maximizing value through traditional fiduciaries. Am Bankruptcy Inst Law Rev 18:337–363
Cork K (1982) Insolvency law and practice: report of the review committee. HMSO, London
Cranston R (2002) Principles of banking law, 2nd edn. Oxford University Press, Oxford
Dada A (30 Apr 2018) AMCON MD calls for stiffer regulation of aviation sector. Available at: http://www.punchng.com/amcon-md-calls-for-stiffer-regulation-of-aviation/. Accessed 4 May 2018
De Lacy J (2010) Personal property security law reform in the UK: comparative perspectives. Routledge, Cavendish
Dhillon US, Noe T, Ramirez GG (2007) Debtor-in-possession financing and the resolution of uncertainty in Chapter 11 reorganizations. J Financ Stab 3(3):238–360
Dickerson M (2003) A behavioral approach to analyzing corporate failures. Wake Forest Law Rev 38(1):1
Dickerson AM (2004) The many faces of Chapter 11: a reply to professor Baird. Am Bankruptcy Inst Law Rev 12:109–137
Dimmling A (2017) Germany. In: Bernstein DS (ed) The insolvency review. Law Business Research, London, p 83
Erhemjamts O, Raman K (2011) Financial restructuring. In: Baker HK, Kiymaz H (eds) The art of capital restructuring. John Wiley & Sons, New Jersey, pp 401–418
Finch V (2005) Control and co-ordination in corporate rescue. Legal Stud 25:374–403
Finch V (2008) Corporate rescue in a world of debt. J Bus Law 8:756–777
Finch V (2009) Corporate insolvency law. Cambridge University Press, Cambridge
Finch V (2012) Corporate rescue: who is interested? J Bus Law 3:190–212
Finch V, Milman D (2017) Corporate insolvency law: perspectives and principles, 3rd edn. Cambridge University Press, Cambridge
Franks J, Sussman O (2005) Financial distress and bank restructuring of small to medium-sized UK companies. Rev Financ 9:65–96
Frost CW (1992) Running the Asylum: governance problems in bankruptcy reorganizations. Ariz Law Rev 34:89–140
Garrido JM (2012) Out-of-Court Debt restructuring. World Bank Study. World Bank, para 60. Available at https://openknowledge.worldbank.org/handle/10986/2230. Accessed 13 Mar 2016
Gilson S (2012) Coming through in a crisis: how Chapter 11 and the debt restructuring industry are helping to revive the U.S. economy. J Appl Corp Financ 24(4):23–35
Gilson SC, John K, Lang LHP (1990) Troubled debt restructurings: an empirical study of private reorganization of firms in default. J Financ Econ 27(2):315–353
Global Turnaround (2007) The lessons of Schefenacker. Global Turnaround, London
Goode R (2005) Principles of corporate insolvency law, 3rd edn. Thomson Sweet & Maxwell, London
Goode R (2011) Principles of corporate insolvency law, 4th edn. Sweet and Maxwell, London. at para 11–17, 393
Gudgeon MR, Joshi SA (2013) The restructuring and workout environment in Europe. In: Larkin B (ed) Restructuring and workout strategies for maximizing value, 2nd edn. Globe, Law and Business, Surrey, pp 7–14
Heery E, Noon M (2008) A dictionary of human resource management, 2nd Rev edn. Oxford University Press, Oxford
Idigbe A (11 Oct 2011) Using existing insolvency framework to drive business recovery in Nigeria: the role of the judges. Available at: http://www.punuka.com/uploads/role_of_judges_in_driving_a_business_recue_approach_in_existing_insolvency_framework.pdf. Last accessed 5 July 2016
Idigbe A, Kalu O (5 Oct 2015) Recent strides in Nigerian insolvency law – banking insolvency & AMCON Act. Available at: http://www.mondaq.com/Nigeria/x/431946/Insolvency+Bankruptcy/Recent+Strides+In+Nigerian+Insolvency+Law+Banking+Insolvency+AMCON+Act. Last accessed 7 Oct 2016

Insolvency Service (May 2011) Proposals for a restructuring Moratorium—summary of responses para 4, 5. Available at: http://webarchive.nationalarchives.gov.uk/20120407195242/http://www.bis.gov.uk/assets/insolvency/docs/insolvency%20profession/consultations/restructuring-response/restructure-response-2-summaryofresponses.pdf. Accessed 14 June 2016

Jackson TH (1982) Bankruptcy, nonbankruptcy entitlements, and the creditors' bargain. Yale Law J 91:857–907

Jackson TH (1986) The logic and limits of bankruptcy law. Beard Books, Washington DC, pp 11–12

Jensen MC (1989) Active investors, LBOs, and the privatization of bankruptcy. J Appl Corp Financ 2(1):35–44

Jones EH (1992) Chapter 11: a debt penalty for debtor and creditor interests. Cornell Law Rev 77(5):1088–1092

Jostarndt P, Sautner Z (2010) Out-of-court restructuring versus formal bankruptcy in a non-interventionist bankruptcy setting. Rev Financ 14:623–668

Kamlah K (1996) The New German Insolvency Act: Insolvenzordnung. Am Bankruptcy Law J 70:417

Kann J, Redeker R (2012) Reform Act on German insolvency law: new opportunities for distressed investors? Pratt's J Bankruptcy Law 8(5):436–442

Keay A, Walton P (2008) Insolvency law: corporate and personal, 2nd edn. Jordans, Bristol

Kelch TG (1992) The phantom fiduciary: the debtor in possession in Chapter 11. Wayne Law Rev 38:1323

Kerkman J (1987) The debtor in full control: a case for adoption of the trustee system. Marquette Law Rev 70(2):159–209

Klein J (2012) Pre-pack administration: a comparison between Germany and the United Kingdom: Part 2. Company Lawyer 33(10):302

Kuney GW (2005) Hijacking Chapter 11. Emory Bankruptcy Dev J 21:19–112

Larkin B, Smolinsky J (2015) Restructuring through US Chapter 11 and UK prepack administration. In: Mallon C, Waisman SY (eds) The law of restructuring in the US and the UK. Oxford University Press, Oxford, pp 213–246

LoPucki LM (2004) The myth of the residual owner: an empirical study. Wash Univ Law Q 82(4):1341–1374

McCormack G (2007) Control and corporate rescue - an Anglo-American evaluation. Int Comp Law Q 56(3):515–555

McCormack G (2008) Corporate rescue law: an Anglo-American perspective. Edward Elgar, Cheltenham

McCormack G (2009) Apples and Oranges? Corporate rescue and functional convergence in the US and UK. Int Insolv Rev 18:109–134

McCormack G (2018) Security rights and insolvency law in the common law system. In: McCormack G, Bork R (eds) Security right and the European insolvency regulation. Intersentia, Cambridge, pp 313–414

Moss G (1998) Chapter 11: an English lawyer's critique. Insolv Intell 11:17–21

Moss G (2004) On the edge of non-recognition? Appointment of administrators under the Enterprise Act and the EC Regulation. Insolv Intell 17:13

Moss G, Bayfield D, Al-Attar A, Seife H, Rivera S (2011) Giving effect to debt compromise arrangement - binding the minority or out of the money classes of creditors. In: Mallon C, Waisman SY (eds) The law and practice of restructuring in the UK and US. Oxford University Press, Oxford, pp 165–212

Paterson S (2014) Bargaining in financial restructuring: market norms, legal rights and regulatory standards. J Corp Law Stud 14:333–365

Paterson S (2015) Rethinking corporate bankruptcy theory in the twenty-first-century. Oxf J Leg Stud 36(4):697–723

Paterson S (2017) Debt restructuring and notions of fairness. Modern Law Rev 80(4):600–623

Payne J (2013) Cross-border schemes of arrangement and forum shopping. Eur Bus Organ Law Rev 14(4):563–589

Payne J (2014a) Debt restructuring in English law: lessons from the United States and the need for reform. Law Q Rev 130:282–305

Payne J (2014b) Schemes of arrangement: theory, structure and operation. Cambridge University Press, Cambridge

Payne J (5 Oct 2016) The future of UK debt restructuring. Available at: https://doi.org/10.2139/ssrn.2848160. Accessed 14 Mar 2017

Payne J (2018) The role of the court in debt restructuring. Camb Law J 77(1):124–150

Pottow JAE (2014) Mitigating the problem of vulture holdout: international certification boards for sovereign-debt restructurings. Tex Int Law J 49:221–243

Rajan R, Winton A (1995) Covenants and collateral as incentives to monitor. J Financ 1(4):1114–1146

Riesenfeld SA (1987) Classification of claims and interests in Chapter 11 and 13 Cases. Calif Law Rev 75:391–404

Rotem Y (2008) Contemplating a corporate governance model for bankruptcy reorganizations: lessons from Canada. Va Law Bus Rev 3:125

Schiessl M (1988) On the road to a new German reorganization law. Am Bankruptcy Law J 62:233

Schwarcz SL (1999) Rethinking freedom of contract. Tex Law Rev 77:515–604

Segal N (2007) The effect of reorganization proceedings on security interests: the position under English and U.S. Law. Brooklyn J Int Law 32:927–981

Seidman A, Seidman RB (1994) State and law in the development process: problem solving and institutional change in the Third World. Macmillan Press, London

Shutter A, McLaughlin D (2011) Waivers, amendments and standstills. In: Mallon C, Waisman SY (eds) the law and practice of restructuring in the UK and the US. Oxford University Press, Oxford, pp 149–162

Skeel D, Ayotte KA (2013) Bankruptcy law as a liquidity provider. Univ Chic Law Rev 80:1559–1560

Stiglitz J (2001) Bankruptcy law: basic economic principles. In: Claessen S (ed) Resolution of financial distress: an international perspective on the design of bankruptcy laws. The World Bank, Washington DC, pp 1–22

Tajti T (2018) Bankruptcy stigma and the second chance policy: the impact of bankruptcy stigma on business restructurings in China, Europe and the United States. China-EU Law J 6:1–31

The Insolvency Service (2016) Summary of responses: a review of corporate insolvency framework, Sept. 2016. Available at: https://www.gov.uk/government/uploads/system/uploads/attachment_data/file/578524/Summary_of_responses_26-10-16_Redacted.pdf. Accessed 4 Feb 2018

Tilley A (2005) European restructuring: clarifying Trans-Atlantic Misconceptions. J Private Equity 8(2):99–103

Tschauner H, Wolfram D (2010) Revision of German bond act: new restructuring options for German bonds. ICR: 40

Walters AJ (2015) Statutory erosion of secured creditors' rights: some insights from the United Kingdom. Univ Ill Law Rev:543–570

Watson AF (2000) Left for dead? The Supreme Court's treatment of the new value exception in Bank of America National Trust & Savings Association v. 203 North Lasalle Street Partnership. N C Law Rev 78:1190–1224

Westbrook JL, Booth CD, Paulus CG, Rajak H (2010) A global view of business insolvency systems. The World Bank, Washington DC

Westpfahl L (2010) Vorinsolvenzliches Sanierungsverfahren [Pre-Insolvency Restructuring Procedure]. ZGR:385

Westpfahl L, Schonen S (2015) Expedited corporate debt restructuring procedure in Germany. In: Olivares-Caminal R (ed) Expedited corporate debt restructuring in the EU. Oxford University Press, Oxford

White M (1994) Corporate bankruptcy as a filtering device: Chapter 11 reorganizations and out-of-court debt restructuring. J Law Econ Org 10(2):268–215
Wood PR (2007) Comparative law of security interests and title finance, 2nd edn. Sweet and Maxwell, London
Yeowart G (2009) Encouraging company rescue: what changes are required to UK insolvency law? Law Financ Mark Rev 3:517–531

Chapter 4
Financing the Restructuring Process: Incentivizing Through Law

4.1 Overview

The trajectory of this book so far has done two things. On the one hand, it has (amongst other things), analyzed the financing options open to financially distressed businesses.[1] On the other hand, it has analyzed the existing restructuring regimes, and the mostly generally agreeably procedural pre-requisites for the restructuring of distressed businesses and how they contribute to liquidity.[2] Although such tools as automatic stay or its functional equivalents may help preserve liquidity, it may not necessarily take the place of new funds. Such new funds are key to the resolution financial distress for businesses undergoing a restructuring. Funding the process also requires incentives, to encourage the lenders to do so. The whole notion of incentives through the law has pit economists against social psychologists. Since for the most part, financing decisions are more economic ones, the use of incentives to facilitate distressed lending cannot be called to question.[3] More so, a closer look at the arguments of social psychologists provide ample support for creating incentives through the law for new financing. This chapter focuses on these two aspects of new lending incentivizing. It examines on the one hand, negative protections of new lending, using the EU recommended approach as a model, whilst highlighting its very modest usefulness as incentive for new financing.

On the other hand, it focuses on the use of priority as new financing incentive. Paying particular attention to how repayment priority is recognized and used as an incentivizing device, this chapter notes that what policymakers across jurisdictions appear not to be agreed on are the approaches. This chapter therefore identifies two

[1] See generally Chap. 2 above.

[2] See generally Chap. 3 above.

[3] For an exposition on the importance of incentives to economics, see Sonnenschein (1983), pp. 79–92. See also Myerson (1999), p. 1068 (noting that economists define their field more broadly as being an analysis of incentives).

S. U. Mba, *New Financing for Distressed Businesses in the Context of Business Restructuring Law*, https://doi.org/10.1007/978-3-030-19749-0_4

dominant approaches decipherable from the practices of the selected jurisdictions. While on the one hand there exists a prescriptive approach, where states specify priority positions as incentive for new lending, on the other hand, there exists an approach describable as a market approach, which essentially allow market players work out for themselves what priorities (if any), and the consideration for same.

An examination of either approach represented by the paradigm of the US and the UK in this book provide support for their approaches. It is however argued that theoretically, the key question that arises from new financing in the context of restructuring policy is how to strike the balance between the protection of pre-distress lenders, and the meeting of the financing needs of the distressed business. A prescriptive approach is better suited to address these issues. In the context of frontier markets with a focus on Nigeria, the chapter points out that that the prescriptive approach that affords superpriority will better incentivize new lending.

4.2 Incentivizing Through Law: Why Extrinsic Motivation Matters for New Financing

The use of incentives to motivate behavior is not new to the field of economics and social psychology. Economists suggest that human behavior characteristically respond to incentives. Several economic studies show that contingent rewards serve as "positive reinforcers" for anticipated behavior.[4] On their part, social psychologists tend to differ on the point. For them, rewards may be counter-productive, so that it may well contribute to negative reinforcement of behavior in the long run. Indeed, several experiments validate the notion that behavior induced by external incentives (extrinsic motivation) may well conflict with the innate desire to see to the accomplishment of that thing.[5] This negative reinforcement has played out in the realm of private law and have been addressed by legal scholars. Wendy Gordon for instance has noted that when we pay people to refrain from the doing harm, such extrinsic motivation may likely inspire the wrong behavioral outcomes in the agents. Ordinarily "moral people might (inaccurately) infer that one has no moral obligation to do the right thing unless one is paid."[6] The author makes a similar point in the context of intellectual property, noting that external incentives designed to

[4] Benabou and Tirole (2003); Lazear (2000) (on how extrinsic motivation of employees can lead to increased workers' efforts and profit for employers).

[5] See for instance, Krepps (1997) (on the negative effect of extrinsic motivation on the intrinsic motivation of workers); Deci et al. (2001) (on the substantially undermining effect of tangible rewards systems in schools). This narrative regarding the negative effect of extrinsic motivation has also been challenged. See for instance, Cameron et al. (2001) (suggesting that in general, rewards are not harmful to motivation to perform a task).

[6] Gordon (1992), p. 457.

induce creativity may produce the contrary effect of degrading "the creativity of or the efforts invested in resulting works."[7]

There is also the signaling effect of incentives. By this, social psychologists note that incentive may serve as proof that an intrinsic motivation does not suffice to promote a particular behavior. Alternatively, positive motivation prescribed by the law may be another way of suggesting that the existing social norms are not supportive of the activity for which the incentive is prescribed.[8] If one applies this to the context of restructuring and the provision of distress financing, it would mean that the provision of incentives through the law may signal to both pre-distress and new lenders that the provision of new financing is not something which the law ordinarily support.

It is arguable that some of the considerations considered by social psychologists justify the use of incentives in motivating new financing for the distressed debtor. For instance, no doubt, lenders are people in business and are in it for improved return on investment. Generally, there is no obligation on the part of the prospective lender to provide new financing to the debtor. Assuming there is a moral obligation, there is no legal obligation on a lender to do so, no matter how compelling the morality of the situation may be. Although it might appear too early in the chapter to point this out but suffice it to say that incentives in the law may fill in the gaps that arise as a result of the absence of a moral obligation to lend, by statutorily encouraging prospective lenders to do so in appropriate circumstances, either through negative protections or priority positions. In addition, regarding the signaling of insufficiency of intrinsic motivation, it is often crystal clear the case that new financing is considered a risky venture, or at least the mere thought that a firm is in trouble triggers alarm bells for lenders. It has also been established that new financing is often required to facilitate the restructuring of a distressed business. Hence, whether or not there is a signal, new lenders or old lenders already consider the situation a risky one.[9] Identifying intrinsic incentives is not always an easy task.

In addition to the above, financing distressed businesses is one of such areas that obfuscates this distinction between intrinsic and extrinsic motivation for behavior. Indeed, there has been much debate about the distinction between intrinsic/extrinsic motivations.[10] Some scholars have highlighted the difficulty in pinpointing exactly what amounts to an intrinsic motivation. This is relatable to motivations in the context of financing debt restructuring. As already noted, a prior secured lender may

[7] Gordon (2010), p. 749.

[8] Underhill (2016), p. 239 (Noting that "[A]gents may interpret an incentive … as evidence that intrinsic motivation is Insufficient-that is, incentives are necessary because social norms do not support the task.").

[9] At least this is explained by the higher interest rates charged by providers of new financing to distressed borrowers and the desire for priority repayment.

[10] See for instance, Feldman (2011), pp. 18–19 (noting the difficulty in demarcating the line between intrinsic and extrinsic motivation); Hollander-Blumoff (2011), pp. 55–59; Guzzo (1979) (noting in the context of work behavior that "a single definition separating intrinsic and extrinsic rewards is not widely shared ….").

provide financing to prop up the value of the asset over which it has a lien, strengthen its strategic position, or to exert more control over the debtor.[11] In addition, for a pre-distress lender, the motivation may be that it continues its lending relationship, or if a new lender, that it starts a new (and hopefully lasting) relationship with the distressed debtor when it rebounds.[12] Now each of these motivations considered as intrinsic may also be susceptible to being defined as extrinsic, given that actors do so in anticipation of a future benefit.[13] It is therefore arguable that in the first place, there is hardly that distinction between intrinsic and extrinsic motivation in the context of new financing for distressed businesses. In addition, although business people as economic actors may not be necessarily driven by social norms as envisaged by the social psychologists, the whole idea of distress financing presupposes some risk and the signaling by incentives may only make the already existing risk the more conspicuous.

In debt restructuring, national policymakers and international experts already recognize the importance of access to financing in the process of restructuring.[14] In line with this recognition, they continue to forge strategies designed to incentivize the provision of new financing for the restructuring of distressed but viable businesses.[15] Supporting the incentivizing of lending may be achieved in the context of formal restructuring as well as informal restructuring. In the case of the former, the incentives may be expressed in the form of positive incentives. Incentivizing the latter may be more challenging especially given that much of it goes on without regulation, and it present an opportunity for abuse, in ways that may conflict with the goals of bankruptcy itself.

---

[11] See Chap. 2, Sect. 2.2. On creditor control, see Chap. 5.

[12] Of course, assuming the borrower is a desirable one.

[13] See Cooter (2000), p. 19 ("people will tend to make moral commitments when doing so causes a sufficiently large increase in their opportunities."); Cameron and Pierce (1994), p. 364 ("although human behavior appear to occur in the absence of any obvious or extrinsic consequences, they may, in fact be due to anticipated future benefits.").

[14] UNCITRAL Legislative Guide on Insolvency Law (2005), para 94, 113. ("To maintain its business activities, the debtor must have access to funds to enable it to continue to pay for crucial supplies of goods and services, including labor costs, insurance, rent, maintenance of contracts and other operating expenses, as well as costs associated with maintaining the value of assets.").

[15] Ibid, at para 97, 114–115 (noting that the central issue in restructuring financing is "is the scope of the power and, in particular, the inducements that can be offered to a potential creditor to encourage it lend."); Also EU Recommendation on Business Failure (recommending the protection of providers of restructuring financing); Proposal for a Directive on Restructuring Frameworks ("Member States shall ensure that new financing and interim financing are adequately encouraged and protected ….").

On the UK, see para 10.3 ("… the Government is keen to encourage greater access to finance for distressed companies seeking new funding."). In Singapore, see Report of the Committee to Strengthen Singapore as an International Center for Debt Restructuring (20 April 2016) at para 4 (advocating the introduction of additional incentives for the providers of new financing).

4.3 Incentivizing New Financing Through Negative Protection: The Insufficiency of the EU Recommendation Regime

In the quest to facilitate the provision of new financing to support the restructuring of distressed businesses, an approach to encourage such lending is the protection of the financing provided from adverse bankruptcy rules, the implication of which may be the inability of the provider of the distress financing to recoup its financing upon the commencement of bankruptcy proceedings. This takes the form of protecting such investments from the transaction avoidance regime of bankruptcy law. Recommendation on a New Approach to Business Failure and Insolvency (hereinafter: EU Recommendation) adopts this approach of negative protections.[16] In a bid to achieve this protection, it is recommended that new financing which is provided to the restructuring debtor, after it has been agreed upon in the restructuring plan and confirmed by the court, should not be treated as voidable, void or as unenforceable.[17] Such a provision protecting the interest of financers of the distressed (restructuring) debtor owes to the centrality of transaction avoidance actions to bankruptcy law which in a nutshell, ensures that the assets of the debtor is not depleted to the detriment of the general body of creditors.[18]

The above notwithstanding, it is important that transactions such as new financing, set out to facilitate the rehabilitation of the debtor for the benefit of the general body of creditors, should be treated differently from that which set out to harm the general body of creditors.[19] This is clearly what the recommendation sets out to

[16] See generally, EU Recommendation on Business Failure.

[17] S. 27 of THE EU Recommendation on Business Failure. See also Article 16(1) of the proposed Directive.

[18] Avoidance of transactions which are detrimental to creditors (action *Pauliana*) is derived from Roman law. Action Pauliana alongside *missio in possessionem* and the *venditio bonorum*, is considered a precursor to bankruptcy law. A historical account of the origin of action Paulina is given by Layton B. Register as follows:

> ... By the Law of the Twelve Tables the creditor might put his debtor to death or sell him into slavery. This was moderated to imprisonment and attachment of the debtor's property. The creditors were placed in possession (*missio in possessionem*) of the entire estate of the debtor which, after a certain period, was sold in a lump to the highest bidder (*venditio bonorum*). But up to the time when his creditors were placed in possession there was no restraint upon the debtor, who was left free to commit any fraud he pleased upon his creditors, increasing his insolvency by alienating his property and assuming new debts. The praetor, through the action *Pauliana*, corrected this by permitting the creditor to follow the property alienated in fraud through the hands of as many persons as it might have passed, provided that they had knowledge of the fraud.

Register (1913), p. 438.

[19] See Mevorach (2011), p. 236. ('If transactions conducted for the purpose of benefiting the company are not attacked but only those which have worsened the company's position, a proper balance is struck between the need to ensure the ultimacy of the transaction, certainty and stability and the need to remedy the harm caused to creditors.').

achieve as the protection afforded the lender from "criminal, civil or administrative liability"[20] is to the extent that the financing transaction is not subsequently tainted by fraud.[21] However, one may wonder: what has this recommendation concretely provided that is not already part of formal restructuring regimes?

The provision of the EU Recommendation does not bring anything new to the discourse of incentives to the providers of new financing, as far as the restructuring regime proposed is designed to apply to formal restructuring.[22] Even if one assumes that it is designed to be applicable to informal restructuring regime, broad enough safe harbors exist, which can assure providers of new financing of protection.[23] In the case of formal restructuring regimes, it is often the case that such regimes are linked to bankruptcy laws already, so that the new financing is already a part of the agreement reached by the parties as a part of the bankruptcy proceedings. In such a case, it is unlikely that such financing approved as a part of the restructuring process will be subsequently disregarded by the courts as falling short of the provision of bankruptcy law that seeks to protect the general body of creditors.

If the restructuring contemplated by the EU Recommendation is informal, or perhaps contained in a legislation that is not bankruptcy law,[24] safe harbors provided for in avoidance laws also afford some respite. This respite guarantees that in certain circumstances, the security interests created in favor of the lender in exchange for the loan, the repayment of the loan, or repayments already made to the lender are protected. As an example, assume a new lender provides financing to the debtor in exchange for the creation of security over an asset of the debtor. Generally, such transaction is protected where value flows from the lender to the borrower, and the transaction is contemporaneous.[25] As far as such security interest created in favor of

[20] Para 28 of the EU Recommendation on Business Failure. See also article 16(3) of the EU Proposal for a Directive on Restructuring Frameworks.

[21] Para 29 of the EU Recommendation on Business Failure.

[22] Formal restructuring is used here in terms of any court-connected restructuring framework, whether targeted or collective (see Chap. 3 above). Hence, although the preventive restructuring regime proposed by the recommendation emphasizes flexibility and limited court involvement (see para. 17 preamble of the recommendation), the invocation of the imprimatur of the state qualifies the regime under the classification used in the book as a formal restructuring regime.

[23] McCormack (2017), p. 191 (pointing out that "[t]he [EU] Recommendation, however, only offers the negative protection already alluded to in the form of protection from civil or criminal liability and in the event of avoidance proceedings.").

[24] See generally, Eidenmüller (2018) (on the characterization of proceedings as bankruptcy proceedings and the implications of such characterization).

[25] The contemporaneity requirement assumes nuances, based on statutory wordings but are not radically different. In the US, contemporaneity in respect of a purchase money security interest is exempted from avoidance, which otherwise apply to transactions concluded within 90 days of bringing bankruptcy petition, if perfection is done within a statutorily prescribed period of 30 days (see 11 USC §547(c)(3)). In the UK, the Insolvency Act invalidates floating charges created on the assets of the debtor within 12 months before the commencement of insolvency proceedings unless the charge serves as consideration for money paid, goods or services supplied, discharge or reduction in the debt owed by the debtor, and "the consideration was given *at the same time as or after the creation of the charge* [emphasis supplied]" (see s. 245(2) IA, 1986). There are conflicting

the lender does not pertain to a pre-existing debt, the lender may not have much to worry about. This is essentially because avoidance laws apply to pre-filing creditors.

As things stand, although negative protection afforded the distressed debtor is characterized in the recommendation as an incentive to attract providers of new financing, it would appear that the drafters sought to take tread carefully, knowing that positive incentives did not feature explicitly in any of the restructuring regimes of member states. As such, there may well be resistance to an approach which introduces positive incentives. It may well be that there has been a rethinking of the approach to incentivizing, with the introduction of a more concrete yardstick which has formed the plank of new lending incentive, on which the rest of the chapter turns. This yardstick is the creation of priority position for new lenders.[26]

4.4 Distressed Debtor Financing: A History of Priority as Incentive

The history of corporate re-organization provides insights into how financing within the context of corporate restructuring has evolved. This history points us in the direction of nineteenth century railroads in the United States.[27] The strategic importance of the railroad industry for commerce necessitated massive expansion and this expansion did require intense capital injection. Within the expansion and capital injection mix were a couple of challenges which the railroads had to grapple with. One of such challenges pertained to the huge fixed costs incurred in the payment of its creditors, dealing with current expenditure, as well as costs to pursue their massive expansion. To make matters worse, the railroads had to deal with a downward pressure on rates charged, to attract patronage, even when the railroads were unable

decisions on the approach of the court on how much lapse of time may be accommodated to protect the charge from avoidance. McCormack has however argued that what should be paramount is whether there is a causal link between the charge granted to a financer for valuable consideration instead of placing emphasis on whether there was an obvious lapse in time between when the lender provided the financing and when the charge came into effect. See McCormack (2006), p. 52. In the case of Germany, an immediate exchange of cash or other form of compensation immediately between the distressed debtor and the creditor is considered a "cash transaction" (and protected under the Code. See s. 142 InsO. See generally, Spahlinger and Kortz (2015), at para 10.42, 212.

[26] Article 16(2) of the Proposal for a Directive on Restructuring Framework now provides that Member States of the EU "may afford grantors of new or interim financing the right to receive payment with priority in the context of subsequent liquidation procedures in relation to other creditors that would otherwise have superior or equal claims to money or assets."

[27] Skeel Jr. (2001), p. 48. ("In a very real sense, the history of corporate reorganization is the history of nineteenth-century railroad failures.").

to break-even.[28] This in addition to other challenges[29] resulted in the inability of the railroads to meet their operational costs as well as debt obligations, and the eventual failure of a good number of the railroads.[30]

Equity receiverships came in handy to help the railroads re-organize, but during the usually lengthy process of negotiations between the stakeholders, the railroads had to continue operation. Capital injection proved difficult in such times especially because of the terms of the pre-distress loans, which chilled the enthusiasm of new money investors.[31] Expectedly, percipient lenders were unwilling to risk subordination of its claim in a firm with senior claimants who already have the privilege of strong legal rights.[32] As such, new money was difficult, if not impossible to come by. However, the court was to devise a way around this. Through the intervention of the courts, the receivers were able to interfere with the claims held by prior creditors. How did this work? With the nod of the courts, receivers issued debt instruments known as "receiver certificates".[33] The certificate was essentially designed to provide the railroads with liquidity until when the restructuring of the debt of the roads could be effectuated.[34] It also served as an incentive to providers of the funding.

By virtue of the receiver certificate, an investor in the distressed corporation was assured by the court that where negotiations break down, and the parties were unable to come to an agreement on the re-organization, the holders of the certificates would be repaid from the sale of the asset, which secured the certificate.[35] In the strict sense, the obligation arising from the issued certificate was on the receiver, and not the railroad debtor itself.[36] However, in fact, the obligations on the certificates were paid from the assets of the estate of the debtor.[37] As the financing was important to preserve and operate the railroad property, the court readily approved the priority even when it undercut the mortgage of prior lienholders.[38] At least in one

---

[28] Ibid, pp. 50–51.

[29] Id. Some other challenges included the haphazard nature in which the rail tracks were laid, the advancement in technology, which saw preference for the steel tracks, rather than iron gauges which were narrower and also importantly, the mergers, acquisitions and power play by investors, which adversely affected the financial health of many of the railroads. See also Tufano (1997), p. 3 ("The railroads fell into distress so often because they had exceptionally high fixed costs while facing bitter competition in many regions of the country.").

[30] See Swaine (1898) (table shows that between 1872 and 1898, about 700 firms had failed).

[31] Tufano (1997), p. 3.

[32] On how corporate debt serves as a disincentive to investment in a distressed debtor and the pursuit of good future investment by the debtor, see Myers (1977).

[33] These were also known as certificates of indebtedness.

[34] Baker (1976), pp. 2–3 (noting that "the purpose of the certificate was to tide over the corporation until such time as a workable plan for readjustment of debts and rehabilitation of the debtor could be adopted, particularly where the debtor's continued survival and operation was in the public interest.").

[35] Dickson (1896), p. 523.

[36] See Baker (1976), p. 3.

[37] See Skeel Jr. (2004), pp. 1911–1902.

[38] Ripley (1915), p. 386 ("…in order to obtain additional capital these certificates must take precedence even over the first-mortgage bonds, as a prior lien both on assets and earnings.").

case,[39] the US Supreme Court endorsed the issuance of a priority certificate by a receiver in spite of oppositions by pre-restructuring lienholders, whose interests had been primed.[40]

The issuance of receiver certificates by the receivers, and the approval of superpriority by the equity courts disclosed a particular pattern, which is quite instructive. It was restricted to businesses in which the public had an interest. Public or quasi-public corporate entities fell into this category, and railroads again were easily an example of either types of business entities.[41] For these railroads, the courts were disinclined to suspend their operations, as their continued operation was necessary for employees, connected businesses and the communities where they operated. Hence, even when the entities were operating at a loss, receiver certificates were authorized, to enable the receiver to continue to operate the business of the railroad.[42] It appears that the courts justified this position on the public interest role which the railroads served. On this basis, the court at the time were willing to justify the likely impairment of prior secured creditors "so far as [it] is necessary to the conservation of the [rail]road and the performance of its public and private duties."[43]

The foregoing notwithstanding, it is not to say that the courts were not conscious of the extent to which the impairment of the claim of secured creditors were to be tolerated. For in situations where the court considered that the continued operation of the railroad will result in unmitigated loss for the secured creditors, and the erosion of their interest, it refused to approve superpriority for the issuance of receiver certificates. In one case,[44] the 4th Circuit reversed a decision which sought to allow the issuance of superpriority certificates to facilitate the continued operation of a railroad. This was particularly as the result of the approval would be the erosion of the assets of the company, to benefit the limited number of stakeholders who sought the continued operation of the road.

---

[39] Ibid (cites the example of the Wabash receivership, where notwithstanding protests by bondholders, the court recognized the validity of certificates issued with priority over their claims). See also *Wallace* v. *Loomis* 97 US 146 (1877).

[40] Ibid, p. 162:

> The power of a court of equity to appoint managing receivers of such property as a railroad, when taken under its charge as a trust fund for the payment of incumbrances, and to authorize such receivers to raise money necessary for the preservation and management of the property, and make the same chargeable as a lien thereon for its repayment, cannot, at this day, be seriously disputed.

[41] Contrast *American Eng'r. Co. v. Metropolitan By-Products Co.*, 275 F. 34 (2nd Cir.) (the 2nd Circuit held that there was insufficient public interest in the refuse collection activity of the debtor in New York City).

[42] See *American Brake Shoe & Foundry Co. v. Pere Marquette R. Co.* 205 F. 14 (6 Cir.) (The circuit court authorized an interim receiver certificate for the railway company, noting, "[a] railroad company owes a duty, not only to its creditors and stockholders, but, by virtue of its franchise, to the public as well….").

[43] Ibid, p. 22.

[44] *Central Bank & Trust Corp. v. Cleveland* 252 F. 530, 534 (4th Cir. 1918).

Where private (non-railroad) companies were involved, the prevailing attitude of the courts was to decline approval of receivership certificates with superpriority for continuing the operation of the business. Thus, even where a majority of the lienholders of a mining company were agreeable to the priming of their interests to raise new financing, the court sided with a minority of the lienholders who opposed the use of receiver certificate, arguing that the company was a private one.[45] In the same vein, new financers who dealt with a receiver appointed by a state court over a brewery were deprived of the superpriority, which induced the investment in the first place. Amongst other things, the reasoning of the court was informed by the status of the corporation as private one, as distinct from a public or quasi-public one, the former being ineligible for raising operational financing with such heightened priority.[46]

This difference in treatment of distressed borrowers soon changed as statutory incentives began to evolve for the restructuring of distressed businesses.[47] Whether or not the distressed borrower was a railroad, or whether the financing was for the purpose of preserving assets or facilitating operations, the authority of a bankruptcy court to authorize the issuance of trust certificates became expressly provided for in statutes.[48] It is arguable that these changes were consistent with recognition of the importance of incentivizing new financing, as a key component of the restructuring of a distressed debtor. Subsequent iterations of this incentive in bankruptcy legislation instead paid better attention to the importance of balancing the need for new financing with the need to protect prior lenders. Hence it makes sense to highlight the role of priority as one important means of expressing the new financing incentive.

4.5 Claim Ranking as Incentivizing Tool and Superpriority Position

Today, the priority arising from the ranking of claims has become an important incentivizing tool for restructuring in the US, and this model (or idiosyncratic modifications of it) continue to come up for consideration in the reform efforts of

[45] See *In re Farmers Loan and Trust Co. v. Grape Creek Coal Co.*, 50 F. 481 (S.D. Ill. 1892).

[46] *In re Benwood Brewing Co.*202 F. 326, 328 (N.D.W.Va. 1913) ("In the first place, a sound distinction is to be drawn between these purely private corporations and quasi-public ones, such as railroad, telegraph, and telephone ones. In the latter the public at large has interest, in the former none whatever").

[47] The issuance of receiver certificates in the restructuring of large non-railroads was made possible for the first time by virtue of s. 77B Bankruptcy Act amendments of 1934. See generally Baer et al. (2012).

[48] Skeel Jr. (2004), p. 1915 (noting that as a consequence of the 1978 Bankruptcy Code, the distinction between the kind of corporation and the purpose of the financing was completely removed).

restructuring law in other jurisdictions.[49] Priority through claim ranking is attributable to bankruptcy law. An essential role which bankruptcy law plays is the distribution of the assets of the debtor to its creditors.[50] To allow such distribution, the claims of all claimants need follow a particular system of ordering, unless (in the sometimes unlikely situation) the assets of the debtor is sufficient to ensure that all creditors receive full payments in respect of their claims.[51] The significance of the claim ranking of bankruptcy law to debt restructuring is that the restructuring of distressed debtors often largely follow the same distributive pattern of bankruptcy law. Even where the restructuring procedure is not designed to immediately distribute claims to creditors, it will necessarily respect the hierarchy of claims in a liquidation context. Indeed, the liquidation context always forms the backdrop against which the bargains are negotiated.[52] In the same vein, the ranking of claims in bankruptcy plays a significant part for distressed financing. It is through this priority system that we can identify what (if any), and the quality of incentive, a financer of a distressed business undergoing restructuring may enjoy. It is against this background that a prospective lender considers its new lending protected and its

---

[49] Some countries have carried out reforms to provide for superpriority incentive for new lenders. Such countries include: i. Canada. S. 50.6 the Bankruptcy and Insolvency Act (as amended) (BIA) and s. 11(2) Companies' Creditors Arrangement Act (as amended) (CCAA) provide for superpriority in favor of an interim financer over pre-filing secured creditors. It is noteworthy that before the prescriptive approach to incentivizing new lending, Canadian courts assumed jurisdiction to grant such priorities under what was considered their remedial authority. See McCormack (2008), pp. 200–201; see also Sarra (2013).

South Africa: s. 138 of the South African Companies Act, 2008 creates superpriority for providers of post-commencement financing in the course of business rescue proceedings. See generally, Calitz and Freebody (2016).

ii. Brazil. See Felsberg and Filho (2009).

iii. Spain: the Spanish Insolvency Act (Amendment) 2011, which came into force on January 1, 2012 incentivizes new financing by allowing 50% of the new funds to be elevated as a claim against the estate of the debtor, whilst the other 50% enjoys priority over ordinary creditors, but junior to preferred claims. See Pallares (2012) Spanish Act Changes. Available at <https://m.lw.com/thoughtLeadership/spanish-insolvency-act-changes-january-amendments>. Accessed 10 Aug 2017.

iv. Italy: pursuant to Law Decree No. 83, of June 22, 2012, which was later converted into Law No. 13 of Aug. 11, 2012 and now a part of the Italian bankruptcy law, new providers of financing may be granted senior ranking repayment position for bridge financing, although this is subject to the approval of the bankruptcy court as well as the pre-distress creditors. See Gallagher and Lombardo (2013).

v. Singapore, S. 211(E) of the Singapore Companies Act now provides for superpriority position for new financers over all other creditors. See Rajah (2017).

[50] Garrido (2011) (arguing that claim distribution is at the center of bankruptcy law).

[51] Tabb (2014), p. 622.

[52] See Paterson (2014), p. 339 ("All financial restructuring negotiations happen in the shadow of insolvency law"); McCormack (2017), p. 179 ("Priority systems are important in a business restructuring context because parties bargain in the shadow of the framework provided by liquidation law.").

repayment assured. It also forms the backdrop against which pre-distress lenders agree to the infusion of the new financing into the distressed debtor.[53]

In analyzing priorities, there is a strong temptation to undertake a mechanical retelling of the priority systems in the jurisdictions examined. One reason for this is that resulting from various jurisdiction-specific considerations,[54] insolvency priority systems are hardly ever identical because.[55] Another reason for this temptation is the difference in priority regimes that may exist depending on whether there is an outright liquidation, or whether a formal restructuring is to be undertaken.[56] Nevertheless, one can still draw a categorization which the jurisdictions follow albeit with certain nuances. This categorization typically starts with the position of the secured creditor, followed by the cost of administering the estate (administrative expense) and ending with the holders of common equity in the business.[57]

In the context of financing a distressed debtor undertaking a restructuring, the tendency has been to encourage new financing based on administrative expense priority (or its treatment as estate liability), a superpriority position, or even the grant of security interest to a potential new lender. In this book, superpriority is used to mean higher priority that exceeds administrative expense priority. Such higher priority positions may involve priority over other administrative expense claims, the creation of security interests in favor of the new lender either over unencumbered assets of the debtor or the subordination of the claim of a new lender over an already encumbered asset. In extreme cases, it may well even involve the creation of a priming security interest in favor of prospective lenders. Of course, all of these forms of priority position have their implication for existing creditors. These are analyzed below, in addition to the statutory designs and how priority incentive is approached within the statutory design.

---

[53] See generally, Gaa (1993), p. 885 (highlighting the desirability of predictability of outcomes, efficiency in the administration of debtor's estate, the equitable distribution of the estate, and the finality of results).

[54] McCormack (2017), p. 179 (Noting that these reasons range from history, culture, experiences and pressure group politics).

[55] Garrido (2011), p. 481 ("It is next to impossible to find countries that have exactly the same priorities.").

[56] The difference in treatment is most noticeable in the treatment of unsecured claims in Chapter 7 and 11 of the US Bankruptcy Code. See generally, See Baird (2010).

[57] It is important to note that in Germany, secured creditors are typically considered to be outside the ranking of insolvency claims. One class of creditors regarded as owners of the assets (pursuant to a retention of title clause for instance) are entitled to exercise a so-called right of segregation (*Aussonderungsrechte*), where the asset is separated from the estate. Another class of creditors are considered to have a right to a claim of privileged distribution (*Absonderungsrechte*), where the asset is exclusively reserved for discharging the secured claim. Given the effect of their claims, one may still argue that their claims rank as the highest priority in German insolvency. See generally Paulus and Berberich (2016), at para 10.44, 273; see also, Spahlinger and Kortz (2015), at para. 10. 59, 216.

4.5.1 Administrative Expense Priority

Generally, the cost of administering the estate of the debtor in a restructuring often falls below the claim of secured creditors and above that of ordinary unsecured creditors.[58] The ranking of new financing for the restructuring of the debtor, ahead of unsecured creditors as an administrative expense has a plausible justification. When a distressed debtor chooses to restructure, there is the already now familiar presumption that the value of the assets of the debtor have a higher "going concern" value than a piecemeal sale of the assets will yield, hence the choice of a restructuring rather than a liquidation.[59] It follows that added to the other gains of a restructuring; unsecured creditors have a chance at recovery if debtor continues in business. If this is the case, they should be amenable to bearing the cost of the new credit in consideration of the higher value.[60]

In addition to the above justification, the ability to incur debt considered an administrative expense should be co-extensive with the restructuring policy, which at least envisages that the business of the debtor continues to operate, as the restructuring is underway.[61] If the authorized management is also empowered to trade and enter into credit transactions, such management should also be able to borrow and make cash payments as it becomes necessary. This is even more important where the creditworthiness of the business may have been negatively impacted as a fallout of its financial distress. Incentivizing new financing so that it enjoys priority ranking as a cost of administering the estate should be the least a jurisdiction should offer.[62] These theoretical arguments could serve as a multi-jurisdictional basis for the convergence of jurisdictions around the administrative expense priority offered to lenders of new financing to the distressed debtor undergoing restructuring. In the light of this, this section will deal with jurisdictional nuances on administrative expense priority for a prospective lender.

---

[58] The English law may be the exception to this, as for practical reasons, administrative expense ranks ahead of the floating charge (which is itself a secured claim) in an administration procedure. The position is different in the US for instance, where administrative expense claims rank below secured claims. See *Hartford Underwriters Insurance Co. v. Union Planters Bank N. A.* 530 U.S. 1 (2000).

[59] At least that is the premise of the analysis in the chapter.

[60] Adler et al. (2007), p. 475.

[61] See Chap. 1, Sect. 1.5.1. See also, Gilson (2012), p. 25 ("debt restructuring creates value by enabling temporarily overleveraged companies to continue to operate their businesses ....").

[62] See UNCITRAL Legislative Guide on Insolvency Law (2005), para 101, 116. (Noting that it is only upon such assurance that creditors will continue to provide credit if they have assurance of repayment priority ahead of pre-filing unsecured creditors).

4.5.1.1 US: Prescriptive Approach to Administrative Expense Priority

Chapter 11 takes a dual approach to the creation of administrative expense priority for providers of new financing to the distressed business. This elaborate approach considers the likely immediate concerns of the business, to seek funding meant to take care of pressing routine demands that arise as the business carries out its operations. Consequently, it allows the DIP to obtain new financing on an unsecured basis, in the "ordinary course of the debtor's business".[63] It also considers those financing needs that are not so routine but for which the debtor seeks financing. Such financing needs are not considered to fall within this "ordinary course of business" rubric. It does matter that the borrower is able to make the distinction between needs that fall within its ordinary course of business, because of the procedural implications that flow therefrom. The debtor is allowed to source for unsecured credit to finance its operations pending the approval of the reorganization plan, and to grant an administrative expense status to the lender. A distressed borrower may obtain the unsecured financing with administrative expense priority in the ordinary course of its business without an order of the Bankruptcy Court.[64] In other words, the authorization of the court is not required.[65]

On the other hand, if this financing is not in the ordinary course of the business of the debtor, then such financing will require the approval of the Bankruptcy Court, following a hearing and notice to interested parties.[66] The implication for making assumptions on whether a transaction falls within the ordinary course of business of the borrower can be dire for the provider of financing. It is not very easy to tell whether new financing is obtained in the ordinary course of business.[67] However, the courts have adopted a narrow construction to the question of the activities of the debtor that fall within this rubric.[68] Adopting this narrow construction approach makes practical sense, as to do otherwise will expand the scope of financing obtained without providing the opportunity for input from other relevant stakeholders who

[63] See 11 U.S.C. § 364(a). It is worthy of note that this priority is often applicable to trade creditors, for the purpose of keeping the lines of supplies open. See Baiser and Epstein (1992), p. 109.

[64] 11 U.S. Code § 364(a).

[65] In *re James A. Phillips Inc*. 29 B.R. 391, 393-94 (S.D.N.Y. 1983), the District Court of the Southern District of New York clearly points out that the "payments *in the ordinary course* need not be authorized by a Bankruptcy Court at all."

[66] 11 U.S. Code § 364(b).

[67] Triantis (1993), p. 905 ("Whether a loan is in the ordinary course of business is often difficult to predict.").

[68] For instance, *In re Massetti,* 95 Bankr. 360, 363 (E.D. Pa. 1989); *In re Lockwood Enter.,* 52 Bankr. 871, 874 (S.D.N.Y. 1985) (since the borrower had not typically sought financing for its operating and payroll expenses, financing obtained to defray such expenses was not in the ordinary course of business). But see also, Henoch (1991), p. 586 (distinguishing transactions usually qualifying as ordinary course of business from those that do not: "… servicing debt, purchasing capital assets, purchasing abnormally large amount of supplies, or advancing funds to assist in the liquidation of the business. This leaves everyday expenses such as rent, utilities, and just enough pencils to get the job done.").

may be impacted by the borrowing, or the bankruptcy courts.[69] Of course, what is important is that such stakeholders are afforded the opportunity to protect their interests. Such borrowing may therefore proceed in certain cases without the notice or hearing.[70]

4.5.1.2 The Implied Approach: English Administration and German Restructuring as Examples

Unlike the US, which boasts of a longer formal restructuring history, with explicit statutory provision on new lender incentives entrenched in its statute, the history of formal restructuring is comparably recent. Incentivizing the financing of distressed businesses undergoing formal restructuring did not have so much attention devoted to it in the UK until the period prior to the passage of the Enterprise Act in 2002.[71] The Insolvency Act, 1986 is silent on the provision of financing for the process of administration, in terms of clearly spelt out rules. However, a case has been made to show that an implied administrative expense priority exists in favor of the provider of formal restructuring financing, using the administration procedure.[72] As a starting point, the Insolvency Act grants to the administrator powers which ordinarily should be exercised by the pre-commencement management of the debtor, part of which includes the right to issue debt and the creation of security over the assets of the debtor.[73]

Furthermore, under the Insolvency Act,[74] the insolvency practitioner (administrator) is by implication considered to be empowered to incur loan obligations

---

[69] See *In re James A. Phillips Inc.* 29 B.R. 391, 393-94 (S.D.N.Y. 1983), at 394 (noting that borrowing in the ordinary course of business does not require a hearing hence the financing obtained should be such that enables the distressed debtor to operate the business).

[70] Pursuant to §102 of the US Bankruptcy Code, the requirement for a notice and hearing is as appropriate in the particular circumstances of the case. If no interested party requests for it timeously, its requirement may be waived. It may also be waived if insufficient time exists for the court to commence a hearing before authorizing performance of the act in question.

[71] It is worth noting however that, the Cork Report had recommended what by implication is a recognition of priority for the lender to the distressed business especially where an administration order is discharged by the court. The Cork Committee recommended that:

> [I]f the order is discharged, all creditors should revert to the position as it was when the original application was made, subject to the rights of priority of payment to anyone who in the meantime has given money or advanced credit to the administrator, to enable the company's business to be carried on as a going concern [....] The cost of the administration should be paid in priority to all other debts, except those secured by fixed charges but not floating charges, whether they have crystalized or not.

See Cork (1982), at para 514.

[72] McCormack (2008), p. 194.

[73] Schedule 1 para 3, IA, 1986.

[74] Schedule B1 para 99(3) essentially provides that the remuneration and the expenses of an erstwhile administrator is chargeable on, and payable out of the pool of assets over which he had

which are payable from the estate of the debtor which the administrator manages, and to have such obligations repaid as an administrative expense.[75] The contractual obligations incurred by the administrator are actually repayable ahead of, not only the remuneration of the administrator, but also other expenses.[76] This line of reasoning has found support in the decision of the English High Court in *Bibby Trade Finance Ltd v. McKay*[77] where the court agreed with the administrator that the loan provided by a financer to the administrator, to enable him complete a lucrative order of the debtor, qualified as an administrative expense. In a similar vein, the English House of Lords in *Centre Reinsurance v. Freakley*[78] stated emphatically that a holder of administrative expense claim enjoys superpriority position in the debtor company.[79] Such decisions point to the important role the court can play in applying the law in such a manner that conduces to the success of the restructuring process.[80]

Both cases before the courts were not directly on the new financing provided for the administration.[81] Consequently, it has been argued that there is no assurance, that when the priority to be accorded the new lender is the primary issue to be decided by another High Court, it will be inclined to follow in the steps of the *Bibby* court.[82] However, the pronouncement of the House of Lords should settle any ambiguity. Moreover, against the backdrop of the desire to support the rescue of the business, it is doubtful that a court might be unwilling to grant priority position to a provider of new financing in justified cases. Of course, this argument does not do away with the need for statutory clarity on administrative expense as rather than

custody or exercised control immediately before the administration ceases and the remuneration and expenses is paid ahead of any floating charge.

[75] Professor McCormack does argue that the "wordings of para 99(3) is sufficiently broad to encompass liabilities under contracts of loan entered into by the administrator on behalf of the company." See McCormack (2008), p. 198.

[76] See Schedule B1 para 99(3) and (4). Note that although the (4) refers to the position when an administrator has ceased to hold the office of an administrator, the English Court of Appeal in *Re Paramount Airways Ltd* [1994] 2 All E.R. 513, 522 resolved this in the context of administration. There the court reasoned that for practical purposes, payments to be made by an administration may have already been made before the administrator vacates office. See Parry (2008), p. 109. (Suggesting that the statutory provision may well be applicable to outstanding payments).

[77] [2006] EWHC 2836 (Ch.).

[78] [2006] All ER 943.

[79] Ibid, at 947 (Lord Hoffmann stated: "The administrator's expenses have priority over a floating charge and of course over unsecured creditors if there is a liquidation.") It bears restating that the fixed charge enjoys priority over the expense of the administration and that of other creditors.

[80] Bacon (2007), p. 4. Also, Finch (2009), p. 410 ("The significance of the *Bibby* case lies in its demonstrating that the English courts are capable of authorizing superpriority funding without there being any need for new legislation.").

[81] In the *Bibby* case, directors who had guaranteed the company's indebtedness to a financier contested the deductions made by the administrator, arguing that payments made to the financier ought to have reduced their indebtedness. The *Centre Reinsurance v. Freakley* case related to an insurer who claimed reimbursement from an administrator for actions carried on before the commencement of administration proceedings.

[82] Fletcher (2007), p. 4.

await the resolution of this issue by the courts, a statutory resolution may well make for certainty especially for would-be lenders. More so, as shall be seen a little later, it remains to be seen how this priority plays out where for any reason, the estate of the debtor is insufficient to cater for all administrative expense items. This notwithstanding, there is the possibility that some challenges may yet arise for this implied superpriority regime.

This implied superpriority regime may be without any challenge especially where the prospective lender is the same as the holder of the floating charge. It becomes potentially problematic if the provider of new financing is different from a pre-distress lender secured by a floating charge.[83]While the administrator can exercise control over assets subject of the floating charge, the priority position of the floating charge holder is still preserved. Intuitively, the reason a pre-distress lender would provide the new financing is clearly that the financing that it provides would enhance its returns on the floating charge, even after the new financing has been fully repaid. On the other hand, if a new financer emerges for whom a new priority position is created, the administrator may face legal challenge by the floating charge holder who's already weakened position is further emasculated by the action of the administrator. Granting such priority interest may harm the interest of the floating charge holder as a creditor and the law permits the floating charge holder to contest such payment.[84] The floating charge holder can contest before the court "that the past, present or proposed acts of the administrator are harmful to their interests or that the administrator is acting inefficiently."[85] More so, as already noted, the provision of this implied priority approach notwithstanding, a new lender is only assured a *pari passu* repayment in the event that the available assets are not sufficient to pay up administrative expense claims.

Although German insolvency law, like English law, does not name new financing, designating it as enjoying some higher priority, this may be inferred, when we think of the items which fall to be treated as administrative expense. As already noted, German bankruptcy law provides a single-entry point to liquidation or restructuring. Upon the appointment of an interim insolvency administrator, he may incur costs in the course of its management of the estate of the distressed business. Hence, obligations that arise in the restructuring and at the hand of the interim insolvency office holder, constitutes a liability on the estate of the debtor

[83] Typically, most lenders in the UK will take a fixed and a floating charge over the assets of the debtor. Generally, there is often no problem regarding the fixed charge given that the charge is on a specific or particular asset of the debtor and enjoys the highest priority as a secure claim. See *Centre Reinsurance v. Freakley* [2006] All ER 943.

[84] See sch B1, para 74(1) IA, 1986, a creditor (which includes a floating charge holder) may bring an action challenging fee payment by an administrator, claiming that:

(a) the administrator is acting or has acted so as unfairly to harm the interests of the applicant (whether alone or in common with some or all other members or creditors), or
(b) the administrator proposes to act in a way which would unfairly harm the interests of the applicant (whether alone or in common with some or all other members or creditors).

[85] See *Hosking and Mackay (as joint liquidators of Hellas Telecommunications (Luxembourg) II SCA (In Liquidation) v Slaughter and May (a firm)* [2016] EWCA Civ 474, para 37.

(*Masserverbindlichkeiten*), being a loan to the estate (*Massedarlehen*).[86] In other words, the financing provided by way of a new loan, enjoys administrative expense priority as a claim incurred in the course of administering the estate.[87]

Beyond this, the loan provided by the lender must be paid in full. However, this full repayment is subject to the availability of assets to liquidate the obligations of the estate of the debtor. This limitation of repayment by the availability of sufficient assets means that lenders will only advance financing to the distressed debtor when the former can assure themselves that the debtor will have sufficient assets to cater for administrative expense claims. The other alternative is for the lenders to provide financing only on the availability of security but not so that it interferes with pre-insolvency security interests.[88] To this extent, it is arguable that the financing provided by a new lender enjoys an implied priority position just like in the UK. Also, German courts have risen to the occasion by authorizing (on a case by case basis), an insolvency office holder to treat payment obligation arising during the restructuring, as administrative expense.[89]

4.6 Security Interest for New Lender: A Technique in Contest

4.6.1 Why Security Interests for New Financer or Why Might Administrative Expense Priority Not Suffice?

So far, the prevailing technique to the provision of new financing has been examined on a jurisdictional basis. In view of the importance of incentives for new lenders, it does appear however that the administrative expense technique will not always do. In other words, there may well be need for providing security interest assurance for prospective lenders in the course of the restructuring of the distressed lender. Three key reasons make the creation of security position something to consider. The first is an intuitive argument. The second flows from the first, when we consider the practical implications of statutorily prescribed administrative expense priority in the event of the failure of the restructuring effort. The third reason is grounded in financial economics and touches on the importance of financing entering the capital

---

86 See s. 55(2) InsO. See also, Spahlinger and Kortz (2015), at para 10.70, 219.

87 Id (noting that such loans enjoy priority over insolvency claims). See also Schultze & Braun, German Insolvency Law in a Nutshell. Available at: <https://www.schubra.de/downloads/broschueren/0027_en.pdf> accessed 6 Mar 2018. ("These loans will be treated as debts of the estate (administrative claims) if they are granted after the opening of the procedure.").

88 Spahlinger and Kortz (2015), at para 10.70, 219.

89 See for instance, BGHZ 151, 353, 365 (the court pointed out that bankruptcy court may on a case-by-case basis, decide that the new loan is entitled to priority repayment by the treatment of the debt as an "estate obligation" which in other words amount to its treatment as administration expense).

structure of the distressed firm based on a heightened priority position, such as is provided by a security position.

On the intuitive argument, it is worth reiterating that the default-incentivizing tool (whether statutorily expressed or implied), is the administrative expense priority. Many jurisdictions agree on this. The problem however is that financing a distressed debtor is intuitively one that involves risk. Ordinarily, one of the most compelling reasons for obtaining security for financing is the severity of the risks associated with such lending.[90] Obtaining security before lending becomes even more compelling when a distressed business seeks to restructure through a channel provided for in bankruptcy law.[91] Given the circumstances of the debtor, potential lenders will consider lending to the debtor without security or without adequate security, a risky venture, especially where repayment is dependent on the successful restructuring of the distressed business.[92] Few lenders may come forward under these conditions.

Another way to explain the importance of secured new financing as a device for incentivizing lending is to consider the implication of a failed restructuring. The design of the formal restructuring frameworks under consideration show just how much administrative expense priority will not do, if the debtor is unable to wade through its distress and successfully restructure. To buttress this assertion, examples will be drawn from the US, UK and Germany. In the US for instance, new financing is only one example of an item granted administrative expense priority.[93] In fact, the list of administrative expenses provided for in the statute is not limited, meaning that more and more items may very well find their way into the list.[94] When this happens and creditors are to share on a pro rata basis, it simply reduces the value that may accrue to the lender.[95] Furthermore, the non-exhaustive list of administrative expenses provided for in the statute does not create hierarchy for claims listed therein, or the class of creditors who enjoy this priority.[96] This means that a distressed financer who has this level of priority is assured of full repayment to the extent that the formal restructuring is altogether successful or even where the attempt fails, the unencumbered assets of the debtor is sufficient to satisfy adminis-

[90] See Kripke (1985), p. 949 ("Looking to the facts of commercial transactions ... one finds that the types of financing usually undertaken on a secured basis often involve situations of severe risk....").

[91] Finch (2009), p. 405 ("When a company enters into formal insolvency process, the difficulties of obtaining financing may increase considerably.")

[92] Ibid.

[93] See 11 U.S. Code § 503 (b) on allowable expenses.

[94] See Tabb and Brubaker (2010), p. 215. The list of items in the subsection is preceded by "including". The rules of construction in § 102(3) clearly provides that the use of "including" is not limiting, meaning that the list is not exhaustive.

[95] Schorer and Curry (1991), pp. 15–16.

[96] It is important that the reader bears in mind that although 11 USC §507(a) specifically provides for 10 items, the second item on administrative expenses is expansive, meaning that more items can be accommodated as administrative claims.

trative expense claims. For if the debtor becomes administratively insolvent,[97] then the claims of the creditors are repaid on a pro rata basis,[98] meaning essentially that the lender with an administrative priority may not receive the full value of the financing provided. Furthermore, the presence of pre-petition secured creditors contribute to weaken the position of a post-petition lender who settles for administrative expense priority position.[99] The lender with an administrative priority position may find itself in a difficult situation, where the restructuring efforts fail, and liquidation proceedings commence. This is because such a lender may not receive any payment at all, as the administrative expenses of the liquidation proceedings take precedence over that of the restructuring DIP lender who held an administrative expense priority.[100]

In the UK also, a similar argument can be made with regard to the administrative expense priority in an administration.[101] As noted already, the administrative expense priority may be implied from the provisions of the English Insolvency Act, 1986. The loan obligation incurred by the administrator enjoys priority ahead of the other administrative expenses.[102] In other words, this gives rise to a priority not just over administrative expenses, but also over the interest of floating charge holders. Reading the statute this way suggests that it creates a superpriority position for a prospective lender.[103] The question however is: to what extent does this "superpriority" live up to that billing?

Even if one agrees that the priority created here is a superpriority, in view of present day lending realities, it is doubtful what incentive it affords prospective lenders. In the first place, present day lending reality especially for SMEs is that their prime asset is typically their receivables, and it is against this asset that they borrow.[104] This means in effect that such businesses may have little or no assets secured by the floating charge.[105] Hence, while it may be easy to say that a superpriority position is impliedly created because it ranks ahead of pre-distress lenders secured by a floating charge, it may not provide any significant incentive. Secondly,

---

[97] This means that the debtor is unable to pay all the claims that fall within the class of administrative expenses. See Squire (2016), p. 237.

[98] See Schorer and Curry (1991), pp. 15–16; Tabb (2014), p. 676.

[99] Squire (2016), p. 237.

[100] See 11 U.S. Code § 726(b).

[101] It need be pointed out that all other formal restructuring procedures in the UK make no provision for priority as a tool for incentivizing new financing.

[102] It is argued that from a combined reading of paras 70, 99(3) & (4) IA, 1986, it can be deduced that the restructuring financing obtained by the administrator is paid in ahead of the remuneration and expenses of the administrator, which is itself payable ahead of the payment of creditors secured by a floating charge. See McCormack (2008), p. 199.

[103] Bork (2012).

[104] See Gullifer and Payne (2015), p. 306 (noting that administrative expense is paid from assets subject to floating charge and receivables financing means fewer assets subject to the floating charge).

[105] Id.

the practical effect of such a superpriority still leaves much to be desired. This is because where for instance, the estate of the debtor is insufficient to satisfy administrative expense claims, the members of the administrative expense class will have to be paid *pari passu*.[106] Therefore, although the provider of financing for the administration may be paid ahead of many other claims, a provider of new financing may very well be weary, given the risks involved.

While German law essentially follows a similar path in the creation of administrative expense priority for creditors on a case-by-case basis, it takes a somewhat different approach where the restructuring collapses and a second insolvency (liquidation) proceeding is opened. It bears restating that the restructuring of a German debtor is carried out within bankruptcy framework. Where the restructuring effort fails, German law provides for priority repayment for the providers of new financing. Although the repayment is capped,[107] it ranks ahead of the pre-restructuring creditors as well as other creditors whose claims arose in the course of the restructuring period.[108] This certainly does not include secured creditors. The above notwithstanding, there is still the open question of what happens where estate of the debtor is not enough to cater for all the claims including that of the new lender. On the other hand, what happens where following subsequent insolvency proceedings, there are insufficient assets to meet the priority of the restructuring loan provider? Such new lender as it appears does not necessarily enjoy this superpriority position.

The third consideration that has informed the use of superpriority as a device for incentivizing lending rests on the importance of financing entering the capital structure of the distressed debtor based on heightened priority. Sometimes, debtors with otherwise good prospects may be heavily leveraged, so that it may be difficult or even impossible to raise more debt. At this time, the prior lenders may be secured by all the assets of the debtor, with guarantees from the debtor that the lender will enjoy priority over any subsequent financing, which the debtor may obtain. If the proceeds of the new financing will be captured by prior lenders, it is most improbable that the prospective lender will find sufficient incentive to lend. This is even so, when the debtor intends to plough the financing raised into a profitable project with a good return on investment to pay for itself and yield profits for the debtor. The difficulty in raising new financing for the profitable project is essentially because any value generated by the new project is partly or wholly swallowed up by pre-existing debt holders. Financial economists describe this as the "debt overhang problem."[109] In view of the extant capital structure, if the source of financing is a junior debt or mere equity, a prospective lender may be disinclined to advance new

[106] See *Re MK Airlines Ltd* [2013] 1 BCLC 9, at para 10 (noting that administrative expense claims will be paid in full if assets subject to the charge is sufficient, or *pari passu* if they were not). See also, Anderson et al. (2016), at para 8.101, 244.

[107] The repayment may not exceed the value of property listed in the survey of assets contained in the plan. See s. 264 Abs 1 InsO.

[108] See s. 265 InsO.

[109] See Myers (1977), pp. 149–55.

funds; neither will new lenders be willing to finance such projects.[110] How then does superpriority position solve this problem?

The more assured a prospective lender is of the repayment of the new financing it provides, the more it is inclined to provide the financing. A priority position in the nature of a secured interest raises the stakes that the new lender will be repaid, hence appropriately calibrating its risk. The availability of collateral over which it may secure its claim, the chances of subordinating its claim to an existing security, or the chances of priming its claim over that of prior secured claims if permitted, may ease the problem of debt overhang. With the knowledge that it stands at the top of the bankruptcy waterfall or somewhere close to the top, the new lender will be willing to lend, and even at possibly lower rates of interest.[111] The less risky the new lending is for the lender, the lower the cost of the new lending and the more likely that the distressed borrower is likely to access new financing for its restructuring efforts.

While it is agreed that providing secured lending position for the provider for new financing may be useful as an incentivizing tool, the approach to the provision of that heightened priority position differs. Two paradigms are discernible. On the one hand, there exists a deregulated approach (referred to in this book as the market-based approach). On the other hand, there is the regulation of the priority incentive by the formal restructuring regime (referred to in this book as a prescriptive approach). Underlying each of the paradigmatic approaches are a number of factors, which are now examined below.

4.6.2 *Incentivizing New Financing: Market-Based Approach Versus Prescriptive Approach*

4.6.2.1 The UK Approach as Market-Based

The alternative approach to the financing of the distressed debtor is one that leaves questions of incentivizing through priority to the decision of the market. The market approach here simply means that questions such as how much finance, who provides it and the extent of the incentive for such financing, is left to the management of the distressed business,[112] its creditors, as well as potential lenders. The law only lays down the framework within which the parties may reach their decisions, without prescribing any specific rules touching on new lending incentives. Incentivizing

---

[110] The firm may be financed with internal funds, but it may be the case that there is no available cash pool at the disposal of the firm. See Triantis (2000), p. 38.

[111] Berkovitch and Kim (1990), p. 766 (noting that such "seniority position in turn reduces the promised interest rate on the new borrowing…"). See also Skeel Jr. and Ayotte (2013), p. 1577 ("If the new lender knows that he will move to the front of the priority line, he will be more willing to lend, and at a lower rate of interest.").

[112] Depending on the procedure, this may mean the restructuring officer, or the pre-distress management.

the financing of distressed businesses undergoing formal restructuring did not have so much attention devoted to it until the period prior to the passage of the Enterprise Act in 2002.[113] The Insolvency Act, 1986 is silent on the provision of financing for the process of administration, in terms of explicitly spelt out rules.[114] In the build up to the passage of the Enterprise Act, policy makers extensively considered the subject, although it did not eventually find its way into the legislation.[115] Further consultations have followed in 2009, as well as recently as in 2016, but it appears "that there is not much appetite for such legislative changes."[116]

What however stands out in the course of the various attempts at providing a prescriptive basis for new financing incentivizing in the UK has been the insistence that the market, not law makers can better decide on lending in distressed situations. For instance, one of the strongest arguments in opposition to the prescriptive approach in 2002 turned on the need to leave lending decision to the commercial judgment of the lending market as well as the undesirability of creating a system that guarantees returns to lenders, whether or not the rescue proposal is satisfactory the market.[117] Consistent with the market-based approach, the lender it was believed could make its lending decision based on its assessment of the "viability of the rescue plan", the negotiations reached by the market players, as well as the availability and priority position available to it.[118]

Although the UK has been cited as the paradigm for the market approach, it may be argued that other systems, which leave financing of the distressed borrower to the decision of the lenders and the market, may be grouped into this category. Take Germany for instance, the consent of the creditor's committee is required, especially where the insolvency administrator seeks to obtain financing which may result in a burden on the estate of the debtor.[119]

---

[113] It is worth noting however that, Cork Report had recommended what by implication is a recognition of priority for the lender to the distressed business especially where an administration order is discharged by the court. The Cork Committee recommended that:

> [I]f the order is discharged, all creditors should revert to the position as it was when the original application was made, *subject to the rights of priority of payment to anyone who in the meantime has given money* or advanced credit to the administrator, to enable the company's business to be carried on as a going concern [....] The cost of the administration should be paid in priority to all other debts, except those secured by fixed charges but not floating charges, whether they have crystalized or not. [Emphasis supplied].

Cork (1982), at para 514.

[114] Indeed, the statutes, which provide for the several formal restructuring regimes in English law do not have express provisions on the financing of distressed debtors.

[115] See McCormack (2008), p. 194 (noting that ultimately, the topic of funding for the administration procedure proved too difficult for policy makers to add to the legislative framework).

[116] See Finch (2009), p. 349 (noting that based on the 2016 consultations, "there is support for a new restructuring tool, but little support for reforms on rescue finance.").

[117] See the House of Lords Debate of 28 July 2002, vol. 638, cc763-806 at 789.

[118] McCormack (2008), p. 195.

[119] See § 160 (2) InsO.

4.6.2.2 Justification for the Market-Based Approach

One must first remember that UK law provides multiple restructuring avenues. Each of these avenues have lent credence to the opposition of a statutorily prescribed approach to incentivizing new financing. In addition, each of these avenues provide justification for an approach that advances a market-based approach over a prescriptive one. These arguments are broadly classified as policy related, the existence of a framework that allow market participants facilitate the needed financing, and the existence of what may be described as a quasi-prescriptive regime (implied prescriptive regime).

4.6.2.2.1 A Financing Facilitative Regime

Absent a prescriptive incentivizing regime, it is arguable that the framework of some restructuring procedures affords the borrowers and key stakeholders the framework within which debt is restructured, and market players can agree on the terms, the basis on which new financing can be achieved. A case in point is the scheme of arrangement procedure.[120] In other words, it should suffice that the law lays down a regime within which the relevant stakeholders of the distressed business may resolve issues pertaining to the restructuring of the distressed debtor, its financing needs inclusive. Although the scheme of arrangement procedure does not prescribe any financing incentive,[121] a number of financially distressed businesses have—through the procedure—achieved debt restructuring, received interim financing and reached agreements on restructuring financing.[122] As one court noted, the schemes of arrangement procedure have been adapted as a means of providing liquidity for distressed businesses seeking to restructure.[123] Market participants have therefore evolved solutions to achieve this end.

The market solutions evolved by market participants to finance their restructuring are in the form of contractual terms designed to achieve consent to the restructuring plan through privately generated incentives to induce the consent of creditors

[120] On the scheme of arrangement procedure, see Chap. 3, Sect. 3.3.2.1.

[121] Recall as already stated in Chap. 3, Sect. 3.3.2.1, the scheme of arrangement does not provide any specific contents. This flexibility means that parties can use the procedure to achieve such goals that include accessing financing for debt restructuring.

[122] The following cases (amongst others) support the use of the scheme procedure to raise new financing: *In the Matter of Rodenstock GmbH*[2011] EWHC 1104 (Ch)(The court sanctioned a scheme comprising of a €40m New Money Facility to be provided to the Company on a super senior basis, comprising a super senior revolving facility and a super senior term facility); *Re: La Seda De Barcelona Sa [2010]* EWHC 1364 (Ch) (the English courts sanctioned a scheme comprising new equity injection of €150m into the distressed restructuring company).

[123] See for instance in *Primacom Holding GmbH v A Group of the Senior Lenders & Credit Agricole* [2012] EWHC 164, 209 (Ch.) (Justice Hildyard noted that the "purpose of the proposed restructuring, including the scheme is, first, to deliver the required liquidity to the group and the company and, secondly, to significantly reduce the company's ongoing debt burden.").

and in the absence of any express provision for heightened priority position for prospective financers, superpriority position for prospective lenders. In cases where the prospective lenders are pre-distress lenders, the financing agreement may be amended to create a priority position for the providers of the new financing. The new financing may also be achieved through agreements that require secured pre-distress lenders to turnover payments received to the provider of new financing or subordinate their claims to that of the new lender. Whatever accommodations or agreements reached by the parties are thereafter tested through the voting process designed by the scheme procedure to make the schemes binding, as well as the approval of the schemes court.

In *Primacom Holding GmbH*[124] for instance, the company sought to restructure through the scheme procedure. However, it had even more pressing liquidity needs for the purpose of meeting up two key interest payments, as well as to make vital upgrades to its networks.[125] In a scheme subsequently approved by the court, lenders were able to reorder the priorities of the pre-distress debt, grant superpriority repayment position for the negotiated interim financing, as well as for the new restructuring financing needed by the distressed business. The pre-distress lenders were offered the opportunity to provide the financing and where they were unwilling or unable to do so, the option was left open to new restructuring investors.

In another case,[126] the scheme companies were more creative. With the consent of some scheme creditors, the scheme creditors entered into new financing agreement. Since it could not obtain the consent of all creditors, the borrower designed a turnover agreement.[127] By the agreement, consenting pre-distress lenders were obligated to give over the proceeds, which they receive under the existing financing agreement to the providers of new financing. This contractual arrangement bore the marks of the statutorily prescribed heightened priority in its economic effect. For one, by contract, the pre-distress lenders subordinated their priority position, as well as their right to receive any payment for that matter to the right of the provider of new financing. In addition, the parties were able to define the insolvency (liquidation) implication of the new financing. In the case of a liquidation, the providers of new financing were also allowed priority over the consenting creditors.

[124] Ibid.

[125] Ibid.

[126] *Re Apcoa Parking Holdings GmbH* [2014] EWHC 3849 (Ch).

[127] Note that a result of the contentious nature of the case, two different turnover agreements were drawn up. The difference between both was the exclusion of the scheme companies as parties to the turnover agreement. In substance, the effect of the turnover agreement remained the same. See para 36.

4.6.2.2.2 Policy Considerations

Transitioning from a market-based approach to a prescriptive approach will require policymakers to think through the pros and cons of the switch. Like in the course of making any prescriptive rules, the likely reaction of the subject is often a good starting point in determining the desirability of the proposed legislative change. Thus, policymakers and lawmakers necessarily ought also to be concerned with how agents will act, with knowledge of the existence of that law.[128] Regarding the specific context of financing distressed businesses in the framework of formal restructuring law, the need to carefully calibrate creditors' rights was echoed by Robert Keach, the co-chair of the American Bankruptcy Institute's Commission to Study the Reform of Chapter 11 of the US Bankruptcy Code. He noted as follows:

> I think it's fair to say that the way cases are financed and the way the Code treats secured creditors' rights is something that we are looking at very carefully. And this is something that needs to be frankly looked at carefully and calibrated very carefully because one of the things that we constantly have to remember is that changes that we make to the Bankruptcy Code with respect to creditors' rights, including lenders' rights, not only impact bankruptcy cases but have a ripple effect on the credit community as a whole.[129]

Compared to the US, the lending market in countries like the UK is still marked by their domination by bank lenders.[130] It therefore follows that policy thrusts consider, how the lending market would react to changes in the law.

As research by Davydenko and Franks show, lending and restructuring practices by bank lenders respond to shifts in the costs imposed on them by bankruptcy law.[131] This could be a big deal where bank lenders are typically pre-distress lenders and policymakers are interested (as they always are) in the reduction of the cost of capital. If formal restructuring law imposes a regime that alters the rights of pre-distress lenders, concerns have been raised that lenders will respond by factoring the costs of the alteration of their pre-distress rights in providing financing to borrowers *ex ante*, and internalize the law as a risk to their investment.[132]

---

[128] See Roosevelt III (2000), p. 97 ("legal rules do more than determine the outcome of particular cases; because people know what the outcomes will be, they tailor their actions accordingly").

[129] See Keach (2013).

[130] See Paterson (2015) (noting that borrowing in the UK is still largely made up of bank debt, unlike the US, which favors capital market borrowing). See also The Insolvency Service: A Review Of The Corporate Insolvency Framework (A Consultation on Options for Reform) May, 2016, at 29 ("[t]raditional lenders still provide the majority of lending and alternative sources of debt finance, such as the capital markets, are still in their infancy"); Larratt-Smith (2013), p. 16 ("In Europe, large and lower middle[-]market companies look to their banks for financing an estimated 80% of corporate financing comes from banks, compared to an estimated 20% in the United States.").

[131] Davydenko and Franks (2008).

[132] See for instance, UK Consultations on Options for Reform, para 10.14 ("In exploring attempts to encourage the availability of rescue finance, the Government is mindful of the risk of reducing the availability of business finance generally or of increasing the cost of such finance"); see also Yeowart (2009), p. 524 ("the leverage at which financers would be willing to lend, which could itself have a broader impact on the UK economy.").

Also, as a policy consideration, heightened priority in the statute books may result in the problem of overinvestment and may place no monitoring duty on the prospective lender. The overinvestment problem will arise where, because of "free" money at the disposal of a distressed borrower, who may be inclined to pursue or undertake projects that have a low net present value. Besides, with the new lender assured that it enjoys priority it may have no incentive to monitor the investment, with the prior creditors bearing the risk of the investment. This problem arises when, because of the prescribed incentives of priority over prior lenders, prospective lenders may provide financing without any regard for the efficiency of the financing provided. The result may well be the nurturing of a distress lending market whose attraction is just the prescribed incentive. A statutory regime that guarantees a last-in-first-out return to the distressed lender may also have an unintended consequence for the process of formal restructuring with its avowed goal being the successful restructuring of the debt of the distressed business. In the UK for instance, it has been argued that a prescriptive approach could give rise to a situation where a new financer will provide financing even when there is no well-thought out proposal for the restructuring of the business.[133] Such situations in the long run may not result in the restructuring of the distressed debtor. At best, it could create a lending market with an incentive to lend, but with no incentive to monitor the borrower, ensuring that it invests only in projects with positive net present value.[134] At the end, pre-distress creditors may be left to bear the costs of an ill-thought restructuring effort for which the new lender provided the financing.[135]

---

[133] See House of Lords Parliamentary Debate, July 29, 2002. See also McCormack (2008), p. 195 ("The government however, was reluctant to create a situation that, in essence, would guarantee a return to superpriority new lenders, irrespective of whether rescue proposals passed commercial muster"). See also Finch (2009), p. 334 (noting that in 1995, policymakers also rejected prescriptive superpriority in the CVA procedure on the ground that "the comfort of superpriority might militate against lender's giving proper consideration to the viability of the business.").

[134] McCormack (2017), p. 549 (noting in the UK, the "hesitation about sanctioning a situation that essentially guaranteed a return to credit providers advancing funds on the basis of superpriority and irrespective of the commercial viability of the restructuring proposals.").

[135] This point has been identified as a feature that makes the US prescriptive superpriority approach (analyzed below) controversial. There appears to be an isolated opinion that agrees with the policy argument. Roe and Tung capture this controversy as follows:

> If the bankrupt debtor wastes the cash and the new lender is repaid anyway, this priority process wastes social value and is paid for by the pre-bankruptcy creditors. Beyond ordinary priority for the new lender is the extent of its priority. The Code anticipated that in unusual circumstances, the new lender's priority could extend into the assets of preexisting secured creditors....

See Roe and Tung (2013), p. 1250 (n57).

4.6.3 The Prescriptive Approach: The US as Paradigm

The preceding section has examined the market-based approach to providing for and incentivizing new financing for restructuring distressed businesses. The prescriptive approach represented by the US as paradigm is different. In the first place, as already highlighted above, Chapter 11 of the US Bankruptcy Code expressly provides for administrative expense priority for new financing.[136] In view of the heightened risk that a new financer may lose its investment in the distressed business to pre-distress lenders, a priority over administrative expense claims does provide this comfort. This essentially makes the case for what is now known as the superpriority incentive for providers of distressed financing. Here, the DIP, with the permission of the court, may grant priority to a new lender, which ranks ahead of the claims that are in the class of administrative expenses.[137] The possibility of the DIP obtaining financing as described here requires that it shows an inability to obtain financing with the incentive of administrative expense priority.[138] Thus, the post-filing lender enjoys priority over administrative expenses recognized under the Bankruptcy Code as such.[139]

The fact of superpriority above administrative expenses notwithstanding, it is important to note that as far as the risk of non-payment is considered, the lender with superpriority over administrative expense claims is not radically different the holder of administrative expense claim. The only benefit is that in the event that there are assets free of encumbrance (security interests), the superpriority holder is first to be paid. In the same vein, the DIP may issue secured debt to a prospective lender. This security interest may be granted to the lender over an unencumbered

[136] See Sect. 4.5.1.1 above. It is however worth noting that in the US, it is hardly ever the case that new financing is provided to distressed businesses with administrative expense priority. This is often reserved for trade creditors of the borrower. See *In re AMF Bowling Worldwide Inc.*, 278 B.R. 96, 100 (Bankr. E.D. Va. 2002) ("It is common for a DIP financing agreement to contain a priming provision as this is frequently the sole basis on which lenders will provide financing to a debtor in bankruptcy.").

[137] 11 U.S. Code § 364(c)(1). This has been described as a super-administrative expense priority. See Qi (2008), p. 163.

[138] The statute does not impose any particular burden on the DIP, regarding how much it should have sort out a lender willing to do so on the basis of an administrative expense priority. See *Bray v. Shenandoah Fed. Savings & Loan Ass'n (In re Snowshoe Co.),* 789 F.2d 1085 (4th Cir. 1986), where the court stated that:

> [T]he trustee contacted other financial institutions in the immediate geographic area and was unsuccessful. The statute imposes no duty to seek credit from every possible lender before concluding that such credit is unavailable. This is particularly true when, as the court determined here, time is of the essence in an effort to preserve a vulnerable seasonal enterprise.

[139] *In re Roblin Industries Inc.*, 52 BR 241, 245–46 (Bankr. WDNY), the court allowed post-petition lender, priority over all other administrative expenses, including the fees of the professionals, who as the creditors' committee argued would carry out an "energetic review of the debtor's affairs".

asset of the debtor[140] or is granted in respect of an encumbered asset but is made to rank below the claim of secured creditors.[141] This is the case, unless of course the prior secured creditor is willing to subordinate its claims to that of the new lender.

All the assets of the debtor may be already encumbered, so much so that a mere priority over unsecured claims (administrative priority) or even an unsecured priority over administrative expenses and a junior lien position may not provide the DIP lender sufficient comfort. To this extent, the US provides for prescriptive rules designed to incentivize prospective lenders. The court is statutorily permitted to, after notice and hearing, allow the debtor to obtain financing based on a security interest over an asset of the debtor which ranks equal or senior to pre-existing liens.[142] This without more does certainly prejudice the property rights of pre-filing secured creditors, and precipitates a breach of *ex-ante* contract(s) between the debtor and such secured creditor(s). As such, the grant of such heightened priority position to new lenders is not casually granted to new lenders and prescriptive provisions provide a background against which judges may decide on the grant of such heightened priority.

Indeed, the interest of pre-distress creditors was certainly not lost on the draftsmen of the Code. Hence, the court may approve the issuance of such debt if the DIP is unable to obtain the financing without creating such priority, and only after the adequate protection of the prior secured lender.[143] These conditions are conjunctive, so that fulfilling one of the conditions does not fulfil the requirement of the law and the burden of fulfilling these conditions rest with the management of the borrower. While it will appear that the first condition may well be easy for the trustee to bypass,[144] the second condition on adequate protection has been relied upon by the court to safeguard the interest of prior lenders. The adequate protection requirement is a means to balance the interest of prior lenders protected by liens, over the diminution that may arise as the restructuring of the debtor is underway.[145] The adequate

---

[140] 11 U.S. Code § 364(c)(2).

[141] 11 U.S. Code § 364(c)(3). A debtor in its motion for DIP financing may combine priority positions. See for instance the DIP financing motion of WorldCom, where it sought "Authorization to Obtain Post-Petition Secured Superpriority Financing Pursuant to Sections 105, 362, 364(c) (1), 364(c) (2), 364 (c) (3), and 507 of the Bankruptcy Code."

[142] 11 U.S. Code § 364(d)(1).

[143] 11 U.S. Code § 364(d)(1)(A) & (B).

[144] In at least one case, the bankruptcy court refused the creation of a secured creditor position for provider of new financing because there was no proof that the borrower had approached any lender for new financing other than the proposed lender. See *In re Phase–I Molecular Toxicology, Inc.*, 285 B.R. 494 (Bankr.D.N.M.2002).

[145] In this regard, House Report on the balancing role of the adequate protection concept is instructive. The Report notes as follows:

Secured creditors should not be deprived of the benefit of their bargain. There may be situations in bankruptcy where giving a secured creditor an absolute right to his bargain may be impossible or seriously detrimental to the policy of the bankruptcy laws. Thus, this section recognizes the availability of alternative means of protecting a secured creditor's interest where such steps are a necessary part of the rehabilitative process. Though the creditor might not be able to retain his lien

protection of such earlier priority holders may be provided through cash payments to such prior lienholders, providing them with additional collateral or a collateral to replace the earlier one, and the grant of reliefs, the effect of which is the realization of an indubitable equivalent of the lienholder's interest.[146]

One must note that this heightened priority regime does not come easy, robbing prior secured creditors of their prior bargain. The courts have ensured this. They have been most vigilant, seeing to it that the heightened priority position is approved of, following the adequate protection of lien holders who have provided prior financing. Hence, although an equity cushion[147] has been held by the court to amount to adequate protection,[148] a thin equity cushion has been considered by the courts to be inadequate to serve this purpose. For instance, in cases where there only exists a thin equity cushion on the collateral for which the borrower seeks to create new security, the courts have denied such heightened priority to new lenders.[149]

A successful restructuring and the protection of the bargain of antecedent secured creditors are competing goals, hence a balance has to be maintained. To this end, the courts have shown caution in focusing on the goal of a successful restructuring when the outcome of the restructuring does not consider the adequate protection of the prior secured lender. In one case,[150] for instance, the debtor failed to provide prior lienholders adequate protection for loss of value arising from the priming lien granted to a new financer in Chapter 11. The bankruptcy court had set its sight on the preservation of value for the benefit of all of the creditors when deciding on the necessity for the new loan. Added to this, it was not shown that the loss of value incurred by the prior lienholders will be taken care of, neither was it shown that the improved value arising from the new financing will be higher than the losses to these prior lienholders. The District Court found it hard to see that the interest of lienholders had been adequately protected.

From the foregoing, it will be indeed difficult to assume that the heightened priority regime of the US, by which it incentivizes new financing, hurt secured creditors and radically affect the value of the bargain reached.

over the specific collateral held at the time of filing, the purpose of the section is to ensure that the secured creditor receives he value for which he bargained.
See S Rep No 989, 95th Cong 2d Sess. 53 (1978).

146 See 11 U.S. Code § 361(1) - (3).

147 Equity cushion in simple terms is the difference between the value of the collateral and the value of the loan which the collateral secures.

148 See *In re Lee* (1981) 11 BR 84, 85.

149 See *Suntrust Bank v. Den-Mark Const., Inc.*, 406 B.R. 683 (E.D.N.C.2009) (holding that superpriority sought on the basis of a cushion of 11% and a speculation that the new financing will enhance the collateral, does not satisfy the adequate protection requirement.); see also *In re C.B.G. Ltd.*, 150 B.R. 570 Bkrtcy.M.D.Pa.1992) (holding that a 16% cushion which will further drop to 14% as a result of the proposed superpriority financing does not meet the adequate protection requirement).

150 *In re Fontainebleau Las Vegas Holdings,LLC*, 434 B.R. 716 (S.D.Fla.2010).

4.6.4 *Between a Prescriptive and Market-Based Approach: SMEs in View*

4.6.4.1 A Restructuring Facilitative Regime Without a Financing Component

Indeed, the law could be facilitative of the financing of the distressed businesses, but it does appear that the usage of such facilitative regimes serves certain specific types of distressed businesses only. Let us take the schemes procedure for instance. Typically, only large or larger mid-cap companies are able to take advantage of the facilitative legal regime of the procedure.[151] Also, only sophisticated lenders may be able to incur the costs drawing up the plan, engage the required experts (lawyers, accountants, etc.) and incurring the huge negotiating fees necessary to reaching the desired restructuring goals.[152] Even though bargaining power between the borrower and the lenders in this situation may not be the same, the parties are economic actors who with the benefit of the expertise at their disposal can reach better accommodation.

One cannot say the same for small and medium- sized enterprises (SMEs) for instance. As research show, SMEs are often at the receiving end of "macro-economic and financial shocks."[153] This means that such businesses ought to be accounted for when analyzing the impact of approaches to new financing incentivization. In the first place, the complexity and cost of the scheme procedure may mean that such procedure is not available to them.[154] This means that they are unable to access such a facilitative regime which hitherto is one of the justifications for the market-based approach.[155] What then is the potential danger to which such SMEs may be exposed? This analysis continues with the UK as the paradigm.

4.6.4.2 A Market-Based Approach and Pre-distress Lender Induced Strategic Illiquidity

A statutory prescription of new financing may have a particular advantage especially as it pertains to the tendency of a market-based approach to foist illiquidity on the borrower. When parties negotiate outside of the confines of formal law, they do

---

[151] The procedure is considered to be quite onerous and complex, making it potentially difficult for smaller businesses to navigate it. See Payne (2014), pp. 291–292.

[152] McCormack (2008), p. 276 ("Schemes of arrangement … [are] complex and difficult to organise, demanding of expensive legal resources and generally the preserve of larger companies.").

[153] See OECD (2009) The Impact of The Global Crisis on SME and Entrepreneurship Financing and Policy Responses (2009). Available at <https://www.oecd.org/cfe/smes/43183090.pdf> accessed 10 June 2017 (on the effect of the economic crises on SMEs).

[154] Id.

[155] See Sect. 4.6.2.2.1 and Chap. 3, Sect. 3.3.2.1.

so against the backdrop of their relative rights under formal laws.[156] In the context of debt restructuring, their relative perceived rights also determine their willingness to commence a formal restructuring (or in the worst case, a liquidation) process if informal negotiations break down.[157] While the lender bargains, bearing in mind creditor protections of the restructuring regime, the borrower also bargains, bearing in mind whatever protections offered by law. A market approach to incentivizing new lending may be guilty of ignoring these market dynamics, which in many cases lean in favor of a pre-distress lender for instance. It may also be guilty of ignoring how these market dynamics may influence negotiations between a distressed borrower and for instance, the pre-distress lender. It may also ignore the effect of strategic behavior of a powerful controlling lender, over the chances of access to financing for the debtor that may be key to facilitating a successful restructuring. In view of this influence, trusting the commercial decision of market players to make the decision may yield results that may lead to the collapse of distressed borrowers, rather than supporting its need for new funding to enable its survival and restructuring.

The dominant control exercised by the lender in our market-based paradigm does have implication for access to financing by the distressed business, as well as the successful restructuring of the distressed business. Bank lending is the typical source of lending in the UK. In many cases, the banks hold security interest over all of the assets of the distressed borrower. The implication is that the lender may have the ability to restrict the access of the borrower to funds when the borrower is financially distressed.[158] When the lender controls the distressed borrower's access to funds, it invariably controls the chances that the borrower will survive the distress.[159] Research by Franks and Sussman find that as the business enters distress, it is often unlikely that the bank lender will increase lending to the distressed business.[160] Yet, the borrower is constrained in seeking refinancing from other lenders either because the pre-distress lender will not permit such, or because the new lender may seek certain repayment priority which the pre-distress lender is unwilling to allow.

Without this stranglehold on the ability of the debtor to access financing by keeping out other lenders, the ability to informally control the borrower is diminished. Pursuant to this control which it enjoys, the prior lender can confer certain benefits on itself. In the first place, it puts itself in a position where it can provide the

156 See Paterson (2014), p. 345 ("... where parties negotiate in the shadow of the law, the availability and the limits of the legal process will have an impact on the bargaining power of the parties outside the process.").

157 Levitin (2016), at section II, Chap. 1 ("... bankruptcy sets the background against which all financial restructuring processes occur, because if [informal] restructuring does not work, the usual alternative is bankruptcy.").

158 This issue further discussed in Chap. 4. But see generally, Skeel Jr. and Ayotte (2013), p. 1585 (on how lenders can control distress outcomes).

159 Ibid.

160 See Franks and Sussman (2005), p. 67 ("... the typical response is a significant contraction of lending.").

distressed borrower with the new funds, without the benefit of competition.[161] Absent this competition, the lender can refrain from taking steps directed towards the facilitation of the restructuring of the distressed business, so far as the value of the collateral is still greater or equal to debt owed to it.[162] Secondly, if the bank for some reason is unable to make the loan by itself, it may encourage a liquidation of the borrower especially where the prior lender perceives that continuation of the business poses a greater risk of loss than the gain it will generate.[163] The absence of a statutorily prescribed incentive basis leaves the distressed borrowers at the mercy of prior lenders, and the survival of the former, the prerogative of the latter. Already as this chapter has sought to establish, absent these incentives in the structure of the law, new lenders may already be unwilling to invest. Given that new lenders are unlikely to be attracted to finance the firm, the fate of the distressed debtor rests squarely with the prior lender. The prior lenders' decision to lend or not to lend becomes the determinant of whether the firm will survive or go into a liquidation.

The demise of the UK Christmas hamper savings firm Farepak illustrates how much the capacity of a prior lender to determine the fate of a distressed borrower can stand in the way of new financing and ultimately lead to the demise of the distressed borrower.[164] The case was one seeking a director disqualification order against the directors of the company. Although the case may have been discontinued, some of the facts that emerged from the statement of Justice Smith point to how the uncompromising stance of a prior lender (HBOS) precipitated the failure of its distressed borrower. Farepak ran a savings scheme which allowed its customers to spread their savings for Christmas by making small monthly contributions. Nearer to Christmas, the contributed amount which is deposited with Farepak is used to buy shopping items which include shopping vouchers. These deposits were however used by Farepak to trade. However, under an arrangement between Farepak's parent company and HBOS, all monies deposited in Farepak's account was swept into the group's account with HBOS. Faced with cash flow difficulties, the directors of Farepak had attempted to raise financing through rights issues as well as mezzanine financing. These attempts fell through, just like attempts at debt financing.

In the face of the financial constraint and the financial arrangement in place, Farepak was clearly in a chokehold. Its survival depended on HBOS. Both within and outside the confines of informal restructuring, HBOS was by far the most protected party, being secured by both a fixed and floating charge. This is instructive

---

161 Skeel Jr. and Ayotte (2013), p. 1586 (authors suggest that the absence of competition may also confer the benefit of providing new loans at attractive terms without the constraints of competition).

162 Franks and Sussman (2005), p. 71 ("Such a bank will limit itself to updating the value of the assets, and trigger liquidation at the point in time when value equals the amount owed (or even before).").

163 This is known as the fire-sale bias. Id.

164 See the statement of Mr. Justice Peter Smith in the case of *Secretary of State v Fowler and others* (formerly known *as Home Retail -v- Farepak*. Statement available at <https://www.judiciary.gov.uk/judgments/farepak-judges-statement/> accessed 5 May 2018.

because the key reason for the indifference of the prior lender was its fully secured position and the fact that it was not susceptible to any losses in the event of a liquidation.[165] Indeed, there was therefore hardly an incentive to provide any new financing to the borrower even though it desperately needed it, neither did it have an incentive to make any concessions by agreeing to a subordination of some of its claims, nor deferment of payment to which it was entitled.

To be clear, none of these may well have been suggestive of illegality, being that the HBOS was only insisting on its rights. Yet, this insistence by HBOS on its rights in the view of the court resulted in the eventual failure of the distressed Farepak.[166] However, a statutory prescription of new financing incentives with heightened priority could have worked in two ways. First, it clearly could have served as an incentive for new lenders. Of course, whether HBOS is adequately protected for instance, will be another issue, which will have been up to the court to decide. Secondly, if HBOS felt so strongly about its secured position and its priority, it may well have been nudged to provide the required new facility and avoid any complications that may arise from the provision of funds by a new lender.

4.7 New Financing in the Nigerian Landscape: What Lessons Can Nigeria Learn?

It would appear that unlike the prescriptive approach, the market-based approach is a default approach suggestive of deregulation. The debate over new financing in the UK, which has leaned in favor of the market-based approach, gives insights into the choice of a deregulated approach. In other words, other than being the default approach, the debate suggests that it is an informed choice, notwithstanding the counterarguments that support a prescriptive approach. In frontier markets like Nigeria, the default choice of a market-based approach is not necessarily one arising from an informed choice. At best, it is so because it happens to be the default position. Arguably, this is so because in the first place, restructuring law is still in its nascent stages and no thought has been given to it. This section asks and answers the question of how have the extant restructuring regimes organized themselves in terms of providing the requisite financing for restructuring and how have they faired? Also, given that the reform of restructuring regimes adopts as a default position a market-based approach, it also asks and answers the question, why will the prescriptive approach better suit the Nigerian market?

---

[165] See the para 21 of statement where Justice Smith noted, "HBOS was not prepared to provide any significant positive assistance to solve the difficulties the group came into. The reason for this was because at all times from the commencement of the troubles HBOS was fully secured and, as was shown in the outcome in October 2006, did not lose anything."

[166] See para 115 where His Lordship noted "Thus it follows that the unchanging attitude of the bank not to give anything during this period was the reason why the companies failed."

4.7.1 The Approach to New Financing Within a Defective Restructuring Regime

As already noted, the extant restructuring regimes in Nigeria are themselves defective as they lack the necessary set of tools for facilitating the restructuring of distressed businesses. Be that as it may, given that financing is equally important for these processes in spite of their defectiveness, it matters to highlight the law and practice in funding the processes. With regard to the receiver/manager appointed by a debenture holder, the practice is that the latter provides or authorizes the former to obtain funding in the nature of a protective advance.[167] The protective advance is new money needed for the protection of the assets under the control of the borrower. Whatever new financing provided will be paid ahead of any other claims, including the original claims of the appointing debenture holder. It is noteworthy that this practice has a statutory basis. CAMA envisages that when a receiver or a manager is appointed on behalf of debenture holders when the company is not to be wound up, debts entitled to priority repayment in a winding up shall be paid out of assets over which the receiver or manager has control. This payment is made in priority to the claims of the holder of the floating charge debenture holder.[168]

A cursory look at the priorities of repayment in a winding up proceeding places the payment of fees and expenses properly incurred in the preservation or realization of the assets of the debtor ahead of all other administrative expenses of the liquidator.[169] Although there is no mention whatsoever of the provision of new financing, a loan which is obtained in the ordinary course by the receiver/manager may be easily accommodated under this heading. In this sense, one could argue that like the English system, there exists a priority position for the new financing afforded the receiver or manager by a lender. The more restructuring inclined AMCON regime is not also different in terms of its approach to new financing, in view of its use adoption of a receivership.

In the case of the Nigerian arrangement and compromise, given that it is in nearly every respect similar to the English schemes of arrangement, one could argue that like the English schemes of arrangement, it provides for a regime that facilitates the agreement of parties, so that rather than a prescriptive approach, market-based

---

[167] In an unstructured interview with 3 legal practitioners and an accountant who have been involved as receiver/manager over a distressed business, they confirm that such funding will be provided by the debenture holder (secured creditor). The secured creditor will typically commit to the providing a certain amount of money to keep the business running and fulfill work orders that can further improve the value of the estate, while the receiver/manager decides how best to recoup the debt owed. They also commonly agree that such new funds will be provided only if there is no other means of obtaining quick liquidity (such as a quick sale of assets) and there is a near absolute certainty of expected inflows.

[168] See s. 182(1) CAMA. See also, Orojo (2008), p. 446 (noting that the priority position does not affect fixed charges).

[169] See Nigerian Companies Winding Up Rules, 2001, Rule 167.

approach is to be preferred.[170] Like the English schemes of arrangement, the Nigerian arrangement and compromise procedure can be (and has been) used to propose and achieve the injection of new financing into businesses whether healthy businesses seeking financing for expansion[171] or distress financing.[172] Again, one must bear in mind that not all companies can take advantage of it. This as noted earlier owes to its complexity and cost implication which only large companies may be able to undertake. It is therefore not such that SMEs may be able to undertake.

Given the difficulty with navigating the regime, lenders provide financing for viable but distressed businesses relying on innovative contractual designs. These designs allow them finance specific projects of a distressed debtor, over which they hold a lien (pursuant to a stock financing facility arrangement for instance), in addition to other security interests over real and personal property of the borrower.[173] The result of such financing has left a sour taste in the mouth of bank lenders like the claimant bank lender in *FCMB v. Capital Oil and Gas Ltd.*[174] FCMB the claimant bank lender had provided two separate facilities to the defendant for what were very lucrative projects. While the first facility of N1,600,000,000.00 (One Billion, Six Hundred Million Naira) was for a Tank Farm Project Expansion Program of the defendant (**Facility 1**), the second facility of $US 60,000,000.00 (Sixty Million Dollars) was for financing importation or local purchase of petroleum products (Automated Gas Oil (AGO) (**Facility 2**). The claimant secured its interest both by a fixed charge over both real and personal property of the defendant, in addition to personal security by way of guarantee by the alter ego of the debtor. Specifically, the claimant was secured by a fixed charge over the AGO financed by the lender.

In the meantime, the borrower had defaulted on other of its earlier loan obligations to secured borrowers who had proceeded to obtain court orders and judgments against the assets of the defendants in different courts both within[175] and outside of

---

[170] See Sect. 4.6.2.2.1.

[171] See the letter of the Chairman in the proposed Scheme of Arrangement of AshakaCem Plc. for Capital Reorganization. Available at <https://www.lafarge.com.ng/sites/nigeria/files/atoms/files/scheme_document_-_print_version.pdf> accessed 4 Mar 2018 (noting that the proposed reorganization is to meet "expansion plans and the funding requirements for the Company's business….").

[172] See Explanatory Letter from Financial Adviser of Scheme of Arrangement for the Reorganization of Share Capital of Starcomms Plc. (on file with author) (on the reason for the proposal, noting that the company "*… is currently facing a significant liquidity crisis and is unable to generate sufficient cash to fund ongoing operations or meets its various debt and trade creditor obligations*" [emphasis supplied]).

[173] See Adebola (2014), p. 166. (On innovative lending approaches: "a lien is taken on the product that they are financing. If the goods are imported, they would be consigned to the order of the bank; that means that they are bought in the name of the bank and the seller cannot sell without the consent of the bank.").

[174] Suit No. LD/1194/2012 (Unreported, at the Lagos State High Court, Commercial Division).

[175] See for instance, *AMCON v. 22 others* Suit No. FHC/ABJ/CS/714/2012 (unreported) (the claimant, an assignee of a prior lender sought and obtained an order of a Federal High Court over property of Capital Oil and Gas, including that over which FCMB had interest) (case on file with author).

Nigeria.[176] Although the case was discontinued,[177] the lessons from the case point not only to the need for an appropriate formal restructuring regime, but one that protects the financing provided in the process.

4.7.2 Is the Situation Any Different with the Secured Transaction Law Regime?

No doubt, reforms to Nigeria's personal property law regime may have improved the rights of financers of specific lucrative projects especially in informal restructuring regimes, but there are still visible challenges. In a bid to improve access to financing by businesses operating within the Nigerian economy, the legislature enacted the Secured Transactions in Movable Assets Act, 2017(ST Act).[178] For the first time, the Act introduces the notion of the purchase money security interest (PMSI) as a form of security interest.[179] By implication, a lender to a distressed borrower may be able to provide financing, and enjoy repayment priority over the movable asset, which it has facilitated the purchase.[180] This is so because PMSI itself is essentially a statutory superpriority. The priority position of the new financer is not affected by the co-mingling of the financed property.[181] This is because the perfected security interest of the new lender continues even when the identity of the financed product is lost.

Ordinarily, going by this legal regime, the financer in the *FCMB* case will have its priority protected in Facility 2. Other potential lenders too may feel better incentivized to lend. The PMSI incentive to priority underscores the optimal investment incentive approach of Triantis, who argues for the limitation of new financing priority to the new value that brought about because of the financing provided.[182] However, two issues may still severely impair the efficacy and appeal of the protection, which the chances of a PMSI provides, to a potential lender. First, is the limited

[176] No. 2012 Folio 1300- *Access Bank Pic v Rofos Navigation & 5 Ors* (the claimant in this suit, (another pre-distress lender) obtained a world-wide asset freeze order against the assets, associated companies, as well as the alter ego of Capital Oil and gas Limited).

[177] Expectedly, the case was one messy maze, which had implications for the stability of the several primary lending institutions involved. Hence the regulatory intervention through the purchase of the loan facilities by the Assets Management Company of Nigeria (AMCON), hence the discontinuation of the case.

[178] Available at <http://nass.gov.ng/document/download/9435> (last accessed 14 Mar 2018).

[179] See s.53 of the ST Act (on the definition of PMSI).

[180] See s. 27 of the ST Act (on the priority of the purchase money provider).

[181] See s. 28 of the ST Act (on the retention of priority by purchase money provider even where goods have been co-mingled).

[182] Triantis (1993), p. 926 (In the context of formal restructuring in the US, proposing that only the post-petition assets secure new financers).

scope of the protection of the PMSI itself, and second, is the power, which the floating charge holder continues to exercise.

On the first issue, the priority position assured a provider of new financing pursuant to the ST Act is good only to the extent that the purpose of the financing is to purchase a given movable asset. It is only in respect of that collateral that the financer enjoys priority. It does not protect priority for a provider of new financing who facilitates other projects not in the character of movable assets, but all the same value enhancing for the distressed borrower.[183] For instance, in the *FCMB* case, the PMSI of the ST Act will protect the lender's priority in Facility 2. It certainly will not protect the priority in the case of Facility 1, where FCMB provided financing for expanding the capacity of the borrower's tank farm. A provider of new financing will need to seek protection through other means.

The second issue that calls to question the efficacy of this priority protection is the practical implication of the powers of the Nigerian floating charge holder. In spite of the introduction of the ST Act regime, the Nigerian floating charge holder retains the right to appoint a receiver or manager over the undertakings and assets of the borrower based on the terms of its financing agreement between itself and the borrower, with or without the involvement of the courts. In other words, the floating charge holder is in the position to effect a change in the management of the borrower, a power, which the PMSI holder does not possess. A receiver/manager who may be appointed at the behest of the floating charge holder hardly has the incentive to see to the maximization of value in the distressed business.[184] This is in spite of the provisions of the Nigerian CAMA, which mandates him to do so.[185] One may argue that the financer can recover the security in a matter of days since the floating lien already attaches.[186] However, in practice, it may be very difficult for the lender to access its collateral if the new management locks the lender out of the business premises where the movable property is in the premises of the borrower. Besides, the lender must wait 10 days following the issuance of the default notice before it may take possession of the collateral. The period from the default notice, until the time when the 10 days elapses is enough for the asset to be appropriated by the receiver or manager.

---

[183] See McCormack (2008), p. 180 (noting that Triantis' optimal investment incentive is less helpful "if the [prospective distress lender] finances expenses such as labor or electricity that enhances the value of existing assets.").

[184] See Chap. 3 on the deficiencies of the Nigerian receivership.

[185] Ibid.

[186] As an important distinguishing characteristic of a floating lien (compared to a floating charge) is the time when it attaches. A floating lien is generally said to have attached upon the execution of the security agreement. See generally, Goldsberry (2002), p. 246. More importantly, upon default, the Nigerian creditor who is secured over a movable property of the borrower is required to give to the borrower and its guarantor, a notice of default and intention to repossess the collateral. Repossession follows ten days after the notice of default. See s. 40 of the ST Act.

4.7.3 A Case for Prescriptive Approach for New Financing in the Restructuring Framework

Although ongoing formal restructuring reform incorporates other restructuring toolkits discussed in Chap. 2, the approach to new financing is still largely market-based in Nigeria. For instance, the Bankruptcy and Insolvency (Repeal and Re-enactment) Bill does not expressly prescribe incentives for new lending; at best, it leaves room for implying an administrative expense approval. For a proposal to be approved by the courts, such proposal must provide for the payment of the "proper fees and expenses of the trustee" which may have arisen from the proposal or incidental to the restructuring proceedings. From the language of the draft, it may be inferred that new loans should attract administrative expense priority repayment.[187] Expectedly, this will be the case where such loans are obtained in the ordinary course of the business of the distressed debtor. In addition, the ongoing reform of CAMA and its proposed formal restructuring toolkit maintains silence on the provision of new financing for the restructuring debtor, neither does it prescribe any incentive to new lenders for providing such financing. Why then should Nigeria reconsider its approach?

It must be stated clearly here that what effect a prescriptive approach to incentivizing new financing may have on lenders is an empirical question with two opposing possibilities. On the one hand, it could facilitate a competitive distress-lending regime and, on the other, as the policy argument in the UK contemplates, it may negatively affect *ex ante* lending rates. In the case of Nigeria, it is argued that the first possibility is considered more likely. There are recent research findings and popular press discussions on the contribution of exorbitant interest rates charged by lenders, to financial distress for businesses, invariably making repayment difficult for borrowers.[188] Nigeria is not an exception. Bank lending rates in Nigeria are very high, negatively affecting the "health" of businesses.[189] A likely advantage that

[187] S. 42(1) of the Bill provides that:

> No [restructuring plan] shall be approved by the Court that does not provide for the payment in priority to other claims of all claims directed to be so paid in the distribution of the property of a debtor and for the payment of all proper fees and expenses of the trustee and incidental to the proceedings arising out of the [restructuring plan] or in the bankruptcy.

[188] See Richardson et al. (1994), p. 12 (based on a case study of the now defunct Imperial Chemical Industries (ICI), authors note "ICI's position was affected in particular by high interest rates"); Young G, Company Liquidations, Interest Rates and Debt, The Manchester School, Suppl., cited in Liu and Wilson (2002), p. 63 (argues that argues that changes in interest rates above expected levels are the primary cause of liquidations particularly in periods of rising debt levels) Jhang et al. (2013), pp. 196–197 (arguing that among macroeconomic indicators of business failure, high interest rate is critical to business, given that such rates will impair the ability of firms to roll over debt, thus precipitating failure).

[189] See High interest rates stifling businesses, economy, Senate tells CBN. In Premium Times, Jun. 14, 2017. Available at: <https://www.premiumtimesng.com/business/business-news/234060-high-interest-rates-stifling-businesses-economy-senate-tells-cbn.html> accessed 10 Aug 2017 (report-

could arise from the existence of an explicit rule may be the provision of new money at competitive interest rates and terms.[190] A pre-distress lender who is unwilling to share priority position with prospective lenders, unwilling to see its interest primed,[191] or who is unwilling to give up its negative pledge clause, may offer better-priced financing to support the restructuring of the distressed debtor. This possibility of a competitive interest rate provides some support for the explicit rule.

In the case of first time borrowers, it may be argued (as the policy argument does) that if heightened priority position is statutorily guaranteed, bank lenders will internalize such an incentive as risk to their initial investment and respond by raising interest premium or pursue other means to cushion such risk.[192] On the other hand, one could argue that Banks would raise their interest rates *ex-ante* to cover their perceived risk of losing their super priority position, which seems unlikely since such strategy may become a self-fulfilling prophecy. As has been argued above, the high interest rates account for business failures. Pushing the interest rates higher may be a means of setting their customers up for failure.[193] Where there is a statutory provision facilitating the incentive to lend by higher priority for new lenders, increasing interest rates in reaction to such incentive will be as detrimental to the bank lender as it is to the borrower. In any case, increasing their interest rates will have distressed borrowers resorting to willing lenders with competitive interest rates, who have the incentive to lend, given the explicit protection of their new money by the statute. It could be argued therefore that creating incentive through an explicit statutory method may well not necessarily chill lending but could in fact help to facilitate a competitive interest rate regime particularly in lending to distressed businesses.

It must be borne in mind that advocating a superpriority regime is done against the backdrop of the provision of protection for pre-distress lenders, whose priority is already guaranteed by law. In other words, the provision of a prescriptive superpriority regime as in the US is advocated on the condition that it incorporates all the protections for prior secured creditor. By this, it is meant that **firstly**, the relevant creditors receive notice of the proposal to grant such heightened priority. **Secondly**, the management of the distressed borrower must be able to convince the court that

---

ing that bank interest rates are between 25 and 30%, making it very hard for businesses to survive within the country); Onu (2017) (noting that "interest rates on loans have also soared to as high as 25 percent, more than double the rate" borrowers are able to pay).

[190] This analysis is clearly in the context of distressed lending.

[191] As in a prescriptive superpriority approach allowing new financing to prime to pre-distress security interest.

[192] See pp. 205–207.

[193] Ekundayo (2017) (reporting that very high bank interest rates "now drive the spate at which Nigerians now patronize the non-banking sector, saying the formal banking sector is fast losing its relevance.") Furthermore, this researcher had informal interactions with 5 randomly selected mid-sized companies operating in Lagos in the following sectors: information technology, distillery, paint manufacturing, pharmaceutical distribution, and haulage. They confirmed that between 2014 to 16 December 2017 (the time of the interaction), they had relied on non-bank lenders for financing especially in respect of specific projects.

it is unable to obtain financing on terms other than on a superpriority basis. The management of the distressed borrower will also have to convince the court in cases where it seeks to create a security interest over any of its unencumbered assets, as well as where it seeks to subordinate the claim of a prospective lender to an asset with a subsisting security interest. **Thirdly** and even more importantly, the management of the distressed borrower must be able to show that the prior secured creditor enjoys adequate protection. Approval by the court of the new financing should only follow when each of these prior lender protections are in place.

4.8 Conclusion: Market-Based Approach as Default Approach

This chapter has examined what is a vital tool in the toolkit for restructuring distressed businesses, but which attract differing treatments in formal restructuring. Incentives to attract such funding is in turn, a critical part of facilitating such funding. Whether one looks at it from the vantage point of economists or from that of psychologist, incentivizing new financing is justified. To be of any serious consequence, such an incentive ought not to be just in the form of negative protections such protecting the lender from transaction avoidance laws. The incentives need to be positive and enough to attract the attention of lenders. In the context of distressed businesses, the most favored incentive from the days of the US railroad receiverships until the present times centers on the creation of explicit priorities in favor of the potential lender.

Whether or not heightened priority is availed the provider of new financing, two approaches are decipherable. On the one hand is a prescriptive approach. As in the US, that prescribes the nature of the priority, the conditions on which such a priority will be allowed and the protection of the claims of prior lenders whose interests are implicated in incentivizing the new lender. On the other hand, is a market-based approach as in the UK or Germany, which leaves the new financing and the details of incentives to the parties involved in the restructuring. The market-based approach itself appears to serve as the default approach for many other countries. In the case of Nigeria, it could be as an accident of history but not much thought has been given to the issue. For such countries like Nigeria still designing their restructuring framework, it may be necessary to rationalize their approach to incentivizing new lending.

However, in spite of the prescriptive approach, there are indications that providers of new financing are relying much more on their market-based liberties in ways that is suggestive of overreaching distressed debtors as well as other stakeholders of the distressed business. These issues are now addressed in Chap. 5.

References

Adebola BA (2014) Corporate rescue and the Nigerian Insolvency System. Unpublished PhD dissertation, University College London. http://discovery.ucl.ac.uk/1385156/7/1385156_Thesis.pdf

Adler BA, Baird DG, Jackson TH (2007) Bankruptcy cases, problems and materials, 4th edn. Foundation Press, St Paul

Anderson H et al (2016) National report for England. In: Faber D et al (eds) Ranking and priority of creditors. Oxford University Press, Oxford, at para 8.101, 244

Bacon A (2007) Administrative costs: some welcome news. Insolv Intell 1

Baer HP et al (2012) The history and statutory basis of debtor-in-possession financing. In: Perlman FB (ed) Debtor-in-possession financing: funding a chapter 11 case. ABI, New York, pp 1–22, at 11

Baird DG (2010) The elements of bankruptcy, 5th edn. Thomson Reuters/Foundation Press, New York

Baiser PM, Epstein DG (1992) Postpetition lending under section 364: issues regarding the gap period and financing for prepackaged plans. Wake Forest Law Rev 27:103–122

Baker HJ (1976) Certificates of indebtedness in reorganization proceedings: analysis and legislative proposals. Am Bankr Law J 50:1

Benabou R, Tirole J (2003) Intrinsic and extrinsic motivation. Rev Econ Stud 70(3):489–520

Berkovitch E, Kim HE (1990) Financial contracting and leverage induced over- and under-investment incentives. J Financ 45:765–794

Bork R (2012) Rescuing companies in England and Germany. Oxford University Press, Oxford

Calitz J, Freebody G (2016) Is post-commencement finance proving to be the thorn in the side of business rescue proceedings under the 2008 Companies Act? De Jure 49(2):265–287

Cameron J, Pierce WD (1994) Reinforcement, reward, and intrinsic motivation: a meta-analysis. Rev Educ Res 64(3):363

Cameron J, Banko KM, Pierce WD (2001) Pervasive negative effects of rewards on intrinsic motivation: the myth continues. Behav Anal 24(1):1–44

Cooter RD (2000) Three effects of social norms on law: expression, deterrence, and internalization. Or Law Rev 79:1–22

Cork K (1982) Insolvency law and practice: report of the review committee. HMSO, London

Davydenko S, Franks J (2008) Do bankruptcy codes matter? J Financ 63(2):565–608

Deci E, Koestner R, Ryan RM (2001) Extrinsic rewards and intrinsic motivation in education: reconsidered once again. Rev Educ Res 17(1):1–27

Dickson C (1896) The rights of material and supply men in railroad foreclosures. Am Law Rev 30:523

Eidenmüller H (2018) What is an insolvency proceeding? Am Bankr Law J 92:53

Ekundayo K (2017) High interest rates push business owners to non-bank lenders. In: Daily trust. https://www.dailytrust.com.ng/news/business/high-interest-rates-push-business-owners-to-non-bank-lenders/206617.html. Accessed 27 Sept 2017

Feldman Y (2011) The complexity of disentangling intrinsic and extrinsic compliance motivations: theoretical and empirical insights from the behavioral analysis of law. Wash Univ J Law Pol 35:11–51

Felsberg TB, Filho PFC (2009) Corporate bankruptcy and reorganization in Brazil: national and cross-border perspectives. https://www.iiiglobal.org/sites/default/files/Felsberg%2C%20Thomas%20B.%20and%20Filho%2C%20Paulo%20Fernando%20Campana.pdf. Accessed 10 Aug 2017

Finch V (2009) Corporate insolvency law. Cambridge University Press, Cambridge

Fletcher D (2007) Time for a DIP? Recovery 30:1

Franks J, Sussman O (2005) Financial distress and bank restructuring of small to medium-sized UK companies. Rev Financ 9:65–96

Gaa TM (1993) Harmonization of international bankruptcy law and practice: is it necessary? Is it possible? Int Law 27:881–909
Gallagher A, Lombardo F (2013) New rules on DIP financing in Italian restructurings. Am Bankr Inst J 32(3):48–49
Garrido JM (2011) No two snowflakes the same: the distributional question in international bankruptcies. Texas Int Law J 46:459–488
Gilson S (2012) Coming through in a crisis: how chapter 11 and the debt restructuring industry are helping to revive the U.S. economy. J Appl Corp Financ 24(4):23–35
Goldsberry JL (2002) Note, perfection of nonpossessory security interests under revised article 9: consequences of the practical and conceptual incompatibility of US and English secured transactions law. Chi J Int Law 3(1):241–246
Gordon WJ (1992) Of harms and benefits: torts, restitution, and intellectual property. J Legal Stud 21:449–482
Gordon WJ (2010) Discipline and nourish: on constructing commons. Cornell Law Rev 95:733
Gullifer L, Payne J (2015) Corporate finance law principles and policy. Hart, Oxford
Guzzo RA (1979) Types of reward, cognitions and work motivation. Acad Manage Rev 4:75
Henoch BA (1991) Post-petition financing: is there life after debt? Bankr Dev J 8:575
Hollander-Blumoff R (2011) Intrinsic and extrinsic compliance motivations: comment on Feldman. Wash Univ J Law Pol 35:53
Jhang J, Bessler D, Leatham D (2013) Aggregate business failures and macroeconomic conditions: a Var look at the U.S. between 1980 and 2004. J Appl Econ XVI(1):179
Keach RK (2013) Examining key developments of ABI's chapter 11 commission during 2013 and the steps to the final report for 2014. Am Bankr Inst 26:16
Krepps D (1997) Intrinsic motivation and extrinsic incentives. Am Econ Rev 87(2):359–364
Kripke H (1985) Law and economics: measuring the economic efficiency of commercial law in a vacuum of fact. Univ Pa Law Rev 133(5):929–985
Larratt-Smith HC (2013) Asset-based lending in Europe today. Secured Lender:15–20
Lazear EP (2000) Performance pay and productivity. Am Econ Rev 90(5):1346–1361
Levitin AJ (2016) Business bankruptcy: financial restructuring and modern commercial markets. Wolter Kluwer, New York
Liu J, Wilson N (2002) Corporate failure rates and the impact of the 1986 insolvency act: an econometric analysis. Manag Financ 28(6):61–71
McCormack G (2006) Swelling corporate assets: changing what is on the menu. J Corp Law Stud 6(1):39–69
McCormack G (2008) Corporate rescue law: an Anglo-American perspective. Edward Elgar, Cheltenham
McCormack G (2017) Business restructuring law in Europe: making a fresh start. J Corp Law Stud 17(1):167–202
Mevorach I (2011) Transaction avoidance in bankruptcy of corporate groups. Eur Company Financ Law Rev 8(2):235–258
Myers SC (1977) Determinants of corporate borrowing. J Financ Econ 5:147–176
Myerson RB (1999) Nash equilibrium and the history of economic theory. J Econ Lit 37(3):1067–1082
Onu E (2017) Unintended result of Nigerian dollar hunt is naira shortage. In: Bloomberg business week. https://www.bloomberg.com/news/articles/2017-09-20/unintended-result-of-nigeria-s-dollar-hunt-is-naira-shortage. Accessed 27 Sept 2017
Orojo O (2008) Company law and practice in Nigeria. 5th edn. LexisNexis, Durban
Parry R (2008) Corporate rescue, vol 109. Sweet & Maxwell, London
Paterson S (2014) Bargaining in financial restructuring: market norms, legal rights and regulatory standards. J Corp Law Stud 14:333–365
Paterson S (2015) The adaptive capacity of markets and convergence in law: UK high yield issuers, US investors and insolvency law. Mod Law Rev 78(3):431–460

Paulus CG, Berberich M (2016) National report for Germany. In: Faber D et al (eds) Ranking and priority of creditors. Oxford University Press, Oxford
Payne J (2014) Debt restructuring in English law: lessons from the United States and the need for reform. Law Q Rev 130:282–305
Rajah I (2017) Enhancing Singapore as an international debt restructuring centre for Asia and beyond. https://www.mlaw.gov.sg/content/dam/minlaw/corp/News/Note%20on%20Debt%20Restructuring.pdf. Accessed 10 Dec 2017
Register LB (1913) Notes on the history of commerce and commercial law: 1. Antiquity. Univ Pa Law Rev 61:431–440
Richardson B, Richardson S, Nwankwo S (1994) Understanding the causes of business failure crises: generic failure types: boiled frogs, drowned frogs, bullfrogs and tadpoles. Manage Decis 32(4):9–22
Ripley WZ (1915) Railroad finance and organization. Longmans Green, New York, p 386
Roe MJ, Tung F (2013) Breaking bankruptcy priority: how rent-seeking upends the creditors' bargain. Va Law Rev 99:1235–1287
Roosevelt K III (2000) Understanding lockups: effects in bankruptcy and the market for corporate control. Yale J Reg 17:94–135
Sarra J (2013) Rescue! The companies' creditors arrangement act, 2nd edn. Carswell, Toronto
Schorer JU, Curry DS (1991) Chapter 11 lending: an overview of the process. Secured Lender 47(2):10
Skeel DA Jr (2001) Debt's dominion: a history of bankruptcy law in America. Princeton University Press, Princeton
Skeel DA Jr (2004) The past present and future of debtor in possession financing. Cardozo Law Rev 25:1905–1934
Skeel D Jr, Ayotte KA (2013) Bankruptcy law as a liquidity provider. Univ Chi Law Rev 80:1559–1560
Sonnenschein H (1983) The economics of incentives: an introductory account. In: Sato R, Beckman M (eds) Technology, organization and economic structure. Springer-Verlag, Berlin, pp 79–92
Spahlinger A, Kortz H (2015) Germany. In: Baer G, O'Flynn K (eds) Financing company group restructurings. Oxford University Press, Oxford
Swaine HH (1898) Economic aspects of railroad receiverships. Proc Am Econ Assoc 3(2):70–71
Squire R (2016) Corporate bankruptcy and financial reorganization. Wolter Kluwer, New York
Tabb CJ (2014) Law of bankruptcy, 3rd edn. West Academic Publishing, St Paul
Tabb CJ, Brubaker R (2010) Bankruptcy law: principles, policies and practice, 3rd edn. LexisNexis, New York
Triantis GG (1993) A theory of the regulation of debtor-in-possession financing. Vand Law Rev 46:901–935
Triantis GG (2000) Financial slack policy and the laws of secured transactions. J Legal Stud 29(1):35–69
Tufano P (1997) Business failure, judicial intervention, and financial innovation: restructuring U.S. railroads in the nineteenth century. Bus Hist Rev 71(1):1–40
Underhill K (2016) When extrinsic incentives displace intrinsic motivation: designing legal carrots and sticks to confront the challenge of motivational crowding-out. Yale J Reg 33(1):213–279
Qi L (2008) Availability of continuing financing in corporate reorganizations: the UK and the US perspective. Comp Law 29(6):162
Yeowart G (2009) Encouraging company rescue: what changes are required to UK insolvency law. Law & Financ Mark Rev 3:517

Chapter 5
New Financing and Lender Capture

5.1 Overview

Chapter 4 examined the approaches to incentivizing new financing, which as noted is vital for a successful restructuring and consequently, ought to be an integral part of the restructuring procedural pre-requisites. While on the one hand, the prescriptive approach represented by the US provides for this regulated incentive structure, English and German laws appear to be favorably disposed to a regime that is market-based, leaving the parties to determine the incentives and basis for new financing. This chapter closely examines what appears to be a capture of the restructuring process by the providers of new financing with pre-distress relationship with the borrower, using the new financing agreements to gain both financial and control advantages over other stakeholder constituencies, as well as over the distressed business as a whole. With this in mind, the chapter focuses on new financing by creditors, financial and control advantages that border on overreach, and the lessons that may be learnt from the dominance of the process of formal restructuring by pre-distress creditors.

Much of the issues that arise with new financing agreements pertain to the provision of new financing by both lenders with prior exposure to the debtor (pre-distress lenders) as well as (new lenders) to the debtor. This chapter however devotes attention to pre-distress lenders and their new financing agreements. The reason for this is not far-fetched, in many cases pre-distress lenders provide new facilities to the debtor.[1] However, new lenders are not left out altogether, given that there is a chance of heightened repayment of the new funds through at least administrative expense

[1] Weijs et al. (2012), p. 2 ("In practice, banks that are willing to provide credit at a time of need, are often banks that have provided credit before. The new credit is therefore often additional credit.") See also Skeel (2004), p. 1926 (author commenting on the US lending market at the time of writing points out that "[n]early sixty percent of the time, the debtor's post-petition financer is a bank or banks that has already lent money to the debtor prior to bankruptcy.").

S. U. Mba, *New Financing for Distressed Businesses in the Context of Business Restructuring Law*, https://doi.org/10.1007/978-3-030-19749-0_5

priority in most jurisdictions.[2] There is therefore the chance that providing new funding "… will bear interest at the rate agreed and both principal and interest will have administrative priority--superior to the priority of the debtor's [existing] unsecured creditors."[3] However, as the chapter will show, pre-distress lenders may be able to achieve more protection for their pre-distress exposure and these sometimes-contentious protections are the focus of this chapter. The problematization of the financing agreement essentially gives the impression of an overreach by new financing. It is in this context that the chapter proceeds. It identifies such clauses designed by pre-distress lenders to protect their claims and enhance the control of the restructuring process and the problems that such lender-inserted clauses may pose. Particularly in the US, many of these clauses are borderline. They are borderline in the sense that are not the subject of express prohibition; neither do they have a broad appeal amongst other stakeholder classes, given the implications of some of such clauses for other stakeholders.

The chapter focuses primarily on the US. This is because these problems, while not necessarily just "US problems", have been left largely unregulated elsewhere. Also, because of the design of the US restructuring regime which is at least conceptually debtor-friendly, lenders seem to be working out innovative ways to maximize value for themselves. Markets like the UK and Germany provide broader principles that may constrain lender overreach and such constraining rules will be examined as well. Also emerging markets reforming their restructuring regimes in the direction of that of the US will find useful, first, the possible justifications for permitting what may otherwise be adjudged lender overreach and to make informed decisions on whether to curtail or leave unregulated such practices.

5.2 Financing Agreements: Unravelling the Devil in the Detail

Consider a distressed debtor involved in the business of constructing condominiums but now seeking to formally restructure its debt and in need of new interim financing to prop up general operations and for improvement on the condominiums. Along comes a prior lender with an offer of new financing. This should ordinarily be a relief for the borrower in view of the importance of this new facility for the survival of the business. Only that things may not always be as they seem. The lender, in the guise of taking security for the new loan which is only a small fraction of the pre-filing loan, secures both the pre-filing loan, as well as the post-filing cash. The agreement may further seek take away from the distressed borrower, rights guaranteed by the formal restructuring regime, such as the automatic stay of pre-filing

[2] See Chap. 4.

[3] White (2004), p. 175.

claims which has been recognized as key to restructuring.[4] Furthermore, by the financing agreement, the new lender takes upon itself, the right to determine the management of the business, to approve the improvements on the condominium and to determine where the proceeds of the debtor's business is kept, and to apply it to outstanding financial obligations.[5]

The above scenario and the demands of the pre-filing lender as the basis for which new financing will be advanced exposes the new financing agreement as a very potent tool in the hands of the lender to assert itself over the debtor in the course of restructuring.[6] The more difficult it is for the borrower to access financing, the more likely that financing agreements with stringent clauses form part of the financing agreements.[7] With the likelihood of undergoing a liquidation if formal restructuring is commenced without new financing, debtors may not necessarily give so much thoughts to the loan agreement which are as a rule very much skewed in favor of the provider of the financing.[8] While the provision of new financing is typically considered as facilitating the rehabilitation of the distressed debtor, there is growing concern that the lenders may have found a way to highjack the restructuring process to serve their interests, at the expense of the other constituencies represented in the distressed firm. The distressed lender does know in most cases what it is getting into, in terms of the costs of the distress financing which the lender is to provide. However, the distressed borrower is motivated by a dire need to ensure continued operation as the details of the restructuring is worked out.[9]

---

[4] See Chap. 3, Sect. 3.4.1.

[5] The above roughly recounts the facts of *In re Tenney Village Co, Inc*, 104 B R 562 (Bankr. D N H 1989).

[6] Carruthers and Parrot (1998), p. 158 (suggesting that financers exert themselves most vigorously during formal restructuring as they can dominate the creditor's committee and shape the restructuring of distressed firms). See Also Mintz and Schwartz (1985) The Power Structure of the American Business Community. University of Chicago Press, Chicago (IL), 83 (authors argue that Chapter 11 of the US Bankruptcy Code is "a legally mandated form of bank control involving the subordination of corporate policy to bank dictation.").

[7] For example, following the financial crisis of 2008. See generally, Rice (2010), p. 314 (attributing the difficulty in accessing financing during the crisis to its impact on the hedge funds and investment banks which were major distress financers; the desire of lenders to pursue safer investments, instead of risky investments; the ease of accessing credit pre-crisis meant debtors had fewer assets to use as collateral for distress loans; finally, the increased number of distressed businesses owing to the crisis).

[8] White (2004), pp. 175–176 ("points out that the prospect of bankruptcy makes the debtor amenable to terms in the loan agreement that would limit its rights. And such debtor would cheerfully accept terms that strengthen the DIP lender's hand ….").

[9] Lee (2009), p. 546 (commenting on distressed debtors in the US, it is argued that "[D]ebtor firms find themselves truly desperate for cash as they enter Chapter 11 because the only real alternative to adequate DIP financing is an organized liquidation…"); see also Adler (2012), p. 211 ("If a debtor has no alternative source of funds to continue operation, even temporarily, a debtor, …, may accede to the secured creditor's demands because the alternative would be immediate liquidation.").

There are basic terms that necessarily form part of the financing agreement and are typical for distressed lending.[10] There are however certain other clauses which by design serve the sole interests of the lender but have somewhat become commonplace in new financing agreements. An analysis of such clauses is undertaken in this chapter, what follows is an examination of the attitude of courts as they exercise the role of approving financing on those terms. For the sake of reiteration, the clauses examined here and their treatment track development in the US jurisprudence.

5.2.1 *Roll-Up and Cross-Collateralization Clauses*

A roll-up occurs when the new loan provided by a lender is used to pay up an antecedent debt owed by the distressed borrower to the lender. In other words, the new loan to be granted to the debtor is the sum of the outstanding pre-petition debt and actual new cash provided, rolled into one.[11] While the contract document indicates

[10] These include (1) increased interest margins chargeable on the loan to the distressed business; (2) affirmative covenants on periodic disclosure; (3) negative covenants which identifies and restricts the use to which the loan is to be put; (4) elaborate covenants. See Squire (2016) (noting that the typical interest rate chargeable by distressed lenders is about 2 percentage points above the rate offered to non-distressed businesses.); Kuney (2005), p. 56 ("[t]he one feature that almost all forms of DIP financing share is an interest rate significantly higher than that of similar loans provided to non-debtors."); Kuney (2005), p. 52 (noting the use of affirmative covenants that require distressed borrower to "periodically disclose financial records and information so that the [new financer] can easily monitor the debtor's performance"). See also, Bussel and Klee (2009), p. 707 (the authors highlight some other conditions to which the new financing may be tied to include "releases, sale and reorganization timelines, use of collateral or priming, additional collateral grants, stipulated claims allowance, current payment of interest, ... standard budgetary controls, and statutory adequate protection and priorities available to post-petition lenders"); see Chatterjee et al. (2004), p. 3111 ("...a majority of the loans have clauses clearly stating that the DIP loan cannot be used for investments in projects and is to be used primarily for working capital needs. Over 63% of the sample restricts the use of proceeds to working capital needs..."). Note that the use of such covenants is not only restricted to new lending in the US. For similar covenants and more, see Wood (2007), pp. 675–676.

[11] The court in *In re Capmark Fin. Grp. Inc.*, 438 B.R. 471, 511 (Bankr. D. Del. 2010) provides an explanation of roll-up clauses as follow roll-up clauses as:

> ...the payment of a pre-petition debt with the proceeds of a post-petition loan. Roll-ups most commonly arise where a pre-petition secured creditor is also providing a post-petition financing facility under section 364(c) or (d) of the Bankruptcy Code. The proceeds of the post-petition financing facility are used to pay off or replace the pre-petition debt, resulting in a post-petition debt equal to the pre-petition debt plus any new money being lent to the debtor. As a result, the entirety of the pre-petition and post-petition debt enjoys the post-petition protection of section 364(c) or (d) as well as the terms of the DIP order.

It is worthy of note that roll-ups (also known as roll-overs) may come in two ways. The first one which is often preferred by lender is as described in the case above (also known as first-day roll-up). The other form of roll-up is that in which a pre-petition lender, pursuant to an agreement to provide new financing, provide for the application of pre-petition receivables to the liquidation of pre-petition debt owed to the lender (also known as creeping roll-up). For this, see 3 Collier on

a certain amount as new financing, in fact, only a nominal cash amount is applied by the debtor to its business, because a good chunk of the loan amount received by the debtor is used in liquidating the pre-petition debt owed to the lender.

Cross-collateralization of debt may arise when a distressed lender offers new money to the debtor, whilst creating security interest over the pre-petition or post-petition assets of the debtor (or both), to cover both the new loan, as well as the pre-petition loan.[12] In ordinary terms, think about cross-collateralization as a pre-distress lender using one stone to kill two birds. A lender may have provided facility to the debtor pre-distress on an unsecured basis, or for some reason, the debt has become partially secured.[13] Following the distress of the debtor, the lender who wishes to provide financing for the restructuring may, through the loan agreement, stipulate that the old unsecured (or the unsecured part of the old partially secured) loan, be fully secured on the assets of the debtor, in exchange for the new loan.[14] Following the definition of roll-ups and cross-collateralization, the reader may be interested to know why these clauses can pose a problem (if at all).

5.2.1.1 The Problem with Roll-Ups and Cross-Collateralization

Both roll-up and cross-collateralization clauses as conditions for distress financing bring up a number of issues as far as the whole framework of restructuring is concerned. The first and obvious challenge is the fact that they create a preference in

Bankruptcy ¶ 364.04[1][e]. See also Bussel and Klee (2009), p. 707 n.209.

[12] This is deducible from the definition of cross-collateralization provided by the second Circuit in *Otte v Manufacturers Hanover Commercial Corp. (In re Texlon Corp.)*, 596 F.2d 1092, 1094, as:

> [I]n return for making new loans to a debtor in possession under Chapter XI, a financing institution obtains a security interest on all assets of the debtor, both those existing at the date of the order and those created in the course of the Chapter XI proceeding, not only for the new loans, the propriety of which is not contested, but [also] for existing indebtedness to it.

In a related sense, cross-collateralization may arise where debtor security interest is created over post-petition assets in favor a pre-petition lender offering new money, so that pre-petition unsecured debt is covered by the post-petition asset. Chatterjee et al. (2004), p. 3100.

There is a less contentious sense in which cross-collateralization may be used. Here, because of new financing provided in Chapter 11 by a pre-petition lender, security interest is created over a pre-petition asset of the debtor. The court in *In re Antico Manufacturing* Co., 31 B.R. 103 (Bankr.E.D.N.Y.1983) noted that this type of cross-collateralization is not as objectionable as the one *In re Texlon*, given that the existing claim of the lender is not necessarily improved, rather is "merely exacting as security for future advances a lien or interest in what may well be the only tangible assets the debtor can offer" (at 105).

[13] This may arise from the depreciation in the value of the assets which serves as collateral.

[14] See Carlson (1993), p. 498 ("[Prepetition] creditors often try to condition new credit on securing payment of the old"). The pertinent facts in *In re Saybrook Mfg. Co.* 963 F.2d 1490, 1491 (11th Cir. 1992) demonstrates this. A pre-distress lender who was undersecured by about $24 million offered to provide distress financing of $3 million provided that the debtor gives the lender security in respect of the unsecured $24 million.

favor of the pre-petition lender providing the new loan.[15] This preference is better understood against the backdrop of the US formal restructuring regime and should be considered different from the superpriority of new financing. Although in general terms, new financing ought not to be used in the settlement of claims arising before the commencement of the restructuring, such contractual provisions have the effect of lumping the new and old facility. Since the new loan is repaid before the confirmation of the plan, the new lender recovers both old and new loans ahead of other creditors. This sort of preference, is not ordinarily envisaged as part of the preference of superpriority incentive for new lending.[16]

The preference received by a pre-distress lender has attendant implication for other stakeholders in the business, particularly preferential and unsecured creditors. Recall that the treatment of the unsecured part of the lender's pre-petition claim ought to be as an unsecured claim. What roll-up and cross-collateralization clauses do however is to elevate and recharacterize the pre-petition unsecured claim to a secured one or to one with heightened priority, in the event of the commencement of liquidation proceedings and thus, possibly leaving the preferential and unsecured creditors with little or nothing.[17]

A roll-up clause can even have a value transfer effect on the debtor and other creditors, as it ensures the concurrent repayment of the (likely unsecured) antecedent loan as a new loan. This means that the new loan(s) now assume priority to which it otherwise may not have been entitled.[18] The repayment of that loan before the confirmation of the plan takes assets in form of cash out of the estate of the debtor. The clause also confers an advantage on the distressed lender's (possibly) unsecured pre-filing loan as it lifts the pre-petition debt from the realm where it can be attacked by an avoidance action or be subjected to a possible restructuring, as formal restructuring is set into motion.[19] It is easy to lift the loan from the reach of avoidance laws. This is because once the roll-up clause is approved by the court as

---

[15] *In re FCX, Inc.*, 54 B.R. 833, 840 (Bankr. E.D.N.C. 1985) ("If an undersecured creditor can obtain unencumbered assets as security for all of its prepetition claims, that creditor is being preferred to the detriment of other unsecured claimants."). Preference as used here need not be confused with voidable preference especially where the financing is provided in the context of a formal restructuring. A hallmark of voidable preferences (transaction avoidance laws) which is somewhat of general application is that the preference liable to be avoided is that given to a particular lender or creditor, prior to the commencement of insolvency proceedings (or formal restructuring). See Tabb (2014), pp. 508–509.

[16] See Chap. 4.

[17] McCormack (2008), p. 190. See also Tabb (1986), p. 113 ("The cross-collateralization clause [...] effectively transform[s] Lender's [unsecured pre-filing] claim from an unsecured claim that shares pro rata with all other unsecured claims and comes behind priority claims into a secured claim which is preferred over all other claims.").

[18] Roe and Tung (2013), p. 1238 ("...bank lenders have convinced judges to "roll up" their possibly unsecured pre-bankruptcy debts—debts that were quite likely not entitled to priority payment—into new, secured, and highly-prioritized loans to the debtor in bankruptcy.").

[19] Bussel and Klee (2009), p. 707 n.209 ("... [the roll-up] is advantageous to the secured creditor primarily because prepetition claims may be subject to avoidance and restructuring, whereas post-petition claims, invariably, are not ....").

part of the financing agreement, there is hardly a chance that the pre-filing loan will be examined to see that a collateral adequately supports it and whether it was made in good faith.[20]

Instructively the roll-up clause that entails the liquidation of pre-petition debt suggests a violation of US Bankruptcy policy as reflected in the provisions of the Bankruptcy Code. This is because the effect of such payment is a violation of the policy of the law to pay pre-petition debts after the confirmation of the restructuring plan by the courts.[21] More than this, as already noted early in this book, Chapter 11 seeks to bind dissenting creditors to the restructuring plan through a cramdown.[22] With a roll-up clause in place, the claim of a pre-filing secured lender cannot be crammed down in respect of the pre-petition loan. This is essentially because the new financing which it has been rolled into is not only entitled to immediate payment as the Chapter 11 plan is approved by the court,[23] but also enjoys the statutory priority incentive which applies to the new financing.[24]

As for the cross-collateralization clause, although it may not leave the other stakeholders with nothing, but it may deplete the assets of the estate of the debtor, leaving other creditors with less than they would have been entitled to but for the clause.[25] As the debtor slides into distress, bankruptcy/insolvency law through its different mechanisms ensures the preservation of the assets of the debtor in the interest of the general body of creditors. An increased pool of assets means better or increased value for the unsecured creditors of the debtor. The result of a cross-collateralization may well be the reduction in the pool of assets available to the unsecured creditors, if it does happen that the restructuring fails and liquidation proceedings are commenced against the debtor.[26] In such a situation, otherwise

[20] Roe and Tung (2013), p. 1252 ("… in roll-ups, the bankruptcy process often does not examine the old collateral's adequacy and the old loan's bona fides carefully. Sometimes the process doesn't examine them at all.").

[21] *Official Committee of Equity Sec. Holders v. Mabey* 832 F.2d 299 (4th Cir. 1987) (the court reasoned that a plan which allowed for the piecemeal, pre-confirmation payments to some unsecured creditors violated the clear policy of the law on formal restructuring of Chapter 11 of the Bankruptcy Code). See also *In re Structurlite Plastic Corp.* 86 B.R. 922 (Bankr. S.D. Ohio 1988) (where the court frowned upon selective repayment of pre-petition debt even where the creditors threatened and sought to coerce the debtor to pay).

[22] See Chap. 3, Sect. 3.6.1.

[23] Zumbro (2016), p. 12.

[24] See Chap. 4 above. See also the argument of the controlling shareholder *In re Colt Holding Co.*, No. 15-11296 (Bankr. D. Del July 2, 2015), Limited Objections of Sciens Capital management LLC (shareholders) to Debtors' Proposed Alternative DIP Financing at 5. The controlling shareholder argued that rolling up the pre-filing debt into the new financing agreement covers "100% of the pre-petition secured claims", making it immune to a Chapter 11 cramdown.

[25] Id (Concerned about the preference that may result when an unsecured creditor receives a preference, the 4th Circuit pointed that "[t]he clear language of these statutes, as well as the Bankruptcy Rules applicable thereto, does not authorize the payment in part or in full, or the advance of monies to or for the benefit of unsecured claimants prior to the approval of the plan of reorganization.").

[26] *In re Saybrook Manufacturing Co., Inc.* 127 BR 494, at 496 (11th Cir. 1991).

unencumbered assets are used to pay up the pre-petition debt of the lender, so that they are unavailable to meet the claim of unsecured creditors.[27]

In a related sense, cross-collateralization conflicts with a priority rule which forms part of bankruptcy law. The consequence of giving effect to a cross-collateralization clause, in favor of a pre-filing distressed lender demonstrates this. A partially secured creditor is unsecured to the extent that the collateral does not cover its debt. However, the result of a cross-collateralization clause, is to make a pre-petition unsecured creditor receive a favorable treatment (full payment) ahead of other pre-petition unsecured creditors. Thus, although courts involved in the restructuring of distressed debtors are usually allowed some discretion in the process, decided cases have shown that bankruptcy courts tend not to grant approval to financing agreements that operate to distort the priority scheme beyond what is expressly allowed under the bankruptcy legislation.[28]

In the US, there is hardly ever any statutory backing for cross-collateralization in the course of providing financing for the distress debtors. Besides, financial economists argue that the cross-collateralization of pre-petition debt may be allowed where the debtor has a potentially lucrative investment opportunity and disallowed when the investment opportunity is not so lucrative.[29] However, it is also true that lucrative investment opportunities do not always result in profits that will take care of the cross-collateralized debt, with sufficient residue to go around all other creditors of the debtor. In view of this, the attitude of the courts to such clauses is now examined.

5.2.1.2 Judicial Treatment of Cross-Collateralization Clauses

US courts have for many years grappled with the legality of cross-collateralization clauses in financing agreements. The clause may arise at two points and these have been the points from which the courts have had to tackle them. At one point, the courts have been faced with its approval in the distress financing agreement. At the other point, the courts have been faced with the question of whether to honor it in the face of a liquidation proceeding. The trajectory of cross-collateralization clauses and their treatment by the courts starts with its consideration as a procedural issue. It progressed from this point to the determination of its legality. It must be however pointed out that even when the courts considered cross-collateralization a procedural issue, there was a lingering and often voiced concern about its propriety.

---

[27] See Gebbia and Oscar (1993), p. 202 (authors argue that the cross-collateralization makes the assets of the debtor unavailable "for pro rata distribution on all unsecured claims.").

[28] *In re Sun Runner*, 945 F.2d 1089, 1094 (9th Cir. 1991) ("[t]here is no … applicable provision in the Bankruptcy Code authorizing the debtor to pay certain pre-petition unsecured claims in full while others remain unpaid. To do so would impermissibly violate the priority scheme of the Bankruptcy Code.").

[29] Dahiya and Ray (2014) ("For borrowers that have an attractive investment opportunity set, DIP financing can be cross-collateralized with the pre-petition debt. Conversely, for borrowers with a poor opportunity, […] DIP financing should not be cross-collateralized.").

In the earliest case where the court was faced with a cross-collateralization clause in a liquidation proceeding,[30] the 2nd Circuit passed up the opportunity to make a categorical statement on the legality of cross-collateralization.[31] This was even though it found it unsupportable by the provisions of the Bankruptcy Code[32] and had upheld the challenge of the clause in the distress financing agreement by the trustee. Its decision was particularly hinged on the failure of the debtor to notify the other creditors and to afford them a hearing.[33] Interestingly, many courts have subsequently read the case to mean that once procedural safeguards have been met, cross-collateralization clauses may be permissible.[34] The procedural safeguard here being the notification of the members of the creditors committee and affording them hearing.[35]

Soon, the attitude of the courts began to shift from treating cross-collateralization clauses as a mere procedural issue to inquiring into its substantial validity. In other words, in addition to the procedural aspects, the courts soon began address substantive objection to the cross-collateralization clause, in view of the preference it conferred on pre-distress lender providing new financing.[36] The 11th Circuit in *In re Saybrook*[37] provided the most definitive statement on the legality or otherwise of cross-collateralization clauses and the powers of the courts to grant or allow such clauses in financing agreements. In this regard, the court emphatically concluded that:

---

[30] *In re Texlon Corp.*, 1092.

[31] The court rather hinged its disapproval of the cross-collateralization clause on procedural the lack of notice and a hearing. The court stated:

> In order to decide this case, we are not obliged, however, to say that under no conceivable circumstances could "cross-collateralization" be authorized. Here it suffices to hold that … a financing scheme so contrary to the spirit of the Bankruptcy Act should not have been granted by an *ex parte* order....

[32] Ibid, at 1098 ("we see nothing in s 364(c) or in other provisions of that section that advances the case in favor of "cross-collateralization.").

[33] *In re Texlon Corp.*

[34] see Tabb (2014), p. 1068 ("Amazingly, post-*Texlon* cases read that decision to as implicitly authorizing cross-collateralization as long as the procedural requisites of notice and a hearing are satisfied.").

[35] In distinguishing its case from *re Texlon*, the bankruptcy court in *Borne Chemical Co. v. Lincoln First Commercial Corp. (In re Borne Chemical Co.)* 9 Bankr. 263 (Bankr. D.N.J. 1981) held that the cross-collateralization order in the case "was not granted *ex parte*, but rather only after notice and hearing" (at 269); *In re Flagstaff Food Services Corp.* 16 B. R. 132, 133 (Bankr. SDNY 1981) (in view of the cross-collateralization clause provided for in the distress financing agreement, the bankruptcy court referenced *re Texlon* as mandating notice and hearing to the creditors (see n.1)); *In re General Oil Distributors, Inc.*, 20 B. R. 873 (Bankr. E.D.N.Y. 1982) ("the law in this circuit is that cross-collateralization provisions may not be approved *ex parte*, but only after notice and a hearing." (At 876)).

[36] See *In re Vanguard Diversified, Inc.*, 31 B. R. 364, 366 (Bankr. E.D.N.Y. 1983) (the court relying on the opinion of scholars proceeded to state that the device "may be utilized as a last resort only when the debtor is otherwise unable to obtain needed financing on acceptable terms." (at 366)).

[37] 963 F2d 1490 (11th Cir. 1992).

> … cross-collateralization is inconsistent with bankruptcy law for two reasons. First, cross-collateralization is not authorized as a method of post-petition financing under section 364 [of the US Bankruptcy Code]. Secondly, cross-collateralization is beyond the scope of the bankruptcy court's inherent equitable power because it is directly contrary to the fundamental priority scheme of the Bankruptcy Code.[38]

In the light of the effect of the preferential effect of cross-collateralization, the court in the earlier case of *In re Vanguard*[39] set forth factors which should be considered before granting approval to a cross-collateralization clause. The court reasoned as follows:

> In seeking to grant cross-collateralization, the debtor-in-possession must demonstrate that: (1) Absent the proposed financing, its business operations will not survive …; (2) It is unable to obtain alternative financing on acceptable terms…;(3) The proposed lender will not accede to lesspreferential terms; and (4) The proposed financing is in the best interest of the general creditor body.[40]

The first of these considerations is that the survival of the business of the debtor is dependent upon the availability of the financing; secondly, alternative financing on acceptable terms is unavailable to the debtor; thirdly, the lender is not willing to accept terms that are less preferential; and fourthly, the financing to be provided by the lender serves the best interest of the general body of creditors. Although a number of courts have relied on the 4-pronged test *In re Vanguard Diversified,*[41] it has its shortcomings that makes its reliability contestable. The first test essentially highlights what is already known of a distressed business. The fact of distress entails that the debtor will require financing to continue, and rehabilitate the business.[42] Consequently, the first ambit of the test appears to only state the obvious.

The second test brings to the fore the difficulty of the debtor in assessing financing as it seeks to formally restructure, as well as the role, which pre-petition lenders may play in this situation. The test therefore has to be examined cautiously. The lender appears to be in an already strengthened position against both the debtor as well as against any other potential financer without a prior lending relationship. The entire pre-petition assets of the debtor may already be subject to a lien held by the pre-petition lender, leaving a prospective lender to either rely upon post-petition assets as security or to seek the priming of pre-petition lien held by the pre-petition lender, which may be particularly difficult, for want of adequate protection.[43] More so, the absence of alternative financing with better terms may not necessarily justify

---

[38] Ibid, 1494–1495.

[39] 31 B.R. 364 (Bankr. E.D.N.Y. 1983).

[40] Ibid, at 366.

[41] See for instance *In re Roblin Indus., Inc.*, 52 B.R. 241, 244 (Bankr. W.D.N.Y. 1985); *In re Antico Mfg. Co.*, 31 B.R. 103, 105 (Bankr. E.D.N.Y. 1983).

[42] McCormack (2008), p. 192 (author describes this as a "needs test", emphasizing the point that the debtor is usually in need of working capital to survive and only a handful of such debtors may have available cash reserves to finance its restructuring).

[43] Tabb (1986), p. 164 (generally analyzes the difficulty a debtor may face when it seeks financing from a new lender, as against a pre-petition lender).

the provision of financing, but may well be a telltale sign of the non-viability of the debtor,[44] so that allowing the cross-collateralization clause may produce results inconsistent with the rehabilitative goal of restructuring. In the first, it may just serve as a cost cutting measure for the obviously self-interested pre-petition lender. If by providing the new loan it is able to protect its pre-distress loan that may otherwise not be paid, the pre-distress lender will do so, whether or not the business will be successfully rehabilitated. Secondly, it may help to finance a drowning debtor seeking to clutch on to any straw. The debtor may have no real prospects of successfully restructuring and returning profits in the future but wants to stay alive. Consequently, allowing such a business to stay alive may turn out to be a drain on the assets that should have served the interest of the general body of creditors.[45]

The third test, relating to the unwillingness of the new lender to accede to less preferential terms does not show much, beyond what is already apparent, that "the bankruptcy court will not grant extraordinary benefits to someone who does not really insist on them."[46] Thus, any lender to a distressed business will expectedly drive a hard bargain and insist on the best protection possible for the loan provided. As the stronger party, it can be expected that the lender will insist on any provision that provides the highest assurances of repayment. Furthermore, what is interesting is that the debtor may fulfill this requirement by testifying to its unwillingness to lend without the cross-collateralization clause.[47] More so, any modification to the clause may face practical difficulties, especially where the financing is to be carried out by a syndicate of lenders.[48]

Finally, the fourth element of the test does assume that the courts can tell with certainty that the creditors of the debtor have at their disposal, all relevant information to help them decide whether the financing arrangement is indeed in their best interest.[49] The best interest of the general body of creditors will usually entail an

---

[44] Perechocky (2012), p. 562 ("Alternatively, if no one would lend absent these special provisions, then perhaps the debtor is not a viable company and would be more valuable if liquidated under Chapter 7.") Note however that it may be argued that the absence of an alternative financing may also have nothing to do with the viability of the firm when we bear in mind that the that the financing in issue here is a temporary one, and is designed by the Bankruptcy Code to be settled as soon as the debtor exits formal restructuring or upon the commencement of liquidation. So, in any case, the lender gets paid.

[45] Id ("The only benefit of allowing these special provisions would be to enable the pre-petition lender to cut its losses and recover more than it would otherwise, and to enable the debtor to gamble to stay alive, at the expense of the other creditors.").

[46] Tabb (1986), p. 166.

[47] Ibid, at n 328 (Explaining that this testimony is conclusive, and also citing *In* re *Roblin,* 52 B. R. 245, where according to the court, an officer of the lender "made the unadorned statement that the Banks were not willing to lend on any terms other than those proposed.").

[48] The officer of the lender testifying may for instance require authorization from the appropriate authority of the lender. Also, even if the modification is to be approved, it may take time, which may not be available to the debtor.

[49] Tabb (1986), p. 171 ("Given the lack of time, the lack of Chapter 11 'experience', and the complexity of financing orders, creditors often do not the information necessary to make informed judgments.").

increased value for the general body of creditors. The consensus appears to be that a formal restructuring as against a liquidation yields this increased value. Herein lies another criticism of this test. If formal restructuring means the availability of new financing, in a sense, the cross-collateralization clause is therefore equated to formal restructuring, so that the debtor and the general body of creditors invariably have to choose between the cross-collateralization clause on the one hand, and the liquidation of the debtor on the other. It may well be that either option i.e. the cross-collateralization clause, or liquidation, may not be in the best interest of the general body of creditors.[50]

Given the inadequacy of the *Vanguard* test, it is not surprising that the attitude of the courts is still divided on how to treat cross-collateralization clauses. While some courts will cautiously approve of financing agreements with such clauses, others continue to frown at, and discourage such clauses.[51]

5.2.1.3 Judicial Treatment of Roll-Up Clauses

In the case of the roll-up clause, the US courts have expressed skepticism on its use by the provider of new financing to the debtor for the purpose of restructuring. The court in *In re Appliance Store, Inc.*,[52] was faced with a roll-up clause in a proposed cash collateral[53] stipulation. The new money lender was granted a superpriority replacement lien against the post-petition goods of the debtors and the proceeds from those goods. Also, the financing agreement authorized the lender to apply the proceeds from the goods to the reduction of pre-petition indebtedness.[54] The court equated the roll-up clause to "a contract of adhesion" which on the one hand, leaves

---

[50] Ibid, at 172 ('The creditors are put to the Hobson's choice of liquidation versus cross-collateralization only because cross-collateralization is allowed in the first place. Neither cross-collateralization nor liquidation is in the creditors' "best interests".').

[51] See for instance: *In re FCX, Inc.* (Giving its proclivity to prioritize unsecured claim of one creditor over that others, the court pointed out that "[c]ross-collateralization should be discouraged."); In re

The International Insolvency Institute has also provided guidelines to aid the determination of the approval of cross-collateralization clauses. These guidelines refer to such indicators as:

> the extent of the notice provided; the terms of the DIP financing and a comparison to the terms that would be available absent the cross-collateralization; The degree of consensus supportive of cross-collateralization; The extent and value of the prepetition liens held by the pre-petition lender (and in particular the amount of any "equity cushion" that the pre-petition lender may have); and whether cross-collateralization will give an undue advantage to some pre-petition debt without a countervailing benefit to the estate. See generally, Kuney (2005), p. 61.

[52] 181 B.R. 237(Bankr. W.D. Pa. 1995).

[53] Cash collateral is defined in 11 USC § 363(a) as "cash, [...] or other cash equivalents, whenever acquired, in which the estate and an entity other than the estate have an interest...".

[54] *In re Appliance*, 243.

the debtor no other option and on the other hand, enables the lender "to exact its pound of flesh without immediately inflicting a mortal wound upon debtors."[55] This description is suggestive of the perception of the court on the effect of the clause.

The above notwithstanding, bankruptcy courts have approved new financing agreements that had roll-up clauses in several cases.[56] Remarkably however, in most of those cases, the courts have not specifically provided indicators on the propriety or otherwise of using the clauses. In others, they have done so cautiously. Even so, one will readily see that in those cases in which the courts addressed the roll-up clause, they have not necessarily justified the clause on its own merit, rather they rely on wider justifications which support the need for access to new financing. For instance, in *Re Aleris International, Inc*,[57] the court relied on the broader rules laid down in an earlier case,[58] which did not include the use of a roll-up clause but pertained generally to the approval of new financing.[59] Similarly, in *In re Lyondell Chemical Company*,[60] the court was particularly wary of the effect of the approval and the use of the decision as precedent, shorn of the economic conditions that warranted the decision at the time.

Finally, one observation on the decisions of the court approving the roll-up clauses is that the courts may have been justified by the credit crunch which was prevalent at the time when most of the decisions were made, given that the restructurings started in the thick of the global financial crises.[61] However, some other

---

[55] Id.

[56] See for instance, in *In re Radioshack Corp*, Case No. 15-10197, Docket No. 947 (Bankr. D. Del. March 12, 2015); *In re Constar Int'l Holdings LLC*, Case No. 13-13281, Docket No. 212 (Bankr. D. Del. Jan. 16, 2014);

In re Uno Restaurant Holdings Corporation, et al., Ch. 11 Case No. 10-10209 (MG) (Bankr. S.D.N.Y. Jan. 20, 2010) (*In re Uno Restaurant*); *In re Foamex International Inc.*, et al., Ch. 11 Case No. 09-10560 (KJC) (Bankr. D. Del. Feb. 18, 2009); *In re Aleris International, Inc.*, et al., Ch. 11 Case No. 09-10478 (BLS) (Bankr. D. Del. Feb. 12, 2009); *In re Tronox Incorporated*, et al., Ch. 11 Case No. 09-10156 (ALG) (Bankr. S.D.N.Y. Jan. 12, 2009); and *In re Lyondell Chemical Company*, et al., Ch. 11 Case No. 09-10023 (REG) (Bankr. S.D.N.Y. Jan. 6, 2009).

[57] Case No. 09-10478 (BLS) (Bankr. D. Del. Feb. 12, 2009).

[58] *In re Farmland Industries, Inc.* 294 B.R. 855 at p. 888 (Bankr. W.D. Mo., 2003).

[59] In the *Re Aleris* case, that case, the court bankruptcy court laid down what it considered as the factors to be considered by a bankruptcy judge when amendments to new financing agreement is sought but is resisted by other creditors. The court factors are: (i) That the proposed financing is an exercise of sound and reasonable business judgment; (ii) That the financing is in the best interests of the estate and its creditors; (iii) That the credit transaction is necessary to preserve the assets of the estate, and is necessary, essential, and appropriate for the continued operation of the Debtors' businesses; (iv) That the terms of the transaction are fair, reasonable, and adequate, given the circumstances of the debtor-borrower and the proposed lender; and (v) That the financing agreement was negotiated in good faith and at arm's length between the Debtors, on the one hand, and the Agents and the Lenders, on the other hand.

[60] Case No. 09-10023 (REG).

[61] See generally, Rapisardi and Davis (2009) (commenting on the economic downturn and how it negatively affected the chances of Lyondell obtaining better priced financing).

cases were decided after the credit crunch, still without any statements on the treatment of the clause, and without any indication that much will change.[62]

5.2.2 *The Use of Waivers and "Immunization" Clauses in New Financing Agreements*

In analyzing waiver clauses for the purpose of this chapter, a distinction can be drawn in terms of the timing and the nature of the clause. Regarding the timing, two types of such waivers need be distinguished. The first is that which is included as part of the original loan document i.e. pre-distress loan agreement between the debtor and a lender. The second is to do with waivers inserted into a subsequent loan agreement between the debtor and a lender, either pursuant to a workout, or as part of negotiations for the provision of new money to finance the formal restructuring. While it would appear that the former is regarded as impermissible,[63] the latter is focused upon here.

In the quest to adequately protect its interest, the provider of new money may introduce waiver clauses into the distress financing agreement. Three types of such clauses may be incorporated into distress financing agreements by the distress financer. The first is to do with the waiver of the pre-petition claims which the debtor may have against the lender. The second is to do with the waiver of the automatic stay, an important right which is afforded the debtor in formal restructuring. Thirdly, the pre-petition distress agreement may preclude junior lenders from providing new money to finance the formal restructuring of the debtor without the consent of the senior lender. These waiver clauses are examined anon.

5.2.2.1 Waiver of Debtor's Pre-Petition Claims

A pre-petition lender has additional cause for concern if it believes that there is the likelihood that validity or enforceability of its prepetition liens can be called into question due to deficiencies in documentation or the possibility of a pre-filing collateral attack.[64] In these circumstances, the extension of credit may be conditioned

[62] See for instance, Hinkes-Jones (2016) https://www.bna.com/dip-loans-costly-n57982065779/ (suggesting that interest rates for distressed lending are still as high as pre-crises period).

[63] See *Inre Atrium High Point Ltd. Partnership*, 189 B.R. 599, 607 (Bankr. M.D.N.C. 1995) where the court suggested this distinction between situations where the waiver of the automatic stay is inserted in the original loan agreement and where it is bargained for. See also the case of *In re Deb-Lyn. Inc*. 2004 Bankr. LEXIS 200 (N.D. Fla. Feb. 20, 2004), at 8–11 (as part of the reasoning of the court in refusing to enforce a waiver, it pointed out that the pre-petition waiver was not part of a confirmed reorganization plan, but was a pre-petition waiver); The latter form of waivers will be further addressed in the analysis of the consideration principle as a justification for financing agreements skewed in favor of distress lenders.

[64] A pre-petition collateral attack is in the nature of a challenge to security interest acquired by the

upon a waiver of actions that would contest the lender's recourse to pledged assets. The financing agreement may provide for the waiver of the right of the debtor to object to the pre-petition loan of the new money lender, this is especially where the new money lender is also a pre-petition lender. This waiver which often relates to a pre-petition loan extended by the lender may relate to questions of the validity, priority, or even the amount of the pre-petition loan.[65] The rationale for this clause is essentially to reassure the financer that after providing the distress financing, it will now be made to the defend its pre-petition interest against an attack by the debtor especially in the context of bankruptcy law.[66]

5.2.2.2 Automatic Stay Waiver (Relief from Automatic Stay)

As already established, the automatic stay is an essential tool for the restructuring of distressed businesses. However, lenders may seek a waiver of the right to an automatic stay when formal restructuring commences. In fact, it used to be the case that lenders may seek to exclude the right of the debtor to even opt for formal restructuring. The idea being to exclude the rights conferred by the Bankruptcy Code on the debtor within the formal restructuring framework.[67] It does however appear that rather than expressly waive the right of the borrower to seek respite from creditor harassment through a Chapter 11 filing, the lender may opt for more subtle language which achieves the same effect.[68] Such language may well easily bring the borrower within the ambits of relief from automatic stay as is provided for under

lender prior to the filing of the Chapter 11 petition.

[65] Kuney (2005), p. 64.

[66] Tabb (1990), p. 89 ("...before supporting the reorganization effort with new financing, the lender wants to be certain that, in a sense, the estate will not turn and bite the hand that fed it.").

[67] Such provisions are very likely to be held to be contrary to public policy. In the US, such provisions in loan contracts have been considered unenforceable by the courts on the grounds of public policy. In *In re Fallick*, 369 F.2d 899, 904 (2d Cir. 1966) ("[A]n advance agreement to waive the benefits of the [Bankruptcy] Act would be void."); *In re Tru Block Concrete Prod., Inc.*, 27 B.R. 486, 492 (Bankr. S.D. Cal. 1983) ("It is a well settled princip[le] that an advance agreement to waive the benefits conferred by the bankruptcy laws is wholly void as against public policy."); *In re Archambault*, 174 B.R. 923, 933 n.8 (Bankr. W.D. Mich. 1994) ("Ample case law exists suggesting that an agreement not to file bankruptcy is unenforceable because it violates public policy"); *In re Heward Brothers*, 210 B.R. 475, 479 (Bankr. D. Idaho 1997) ("... prepetition agreement to waive a benefit of bankruptcy is void as against public policy"). But see also White (2004), p. 186 (arguing that although the courts couch prohibition of such waivers in terms of public policy considerations, the courts are also concerned about redundancy. Author rhetorically asks: "If bankruptcy filings could be promised out of existence, then what is a bankruptcy judge to do for a living?").

[68] Such was the case in *In re Bryan Road LLC*, 382 B.R. 844 (Bankr. S.D. Fla. 2008). Where debtor and creditor had entered into a pre-petition forbearance agreement which entitled the creditor to the right to immediately seek relief from automatic stay if Chapter 11 petition was filed by the debtor.

Chapter 11.[69] It is possible that automatic stay waivers may not necessarily have concrete effect on other creditors especially as it pertains to their earnings where the pre-petition lender holds security over financial assets, or non-financial but liquid assets. This may be because the prior creditor is still entitled to be paid from the proceeds of the security when it is disposed of.[70] However, such a waiver may have a broader effect on other creditors and the distressed business, if the asset in question is such that is required for the purpose of achieving the restructuring of the distressed business. In that case, it may well defeat the purpose of the restructuring, to the extent that the asset is required to achieve a successful restructuring.

5.2.2.3 Waiver of Junior Lender Financing

As between a senior lender and a junior lender in the context of a syndicated lending to a borrower, it is not unusual that apart from the financing agreement which is binding between the borrower and the lenders, the lenders also reach agreement between themselves. These agreements known as inter-creditor agreements define the relationship between the lenders.[71] It is these inter-creditor agreements that define the rights between the tranches of lenders in relation to other tranches.[72] Amongst the several rights typically defined in the inter-creditor agreements is that which relates to the provision of new financing to the distressed business in the event of its formal restructuring. This may be an outright prohibition on the part of junior lenders to provide such financing or to tag-along a new financing provided or supported by the senior lender. Thus, the terms of the syndicated lending may exclude the prospects of the junior lender to provide new financing to the business when it is in distress.

5.2.2.4 The Problem with Waivers

Inherent in the design of waiver clauses is their capacity to inhibit the discretion of the courts, or generally interfere with the workings of the process of formal restructuring.[73] They inhibit the discretion of the court because they seek to co-opt the

[69] See generally, 11 USC § 362 (a) & (d). See Sect. 5.2.2.5 below on the judicial treatment of waivers.

[70] Schwarcz (1999), p. 554 (analyses waivers of automatic stay and how they affect the other creditors of the debtor).

[71] Berman and Lee (2011) Art. 1 (on inter-creditor agreements and their implications).

[72] Id ("including lien and payment priority, modifications of the credit agreement, the pursuit of remedies against the borrower in the event a default shall occur, the right to vote on a borrower's Chapter 11 plan and otherwise be heard in a borrower's bankruptcy case, etc.").

[73] See for instance, Guidelines for Financing Requests: United States Bankruptcy Court for the Southern District of New York, Int'l Insolvency Inst. at 8 (20 Mar 2002) ("Waivers: Extraordinary Provisions are those that divest the Court of its power or discretion in a material way, or interfere with the exercise of the fiduciary duties of the debtor or Creditors' Committee in connection with

direction of the restructuring, requiring the court to respect the agreement reached. The waiver of rights protected by the formal restructuring regime may sometimes go to the root of a successful formal restructuring. One such rule which the lender may seek to extract a waiver of it is the automatic stay. The automatic stay as was highlighted in Chap. 3 plays an important role in ensuring a successful rehabilitation of the distressed debtor.[74] What is more? One may think of the automatic stay as a "structural rule" that plays a significant role in protecting the efficiency of the system of formal restructuring, and a waiver of this right may be detrimental to the process of restructuring. This is because the collateral which is protected by the automatic stay may be more valuable to the firm than it is to the market. If this is the case, then the value of the estate of the debtor is maximized, in the absence of the waiver.

With a waiver of the automatic stay negotiated between the debtor and secured lender (for instance), and a foreclosure by the lender, there may be no way to determine the value of the collateral, resulting in a loss of value to the estate of the debtor, and a possible defeat of the restructuring process.[75] Further, advocates of this waiver justify it as a signal to creditors on the viability of the firm.[76] However, this may not necessarily be true as even bad debtors, in their desperation to restructure their debt may also employ signaling to convince lenders of viability, when indeed they are not. The result of the use of the waiver becomes the increased cost of signaling for good businesses.[77] Hence, allowing waiver of an automatic stay may stand in the way of a proper determination of the value of a collateral, thereby potentially depriving the estate of value and misinforming potential lenders whose participation in the restructuring process is crucial.

Furthermore, a strategic pre-petition lender may leverage on its provision of new financing for the restructuring process to silence possible challenges to transactions which if successful, may have the potential of increasing the value of the debtor's estate far more than the new money may.[78] An example may elaborate this concern. A pre-petition lender Bank X may have, in exchange for a pre-petition loan to Debtor Y, obtained collateral over the assets of Debtor Y. The estate of the debtor may have a credible avoidance claim against the collateral of Bank X. In this situa-

---

the operation of the business, administration of the estate, or the formation of a reorganization plan . . . .").

[74] See Chap. 3, Sect. 3.4.1.

[75] Schwartz (1998), p. 1839 ("to let a secured creditor … foreclose before the value issue is resolved would vitiate the reorganization process.").

[76] Bogart (1996), p. 1182 ("The Waiver of a stay provision might be a signal that borrower is confident that it controls a good project that is worth the effort of a loan workout, presuming that only a borrower convinced that it will not need to file for bankruptcy will waive its most substantial protection.").

[77] Ibid, 1176 (author argues that "[B]ad borrowers will grant concessions to lenders, making the process of distinguishing between good and bad borrowers difficult. The only option open to the good borrower then, is to adopt even more costly strategies of signaling the lender.").

[78] Tabb (1990), p. 87 (analyzes the potential for abuse arising from the use of pre-petition claim waivers in financing agreements).

tion, Bank X may provide financing, with the aim of extracting an agreement which waives the recourse of the estate of the debtor to its avoidance claims.[79] As between accepting the new loan on those terms, and pursuing avoidance claims, the borrower may have been successful in pursuing its avoidance claim, assuming it had the resources to sustain such a claim.

One approach to avoiding the likelihood that lenders exploit new financing to impair the chances of debtor rehabilitation is to prohibit waivers after the debtor has filed the petition for the commencement of formal restructuring.[80] This approach may not necessarily achieve much and may even be a little too late. This is essentially because the financing provided by the lender is often negotiated before the filing or commencement of formal restructuring, meaning that the loan agreement may already be in place at the time the debtor approaches the bankruptcy court with its request. In the light of the foregoing, it makes sense to now examine the treatment of waiver clauses by US courts.

5.2.2.5 Judicial Treatment of Waiver Clauses

The treatment of waiver clauses, like many lender protective provisions in financing agreements is not settled. When faced with waiver contracts, courts have in many cases justified their enforcement.[81] In the US case of *In re Club Tower*[82] involved a single-asset debtor who had entered into a permanent loan agreement with its secured lender, and granting the latter a waiver of automatic stay. The secured lender sought relief from automatic stay and the court granted same. The court in enforcing the waiver reasoned that the debtor has not been deprived of all the protections afforded it by bankruptcy law, but only as it pertains to automatic stay, and in respect of the particular creditor.[83]

On the public policy implication of such waivers, the court opined that the waiver of automatic stay did not violate public policy and that even the Bankruptcy Code did not provide the debtor a guarantee that the automatic stay will always be in

[79] This essentially sums up the situation in *In re Ellingsen MacLean Oil Co.* 834 F.2d 599 (6th Cir. 1987) where in the course of the reorganization proceedings, the consolidated pre-petition collaterals of the lenders running into millions of dollars was already subject to a fraudulent conveyance attack. The lenders thereafter obtained an emergency order from the court, allowing them to provide a financing package totaling about $235,000 in exchange for the waiver of all attacks to its pre-petition claims.

[80] In the US for instance, s. 558 of the US Bankruptcy Code makes unenforceable against the estate of the debtor, any waiver of defenses procured after the filing of the reorganization petition.

[81] *In re Citadel Properties, Inc.*, 86 B.R. 275 (Bankr.M.D.Fla.1988); *In re Club Tower* 138 BR 307, 310–312 (Bankr. N.D. Ga. 1991); *In re Hudson Manor Partners*, No. 91-81065HR 1991 WL 472592 (Bankr. N.D. Ga. Dec. 31, 1991); *In re Powers*, 170 B.R. 480 (Bankr.D.Mass.1994); *In re Atrium High Point Ltd. Partnership* 189 B.R. 599 (Bankr. M.D.N.C. 1995). This will be broadly addressed in the subsequent section on theories justifying the approval of such clauses.

[82] 138 BR 307, 310–312 (Bankr. N.D. Ga. 1991).

[83] Ibid at 312.

place.[84] Given the particular facts of this case, it is arguable that such a reasoning was suspect. This is because although the debtor may be able to rely on the other protections available through formal restructuring under Chapter 11 of the Bankruptcy Code, the other protections do little to facilitate a formal restructuring in the absence of an automatic stay. A closer look at the decision of the court will reveal that a stronger argument in support of that decision would be what the court perceived as the bad faith of the debtor whose reorganization filing coincided with the last day within which the debtor ought to have made payments to the lender under the workout agreement entered into between the debtor and pre-petition lender.[85]

In other US cases, the courts have put resistance to lender waiver clauses. The court *In the Matter of Pease*[86] declined to follow the line of cases approving waiver clauses. The court was faced with similar facts involving pre-petition agreement providing for the waiver of the bankruptcy right to automatic stay and in addition, the waiver of the right to resist the lender's motion to dismiss the case. It concluded that the debtor was not in the position to waive statutory rights conferred on it especially where such rights are fundamental to a successful formal restructuring.[87]

5.3 New Financing as Control Lever Over Distressed Borrower

Generally, the element of control plays a significant role in the process of formal restructuring, as the proper functioning of the process largely depends on its existence In fact, most jurisdictions recognize the place of ceding control and management of the assets of a debtor undergoing formal restructuring to an entity or official empowered to exercise control over, or manage the process of formal restructuring, or in the best case, the management of the business is subject to supervised management.[88] The exercise of control over the assets of the debtor lies at the heart of the bankruptcy procedure, given the necessity to maintain an orderly resolution of the indebtedness of the debtor.[89] The job description of this controller of the assets of

[84] Ibid at 311.

[85] In a similar case where the court enforced the automatic stay waiver, the debtor had filed for Chapter 11 an hour before a scheduled foreclosure in a one-asset debtor case, the court in addition to approving the automatic stay waiver considered the filing to have been done in bad faith. See *In re Citadel Properties, Inc.*, 86 B.R. 275, 276 (Bankr.M.D.Fla.1988).

[86] 195 BR 431 (Bankr. D. N1996).

[87] Id at 434.

[88] Westbrook (2004), p. 253 ("Control of the debtor's assets is a universal characteristic of bankruptcy regimes around the world. Virtually all of them use a property concept to give ownership or management of those assets to a publicly designated official or entity at the time of the opening of a bankruptcy proceeding.").

[89] Westbrook (2004), p. 824 (author highlights the importance of control in the bankruptcy process (including the process of formal restructuring of the debtor) to avoid the rush for the assets of the debtor).

the debtor is essentially to ensure the maximization of the value of the assets of the debtor, whether through a rehabilitation of the debtor, or the liquidation and distribution of those assets in the manner prescribed by law.

Ordinarily, a distinguishing feature of formal restructuring law in the US as conceptually designed leaves the debtor both in control of the business and the process of formal restructuring.[90] Also by its design, the law conceded the least possible control of the restructuring process to the lender,[91] and this was indeed the practice in the early years of formal restructuring.[92] However, secured creditors who lend to the distressed debtor have found a way to contract around the "debtor-centric" formal restructuring regime. The question then, is how does the lender achieve this control, asserting itself over the process of formal restructuring of the debtor?

5.3.1 *The Financing Agreement as Control Lever*

As it makes new money available to the debtor, the lender (who in many cases is the pre-petition secured lender) effectively takes charge of the distressed debtor through a variety of clauses in the financing agreement that effectively places the lender ostensibly in control of the restructuring process.[93] The financing of the distressed debtor has provided secured creditors a means through which they may assert control over the debtor as it undergoes formal restructuring. A known means by which

[90] 11 U.S.C. § 1107 (highlighting duties of company as a debtor in possession).

[91] See White (2004), p. 145–146 (The author enumerates the elements of DIP control in the Code to include the automatic stay, which effectively stopped foreclosure in its tracks, debtors expansive right to use and possibly sell collateral; the cutting off interests on the debt liability of the debtor during the process of formal restructuring, to the extent that the value of the collateral exceeded the value of the debt and; the exclusivity of plan proposal by the debtor, and the early practice of the bankruptcy courts in routinely extending the period of exclusivity).

[92] See Skeel (2004), p. 1916 ("For the first decade after the enactment of the 1978 Bankruptcy Code, the debtor and its managers seemed to control the course of many large-scale Chapter 11 cases.").

[93] See Weiss and Capkun (2007), p. 3 (Pointing out that secured creditors often provided DIP financing "and would thereby increase their influence over the bankruptcy process.") Miller & Waisman itemise some of the provisions of control in the financing agreement as follows:

> (i) requiring debtor to operate within a budget approved by the lenders; (ii) limiting disbursements other than those approved by the lenders in a budget; (iii) limiting the payment of prepetition claims even if approved by the court; (iv) requiring the debtor to meet a variety of performance hurdles related to, among other things, revenue, (v) limiting intercompany disbursements to non-debtors; (vi) requiring the rejection of executory contracts that the lenders believe unfavorable; (vii) requiring the payment of certain lease obligations; (viii) requiring the appointment of a chief restructuring officer approved by the lenders; (ix) requiring that certain assets be sold by certain fixed dates; (x) requiring the filing of a plan of reorganization by a fixed date; and (xi) requiring the debtor to obtain the court's approval of a disclosure statement by a fixed date.

See Miller and Waisman (2004), p. 185.

this is achieved is through the appointment of a third party over the distressed business through the financing agreement.

As it is often the case when businesses are in financial distress, the debtor does not straightway file for formal restructuring. When the debtor begins to undergo the strains of distress and the attendant decline, it begins to default on its loan obligations. This situation would require the debtor to seek to amend the terms of the financing with the lender, and in many cases, to enable the debtor access new funds to meet its cash flow needs.[94] In return for financing the debtor, the lender appoints a third party or institution saddled with responsibility of managing the business of the debtor, as well as in preparing the debtor for formal restructuring.[95] While it appears that the debtor actually does the appointment, the lender very much influences this decision in many a case, by providing a closed list of candidates who may be appointed to fill in the position.[96] This third party is often described as the Chief Restructuring Officer (CRO). As a consequence of the so-called appointment by the borrower, the CRO is compensated by the borrower.[97] In some other cases, the lender may insist on the outright removal of the Chief Executive Officer (CEO) of the debtor as the new financing arrangement is being put in place.[98] It has even been pointed out that a change in management prior to commencement of formal restructuring may well be because the lender has insisted on this.[99]

Another quite significant incident of control by the lender is through the imposition of both affirmative and negative covenants in the financing agreement, requiring the debtor to take particular actions, failure of which may entitle the lender to cut off the supply of financing to the debtor.[100] Given that the terms of the new financing have been worked out prior to entering bankruptcy, and the terms are conditions of the loan approved by the lender, there is nothing preventing the lender

---

[94] See Skeel (2004), p. 1917 (describing the commencement of the incident of control in the case of distressed businesses).

[95] Miller and Waisman (2004), p. 186 ("Major executive functions were vested in the [third party] and it was granted direct reporting and access to the debtor's governing body."); see also Baird and Rasmussen (2002), p. 1807 ("In large formal restructuring cases, the authors found that "at the moment Chapter 11 is filed, a revolving credit facility is already in place that entrusts decision making to a single entity. This entity will often step in to replace the management.").

[96] White (2004), p. 183 ("In the words of several bankruptcy lawyers familiar with the practice, the DIP may appoint anyone in the world--as long as that person is on the secured creditor's list of three approved candidates.").

[97] Id.

[98] See Rasmussen (2007), p. 82 ("The new CEO or the new CRO is often a turnaround specialist. These executives do not plan on staying with a company long; rather, they are attempting to right the ship. They stabilize operations and offer advice to the creditors as to the best course of action for the business.").

[99] Skeel (2004), p. 1918 (suggesting that a management turnover shortly before the company files for bankruptcy is often because the lenders have been pulling the strings).

[100] Id (citing the example of a covenants contained in the financing agreement of FAO Schwartz (the high-end US toy company) which authorized the financer to insist on the liquidation of the debtor if it is either unable to sell off its assets or to confirm a reorganization plan by a fixed date).

from enforcing such terms as a part of the financing agreement, if and when such clauses are breached.

5.3.2 *Lender Control and Its Complication*

When the process of restructuring is dominated by providers of new financing there arises the likelihood of misaligned interests between such a lender and other stakeholders. For this reason, it is doubtful whether the secured lender providing financing may, whilst exercising control, provide the required neutrality to ensure that the other stakeholders are not shortchanged in the formal restructuring process.[101] Recall that the appointed CRO is saddled with managerial responsibilities. In most cases, the interest of the CRO is aligned with that of the financer who has influenced its appointment as this may be its only guarantee for future appointments by the lender, given that both lender and CRO are repeat actors in formal restructuring.[102] As will be shown below, jurisdictions like the UK have devised statutory intervention in response to this issue.[103]

This however is not to say that in the course of protecting its interests through the exercise of control, no incidental benefit may accrue to the debtor or other creditors, or that such control may sometimes not be in the best interest of the debtor or at least a majority of the creditors.[104] The point however is that such control may provide a leeway for the diversion of value from other stakeholders in the estate of the distressed business, as well as precipitating a procedure that borders on the liquidation of the debtor.[105] One may think about this in terms of a fully secured lender who controls the restructuring process as a result of a blanket lien which it holds over the assets of the borrower. In that situation, the distressed borrower obviously has no means to fund the restructuring, and if the secured lender consents to the provision of such funding, then it becomes only available on the terms of that secured

[101] Westbrook (2004), p. 251 (The author rightly expresses doubt that the lender may act with sufficient neutrality, hence "all other parties would be required to discount heavily their chances of recovery in that process given secured party control.").

[102] Rasmussen (2007), p. 83 ("The need to get rehired on a constant basis provides a strong incentive to appease the creditors"); Lipson (2016), p. 278 ("[...] relational theory predicts that [the restructuring managers] may have greater loyalty to those whose relationships matter to them, such as those with who control the debtor's purse.").

[103] See Sect. 5.6 below.

[104] Skeel (2004), p. 1930 (author cites the examples of US Air and United Airlines restructuring, where in the exercise of control over the debtor, the DIP lender threatened a liquidation absent a significant wage concession by the employees, without which the debtor companies might not have been viable).

[105] See Adler (2004), p. 222 (author argues that in its new form, formal restructuring under Chapter 11 may tend more towards the liquidation of the debtor).

lender.[106] With such secured lenders in control of the process, absent any safeguards that assure the protection of other creditors, the result may be a perversion of the restructuring process and the deprivation of other constituent stakeholders that could have benefited from the successful restructuring.[107] These concerns have fueled the preference on the international scene, of a restructuring regime that favors a collective procedure not dominated by the secured lender through the contractual appropriation of the value in the distressed firm through its provision of new financing.

5.4 Lender Overreach Through New Financing Agreement: Critiquing the Theoretical Justifications for Special Clauses

What is most striking in most of the terms analyzed above is that they do not have express statutory backing. In other words, it is becoming even more apparent that in the context of new financing, contract is king.[108] In the same vein, and even more critical is the fact that the law does not expressly prohibit their use. Hence, these clauses may be said to stand in the grey zone, where the discretion of the courts becomes crucial. Instead, it might be necessary to situate them in the overall policy objective of the rehabilitation of distressed businesses, and the equal treatment of similarly placed creditors.[109] In addition, policy considerations may rest on competing objectives and the overall benefit that ensures the greater good or gain to the stakeholders of which the debtor is constituted. Some of the justifications which invariably support the financing agreement will be examined and will be weighed

---

[106] LoPucki et al. (2013), p. 1855 (Noting that even when such secured creditors allow a portion of the collateral to fund the restructuring, then it has to be "scripted to the secured creditors requirements.").

[107] In *In re Tenney Village Co. Inc.* 104 BR 562, at 568 (Bank. D.N.H. 1989), the New Hampshire bankruptcy court succinctly highlights the problem arising from the control of formal restructuring by the financer. It stated that:

> [u]nder the guise of financing a reorganization, the bank will disarm the debtor of all weapons used against it for the bankruptcy estate's benefit, place the debtor in bondage working for the bank, seize control of the reins of reorganization, and steal a match on the other creditors in numerous ways. The financing agreement would pervert the reorganization process from one designed to accommodate all classes of creditors and equity interests, to one specially crafted for the benefit of the bank .... It runs rough shod over numerous sections of the Bankruptcy Code.

[108] For an analysis of the growing use of contracting practices in formal restructuring by which lenders bypass statutory provisions, see Lipson (2016).

[109] For a contrary opinion on the most important goal of bankruptcy laws, see Westbrook (2004), p. 245 (arguing that the maximization of value for distribution to creditors through control is the overriding policy of formal restructuring or liquidation in the Bankruptcy Code).

against the overall policy on financing in the process of the rehabilitation of a distressed debtor.

5.4.1 The "Rehabilitation Goal" Facilitation Theory

If new financing shows better chances of facilitating the rehabilitation of the distressed business, courts may look favorably to the financing agreements, which favor lender. The rehabilitation goal holds a preeminent position as far as formal restructuring is concerned.[110] It is considered the overriding goal of the formal restructuring process.[111] Flowing from this, the role of the court is therefore to ensure that its actions yield this result.[112] To this extent, where there are clauses which are skewed in favor of the new money lender, such clauses should be approved by the court even if they are not strictly within the statutory incentive structure for new financing.[113] The principle that has continued to sustain the drive for incentivizing new money lending has been the unwillingness of lenders to finance failing debtors, hence the necessity of encouraging such lenders.[114] Importantly, this incentivizing is based on a more general policy that favors the successful rehabilitation of the debtor, for which new money is an essential part.

The provider of new financing contributes to the overall goal of achieving the successful rehabilitation of the debtor financing and this role is not lost on the courts who from time to time allow financing agreements often skewed in favor of the provider of new financing.[115] For instance, the court in *In re Ionosphere Club*[116] gives insight into this theory when it stated that the rehabilitation goal of the debtor

[110] Leepson (1996), p. 799 ("…rehabilitation is the predominant goal of chapter 11 reorganization, and that the goal of rehabilitation should be accorded greater weight in reorganizations….").

[111] See for instance the H. REP. No. 595, 95th Cong., 2d Sess. 220 (1978), reprinted in 1978 U.S.C.CA.N. 5787, 6179 ("The purpose of a business reorganization case, unlike a liquidation case, is to restructure a business's finances so that it may continue to operate, provide its employees with jobs, pay its creditors, and produce a return for its stockholders.") The courts have also re-echoed this position. See for instance *NLRB v. Bildisco & Bildisco* 465 U.S. 513, 528 (1984) ("[t]he fundamental purpose of reorganization is to prevent a debtor from going into liquidation, with the attendant loss of jobs and possible misuse of economic resources."); In *Caplin v. Marine Midland Grace Trust Co.* a 406 U.S. 416, 422–423 (1972) ("In contradistinction to a reorganization proceeding where liquidation of a corporation and distribution of assets is the goal, a Chapter X [a precursor to Chapter 11] proceeding is for the purposes of rehabilitating the corporation and reorganizing it.").

[112] See Leepson (1996), p. 803 (urging that courts invoke their equitable jurisdiction in approving special clauses in order to achieve the goal of debtor rehabilitation).

[113] See Chap. 4, Sect. 4.6.3.

[114] See the incentivizing theory below.

[115] Barnett (2003), p. 3 ("Bankruptcy courts understand the role of the DIP lender and, within limits, are willing to approve DIP financing agreements that disproportionately favor the DIP lender over the debt …").

[116] 98 B.R. 174 (Bankr. S.D.N.Y. 1989).

trumps all other goals of bankruptcy.[117] One could relate this opinion to the equitable powers of the court to decide on the manner in which even secured creditors may enforce their claims once a Chapter 11 petition has been filed, given the importance ascribed to the rehabilitation goal.[118] The advocates of this position agree that special clauses such as cross-collateralization or roll-ups are not part of the statutory incentive framework, however, they argue that such clauses draw their validity from their intrinsic role in achieving the overarching goal of rehabilitation as set forth in the Code.[119]

In re Lyondell Chemical Co.,[120] decided over a decade later, the bankruptcy court of the Southern Distress of New York gave approval of DIP Financing with substantial roll-up for the pre-distress lenders.[121] The court supported its approval as follows:

> The DIP financing provides the Debtors and European non[-]debtor affiliates with funding that is essential to their survival, and ultimately, the Debtors' ability to successfully reorganize. Loss of the DIP financing would doom their reorganization, resulting in the loss of billions of dollars of value essential to satisfying creditor claims and a loss of thousands of rank and file employee jobs.[122]

This re-echoes the notion that the approval of the new financing agreement, in spite of its provisions will equally be in keeping with the rehabilitation goal theory.

The difficulty with this theory rests on the assumption that once financing is provided to the distressed debtor, it automatically results in the successful rehabilitation of the distressed business. This is not necessarily so. In fact, what may well be in conflict with the ultimate rehabilitation goal of the distressed debtor is the capacity of some of the special clauses to extract value from the estate of the debtor. This is because, in addition to achieving protection for the post-petition loans, the clauses are couched in such a way that importantly increases the chances of the debtor paying up the pre-petition debt owed to the lender.[123] It is not out of place to argue that the provider of new money is motivated by the maximum recovery of its

---

[117] Ibid 176. Although the court pointed out that the goal of the equality of distribution could trump other considerations in a liquidation. Id.

[118] See Warren and Westbrook (2009), p. 604.

[119] Leepson (1996), p. 799 (arguing that the broad equity powers of the US bankruptcy courts allow them to approve financing agreement with clauses favorable to providers of new financing since it serves the goal of rehabilitation).

[120] 402 B. R. 571, (Bankr. S.D.N.Y. 2009).

[121] The court approved one of the largest DIP Financing provision of $ 8 Billion, about the largest single DIP loans in history. The sum consisted of a new term loan facility of $6.5 Billion, of which $3.25 Billion was in new term loan facility, and the other $ 3.25 Billion was a dollar-for-dollar rollup of pre-petition claims. The other $ 1.5 Billion was made up of ABL new loans which also rolled up the pre-petition ABL. (DIP Financing Order on file with author).

[122] *In re Lyondell Chemical Co.*, at 583.

[123] Tabb (1986), p. 119 ("... [t]he lender preference clauses are designed to enhance in different ways of, and the likelihood of repayment of funds already advanced prior to the filing of the Chapter 11 petition.").

investment, more than the broad policy of the rehabilitation of the debtor. Hence the special clauses which invariably bypass other strictures of the law which add up to ensuring the successful rehabilitation of the debtor. Theoretically therefore, the special clauses inserted into the financing agreements can be struck out from the financing agreement without affecting the rehabilitation goal of the statute.[124] This argument weakens any argument equating new financing to the rehabilitation goal.

5.4.2 *Incentivizing Policy Theory*

Another theory that seeks to justify special clauses in new financing agreements suggests that they are simply an extension of a statutory policy to motivate distress lending and protecting these special clauses in the new financing agreement only contributes to serves this purpose. This is so far as the clauses are not expressly prohibited by the Bankruptcy Code.[125] The principle stems from the reasoning that Chapter 11 envisages that the business of the debtor continues to operate whilst undergoing formal restructuring. It also recognizes the rather obvious need for new financing during this period, which financers are reluctant to provide, not only because of the distress of the debtor,[126] but also because the debtor may have no (or few) unencumbered assets to secure new financing.[127] Hence, allowing the provider of new financing the right to insert these clauses that may in fact exceed the scope of statutory protection invariably achieves the end of incentivizing the lender.[128] The following cases illustrates this.

In re Adams Apple, Inc.,[129] the ninth Circuit was faced with an appeal in which although other creditors had withheld consent to the approval of the distress loan, the bankruptcy judge had approved of the loan, and the district court had affirmed. In the case, the lender had agreed to provide financing to the tune of $450,000 and an optional additional $325,000, to enable the debtors produce crops in 1983, as well to preserve the horticultural quality of the debtors' orchards. In exchange for

---

[124] Id.

[125] See for instance Rickert (1993), p. 250 (on cross-collateralization, author argues that "[t]he Code does not explicitly authorize the practice of cross collateralization; however, it also does not strictly forbid it.").

[126] For instance, see: Telesca (1987), p. 110 (pointing out that the creditor is often uncertain whether outstanding debts will be collectible and is therefore very hesitant to extend further credit); Baiser and Epstein (1992), pp. 103–104 ("To counter the understandable reluctance of financial institutions to lend to Chapter 11 debtors, section 364 of the [Bankruptcy] Code provides incentives to lenders to provide financing to borrowers who are the subject of bankruptcy cases.").

[127] McCormack (2008), p. 177 ("New lenders however have no great incentive to lend since the company is in difficulties, and by definition, any loan will run the risk of not being repaid in full.").

[128] Bohm (1985), p. 290 (commenting on the inclusion of cross-collateralization clauses in the financing agreement, the author argues that it is meant to convince lender to provide additional financing to debtor who has just filed Chapter 11 petition for reorganization).

[129] 829F.2d 1484 (9th Cir. 1987).

these facilities, the lender was to be granted a security interest with superpriority status, ahead of all other creditors in the 1983 crops. In addition, the crops were to secure a pre-petition unsecured loan of $450,000 provided the debtor in 1982. In the hearings held by the bankruptcy judge, the other creditors (secured and unsecured) objected to the cross-collateralization clause.

In analyzing the cross-collateralization clause in the financing agreement, the ninth Circuit first considered the scope of s. 364 of the US Bankruptcy Code, which essentially incentivizes new financing. The court reasoned that the section allows the bankruptcy court to use a variety of financing devices, although there is no indication from the express wordings of the section that allows the pre-petition debt of a lender to move up the priority ladder, ahead of pre-petition debts of equal priority.[130] The court however proceeded to point out that the essence of s.364 of the US Bankruptcy Code is to ensure that debtor can access financing whilst undergoing formal restructuring. Any conditions in the financing agreements necessary to obtain the financing were covered under the section.[131] Relying on an earlier case,[132] the court reasoned that the essence of s. 364 is to motivate lenders who would otherwise be unwilling, to provide financing to a distressed business. In motivating a good faith lender to finance a distressed debtor, the section allows the new financer to rely on the authorization of the loan by the bankruptcy court judge. Instructively, the court proceeded to point out that since protecting the validity of clauses in the financing agreement which motivated the lender to provide financing contributes to overcoming the unwillingness of the lender, it followed that cross-collateralization clauses in this context were protected.[133]

It is important to disclose here that this argument was relied upon by the court in treating a procedural question relating to the mootness of an appeal against a cross-collateralization clause contained in a financing agreement which has been approved by the bankruptcy court. However, the case is instructive because the reasoning of the court offers a justification for the cross-collateralization clause in the agreement. The ninth Circuit preferred to treat the clause as an integral part of the incentive structure of s. 364 of the Code. As such, to the extent that the Code seeks to ensure the availability of new financing for the distressed debtor, a lender who volunteers to lend to a debtor in this state deserves to have his bargain protected.

The sixth Circuit followed the same principle *In re Ellingsen Maclean Oil Co. Inc.*[134] In this case, the debtor who supplied heating oil to homes was hard put to access financing with which to supply its customers in the Christmas week of 1984. The unavailability of cash during this period may well have dealt a deathly blow to the business of the debtor and was as such in dire need of the funds. The debtors' pre-petition secured creditors were to provide new financing, but on the conditions, that require the cross-collateralization of their pre-petition unsecured loan and the

[130] Ibid at 1488.

[131] Id.

[132] *Matter of EDC Holding Company* 676 F.2d 945, 947 (7th Cir.1982).

[133] 829F.2d 1490.

[134] 834 F2d.

immunization of their pre-petition secured loan from all questions pertaining to the validity of their security interests.[135] The bankruptcy court approved the financing agreement which provided for these special clauses. The other creditors of the business appealed. In the meantime, the lender had provided the funds to the debtor.

The court first takes the position that the approval of the financing agreement with a cross-collateralization and a claim immunization clause did not exceed the scope of the protection of new financing in the US Bankruptcy Code. Hence the financing agreement enjoyed the full protection of the Code on new financing. The court went a step further to concede that even if these special clauses exceeded the scope of protection of s. 364 of the Bankruptcy Code, it sufficed that the orders were granted pursuant to the section, and was relied upon by the lender to provide financing to the debtor.[136] On the statutory policy to motivate new lending and how these clauses express this policy, the court stated that the clauses:

> … were necessary to induce the banks to extend more credit in a risky situation. Since the debtor was experiencing continuing losses, more was at risk. The collateral base of the Banks was being depleted. Thus, if [new financing protection] was only limited in all cases to new advances, creditors might not be willing to extend more credit, and debtors will fail, probably after depletion of assets and collateral; all creditors would be losers in that situation.[137]

Both cases tend to treat special clauses in financing agreements as a necessary extension of the incentive structure of bankruptcy law. The principle supposes that special clauses in new financing agreements are allowable costs for the decision to provide new financing to enable the debtor continues as a going concern. The reasoning of the courts in these cases is somewhat problematic. The consequence of this argument followed to its logical conclusion, is to treat the interest of the lender as preeminent over all the competing interests and policies encompassed in bankruptcy law and represented in the restructuring of the distressed debtor. More than this, it becomes difficult to exclude any clauses, irrespective of their practical implication for the restructuring process.[138] It therefore suggests that no matter what the lender inserts into the financing agreement, it is beyond reproach because the focus of the law is to (by all means, and at all cost), incentivize the provision of new money. This certainly cannot be, especially if it is agreed that there may well be clauses that unfairly tilt the balance in the restructuring process so much in favor of the lender who is in any case the stronger party.[139] Hence if the incentivizing

---

[135] Ibid at 600-1.

[136] The court rhetorically asked, "[i]f an order exceeded the scope of s. 364(c), is it not entitled to s.364(e) protection, if purportedly granted under s.364(c) and relied un by the debtor and lending party in good faith?" Ibid at 602.

[137] Ibid at 604.

[138] Tabb (1989), p. 120 (pointing out that this argument tends to suggest that "any clause in a financing order, no matter how egregious or how violative of the bankruptcy laws …" is irreproachable).

[139] Id (suggesting that the courts in both *Adams Apple* and *Ellingson* took into cognizance the fact that the disputed clauses were not in fact very offensive).

argument is stretched this far, it may well create an absurdity unintended by the law, calling the fairness of the formal restructuring process into question.

Furthermore, it is not always true that the inability to access financing stems from the unwillingness of lenders to lend generally. In some cases, it is the pre-petition secured lender who excludes the chance of junior lenders to provide distress finance, for fear of a priority contest. So, the argument that there is no other lender willing to provide financing may be the making of the pre-petition lender offering new money. It is argued here that at least, as far as the pre-petition lender has already shut out a class of possible lenders, it has somewhat stifled or excluded competition. This competition may well have been the game changer and clearly shown alternative source of financing.[140]

The other way to look at this is that if lenders with full information on the debtor are all unwilling to provide financing other than on the basis of such clauses, it may be a pointer to the viability of the debtor, so that a liquidation may better benefit the stakeholders of the business.[141] Taking out the possibility that the unwillingness to lend speaks of the health of the debtor, there are two likely motivations which cannot be considered to be in line with the policy of achieving the rescue of the distressed debtor. In fact, these policies may be regarded as antithetical to the policy of rescuing viable businesses. The first of these motivations will be the desire on the part of the pre-petition lender to put itself in a better position than it would otherwise have been, in the likelihood that the debtor fails and falls into a liquidation. On the part of the debtor, it may just be postponing a liquidation, which if it had been timeously pursued, would have probably better benefitted the other stakeholders of the debtor.[142]

Finally, given the prescriptive approach that already exists in the formal restructuring framework in the US, the incentivizing policy theory proves insufficient to support new financer overreach through such clauses. The policy in formal restructuring is to promote financing advanced during the process of the restructuring.[143] Therefore, it can be argued that clauses that sneak in the favorable treatment of pre-petition loans, through the instrumentality of financing agreements should not be factored into the incentive principle. In other words, there necessarily has to be a

[140] Perechocky (2012), p. 562 (arguing that competition has the capacity to reduce the cost of distress financing for the debtor, or even raise the price of the assets of the debtor in the event that a sale is to be effectuated under s.363 of the Bankruptcy Code, and provide overall benefits for the estate of the debtor and its creditors as a whole).

[141] Although in this case, the lender may not enjoy priority over the providers of financing for the liquidation.

[142] Perechocky (2012), p. 562 ("The only benefit of allowing these special provisions would be to enable the pre-petition lender to cut its losses and recover more than it would otherwise, and to enable the debtor to gamble to stay alive, at the expense of the other creditors.").

[143] See generally, Tabb (1989), p. 119 (Commenting on the s. 364 of the US Bankruptcy Code which incentivizes new financing, author points out that what the law seeks to protect is the providers of financing post-petition "… permitting the lenders to rely on the finality of the authorizing financing order.").

limit to the incentives enjoyed by the new financer, especially where it impairs statutory provisions, and upends the balance of the law.[144]

5.4.3 The "Consideration" Theory

Another argument in support of clauses hugely skewed in favor of the new money lender may draw from the common law contract principle of consideration. Consideration, an elementary principle in Anglo-American contract law, is concerned primarily with the exchange of value between the contracting parties.[145] In other words, as a result of the bargain for exchange between the parties, one party voluntarily takes on an obligation arising from the agreement in exchange for an act or forbearance by the counterparty.[146] The principle of consideration plays a role in providing justification for the terms of the financing agreement between the debtor and its creditor. In this sense, financing agreements are considered to be a part of the package of pre-petition loans, defaults, and forbearances or concessions on the part of the pre-petition lender (especially in respect of pre-petition loans), in addition to the refinancing facility which the lender has agreed to provide the debtor.[147] The forbearance on the part of the lender entitles it to the benefits conferred upon it by the debtor in the financing agreement.[148] According to this principle, the fact of

[144] See for instance, the opinion of the court *In re Saybrook*, where the court reasoned that notwithstanding the objective of restoring the debtor to profitability through the new financing, such an end cannot be justification for the circumvention of the provisions of the Bankruptcy Code.

[145] As provided for in the 2nd Restatement on Contracts § 72, with certain exceptions, performance which is bargained for is considered a consideration. § 71 highlights the constituents of consideration as follows:

(1) To constitute consideration, a performance or a return promise must be bargained for:
(2) A performance or return promise is bargained for if it is sought by the promisor in exchange for his promise and is given by the promise in exchange for that promise.
(3) The performance may consist of
   (a) an act other than a promise, or
   (b) a forbearance, or
   (c) the creation, modification, or destruction of a legal relation.
(4) The performance or return promise may be given to the promisor or to some other person.

It may be given by the promise or by some other person.

See also Arvind (2017), p. 59 (explicates the principle of consideration in English common law as "something of value, which one party gives in exchange for the promise made, or performance rendered by the other party.").

[146] See *E.J.Baehr v. Penn-O-Tex Oil Corp.*, 104 N.W.2d 661, 662. ("Consideration requires voluntary assumption of obligation by one party upon condition of act or forbearance by other.").

[147] See for instance, Miller and Murray (2006), p. 361 ("such agreements are supported by new and valuable consideration in the form of the lender's forbearance from exercising its legal rights and remedies as well as other lender concessions and accommodations.").

[148] Of course, in reality, the clauses are not necessarily negotiated by the parties but is imposed by

forbearance on the part of the lender renders any objections of the debtor to the clauses to be of no effect.[149]

This principle has formed the basis for the decision of bankruptcy courts in a number of US cases, especially those involving the waiver of the automatic stay,[150] a key protection in formal restructuring. *In re Atrium High Point Ltd. Partnership*[151] Pursuant to the contract modification agreement between the debtor and its lender in an earlier bankruptcy proceeding, where the lender had reduced interest rates payable by the debtor, extended the loan maturity date and refinanced the loan, the debtor had undertaken to refrain from challenging any motion the lender may file for relief from the automatic stay in a subsequent bankruptcy case. When the debtor filed for bankruptcy again in the following year, the lender sought relief from the automatic stay, which debtor opposed. The court in granting the debtor relief opined:

> Although an order of this court granting relief from stay may debilitate the Debtor somewhat, the Debtor accepted that risk when it agreed to the prepetition waiver of the automatic stay. There was no prepetition waiver in the original loan agreement or under the First or Second Modification. The agreement not to object to the motion to lift stay was bargained for under the Third Modification and under this Debtor's first confirmed plan of reorganization. The Debtor received a lower interest rate and a five-year extension of the loan. Ohio National received the Debtor's covenant not to oppose a motion to lift stay in a subsequent bankruptcy filing.[152]

The court in *In re Shady Grove Tech Center Associates Ltd.Partnership*[153] reasoned along these lines when it held the waiver in favor of the pre-petition lender (who also provided new financing) enforceable. Amongst other factors which weighed on the mind of the court was the existence of:

> *a material, significant, and substantial consideration given by the lender for the waiver provision*, in the context of a restructuring agreement (including a reduced interest rate, an

---

the lender. See Tabb (1986), p. 170 ("In the reported cases involving cross-collateralization, the financing terms do not appear to be negotiated they seem to be presented more on a take-it-or-leave-it basis.").

[149] In cases (especially involving waivers) where the other creditors object, it is very much likely that the court will take their objection into consideration. The objection must not however come from the debtor who has enjoyed the forbearance on the part of the lender. See *In re Cheeks*, 167 B.R. 819–820 (Bankr. D.S.C. 1984).

[150] The consideration principle could be regarded as relevant in respect of other clauses, such as those that pertain to interest rate. The court *In re Defender Drug Stores, Inc.* 145 BR 312, 316 (B. A. P. 9th Cir. 1992) framed the consideration principle as compensation for the distressed lender for the use of the money of the lenders as well as for forbearance in exercising its rights and remedies following a borrower default.

[151] 189 B.R. 599 (Bankr. M.D.N.C. 1995).

[152] Ibid 609. The bankruptcy court re-echoed a similar sentiment in *In re Powers* 170 B.R. 480, 483 (Bkrtcy.D.Mass.,1994) ("In the instant case the Debtor received relief under the forbearance agreement approximating that which would have been available in a bankruptcy proceeding. The Pending foreclosure sale was canceled, the foreclosure action was dismissed, and the Debtor gained an opportunity to start a new payment schedule....").

[153] 227 B.R. 422 (Bankr. D. Md. 1998).

advance of new money, an extension of the maturity date of the loan, and capitalized interest payment[154] [emphasis supplied].

There is some plausibility in the consideration theory. This is especially so if the dynamics and techniques employed in distress financing by pre-distress lenders are borne in mind. The lender who already has an outstanding pre-distress loan offers to refinance its pre-distress loan, using a line of revolving credit. So, what we have on the one hand, is a loan granted to the debtor before it became distressed. On the other hand, the lender, as distress financer extends distressed financing which is characteristically for a short term, being a revolving line of credit.[155] When the prepetition lender providing new financing, makes liquidity advance, or provides relief to the debtor, modify its loan covenants by making them less restrictive; it is believed that the lender has provided value to the debtor.[156] Argument along these lines supported the decision of the court *In re Colt*,[157] to approve DIP loan which contained a roll-up clause, in spite of shareholder's objection.[158] In that case, attorneys for the management had expressed their preference for the DIP financing terms with the roll-up clause because it afforded the borrower lower interest rates, covenant relief and flexibility.[159] The court in making it final Order approving the DIP, also pointed out the concessions made by the DIP lender in terms of an exchange of value as it noted that "the overall financing terms are appropriate and the roll-up provisions had been softened as a result of concessions negotiated…".[160]

On the face of it, this presupposes two transactions that—as David A. Skeel Jr. suggests[161]—should be treated as distinct transactions. However, the revolving nature of the credit line may be such that for every time the debtor makes a payment on the loan, the pre-petition debt is reduced and for every advance of new money by

[154] Id at 425.

[155] Chatterjee et al. (2004), p. 3105 ("DIP loans are usually made in the form of revolving line of credit (RLC) either for less than one year (25% of the loans) or over a year (60% of the loans) and in many cases (25% of the RLC facilities), the RLC is accompanied by a term loan and/or a letter of credit....").

[156] Schwarcz (1999), p. 564 (arguing that in such situations, the debtor has received something of value which benefits the debtor by easing its illiquidity).

[157] *In re Colt Holding Co.*, No. 15-11296 (Bankr. D. Del. June 15, 2015).

[158] Limited Objections of Sciens Capital management LLC (shareholders) to Debtors' Proposed Alternative DIP Financing at 4, *In re Colt Holding Co.*, No. 15-11296 (Bankr. D. Del July 2, 2015).

[159] See Debtors' Statement in Further Support of Debtor's Motion, *In re* Colt Holding Co., No. 15-11296 (Bankr. D. Del. July 8, 2015), 4.

[160] Final Order: *In re* Colt Holding Co., No. 15-11296 (Bankr. D. Del. July 10, 2015).

[161] Skeel (2004), p. 1928 (the author whilst proposing a solution to the overreach by pre-distress lenders through financing agreements proposed that the transactions (pre-petition loan and distress financing) be treated differently. He further opines that "[t]he ideal way to separate old and new would be to treat them as entirely separate loans, each with its own collateral and bankruptcy treatment. Payments on the new loan will be treated as an administrative expense, and the loan would be secured by whatever lien the court approved. The old loan by contrast, would be entitled to priority to the extent of any collateral, while the remainder would be treated as an unsecured claim").

the pre-petition lender, the principal balance of the so-called new financing is increased.[162] What this (in addition to other concessions) shows is that the lending transaction may in principle, be two different transactions, but in reality, both transactions are often so connected that it may be indeed a tall order to disentangle the contractual elements of each transaction. In other words, it may well be difficult, for instance, to draw the boundaries between the considerations of which the pre-petition loan now consists, as distinct from that of the new money.

The consideration theory may well be considered the building block on which the recommendation of the American Bankruptcy Institute (ABI) recommendation on the approval of cross-collateralization rests.[163] Take for instance the use of cross-collateralization clauses in new financing agreements. It was recommended that approval for such clauses should be allowed by the courts "only for the purpose of providing adequate protection … and only to the extent that such [clause] covers any decrease in the value of the secured creditor's collateral as of the petition date."[164] Adequate protection is suggestive that there is an interference with certain rights of the pre-distress lender whether as a result of the sale of the collateral or the subjection of the asset to security rights. When a pre-distress lender allows such interference with its previously acquired interest, this may be considered a kind of forbearance, for which cross-collateralization is considered permissible.

The plausibility of the consideration principle holds strong until we realize that upon the commencement of formal restructuring proceedings, the transaction between the debtor and the lender takes on more parties with individuated contracts. The business debtor itself is generally involved in a web of contracts and the negotiations in formal restructuring makes this even more so.[165] Therefore, the consideration principle justifying financing agreements skewed in favor of the new money lender will be manifestly unfair to other creditors, especially, unsecured creditors who are not themselves parties to the negotiation of the financing agreement.[166] How is this so? When the debtor, in its quest for self-preservation[167] exchanges

[162] See White (2004), p. 182 (explaining the way the rollup clause works in practice states that "[e]ach payment on the loan reduces the pre-petition debt and each advance on the revolving loan increases the principal balance of the post-petition [s. 364) loan. When the loan has gone through one complete cycle after the filing, it has all become post-petition secured debt entitled current interest and heightened priority.").

[163] See American Bankruptcy Institute, Final Report of Commission to Study the Reform of Chapter 11, Commission to Study the Reform of Chapter 11, 68 (ABI, 2014). It is worth noting that while the Commission recommended the disallowance of some of such clauses such as the granting of lien or waiver of avoidance action as well as rollups that "provide little or no value to the estate."

[164] Ibid, at 68.

[165] For an analysis of the corporation as a web of contracts, see generally, Allen (1993), p. 1400.

[166] See *In re Shady Grove Tech Center Associates Ltd. Partnership*227 B.R. 422 (Bankr. D. Md. 1998). (the court considered as a condition for the approval of a waiver clause, the fact that there was no material impairment of the rights of third parties as there was no equity in the asset of the debtor, and the dispute in the case was between the debtor's equity holders and the lender).

[167] See *In re Texlon Corp.*, 596 F.2d 1092, 1098 (2nd Cir. 1979) (suggesting that the debtor in possession is itself hardly ever neutral and is more concerned about its own survival, even at the cost of treating the creditors equally).

promises and the lender agrees to forbear, the unsecured creditors are much more at the receiving end of the possible negative fallout of the transaction.[168] If it happens that formal restructuring is impossible and the debtor is to be liquidated, unsecured creditors who have not benefited from the so-called consideration will bear the burden of receiving less payment than they will have been entitled to, in the absence of the special clauses.[169]

Indeed, it may be argued that the process of formal restructuring gives the unsecured creditors an opportunity to air their views on the terms of the financing agreement, through the unsecured creditors committee.[170] However, the formation of this committee may sometimes only come into existence after the debtor has already obtained an interim financing order.[171] By this time, there might not be very much the unsecured creditors committee may be able to achieve, in terms of protecting the interest of the unsecured creditors, given that it hardly has time on its hands to prepare to mount a challenge on the financing order.[172] Of course it may well be argued that the other creditors may partake in the overall benefits of the concessions and forbearances, in addition to the new financing extended by the pre-petition lender providing new financing.[173] However, this does not equate to a bargain between the other creditors and the pre-petition creditor provider of new financing.

5.4.4 *The "Whole Package" Theory*

Usually, when the financing agreement is negotiated with the debtor, it is done as a whole, and contained in one financing order. It is on this basis that the whole package theory posits that such financing agreement be entitled to protection as if it were protected under the statutory incentive scheme of s. 364 of Chapter 11. This is so, even when the clauses are beyond what is provided for in the Code. The theoretical

---

168 Goss (1991) Chapter 11 of the Bankruptcy Code: An Overview for the General Practitioner. Utah B.J. 4(9): 6, at 7 (arguing that special lender clauses often are "approved even though the debtor must make significant concessions that affect the interests of other creditors.").

169 White (2004), p. 190 (argues that "…to some degree, the DIP is truly spending the form the unsecured [creditors'] purse when it strikes a deal with the DIP lender.").

170 11 U.S.C.§ 1102(a)(1).

171 Wolfson and Kochis (2013) (Pointing out that for reasons which include difficulty in finding unsecured creditors willing to seat on the unsecured creditor's committee, or a rough start to the restructuring, the interim financing order may have been obtained before the Committee of unsecured creditors is formed, or their counsel appointed).

172 Id ("Hence, [unsecured creditors'] committee counsel may find itself scrambling to understand a large amount of information in a compressed timeframe to prepare to challenge the financing order.").

173 Schwarcz (1999), p. 564 (author argues for instance, that a stay waiver may result in offsetting benefits for creditors where something of value has been demanded and given by the debtor.); Schwarcz (1997), p. 443–449 (arguing that secured lending through pre-bankruptcy contracting not only reduces the chances of default on the part of the debtor, but also facilitates a potential increase in the value of the claim of unsecured creditors).

ground for this position is that the lender had negotiated the financing terms as a single and integrated "package"[174] especially as the lender "may have given up some other potential benefits in exchange for the lender preference clauses."[175] The severance of the special clauses from the financing agreement by the court may therefore tamper with the fairness of the agreement reached by the parties,[176] and may distort the intention of the parties as at the time of the negotiation of the financing agreement. Therefore, the portion of the statutorily protected agreement saves the whole agreement.[177]

It does appear that this theory bears some similarity to the consideration argument especially as it pertains to the argument against severability and the fact that the lender may well have given something of value to entitle the lender to the benefit of these clauses.[178] Again, the problem with this position is that it views the financing agreement as between the debtor and the financer, excluding other interests. In another sense, it is similar to the incentivization argument as it considers the approval of the agreement as consisting of acts and forbearances which ought not to be separated but treated as a whole. Again, the problem with this theory is that it may provide a veritable leeway for lenders to abuse their position, to the detriment of other stakeholders.

From the foregoing, one may see that theoretically, there may not be a very sound basis for the additional benefits which providers of new financing seek to achieve especially in the light of the already prescribed incentives of the US Bankruptcy Code, as well as the broader goals of restructuring. One must also be quick to add that in some cases, lender capture through new financing agreements have been justified on the credit crunch, but it does not appear that much has changed following the credit crunch. On the other hand, on the control by new financers, it clearly appears that there is much concession in favor of providers of new financing, which somewhat indicates a practical shift away from the whole concept of DIP as it used to be known. What therefore is of utmost importance is the balancing of interests between the stakeholder classes, with a view achieving the goals of restructuring without unduly shortchanging other creditor classes. The section that follows examines how new financing and control have been managed in the UK and Germany. Again, it is important to note that the jurisprudence in the US is richer in these issues compared to European jurisdictions like the UK and Germany.

---

[174] The court in *In re Ellignsen* whilst dealing with a claims waiver clause referred to the financing agreement as a package containing this clause. See at 602.

[175] Tabb (1989), p. 122. See the consideration theory in Sect. 5.4.3 above.

[176] See *Evans v Jeff D*, 106 S. Ct. 1531, 1537(Regarding a settlement case, the US Supreme Court reasoned that courts may be allowed to approve or reject a settlement proposal but may not modify the terms of the agreement and compel the parties to accept the modified agreement).

[177] Tabb (1989), p. 122 (suggesting that the theory may be termed salvation by agreement because special clauses which may otherwise be struck down are protected by the part of the agreement that comply with the law).

[178] See the criticism of the consideration theory in Sect. 5.4.3 above.

5.5 Distress Financing and Lender Control: A Case of Practical Convergence Between the US and Europe?

At the core of this chapter are certain problems which have come to be associated with the financing of the business in distress. Particularly regarding control of the distressed business, it would appear that despite strong orientation of US restructuring law towards control by the distressed borrower, in practice, there is a growing shift that makes the practice less reflective of this statutory leaning. While the framework in the UK and Germany for instance are designed in ways that allow creditors control the process, as the prevailing trend suggests, US creditors are achieving the same results through their new financing agreements.

To be sure, some measure of control, exercised by the lender over the distressed debtor plays a significant role in checking the excesses of the management. Most significant is the role the lenders may play in preventing management from pursuing risky investment strategies with available assets, the result being a depletion of the assets which should serve to repay the general body of creditors.[179] This is especially so if we consider the ease with which the distressed business may lose value.[180] Thus, exerting control over the management of the debtor may prove valuable to not just the controlling lender, but possibly to the general body of creditors as well.

What the problems have revealed is that in many cases, the provider of financing seeks to contract its way into achieving the best possible value for financing advanced to the debtor both pre-distress, and that meant to facilitate the formal restructuring. This desire of the lender, achieved through clauses that control the debtor and/or enhance lender recovery interfere with the interests of other constituents, in such a way that may well border on fairness and the survivability of the distressed business. It does appear that until now, the US Bankruptcy Code has not addressed such issues, especially because the design of the law is still debtor-oriented. Even with the growing list of alternatives to formal restructuring which debtors (motivated by lenders) are now inclined to explore,[181] it is of interest to see how and why some of the high.

[179] Armour et al. (2008), p. 152 ("once companies become financially distressed "concentrated creditor" governance may serve to correct any tendency for the directors to "bet the firm" by committing to high risk strategies in which remote future benefits (the pay offs to all stakeholders in the unlikely event that such strategies succeed) are pursued with assets that in economic, if not strictly legal, terms are "owned" by the creditors.").

[180] Baird and Rasmussen (2001), p. 922 (n4) (authors cite the example of the teen fashion retailer Merry-Go-Round, which found itself in Chapter 11 with more than $100 million in cash but had lost the money and nearly all of its assets within 1 year).

[181] Fleet (2012). ('Over the past several years, a growing number of companies have vigorously sought to avoid the bankruptcy court process and have embarked on such trends as out-of-court negotiations, assignment for the benefit of creditors (ABC) or state receivership and Article 9 foreclosures under the Uniform Commercial Code (UCC) ("friendly foreclosures")').

5.6 Secured Lender Control: A Case for Carve-Outs and Fiduciary Duties

Today, what is seen in the US as an increased lender control of the restructuring process is not particularly new in the UK. Traditionally, this control of the restructuring process by the lender explains the description of the English bankruptcy system as "creditor controlled".[182] More so the drive of formal restructuring law in the US towards a contractual model is a trajectory through which the English formal restructuring law has come. Under the English receivership system for instance, the floating charge holder was a concentrated secured creditor who, exercised substantial control over the governance of the distressed debtor.[183] This was achieved at common law through *ex ante* contracting of the allocation of control rights upon the distress of the debtor as well as the allocation of bankruptcy rights in insolvency. Although this was essentially contracting on the face of it, the fate of the distressed business was that of the floating charge holder to decide as it was within its power to appoint a receiver over the assets covered by the floating charge,[184] who is charged with the liquidation of the assets of the debtor for the benefit of the floating charge holder.[185] The choice to restructure the distressed business through the administrative receiver depended on whether it increases the recovery of the appointing creditor.[186] Especially for unsecured creditors, there was indeed a fundamental fairness problem with this system as the US *contractualism* regime today reveals. The lender had more or less the liberty to appropriate the value of the firm for itself, notwithstanding the losses which the unsecured creditors and other constituencies had to put up with.[187] This the lender could do through its receiver.

---

[182] A clear manifestation of this is the growing popularity in the use of blanket liens by secured creditors over all of the assets of the borrower, whose perfection is now largely simplified by Article 9 of the UCC. See Vance and Barr (2003), pp. 379–380 (on the now increased power afforded secured creditors over the assets of borrowers under the reformed UCC Article 9); Ayotte and Morrison (2009), p. 523 (noting that over 90% of new financing facilities are by either all or almost all of the assets of the distressed business); Warner (2011), p. 525 (on how the revision to UCC Article 9 is unduly skewed in favor of secured creditors); Harner (2015), pp. 515–517 (discussing how blanket liens, combined with term lending can now effectively place secured creditors in control over the distressed business).

[183] See Walters (2015), p. 560 ("Before the Enterprise Act, bankruptcy and secured transactions law were structured so as to confer significant formal control rights on secured creditors.").

[184] Indeed, the floating charge has been described as a tool for control, as against fixed charge which is for priority. See generally, Westbrook (2004), p. 820.

[185] Armour et al. (2008), p. 153 (authors point out that prior to reform, "a secured creditor holding an all-encompassing general floating charge was free to contract for the right to appoint an administrative receiver to take control of the company's affairs, realize the charged assets and repay that creditor's debt from the proceeds of realization.").

[186] See Kirshner (2015), p. 527.

[187] See Lightman and Moss (2011), pp. 26–27 (on the powers of the receiver); see also Walters (2015), p. 561 ("Prima facie, receivers had little or no accountability to junior creditors.").

The first wave of corporate insolvency law reform in the UK remarkably introduced the administration procedure, a procedure intended to give heightened attention to the rescue of the company (compared to the interests of the floating charge holder), amongst other considerations.[188] It however still left enormous powers in the hand of the floating charge holder as it could bypass the administration order to appoint an administrative receiver in its place.[189] This therefore meant that the appointment of an administrator required the consent of all the holders of a floating charge. Given that they could bypass such an appointment. This had implications for administration procedure, which bordered on conflict of interest. Commenting on this constraint for an administrator under the initial IA 1986, one author noted that:

> [s]ince an administrator can only be appointed if debenture-holders agree, this procedure cannot be viewed as offering the debtor protection from impatient creditors... Since the administrator himself has to meet with the approval of creditors we may expect that the administrator will, if appointed, like an administrative receiver, *act in the interests of the creditors* although nominally an agent of the creditors and the firm [Emphasis supplied].[190]

This meant that the law still leaned in favor of the control of the process by the lender, leaving the fundamental fairness problem for the underserved constituencies unattended to.

The Enterprise Act ushered in a second wave of reform into English insolvency law.[191] It significantly curtailed the predilection of the lender to strengthen its control over the debtor in insolvency through the floating charge device. This it achieved by restricting the powers of the lender to appoint an administrative receiver and instead gave the administration procedure a notable position as a means of effecting the rehabilitation of the distressed business.[192] Although the administration procedure still places some level of control over the debtor in the hands of secured creditors, it however does so (at least theoretically) with a wider degree of accountability to the other stakeholders.[193]

Even more importantly, one may compare the English floating charge to the blanket lien employed by some lenders who provide new financing to the distressed business, in terms of its control effect.[194] The English floating charge is renowned

---

188 See generally, Chap. 3, Sect. 3.3.1.2.

189 Armour et al. (2008), p. 154 (noting that secured creditors (floating charge holders under the original IA, 1986 could veto an administration, appointing administrative receiver instead).

190 Webb (1991), pp. 152–153.

191 Enterprise Act, 2002 (Commencement No.4 and Transitional Provisions and Savings) Order 2003 (SI 2003/2093). The Act came into force in 2003.

192 Armour et al. (2008), p. 155 ("the Enterprise Act reconfigured corporate rescue law in United Kingdom by simultaneously curtailing the power of a secured creditor to appoint a receiver and elevating the administration regime to a position of structural priority within the overall legal scheme.").

193 IA 1986 Sch.B1 para.3(2) for instance requires an administrator to act in the interest of the creditors as a whole.

194 See McCormack (2008), p. 183 (describing the provisions supporting the US blanket lien as the functional equivalent of the English floating charge). See also Lupica (2005), p. 888 (analyzing the

for use as a tool for control,[195] and the blanket lien equally serves the same purpose.[196] Indeed, as Harner notes, the effect of blanket lien is that "[t]he company and junior stakeholders ... frequently possess little negotiating leverage, and are presented with the choice of accepting the secured lenders' terms or losing the business."[197] In the UK, the tendency of the secured creditor to capture all the value in the distressed business through its control right has also been statutorily regulated through the creation of a carved-out portion of the estate for administrative expense, as well as other creditors who may be at the receiving end of control skewed so much in favor of the secured creditor.[198] In essence, the secured lender who holds a floating charge as an instrument of control soon realizes that its priority position is subordinated to that of statutorily specified administrative expense, bankruptcy preference claims, as well as a carved out portion for the body of general unsecured creditors.[199] This represents the approach of the UK to balancing the control of a floating charge holder with the interest of junior creditors who may be left with nothing.

Indeed, similarly to the UK, such carve-outs have been proposed in the US, in order to facilitate funding for the restructuring and to provide unsecured creditors some measure of protection,[200] in the face of blanket liens, a proposal which has been discountenanced by the regime of revised Article.[201] The result therefore continues to be that pre-distress lenders can exercise control through their all-encompassing security interest, and in the context of a pre-distress lender providing the restructuring financing, it can exercise the same measure of control through its new financing agreement. Although in very few cases, courts have approved such

---

changes in US Article 9 that make easier, the creation of blanket liens over the undertakings of a borrower).

[195] See generally Westbrook (2004), p. 795 (quoting a British bankers' saying, "fixed charge for priority, floating charge for control.").

[196] Westbrook (2004), p. 862 (noting how the expanded security interest under the regime of (revised) Article 9 "... not only changes the basis on which the lender extends credit, but also the control that the creditor can exercise over the business.").

[197] Harner (2015), p. 510.

[198] IA 1986, Sch. B1, para 65 (1) and (2) is to the effect that "[t]he administrator . . . may make a distribution to a creditor of the company" and that "Section 175 shall apply in relation to a distribution under this paragraph as it applies in relation to a winding up." On its part, IA 1986, s. 175(2)(b) is to the effect that designated preferential debt shall "so far as the assets of the company available for payment of general creditors are insufficient to meet them, have priority over the claims of holders of debentures secured by, or holders of, any floating charge created by the company, and shall be paid accordingly out of any property comprised in or subject to that charge". See generally, Wood (2013), p. 227.

[199] See generally, LoPucki et al. (2013), pp. 1853–1857.

[200] See for instance, Warren (1997), pp. 1373–1395; Bossetti and Kurth (1997).

[201] For a criticism of the rejection of the notion of carve-outs for non-secured creditors, see Warner (2001), p. 24.

carve-outs,[202] there is still the problem that such carve-outs are seldom the case.[203] Where such carveouts exist, they can help curtail the hardship of other stakeholders, arising from the diversion of restructuring value to the secured creditor, without necessarily destroying the idea of taking security in the first place.[204]

Instructively, the nature of control exercised by the major lenders of the debtor in the US setting through contracting is quite similar to the UK administrative receivership or even the current administration system in the UK. Thus, although the receiver or administrator displaces the management in the English administrative receivership,[205] the financer in the US may through contracting, decide the de facto management of the debtor, through the appointment of the CRO or the replacement of the CEO. The only practical difference would be that while the goal of the formal restructuring by the CRO is to be determined by the lender or its installed executive in the US,[206] in the UK, the goals of the administrator is statutorily provided for in an order of preference that prioritizes the rehabilitation of the debtor.[207] Furthermore, in the role as administrator, the appointee is required to take the interest of all creditors into account, as against the regime of the administrative receiver which required the receiver to take into account the interest of the appointing creditor.[208] There may therefore be the need to statutorily recognize the place of the CRO in the US bankruptcy regime, and to invest her with duties similar to a fiduciary with clear cut priority agenda, in line with the overriding policy of the rehabilitation of the debtor.

The above is quite similar to the German law approach to situations where a lender takes on the controlling position of the distressed business. Where the lender puts itself in a position that gives it control over the management of the debtor, then it sets itself up to be regarded as a shadow director ((*faktische Geschäftsleitung*) of the debtor,[209] assuming the obligations which the management of the debtor ought to exercise, such as filing for insolvency, where the conditions for insolvency

---

[202] See for instance, *In re Renaissance Park Hotel, LLC*, Case No. 06–04893 (Bankr.D.S.C. Nov. 19, 2007); *In re Pulliam Motor Company d/b/a Pulliam Ford,* Case No. 07–01555–dd (Bankr.D.S.C. Apr. 17, 2007.

[203] LoPucki et al. (2013), p. 1858.

[204] McCormack (2011), p. 610 (such carveouts constitutes "a fair concession to unsecured creditors without destroying the notion of security in its entirety.").

[205] See generally, IA 1986, ss. 388–390.

[206] Baird & Rasmussen state that the appointment of the CRO or CEO (as the case may be) depends on what the lender intends to achieve with the debtor. They point out that:

> At times, creditors put a new head in place after they have already decided the fate of the company. If the creditors have already decided to place the company on the block, they will push for a manager whose talents lie in readying companies for such sales. If they have decided to reorganize the company, they will veer toward a professional whose skills lie in fixing the company's problems. If they have yet to decide what the best course of action will be, they will endorse someone whose judgment they trust.

Rasmussen (2007), p. 83.

[207] IA 1986, Sch B1, para 3(1).

[208] See generally, Walters (2015), p. 565.

[209] Especially in the context of banks as lenders who exert control through their superior knowledge to protect their secured position, see Spindler (2006), p. 345.

exist.[210] It may therefore incur civil and criminal liability where it neglects to do so.[211] While deepening of insolvency may generally not be the worry of a CRO in the US for instance, the imposition of directorial duties on the CRO may play a critical role in ensuring that in their role, they consider the legitimate interests of other creditors other than the one who has facilitated their appointment.

5.7 Treatment of Distressed Lender in the German Law Context

Although as already noted, Germany adopts a market-based approach to new financing,[212] German law takes a strict approach to the provision of new financing and hence provides for checks by way of its detailed transaction avoidance regime, rules on public policy and the deepening of insolvency. These rules set the bounds around which constrain borrower and lender arrangements in ways that ensures that other stakeholders are not left out in the cold, while the provider of new financing enjoys the benefits of its capture through new financing. Again, while it is believed that the motivation for providing new financing in Germany is not necessarily as it is in the US, the possible introduction of the priority incentives for preventive restructuring as envisaged in the proposed Directive may make lenders the more adventurous. This means in essence that the tolerance of German law may be tested to see how it reacts to new financing agreements that is skewed in favor of the provider of new financing. In view of the foregoing, the relevant rules in the German transaction avoidance regime, public policy, and the deepening insolvency are examined below.

---

[210] On the nature of lender involvement that may result in control that may warrant liability of lender, see Hadjinestoros (2013), p. 176.

[211] On the criminal liability imposed, see 2. 15(a)(4) InsO. Regarding the civil liability imposed, see s. 823 Abs 2 BGB. The practice of imposing liability on directors for failing to petition for insolvency also applies in the UK, see s. 214 IA, 1986; See also See also Finch (2009), p. 300. The US presents a sharp contrast. The nearest to liability directors may come is based is based on their fiduciary duty. Attempts to rely on the theory of "deepening insolvency" have been consistently refused by the court as grounding a cause of action against the directors of a distressed and now insolvent debtor. See *In re Hydrogen LLC* 431 BR 337, 357. A powerful statement of the law rebutting deepening insolvency as a cause of action was proffered by Delaware Court of Chancery in *Trenwick Am. Litig. Trust v. Ernst & Young, L.L.P.*, 906 A.2d 168, 205 (Del.Ch.2006) as follows:

> [T]he fact of insolvency does not render the concept of "deepening insolvency" a more logical one than the concept of "shallowing profitability." That is, the mere fact that a business in the red gets redder when a business decision goes wrong and a business in the black gets paler does not explain why the law should recognize an independent cause of action based on the decline in enterprise value in the crimson setting and not in the darker one. If in either setting the directors remain responsible to exercise their business judgment considering the company's business context, then the appropriate tool to examine the conduct of the directors is the traditional fiduciary duty ruler….

[212] See Chap. 4, Sect. 4.6.2.2 above.

Importantly, at the heart of the transaction avoidance regime of German law is whether through an unfair advantage gained by a lender even by omission, the creditors as a whole have been disadvantaged.[213] In this sense, one may look particularly at German transaction avoidance regime as it relates to the willful disadvantaging of the general body of creditors. German law lays a provider of new financing to the distressed business bare to avoidance of the benefits received from the transaction, if the lender knew that the borrower acted with the intention to disadvantage its creditors. Where the debtor willfully performs a transaction to create a disadvantage for its creditors, the look back period is extended to a period of 10 years before the request for the commencement of insolvency proceedings.[214] Two important points need to be noted regarding the borrower's intention and the lenders knowledge. Regarding the debtor's intention, it suffices that the transaction with the lender will result in a disadvantage for the other creditors.[215]

More concretely, the intention is imputed to the borrower who recognizes that the satisfaction of a [new lender] or the granting of a security to [the lender] is likely to cause disadvantages to the other creditors, e.g. the other creditors cannot be paid out of the remaining assets of the company, and accepts this as a consequence of its acts."[216] Regarding knowledge on the part of the lender, it has also been argued that presumption of knowledge can be imputed to the lender if it knows that the borrower is imminently illiquid, and "the transaction constituted a disadvantage to the creditors."[217] Thus, even where there is a statutory safe harbor for new value exchange, the statute still subjects the new value transaction to the scrutiny of transactions that willfully disadvantages the creditors.[218] One may therefore conclude that the provision on willful disadvantaging of the creditors may be sufficiently wide to deal with situations where a new financer, in a bid to provide new financing to support a restructuring, takes advantage of the new financing agreement in such ways that interfere with the right of other creditors. This is particularly so where the restructuring efforts fail.

A second line of protection that may possibly interfere with the overreach of a lender, through its new financing agreement will be how it meets up with public policy concerns. The whole notion of being contrary to public policy has its roots in the usury concept. From the medieval times, the essence of usury was to preclude lenders from increasing the capital in loan transactions. In essence, the consent of the debtor to the transaction notwithstanding, the general belief was that the debtor has only done so as a result of its necessity and when the law provides protection for the necessitous debtor, it does not depend on the showing that the lender had exercised undue influence on the debtor. Rather, the protection of the law is based on

---

[213] See s. 129 InsO.

[214] See s.133(1) InsO.

[215] See Weijs et al. (2012), p. 11.

[216] Id.

[217] Id.

[218] See s. 142 InsO.

both considerations of morality and social policy.[219] As has already noted early on in this book, a contemporaneous exchange of value between the lender and the borrower does not fall to be voided under the avoidance regime of German law.[220]

Even when Northern Germany repealed its usury laws in the nineteenth Century in pursuit of a regime of free competition, overreaching by lenders saw the introduction of criminal sanctions against lenders who provided loans, on the strength of a promise of returns above the customary interest rates or for performance which was strikingly out of proportion with the lenders performance.[221] The German Civil Code which came into effect in January 1, 1900 also provided place for this important principle of German law.[222] The implication for new financing providers even in present times is enormous. The debtor is distressed and may ordinarily be considered the weaker of both parties. Although the lender is put on its toes by ensuring the financing provided suffices for the restructuring, it is required that it closely considers the rates of return such that it is not disproportionate. Hence, such clauses as cross-collateralization or roll-ups may very well be considered to be contrary to public policy as such clauses characteristically hand the lender much more value than the immediate financing it is providing.

The third point as already stated is directed towards the prevention of complicity on the part of the lender, in the deepening of the borrower's insolvency. The management of a debtor that is illiquid and over-indebted has an obligation to file for insolvency within a time period of about 3 weeks following the illiquidity of the company or its over-indebtedness.[223] The management of a debtor that is illiquid and over-indebted has an obligation to file for insolvency within a time period of about 3 weeks following the illiquidity of the company or its over-indebtedness.[224] Financing in order to serve its ends by prolonging the life of a company which does not have survival prospects. Especially for the purposes of restructuring, a lender is expected to only provide such loans on the basis of a restructuring opinion which points to the prospects of a successful restructuring.[225] In addition, the lender may lay itself bare to the payment of damages if, through the provision of financing, the

---

[219] Dawson (1937), p. 45 ("The protection received by the borrower did not depend on proof of economic pressure in the particular case but was explained on broad grounds of morality and social policy.").

[220] See the discussion on contemporaneity in Chap. 4, Sect. 4.3 above.

[221] Ibid, 48.

[222] S. 138 BGB:

(1) A legal transaction which is contrary to public policy is void;
(2) In particular, a legal transaction is void by which a person, by exploiting the predicament, inexperience, lack of sound judgement or considerable weakness of will of another, causes himself or a third party, in exchange for an act of performance, to be promised or granted pecuniary advantages which are clearly disproportionate to the performance.

[223] S. 15a para 1 InsO.

[224] S. 15a para 1 InsO.

[225] Such opinions are typically provided by auditors based on the standards set by the Institute of Public Auditors in Germany (IDW). The standard for many years has been the IDW S6. Proposed reform (IDW ES 6 n. F.) is designed to make such opinions more concise especially for SMEs.

debtor succeeds in deepening the insolvency to the detriment of the other creditors of the debtor.[226]

One may conclude from the foregoing that German law provides stricter guidelines that can serve as a line of defense for creditors who may be disadvantaged by lender capture through new financing agreements. The provision of financing to the distressed debtor. These rules can be gleaned from transaction avoidance rules, public policy, as well as the requirement that a lender does not take part in the deepening of the insolvency of the borrower. Admittedly, it is a challenge to see how exactly these rules may work in practice. Again, the reader need be reminded that German law tends to be positivistic, with few academic or empirical resources available especially in the English Language.

5.8 UK Law and New Financing Agreements: Reflecting on New Financing Problematic Clauses

English law like German law, follows a market-based approach as already pointed out early on. Ordinarily, this means that the parties can bargain for new financing and reach agreements on the incentives and concessions that may be agreeable to the parties. Generally, it may therefore be of interest to see or understand how such clauses that suggest a lender capture of the restructuring process are dealt with by the law, to ensure that in the course of the restructuring, other creditors are not short-changed, and value diverted to the new lender, at the expense of other creditors. On the one hand it has been argued—like in Germany—that such provisions may be excluded already on the basis of both transactional avoidance rules, as well as the regime that regulates an administration procedure.[227] On the other hand, it is argued here that the market-based approach of the incentivizing regime for new financing in the UK may well explain why problematic clauses in the new financing agreements never come to the fore.

In the UK, its transaction avoidance rules follow the common policy geared towards the protection of "the general body of creditors against the diminution of the assets available to them, by a transaction that confers an unfair or improper advantage on the other party."[228] Consequently, for instance, where pursuant to a new financing agreement, a lender obtains new security interest to cover both new and old exposure, such may be considered as a preference.[229] Where the security interest created is a floating charge, the law requires that the validity of the security interest depends on whether it provides certain specified new value. This, McCormack argues can be applied to roll-up clauses. A floating charge created in

[226] S. 826 BGB: A person who, in a manner contrary to public policy, intentionally inflicts damage on another person is liable to the other person to make compensation for the damage.

[227] See generally, McCormack (2008), p. 205 ff.

[228] Goode (2011), pp. 522–523.

[229] See generally, s. 239 IA, 1986.

favor of a lender before the commencement of insolvency or administration proceedings are void to the extent that they are meant to discharge pre-existing debt.[230] He therefore points out that a roll-up is not new money and therefore falls to be voided under transaction avoidance rules.[231]

Regarding the regime of administration, in the case of a cross-collateralization clause, McCormack argues that since the Insolvency Act refers to contracts entered into by an administrator as being entitled to priority,[232] it invariably excludes pre-administration debts. Hence, it is unlikely that a lender will be able to leverage on its new financing to effect a cross-collateralization of pre-distress debt. Likewise, a pre-administration debtor cannot by contract make its pre-administration debt enjoy priority payment as the administration debt.[233]

The above security interest creation argument is valid to the extent that the new money financer enters into the loan agreement prior to the commencement of formal restructuring. This is because, then it may be caught by avoidance rules.[234] Otherwise, the transaction avoidance legislations hardly have effect on agreements reached during the formal restructuring itself. There is however the possibility that the administration may fail, and liquidation proceedings is commenced. In that case, perhaps, transaction avoidance rules may be relied upon to render void the portion of the financing agreement which has conferred roll-up benefit to the lender. Consequently, it is still not clear how the law may deal with such a clause given that as far as it is known to this researcher, there is hardly a case on the point. One may however suggest a reason for the absence of such cases.

It is however not clear what happens where clauses which create these incentives in favor of new lenders are included for instance in a CVA or a scheme of arrangement. Given that the approach of English law to new financing is a market-based one,[235] one would expect that it is unlikely that the courts will interfere where the parties agree to the demands of the provider of new financing, as the basis for the new loan. It will be considered as a product of the bargain of the parties. The agreement will be reflected in the approval of the scheme or proposal by the requisite majority, and unless the scheme is challenged as being unfair, it may not give rise to concerns that may warrant intervention.

---

[230] S. 245 IA, 1986.

[231] McCormack (2007), p. 729.

[232] Ibid, at 205. This position is based on the expansive reading of para. 99 of the IA, 1986.

[233] Id.

[234] See the analysis in Chap. 4, Sect. 4.3.

[235] See Chap. 4, Sect. 4.6.2.1 above.

5.9 Conclusion: Reflections for Frontier Markets and on the Future of New Financing

5.9.1 The Quest for Control Through Financing Agreement: Is There a Problem with the DIP Construct?

In view of the analysis on the seemingly overbearing influence of pre-distress lenders as providers of new financing to the distressed debtor, one issue that arises for consideration is the need for rationalizing the quest for control, using the financing agreement as the basis for achieving same. As already highlighted early on, the management of distressed businesses may take the pattern of a retained management, the displacement of management as prescribed by the restructuring law framework, or a system of supervisory management over the management retained in place.[236] Admittedly, there are justifications that support the use of any one of these approaches. It would however appear that there exists a correlation between the retention of management in place, and the quest for pre-distress lenders providing new financing to seek to control the restructuring through the instrumentality of the financing agreement.[237] This may hold crucial lessons for frontier markets desirous of designing the management of their restructuring toolkit.

From the analysis above, although the framers of Chapter 11 of the US Bankruptcy Code intend to leave the debtor in possession, the realities on ground mean that prior secured lenders who provide new financing can contractually determine the management of the distressed borrower. The prescriptive approach to incentivizing new lending notwithstanding, the provision of new financing has largely become a means by which providers of new financing protect their pre-distress bargains and assert themselves in the governance of the business while in distress. The danger that has been created therefore is that while systems like the UK or Germany that have been favorably disposed to the displacement of pre-distress management already impose duties on an administrator in a bid to protect other classes of stakeholders for instance, the same may not be said of the US.

In the light of the above, as frontier markets evolve their restructuring regimes and think about how to design the management structure of the business in formal restructuring, it may be of importance that they take into consideration certain permutations. The first being that when pre-distress management is left in place, one motivation for their willingness to lend will be to be able to exert control over the direction of the restructuring. If the restructuring framework is designed in such a way that a statutorily recognized restructuring officer who on the one hand pre-distress lender has some measure of control over his appointment, and on the other hand has statutorily imposed duties; there may be less appetite to control the restructuring process.

[236] See Chap. 3, Sect. 3.7 above.

[237] See for instance, McCormack (2008), p. 206 (explaining why secured creditors in the UK will be unwilling to seek control through financing agreements).

In a bid to incentivize new lending for distressed borrowers, one likely fallout will be that prior lenders will be in the position to provide such financing. But doing so may provide further incentives to enhance their recovery through such new loans. In addition, new financing agreements may provide a path to the control of the restructuring in ways that maximize the returns of such lender, in ways that may be detrimental to the other stakeholders in the distressed business. In this wise, a statutory framework that ought to be pro-restructuring may fall to serve the benefits of only a secured prior lending providing new financing. This is the practical experience from the otherwise pro-restructuring regime of Chapter 11 of the US Bankruptcy Code. In spite of the design of that formal restructuring regime for distressed businesses, it would appear that pre-distress lenders have put to maximum use, the possibilities of new lending agreements. They have used that instrument in ways that implicate protection of their pre-distress interests and in ways that enhance their control over the firm.

For frontier markets, they will find that most of the theories that have been put forward to support the use to which new lenders in the US put the financing agreements will not stand up to a restructuring goal which is designed to achieve a rehabilitation or maximize value for all the creditors. Consequently, market practices which interfere with the goal of achieving a successful restructuring of the business should as a matter of policy be subject of legislative and judicial scrutiny. This is assuming some of those terms are not illegal or contrary to public policy.

More than envisaged by the drafters of Chapter 11, the financing agreement has drawn the restructuring regime in the US to mirror the restructuring regimes in the UK and Germany, where creditors have always held sway. In this wise, it becomes critically important to be able to balance the gains of financing the restructuring with the gains that may arise from a lender whose strategy includes active management of the distressed debtor and whose involvement may be aligned to value maximization. As one author succinctly points out, there is the need for a "workable proxy who may be able to represent the interests of unsecured creditors."[238] Could that search be leading us in the direction of distressed debt investors? Chapter 6 focuses on this issue.

References

Adler BE (2004) Bankruptcy primitives. Am Bankr Inst Law Rev 12:219–244

Adler BE (2012) Game-theoretic bankruptcy valuation. J Leg Stud 41(1):209–238

Allen WT (1993) Contracts and communities in corporation law. Wash Lee Law Rev 50:1395–1407

Armour J, Hsu A, Walters A (2008) Corporate insolvency in the United Kingdom: the impact of the enterprise act 2002. Eur Company Financ Law Rev (2):149–171

Arvind TT (2017) Contract law. Oxford University Press, Oxford

Ayotte KM, Morrison ER (2009) Creditor control and conflict in Chapter 11. J Legal Anal 1:511–551

[238] Walters (2015), p. 568.

Baird DG, Rasmussen RK (2001) Control rights, priority rights, and the conceptual foundations of corporate reorganizations. Va Law Rev 87:921–959

Baird DG, Rasmussen RK (2002) Four (or five) easy lessons from Enron. Vand Law Rev 55:1787–1812

Baiser PM, Epstein DG (1992) Postpetition lending under Section 364: issues regarding the gap period and financing for prepackaged plans. Wake Forest Law Rev 27:103–122

Barnett W (2003) Test your expertise - DIP financing no. Bankr Strat 20:3

Berman MN, Lee D (2011) The enforceability in bankruptcy proceedings of waiver and assignment of rights clauses within intercreditor or subordination Agreements. Norton J Bankr Law Prac 20:Art. 1

Bogart DB (1996) Games lawyers play: waivers of the automatic stay in bankruptcy and the single asset loan workout. UCLA Law Rev 43:1117

Bohm J (1985) The legal justification for the proper use of cross-collateralization clauses in Chapter 11 bankruptcy cases. Am Bankr Law J 59:289

Bossetti LM, Kurth MH (1997) Professor Elizabeth Warren's Article 9 carve-out proposal: a strategic analysis. UCC Law J 30:3

Bussel D, Klee KN (2009) Recalibrating consent in bankruptcy. Am Bankr Law J 83:663–748

Carlson DG (1993) Postpetition security interests under the Bankruptcy Code. Bus Lawyer 48(2):483–533

Carruthers BG, Parrot JS (1998) Weakening the strong: banks and secured lenders. In: Carruthers BG, Halliday TC (eds) Rescuing business. Clarendon Press, Oxford

Chatterjee S, Dhillon US, Ramírez GG (2004) Debtor in possession financing. J Bank Financ 28:3097–3111

Dahiya S, Ray K (2014) A theoretical framework for evaluating debtor-in-possession financing. Available at SSRN: https://ssrn.com/abstract=2447868. Accessed 12 June 2017

Dawson JP (1937) Economic duress and the fair exchange in French and German law. Tulane Law Rev 12:42–73

Finch V (2009) Corporate insolvency law. Cambridge University Press, Cambridge

Fleet J (2012) Chapter 11 on decline? Changes are here to stay. Am Bankr Inst J 31:16

Gebbia KM, Oscar LE (1993) Saybrook manufacturing: is cross-collateralization moot. J Bankr Law Prac 2:163–243

Goode R (2011) Principles of corporate insolvency law, 4th edn. Sweet and Maxwell, London

Goss RW (1991) Chapter 11 of the Bankruptcy Code: an overview for the general practitioner. Utah Bus J 4(9):6

Hadjinestoros E (2013) Fear of the dark: banks as shadow directors. Comp Law 34(6):169, 176

Harner M (2015) The value of soft variables in corporate reorganizations. Univ Ill Law Rev:509–525

Hinkes-Jones L (2016) DIP loans still costly. Bloomberg BNA. Available at: https://www.bna.com/dip-loans-costly-n57982065779/. Accessed 30 Dec 2017

Kirshner JA (2015) Design flaws in the bankruptcy regime: lessons from the U.K. for preventing a resurgent creditors' race in the U.S. Univ Penn J Bus Law 17(2):527

Kuney GW (2005) Hijacking Chapter 11. EmoryBankr Dev J 21:19–112

Lee BP (2009) Chapter 18? Imagining future uses of 11 U.S.C. § 363 to accomplish Chapter 7 liquidation goals in Chapter 11 reorganizations. Colum Bus Law Rev 520

Leepson B (1996) Note, a case for the use of a broad court equity power to facilitate Chapter 11 reorganization. Bankr Dev J 12:775–807

Lightman G, Moss G (2011) The law of administrators and receivers of companies, 5th edn. Sweet & Maxwell, London

Lipson JC (2016) Bargaining bankrupt: a relational theory of contract in bankruptcy. Harv Bus Law Rev 6:239–295

LoPucki LM, Abraham AI, Delahaye BP (2013) Optimizing English and American security interests. Notre Dame Law Rev 88:1785–1864

Lupica LR (2005) The impact of revised Article 9. Ky Law J 93:867–913

McCormack G (2007) Super-priority new financing and corporate rescue. J Bus Law 701–732

McCormack G (2008) Corporate rescue law: an Anglo-American perspective. Edward Elgar, Cheltenham
McCormack G (2011) American private law writ large? The UNCITRAL secured transactions guide. Int Comp Law Q 60(3):597–625
Miller HR, Waisman SY (2004) Does Chapter 11 reorganization remain a viable option for distressed businesses for the twenty-first century? Am Bankr Law J 78:153–200
Miller JG, Murray JC (2006) Waivers of automatic stay: are they enforceable (and does the new bankruptcy act make a difference)? Real property. Probate Trust J 41(2):357–380
Mintz B, Schwartz M (1985) The power structure of the American business community. University of Chicago Press, Chicago
Perechocky D (2012) Should ad hoc committees have fiduciary duties?: judicial regulation of the bankruptcy market. Am Bankr Law J 86:527–568
Rapisardi JJ, Davis GA (2009) Lyondell: the largest commercial DIP in history. Butterworths J Int Bank Financ Law 393–394
Rasmussen RK (2007) On the scope of managerial discretion in Chapter 11. Univ Pa Law Rev 156:77–87
Rice J (2010) Developments in banking and financial law: 2010: changes in debtor-in-possession financing following the financial collapse of 2008. Rev Bank Financ Law 29:312
Rickert JJ (1993) Bankruptcy-cross collateralization: an appropriate method of Section 364 Post-Petition Financing-In Re Saybrook Manufacturing Co. Temp Law Rev 66:239–256
Roe MJ, Tung F (2013) Breaking bankruptcy priority: how rent-seeking upends the creditors' bargain. Va Law Rev 99:1235–1287
Schwarcz SL (1997) The easy case for the priority of secured claims in bankruptcy. Duke Law J 47:425–489
Schwarcz SL (1999) Rethinking freedom of contract. Tex Law Rev 77:515–604
Schwartz A (1998) A contract theory approach to business bankruptcies. Yale Law J 107: 1087–1851
Skeel DA Jr (2004) The past present and future of debtor in possession financing Cardozo. Law Rev 25:1905–1934
Spindler G (2006) Trading in the vicinity of insolvency. EBOR 7(1):339–352
Squire R (2016) Corporate bankruptcy and financial reorganization. Wolter Kluwer, New York
Tabb CJ (1986) A critical reappraisal of cross-collateralization in bankruptcy. South Calif Law Rev 60:109–175
Tabb CJ (1989) Lender preference clauses and the destruction of appealability and finality: resolving a Chapter 11 dilemma. Ohio State Law J 50:109–162
Tabb CJ (1990) Emergency preferential orders in bankruptcy reorganizations. Am Bankr Law J 65:75–115
Tabb CJ (2014) Law of bankruptcy, 3rd edn. West Academic Publishing
Telesca NB (1987) Section 364(d) superpriority financing: has a secured creditor met his match? Bankr Dev J 5:109
Vance CE, Barr P (2003) The facts & fiction of bankruptcy reform. DePaul Bus Commer Law J 1(3):361–416
Warner GR (2001) The anti-bankruptcy act: revised article 9 at bankruptcy. Am Bankr Int Law Rev 9:3
Warren E, Westbrook JL (2009) The success of chapter 11: a challenge to the critics. Mich Law Rev 107:603
Walters AJ (2015) Statutory erosion of secured creditors' rights: some insights from the United Kingdom. Univ Ill Law Rev 543–570
Warner GR (2011) Article 9's bankruptcy proceeds rule: amending Bankruptcy Code Section 552 through the UCC "proceeds" definition. Gonz Law Rev 46:521–553
Warren E (1997) Making policy with imperfect information: the Article 9 full priority debates. Cornell Law Rev 82(6):1373–1395

Webb D (1991) An economic evaluation of insolvency procedures in the United Kingdom: does the 1986 insolvency act satisfy the creditors' bargain? Oxf Econ Pap 43:139–157
Weijs RJ, Verwey EJR, Barenz C, Connel R (2012) Financing in distress against security from an English, German and Dutch law perspective: a walk in the park or a mine in the field. Int Insol Law Rev:1–23
Weiss LA, Capkun V (2007) Bankruptcy resolution: priority of claims with the secured creditor in control. Am Law Econ Pap:1–26
Westbrook JL (2004) The control of wealth in bankruptcy. Tex Law Rev 82:795–861
White JJ (2004) Death and resurrection of secured credit. Am Bankr Inst Law Rev 12:139–192
Wolfson SA, Kochis AJ (2013) Unflopping the debtor: finding fairness in financing. Am Bankr Inst J 32:42–96
Wood PR (2007) Law and practice of international finance: principles of international insolvency, 2nd edn. Sweet & Maxwell, London
Wood PR (2013) The bankruptcy ladder of priorities. Bus Law Int 14:209
Zumbro PH (2016) DIP and exit financing trends and strategies in a changing marketplace. Aspatore, Boston

Chapter 6
The Role of Distressed Debt Investors in Financing Distressed Debtor Restructuring

6.1 Overview

The underlying theme of every debt restructuring is the existence of debt, which requires adjusting. Disagreements between investors, distressed debtors and other stakeholders largely revolve around what to do about the debt: the desire for immediate repayment, the need to make compromises to facilitate the survival of the business, the desire to be divested from the business, amongst other considerations. During the period when the company mulls commencing a restructuring, some creditors for varying reasons may be unwilling to remain invested in the distressed business and unwilling to provide further capital. When pre-distress creditors find themselves unwilling to invest or stay invested, the existence of a market for the trading of their debt portfolio matters a great deal.[1] Furthermore, the existence of a market, which has the capacity to participate in the process of financing the restructuring, and actually does so in a number of cases, is indeed deserving of attention.

The distressed debt market, through distressed debt investors, trade in the debt of financially distressed firms at a price which is discounted against the nominal value of the debt.[2] The discount rate varies depending on the individual circumstances of the debtor or projections of the investors. Typically, the investor expects to reap a profit either by reselling the debt, by liquidating the claim in the process of restructuring, or by taking an equity position in the debtor as it exits restructuring.[3] Essentially, these investors take advantage of their superior knowledge of the

[1] See Miller (2007), p. 377, quoting Macleod (1872) ("If we were asked … who made the discovery which has most deeply affected the fortunes of the human race? We think, after full consideration, we might safely answer - The man who first discovered that a Debt is a Saleable Commodity.").

[2] Reference to debt here includes all forms of debts. See Gilson (2001), p. 189 (noting that such debts include "bank loans, debentures, trade payables, private placements, real estate mortgages, even claims for legal damages….").

[3] See Harner (2008a), p. 98 (explaining the role of the distressed investor in the life of a financially distressed debtor).

S. U. Mba, *New Financing for Distressed Businesses in the Context of Business Restructuring Law*, https://doi.org/10.1007/978-3-030-19749-0_6

situation of the debtor to reap a profit from the difference in the purchase and sale process of the underlying asset.[4]

While it is true that the distressed debt market is actively competing, or seeks to actively compete with traditional lenders, the depth of the involvement of distressed investors in troubled companies is becoming even more pronounced. It is particularly suggested that the players in the distressed debt market are not only powerful but are gradually and surely displacing traditional lenders as the provider of financing to troubled companies.[5] Indeed the jurisdictions covered in this book have quite different capital markets. However, the regulatory constraints faced by traditional lenders is essentially the same, so that although there might not be a uniform growth trend in the influence of distressed debt investors across board, an upward trend can be justifiably predicted.[6] The same can be said for frontier markets or developing economies, as the intervention of the distressed debt market has the capacity to bridge the gap in the ability of traditional bank lenders to support distressed debtors undertaking corporate restructuring.

Furthermore, there appears to be noticeable convergence in restructuring practices in spite of the nuances in the extant formal restructuring regimes. This convergence largely owes to the distressed debt market.[7] There are two reasons which may well account for this. On the one hand, there appears to be a noticeable movement of distressed debt market players from the US to capital markets on the other side of the Atlantic and dominating the markets there.[8] On the other hand, there is a current trend which seem to support the globalization of the "corporate rescue policy" which is gaining traction in many countries. Expectedly, the rescue policy will be accompanied by skills and techniques and possibly the legal ecosystem associated

---

[4] See Krasoff and O'Neill (2006) (describes distressed investing as often involving "an arbitrage play, making use of superior knowledge of a particular situation.").

[5] Miller (2007), pp. 393–394 (author points out that hedge funds, a leading player in the distressed debt market, have edged aside traditional lenders, such as banks and insurance companies, to become the primary lendersand major participants in providing the apparently endless flow of financing to troubled companies …"); see also, Baird and Rasmussen (2007), p. 939 n.43 ("For those who fret that bankers have a culture that makes them overly cautious, one need only remember that many of today's lenders are not traditional banks. Private hedge funds are on the prowl for investments that promise above market returns.").

[6] See for instance, McNee (2005) (on the involvement of opportunity funds, hedge funds, private equity firms, and the proprietary arms of investment banks in the Non-Performing Loans of financially distressed firms held by German banks).

[7] Harner (2008b), p. 709 (pointing out that distressed debt investing is causing a slow, but noticeable, convergence of the U.S. and the U.K. corporate restructuring processes).

[8] See also KPMG (2016) (pointing out the dominance of the distressed debt market in the UK by players from the US); Paterson (2014), p. 337 (commenting on the advent of the distress debt market in the UK, author states that "[a] number of US investors arrived in the English market to implement a highly successful strategy which they had pursued at home for some time."); see also Chassany and Sender (2013) (suggesting that American investors are becoming more visible in Europe partly because of their belief that European distressed debt offer better prices when compared to the US debt); See Wollaston (2005) (suggesting that the migration of distressed debt investors to Europe include the growth potential offered by the undeveloped European market, the narrowing spreads for distressed debt investors in the US, leading them to explore new markets).

with its exploitation.[9] In view of these two factors, the more adventurous distressed debt investors become, and the more restructuring friendly jurisdictions become, there is bound to be predictable increase in the reach of the distressed debt investors across jurisdictions.

Recall that one of the main considerations in Chap. 5 was the influence which pre-distress lenders exerted through their new financing agreement.[10] The role of distressed debt investors raises similar concerns. Their investing strategies tend to yield somewhat similar results especially as regarding the exertion of influence over the management of the distressed debtor, in the course of formal restructuring, and if the business happens to emerge from the process of restructuring, the ownership structure of the business upon emergence from the process.[11]

Consequently, the role of distressed debt investors in the restructuring process has divided scholars, in terms of their effect on the value of the distressed debtor and the distribution of that value to the stakeholders of the distressed business. Thus, while some scholars perceive the involvement of such investors in distressed businesses as value destructive, and possibly precipitating the failure of the debtor,[12] others insist that their role in the distressed business can, and does facilitate value enhancement first for themselves, and for other stakeholders of the business also.[13] Indeed, positive evidence still points to the salutary impact of distressed debt investors on the survival of distressed debtors. It is worth noting, however, that it is not to say that there are no practices of distressed debt investors that result in value destruction for the distressed debtors. It is on more concretely this point that the chapter

---

[9] See Flood (2001).

[10] See Chap. 5, Sect. 5.3.

[11] Harner (2008b), p. 709 (writing about the US and the UK, the author points out that "distressed debt investors are increasingly taking charge of the restructuring process and placing the management of the troubled company in a secondary or supporting role.") It is important to state that the influence which distressed debt investors may wield will often depend on many other factors other than the provision of financing. Such factors will necessarily include the nature of the restructuring regime and the local prevailing disposition towards corporate restructuring (as against a liquidation).

[12] Thomas (2010) (arguing that predatory distressed debt trading undermines the traditional purposes of formal restructuring under Chapter 11 of the US Bankruptcy Code); Lipson (2009), pp. 1614–1615 (arguing that chapter 11 creates a "shadow bankruptcy" system where "[s]ophisticated and aggressive private investors exploit interstices in Chapter 11, and between Chapter 11 and other laws—in particular federal securities laws—that might check their behavior"); Miller and Waisman (2007), p. 170 (on the control wielded by creditors (including distressed debt investors, authors point out that "[e]excessive creditor control remains undesirable because such influence may cause the debtors operations to be managed solely in the interest of the particular controlling creditor group, thereby foreclosing the debtor's restructuring options.").

[13] See for instance Altman (2014), p. 76 (highlighting the depth and liquidity providing role of distressed debt investors in the loan and bond market); Harner (2011), pp. 169–170 (underscoring the positive implications of distressed debtor investment for the distressed corporations and their stakeholders); Agarwal and Meneghetti (2011), pp. 242–243 (finding that hedge funds add "value through their lending relationships and financial markets perceive these activities as good news for the firms"); Goldschmid (2005), pp. 267–268 (emphasizing the role of distressed investors in promoting market liquidity).

contributes a perspective to analyzing the role of distressed investors and proposes a principled approach for the courts in the context of a formal restructuring.

In the light of the above, this chapter proposes a perspective through which distressed debt investors involved in formal restructuring may be perceived. This perspective recognizes distressed debt investors as rational economic actors operating in a free market, characterized by self-interest. In the best case, the success of the distressed debt investor is tied to the success of the firm so that their participation creates or maximizes value, in line with the identified goals of restructuring. This twinning of the goals of restructuring with the profit-maximization goal of the distressed investors should typically result in the overall value maximization for the creditors and for the firm. However, because the best case is not always the case, distressed debt investors have employed strategies that solely drive their profit goals and have sometimes led to the destruction of value in the distressed debtor. When this self-interest conflicts with the creation of value for the firm as envisaged by corporate restructuring law, it is in such cases that the courts should (and as the latter part of the chapter shows, need) intervene.

This Chapter—as this book—notes that the distressed debt market indeed plays an active, and increasingly significant role in the restructuring of distressed businesses, and consequently, may contribute to the successful restructuring of distressed businesses. This is the case, irrespective of the portion of the capital structure in which the distressed investor is invested in. Even though this comes at a price, a general theoretical framework is adopted to capture this price as the result of the self-interest of distressed debt investors as rational economic actors. However, as this self-interest begins to move away from the point of coterminous benefit as envisaged by corporate restructuring law, the courts must intervene to push the distressed investors back within this sphere which should not altogether undermine the interest of the investors but allow for shared benefits for the business and its stakeholders. This intervention as proposed in the book is grounded on the collateral purpose and effect principle.

This chapter proceeds as follows. The first section recognizes the role of distressed debt investors as providers of an alternative to traditional lending institutions. The section which follows identifies the players in the distressed debt market and their loan-to-own strategy. The next section undertakes an examination of the virtues of the involvement of the distressed debt market in the financing of distressed businesses, capturing the shades of theoretical arguments that point out the virtues of their preferred position (unsecured creditors or shareholders) in the distressed business. It is not for nothing that the players in today's distressed debt market were once described using pejoratives such as "vultures",[14] or "locusts".[15] Hence, this section identifies problematic consequences of investors' strategies. In the light of these challenges, the penultimate section goes on to propose a

---

[14] The pejorative has its origins in an analogy where these investors were said to earn their profits "... by feeding on the carcasses of corporate America." See Henriques (1992), p. 1.

[15] See Landler (2005), p. C6 (reporting the perception of hedge funds by German politicians who thought of hedge funds as dubious and invading the EU financial space).

two-pronged test on a principled approach to dealing with the aggressive behavior of distressed debt investors that negatively impact the value of the firm. To conclude, lessons are drawn for frontier markets like Nigeria, where distressed debt investing is beginning to take a foothold.

6.2 The Distressed Debt Market as Alternative to Traditional Lenders

The distressed debt market of today appears to be partly a response to the challenge traditional lenders face, particularly with regard to the failure of the management of debtors to meet projected revenue targets, as well as the failure to abide by loan covenants. Traditional lenders such as commercial banks and insurance companies are characteristically subjected to regulations that largely determine their willingness to remain invested in a financially distressed debtor.[16] Recall that traditional lenders (as prior lenders) who provide distressed lending to businesses may do so with the intention of ensuring that their existing risk exposure is not only protected, but also their recovery is maximized.[17] However, as will be seen shortly, regulations to which these traditional lenders are subject now appear to adversely impact the ability of traditional lenders to pursue such strategies. In the face of such lending constraints, what role (if any) does the distressed debt market play?

6.2.1 Buyers of Distressed Portfolio

The willingness of traditional lenders to support the restructuring of their distressed borrowers is being replaced by a heightened incentive on the part of these lenders to dispose of their distressed debts to willing buyers. But how exactly has regulation impacted traditional lenders in their support for the distressed borrower? When the debtor fails to meet its projected earnings, with the possibility of default, regulators require the lender banks to make provisions (or reserves) for the likelihood of default.[18] Such provisioning by the banks simply means that the bank has got more money tied down in respect of a debt, the repayment of which is uncertain. While the imposed regulatory adjustments may better facilitate prudence, for bankers,

---

[16] Donegan (1998), pp. 384–385 (noting that banks' motivation to sell claims may be influenced by increased minimum capital requirements). See Jensen (1996), p. 329 (on how regulation is drying up traditional sources of credit, increased the cost of debt and also increased the rate of default). These regulations such as contained in Basel III and other localized regulations such as the Dodd Frank/Volker Rule are typically intended to de-risk the banks.

[17] See Chap. 2, Sect. 2.2.1.

[18] See Chap. 2, Sect. 2.6.2.1 above. It is this author's opinion that this changed approach may even further constrain the willingness of traditional bank lenders to lend to distressed businesses.

these adjustments do not make economic sense for bank accounting.[19] In such situations, it makes even less economic sense for such lenders to provide additional financing to distressed debtors. It is here that distressed debt investors come to the rescue. This is because one of the strategies of distressed debt investors is the purchase of these distressed debts off the books of traditional lenders.[20]

This is not to say that traditional lenders do not take a haircut when they dispose of their distressed debt. This haircut is a discount which reflects the risk with which the investment is associated.[21] However, compared to the risk of a fire-sale following insolvency or bankruptcy enforcement, it is arguable that traditional lenders are better off with a predictable loss arising from the sale.[22] Besides, traditional lenders may prefer cash to a possible debt for equity exchange which the debtor may wish to propose as part of its restructuring plan.[23] Also, in their capacity as buyers of distressed portfolios, the distressed debt market throws up new investors who are not particularly under regulatory pressure and who should (ideally) be willing to partake in the process of corporate restructuring.

6.2.2 *Potential Exit Route and Liquidity Providers*

As traditional financial institutions adjusted their lending strategies to meet their regulatory realities, distressed debt investors now serve a dual role which potentially benefits the restructuring process and the economy as a whole. While on the one hand, distressed debt investors serve as a potential exit route for the creditors,[24] on the other hand, they serve as a source of liquidity for both creditors and even the distressed borrower. In addition to regulatory reasons already highlighted, creditors may be desirous of divesting from the distressed business.[25] Of particular

---

[19] Krasoff and O'Neill (2006), p. 18 (Suggesting that bank regulators usually require traditional lenders to make provision for possible losses arising from non-performing loans "making most [...] loans uneconomical from a bank accounting perspective.").

[20] Sharfman and Warner (2014) (commenting on hedge funds, authors argue that buyers of financially distressed securities provide a valuable outlet for lenders who wish to exit the markets).

[21] See for instance, Harner (2008b), p. 715 ("Investors purchase distressed debt at a discount off of its face value, reflecting the risk associated with the investment.").

[22] For a similar argument in the context of the UK distressed debt market, see Paterson (2016), p. 507.

[23] Gilson (2010), p. 54 (noting that banks may prefer to take cash upfront where there is a likelihood that the debtor will be proposing a debt for equity swap).

[24] Creditors here include both money lenders as well as trade creditors.

[25] Creditors may be inspired by other reasons to dispose of their claims. These reasons include: negative covenants placing restraints on holding defaulted bonds, limited stake in the debtor to warrant participation in restructuring proceedings, or an unwillingness to participate in (the sometimes acrimonious) restructuring proceedings, for the sake of the relationship existing between seller and the debtor. See Fortgang and Mayer (1990), p. 4. See also Rasmussen (2007), p. 1001 (observing that "[t]hose creditors who want no part of bankruptcy have an exit option: they can sell out to the various hedge funds that take a stake in many cases" and explaining debt strategies of

importance is the point that creditors may not possess the expertise to profit from distress, or even the willingness to remain invested in the debtor through its distress and the process of restructuring.[26] For such lenders, nothing could be more soothing than to be able to cash out.[27]

The availability of an exit strategy allowing traditional lenders to cut their losses benefits traditional lenders, distressed borrowers, as well as other potential market borrowers. As already pointed out, thanks to the distressed debt market, traditional lenders may provide financing for potentially troubled businesses in need of financing, knowing that the debt may be disposed-off even if at a discount.[28] The liquidity provided by the distressed debt market also swings favorably in the direction of the distressed debtor undergoing restructuring. As it is the case with debt restructurings, one device which is often employed in the restructuring process is the debt for equity swap. The debt equity swap helps the borrower reduce the debt burden on its balance sheet. Taking the place of the original lenders unwilling to remain invested in the debtor business, players in the distressed market may willingly take equity in the debtor, giving the debtor improved debt to equity ratio and deleveraging its balance sheets.[29] More than this, the distressed debt investor may inject new money as equity investment, which may be key to the survival of the distressed business.[30]

---

hedge funds and similar investors). The claim in which they invest is not limited to bank loans, it also includes such claims as "publicly traded debt, …, trade claims, personal injury claims and claims for the rejection of executory contracts tort claims." Goldschmid (2005), p. 207.

[26] The recent EU Non-Performing Loan Consultation ("EU/NPL consultation") document aptly captures this reasoning. It posits that:

> If banks were better able to off-load legacy assets from their balance sheet via secondary markets for credit, they could use their managerial capacity more on evaluating new lending business, while other firms could specialize in related services such as debt collection, collateral administration and credit restructuring. Economies of scale and increasing specialization as well as a better potential to exploit technological progress might be fostered if banks had better possibilities to unbundle pre and post contractual credit services.

See EU Commission, Development of Secondary Markets for Non-Performing Loans and Distressed Assets and Protection of Secured Creditors from Borrowers' Default, 3. Available at: https://ec.europa.eu/info/sites/info/files/2017-non-performing-loans-consultation-document_en.pdf accessed 14 Jan 2018.

[27] See Yap (1995), p. 158 (noting that claim purchasers offer creditors a way to remove themselves from bankruptcy in exchange for a specific sum of money); Altman (2014) (noting that the distressed debt market "provide[s] a potential outlet for original investors to monetize their troubled assets over a period that can stretch from a year or more before the bankruptcy filing and lasting throughout the duration of the bankruptcy process."); Similar arguments have been made in the case of the UK. See Paterson (2014), p. 338 ("A bank which had lent to a financially distressed borrower now had… [the] option to sell its debt to a specialist fund at a certain price and a predictable level of loss."); See also Wollaston (2005), p. 149 (commenting on the implication of the distressed debt market on relationship lending by banks in Europe).

[28] Harner (2008a), p. 98 ("… the existence of a readily available exit strategy may make institutions more willing to lend to potentially troubled companies.").

[29] Harner (2008b), p. 757 (such deleveraging can give the company a second chance).

[30] Altman (2014), p. 87 ('Usually, the new owners of the equity are the "old" creditors, based on

Finally, the distressed debt market can engender economy-wide benefits through lender competition which can reduce the cost of capital and improved lending within the economy. It is generally the case that as businesses become financially distressed, the cost of equity or debt capital for such businesses increases.[31] While the distressed debt market does not altogether eliminate the costs of capital, there is a fair chance that an active distressed debt market can mitigate the costs, through the provision of financing options, thereby engendering competition amongst lenders.[32] Furthermore, traditional lenders are able to channel their resources towards healthier undertakings, thereby improving economic activities.[33] Even in markets where lending is a heavily regulated activity and dominated by traditional lenders, distressed debt investors involved in lending will typically fall within exceptions that allow them to participate in the market, thereby contributing to market liquidity.[34]

Given that the distressed debt market provides an important alternative to the traditional lenders, the next section identifies the players or actors in this market, as well as the reasons why they are able to play the role originally reserved for traditional lenders.

---

either the conversion of debt to equity or the injection of new equity financing, the latter providing critical new liquidity for the debtor to compete'); Gilson (2010), p. 12 (Explaining how creditors may agree to an equity swap or actual equity finance injection, the latter providing the debtor with new money which bolsters the chances of the distressed debtor to compete); Also, see for instance, IPE Real Estate (2014) (Quoting CBRE Group Inc., a world leading commercial real estate services and investment firm, suggesting that German borrowers have now turned to alternative lenders such as insurance companies and debt funds for easier distress funding).

[31] See, e.g., Shaked and Michel (1999) (discussing costs of capital for distressed companies).

[32] See Tung (1996), p. 1701 (noting that claim trading may indirectly result in the reduction of borrowing costs.); see also, Harner (2008a), p. 71 (pointing out that the distressed debt market introduces an additional source of financing for troubled companies, i.e., hedge funds, private equity firms and other nontraditional lenders).

[33] When traditional lenders have their resources tied down in distressed businesses, it may negatively impact other market borrowers, cutting them off from much needed financing so that "they are unable to purchase new raw materials or invest in new projects thus contributing to the slowdown in economic activity." See Neyens (2002), p. 374.

[34] Germany is an example of such a regulated lending market, which generally requires a banking license for lending activities. However, exemptions have been created for the EU and EEA Alternative Investment Fund Managers (AIFMs). See Schmies et al. (2017), p. 93 ("… EU/EEA AIFM may, depending on the laws of their home state, be allowed to originate loans for alternative investment funds (AIFs) they manage. As the origination of such loans for AIFs managed by an AIFM is part of the AIFM's portfolio management activities, an EU/EEA AIFM can extend such loans to borrowers domiciled in Germany without being exposed to licensing requirements under the German Banking Act.").

6.3 The Players in the Distressed Debt Market and Their Capacity to Add Value

Like every other market, the distressed debt market has its own players (investors). These players are sometimes referred to as "special situation investors", given their interest in the securities of distressed entities seeking to restructure.[35] The players in the distressed debt market are a mixed crowd, ranging from dedicated distressed funds, to diverse non-traditional lenders (alternative investment) capital funds, states through their Central Banks, as well as states-connected "bad banks".[36] The array of players notwithstanding, some players are more prominent in investing in distressed debt than others and this section focuses on these prominent players. However, a common characteristic shared by all of these participants (albeit to different degrees) is that they are primarily driven by the opportunities of value return from their investment in the financially distressed business. In other words, at the heart of their investment are returns from the purchased claims either during restructuring, or at a later time i.e. post-restructuring. Given the prominence of hedge funds and private equity firms in distressed debt investing, the analysis below focuses on them, while other investing subsets are also collectively considered.

6.3.1 Hedge Funds

Hedge fund is today used to describe a whole range of non-traditional investment vehicles.[37] It is difficult to define hedge funds with precision,[38] given the wide-ranging investment strategies they employ,[39] as well as the various markets in which they operate.[40] Hence, some experts find it convenient to define hedge funds in terms

---

[35] INSOL International (2007), p. 4.

[36] The list of distressed debt investors will include: investment banks, hedge funds, pension funds, private equity funds, mutual funds, specific distressed debt funds, "bad banks" often backed by the government, central banks, as well as vehicles that issue collateralized debt obligations (CDOs), university endowments, foundations, and sophisticated individual investors.

[37] INSOL International, at 1 (Noting that historically, hedge fund referred to the strategy which involved investment in equities while using short selling and leverage to hedge exposure in the equities market. the strategy was focused on offsetting investment risk). On the history and origins of hedge funds in the US, see Stulz (2007), p. 176 ff.

[38] See Hammer et al. (2005), p. 1 (stating that "'Hedge fund' has no uniformly accepted meaning, but commonly refers to a professionally managed pool of assets used to invest and trade in equity securities, fixed income securities, derivatives, futures and other financial instruments.'").

[39] Kahan and Rock (2009), p. 282 ("What distinguishes hedge funds from other investors is that hedge funds tend to pursue active and aggressive investment strategies. Thus, hedge funds use leverage, sell short, and invest in derivatives. They trade much more frequently than other investors.").

[40] See Bianchi and Drew (2014), p. 6, 8 ("Hedge funds tend to own holdings and exposures in a wide range of asset markets and investment strategies, making them difficult to clearly define within a concise set of definitive terms.").

of observed characteristics.[41] Notwithstanding the absence of a universally accepted definition of hedge funds, it is broadly used to refer to privately held investment funds which manage funds for high net worth individual investors, as well as public trusts,[42] without their interest sold in registered public offerings.[43] While hedge funds generally play an important role in capital markets, credit-oriented hedge funds now also play a very active role in the distressed debt market, participating in different positions in the corporate structure of the distressed debtors, and providing exit financing for distressed businesses.[44]

While other investors may generally decline to invest in poorly performing companies, credit-oriented hedge funds take a different approach. As Macey puts it, "rather than seeing bad performance as something to avoid, hedge funds [...] see investment opportunities."[45] Their investment in such distressed businesses differentiates them from traditional lenders in that while such traditional lenders are preoccupied with salvaging their investment in the debtor, distress-investing hedge funds are strategically investing in the distressed businesses, with a view to making huge returns.[46] Their capacity to feature in the distressed debt market may be attributed to the flexibility of their structures, so that unlike traditional lenders, they may participate either as equity or debt investors in distressed businesses whether undergoing formal or informal restructuring.[47]

---

[41] For instance, the Australian Prudential Regulation Authority (APRA) describe hedge funds as funds which possess some of the following characteristics, funds that rely heavily on a single strategy, with broad delegations for the use of gearing and derivatives, funds that have a reliance upon a single individual to execute the investment management process, a relatively short trading history; and/or target an absolute return rather than a benchmark return. See APRA Alerts (2003).

[42] Such public trusts may include pension funds, charity organizations, university endowments, as well as foundations.

[43] US Securities Exchange (2003), p. viii (stating that hedge funds generally refer to entities that hold a pool of securities and perhaps other assets, whose interests are not sold in a registered public offering and which is not registered as an investment company under the *Investment Company Act*).

[44] Credit oriented hedge funds refer to hedge funds willing to invest in fixed income securities. Such hedge funds may invest directly by buying securities from original creditors, or by purchasing portfolios of loans or bonds from structured debt vehicles such as collateralized bond obligations (CBOs) or collateralized loan obligations (CLO). See Krasoff and O'Neill (2006), p. 18 (pointing out that "Credit-oriented hedge funds typically make leveraged investments in subordinated and equity tranches in a CLO securitization funding."); see also Jiang and Wang (2012), p. 513 (where the authors undertake the examination of the "roles of hedge funds in Chapter 11 and the effects of their presence on the nature and outcome of the bankruptcy process.").

[45] Macey (2008), p. 247.

[46] Dai (2013), p. 572 ("rather than striving to contain damages on their existing investments in distressed firms like traditional creditors, hedge funds strategically invest in distressed firms as profitable opportunities.").

[47] Kamensky (2014), p. 236 (pointing out that owing to the flexibility of hedge funds, they can provide capital for distressed businesses in times of volatility and can participate in any part of the capital structure of the distressed business).

Overtime, there has been an increase in hedge funds with particular interest in distressed investing with huge funding, moving across the Atlantic.[48] Their influence in distressed debtor financing has seen so much growth in the US such that they have been touted as having overtaken traditional lenders in providing the financing for troubled companies.[49] With their help, these companies are able to avoid default, albeit at the price of increased leverage.[50] Again, while this might not exactly be the case in Europe or other frontier markets, there is no disputing that credit-oriented hedge funds have a competitive advantage in distressed lending, over the more closely restricted traditional lenders. The more pro-restructuring the regulatory environment becomes, the more their participation in the European distressed debt market is likely to see an increase.

6.3.2 *Private Equity Firms*

In simple terms, private equity entails the infusion of investment capital into a privately-held business, with the aim of sharing in the profits of the company receiving the investment capital.[51] Typically, private equity investment sees the investors investing in the equity (or equity related securities) of privately held companies.[52] Although the advent of private equity has been traced to an older time in history,[53] a more concrete history dates back to the post-World War 2 period in New England. The burgeoning technological development companies were faced with lack of financing especially because they required "patient capital" (equity or debt), which banks at the time were unable to provide.[54]

The attention of private equity firms was not originally focused on distressed businesses.[55] For some reasons, they kept their distance from distressed debt. In the

---

[48] See for instance, Stevenson (2014) (reporting that Marathon, a $11 billion hedge fund was looking to invest in Europe's distressed debt market by buying "nonperforming loans from local banks, distressed real estate loans and mortgage-backed securities."); Johnson and Fortado (2017) (reporting that Halcyon Capital Management, a 9.2 billion New York-based hedge fund with about 20% exposure to European corporate distressed debt was looking to increase its exposure).

[49] Miller (2007), pp. 393–394 (stating that "hedge funds have edged aside traditional lenders such as banks and insurance companies, to become the primary lenders and major participants in providing the apparently endless flow of financing to troubled companies.").

[50] Ibid (explaining that hedge funds typically do this through convoluted debt structures that may consist of different tranches of debts which include first and second liens).

[51] See Mccahery and Vermeulen (2008), p. 181.

[52] This may also include taking publicly listed companies private. Ibid, at 181–184.

[53] Dixit (2007) (author posits that the first known private equity investment is traceable to a daring Christopher Columbus, who although was not known to be successful, sought capital from the Spanish royalty to undertake an ambitious project).

[54] See generally, Hsu and Kenney (2005).

[55] This may also include taking publicly listed companies private. See generally, Mccahery and Vermeulen (2008), pp. 181–184 (noting that private equity firms were primarily concerned with

first place, the prevailing thinking at the time was that the investment in distressed businesses was complicated and time consuming.[56] Given that private equity firm owners were not particularly confident of their expertise in operational turnaround, it made sense to leave this to those with such expertise.[57] Furthermore, there were investors focused on distressed funds and the sponsorship of these funds were different from those on which private equity firms relied for their own sponsorship.[58]

Private equity firms are now a lot less hesitant to adopt distressed funds as one of their investment areas.[59] This change is not unconnected to the market changes that followed after the 2008 financial crisis. The market changes led experts to forecast the potentials of distressed debts to yield immense profits.[60] What had happened to bring about this change? Before 2008, companies with huge debt portfolios could easily refinance their debts. However, as the financial crisis took its toll, the stress faced by the financial market meant that the market could no longer correctly price assets.[61] This resulted in illiquidity, and to survive the illiquidity, the businesses looked to private equity. Private equity firms which previously would not be bothered about distressed businesses, took advantage of the distressed sale value at which the businesses and their securities were being offered.[62] Evidently their capacity to participate in the market for distressed debt is informed by the control it gives them to effect strategies aimed at maximizing profits for their investors.

6.3.3 Other Institutional Investors

As already noted, a list of investors may take on distressed debt investing.[63] However, the regulatory constraints, the nature of the funds, as well as the nature of distressed debt limit their ability to directly participate. For instance, in the US, banks with proprietary trading desks may participate in distress investing. It is, however, noteworthy that regulatory interventions post-2008 have somewhat affected proprietary

financing high-growth and hi-tech start-ups as venture capitalists or angel investors.); see also Schwartz and Breslow (2016) (listing investment areas of private equity firms to include mezzanine funds, real estate funds, activist funds, credit opportunity funds, structured product fund, etc.).

[56] Schwartz and Breslow (2016) § 1:4:6.

[57] Id.

[58] Id.

[59] Id.

[60] See for instance, Widows (2008) (suggesting "huge profits are waiting to be made in distressed securities.").

[61] This is known as market dislocation. For an analysis of financial market dislocation and its prevention, see Kashyap et al. (2011).

[62] Holzman (2007) (author compares the profitability of investing in distressed companies by private equity sponsors, compared to investment in non-distressed businesses).

[63] See Sect. 6.3 above.

trading by such banks.[64] Furthermore, distressed debt is quite illiquid and realization on them could take several years, meaning that investors in this class of asset need to be prepared to be invested for a relatively longer term.[65] Alternative investment funds such as pension funds and insurance companies have limitations on their capacity to invest in such illiquid assets, compared to hedge funds and private equity firms.[66] Also, compared to a hedge fund or a private equity firm that privately source for their fund, mutual funds which sell assets to the public are more constrained in terms of the amount of illiquid assets that they may hold.[67] Given that distressed debt are by their nature illiquid, it may be unlikely to find mutual funds pursuing distressed debt investment strategies. In most cases therefore, it is likely to find most distressed debt funds structured as either hedge funds or private equity firms.

Now that the players in the distressed debt market have been identified, an understanding of their strategies in engaging with distressed investors is appropriate. This is because their strategies underscore their value creation (or destruction) in a distressed business.

---

[64] Following the Volcker Rule introduced as part of the regulatory regime of the Dodd-Franks Act, traditional lenders (deposit taking banks) face restrictions (with limited exceptions) from short term proprietary trading i.e. trading on the market with their own capital. Admittedly, it is not very clear whether distressed debt investing is specifically prohibited by the Rule. However, some investment banks (e.g. Goldman Sachs) closed down their proprietary trading desk, others (e.g. JPMorgan Chase) had plans to spin off their proprietary desks. See Ben Protess (2011). The Council of the EU on its part is mulling a draft regulation aimed at preventing systemic risks, by separating the proprietary trading activities of banks from their "core" businesses such as deposit taking or retail payment. See Council of the EU, Structural Reform Of EU Banking Sector: Improving the Resilience of Credit Institutions. Available at: http://www.consilium.europa.eu/en/policies/banking-structural-reform/# (accessed 10 Mar 2018).

[65] Sakoui and Jones (2010). But see also Mietzner and Schweizer (2014), p. 185 (noting that when compared to private equity firms, hedge funds have a shorter investment horizon and face the threat of illiquidity, hence their preference for "investments where they can achieve a faster turnaround.").

[66] Harner (2008b), p. 714 (noting that "[p]ension funds and certain other institutional investors often are prohibited under their charters or applicable regulations from holding below investment grade securities.").

[67] See for instance, Flood (2017) (on liquidity rules for mutual funds); see also, Anabtawi (2006), p. 580 ("Hedge funds, like mutual funds, hold pools of assets. Unlike mutual funds, they engage in a wide variety of investment strategies, including investing in distressed securities, illiquid securities, securities of companies in emerging markets, derivatives, and arbitrage opportunities."), Macey (2008), p. 243 ("When most companies, including investment companies or mutual funds sell securities to the public, they are required to register the securities being sold with the SEC and to make all sorts of disclosures about themselves and the securities.").

6.4 Financing Strategies of Distressed Debt Investors

Distressed debt investors adopt different strategies when dealing with the distressed debtor, depending on the goals of the distressed debt investor. These goals also influence their broad categorization as passive or active investors.[68] For instance, as a passive investor, the investor may simply be a trader, buying a portion of the debt of the distressed business, with a view to profiting from the arbitrage arising from the chances of a higher valuation of the claim in the course of restructuring.[69] This strategy is characteristic of passive investors.[70] This chapter is not particularly concerned with this sort of investment, but with those which in addition to purchasing the distressed claims, extend financing to the distressed debtor, to support the restructuring of the distressed businesses,[71] as well as the intention to acquire ownership of the distressed company.[72]

A distressed debt investor may provide new financing as debt, structured equity, or through direct equity investing. For the strategies that involve the provision of debt (or debt like financing), the debt may be ranked as a senior debt, so that the investor may wind up as the distress financer of the debtor.[73] Depending on the bargain reached, the new money may be provided as senior secured debt for two strategic reasons. First, if the debtor needs to provide collateral for the debt, then that collateral will be pledged to the distressed investor, further strengthening the leverage of the investor over the debtor. Even if the debt is not a senior secured debt, the loan will usually be backed by strict debt covenants in order to ensure that the restructuring process goes as planned by the investor.[74] Secondly, providing senior secured debt puts the lender in a position where it is able to access relevant information on the debtor.[75] This information advantage helps the lender make the decision

---

[68] Altman (2014), p. 84 (author includes a third category of "active-control").

[69] See Levitin (2007), p. 87 (Noting that a strategy may be "to arbitrage the bankruptcy payment risk for a profit, buying the claims at a lower price than the expected payout."); Gilson (2010), p. 21 (noting that passive distressed debt investment does not require the investor to directly intervene in the operation of the firm or its restructuring).

[70] Gilson (2010), p. 193 (Pointing out that investors employing this strategy who correctly identify a claim incorrectly priced by the market, buy such claims and hold them until their market value appreciates).

[71] Harner et al. (2014), p. 178 (noting that these loans are given at quite high interest rates, to account for the higher risk of default).

[72] Id ("Lenders issuing these types of distressed loans are often said to be loaning to own.").

[73] For instance, during the informal restructuring of Stabilus, a German company that design, build and manufacture spring systems, Triton Partners, a private equity fund had purchased about 28% of the senior debt of Stabilus in the secondary market, while injecting €36 million into the Stabilus Group. It provided both interim financing and exit financing.

[74] In the case of the US, it may be backed by a DIP financing order, through which the lender may exert more control on the restructuring process. See generally, Peterman et al. (2014).

[75] See generally Jensen (1996), pp. 333–334 (on the challenge resulting from inaccurate information in the distressed firm).

whether to maintain a mere lender-borrower relationship, or to negotiate for the equity of the debtor, following the provision of new money.[76]

One last point to note, the strategies classified below are not set in stone. In some cases, combining all of the strategies is possible. These strategies are based on observations of case studies involving distressed debt players. It bears restating also that each of these strategies involve the provision of new money to the distressed business either as emergency funding or restructuring exit financing. It would, however, appear that whatever strategy is employed by distressed investors pursuing a proactive investment strategy entails the exercise of influence over the debtor, with a view to controlling both the restructuring process and how the debtor emerges from the restructuring.

6.5 Distressed Debt Investors: Driving Value Through Self-Interest?

This section focuses on the value creation/enhancement analysis in support of distressed investors' involvement with distressed businesses. One thing must be made clear from the outset. The sometimes-hardline puritanism with which some distressed investors drive their personal value orientation (i.e. their personal profit) gives the impression that all the other stakeholders in the company are inherently worse off. This is against the backdrop of their capacity for value creation/maximization for the distressed firm. In fact, as a building block of the book, it is agreed that both situations are possible and there are practical examples showing this. This, however, is not the subject of this section. This section characterizes the distressed debt investor as what it is: a self-interested participant. But the question is whether the self-interest of the distressed debtor rubs-off on the restructuring process, to the benefit of not just the distressed debt investor, but also, creates or maximizes value for the distressed debtor and its stakeholders.[77]

[76] Peress and Prinzhorn (2006), p. 48 ("By becoming a secured lender, the "investor" gains access to restricted information. This information advantage is a key value driver and ultimately influences the decision to either stay put as a lender or negotiate for equity after the company refinances.").

[77] See for instance Rosenberg (2000), p. 29 (author points out that vultures (distressed) investors "throw their fate in with a company for the long term, staying with it after it has climbed out of the depths"); Bratton (2007), pp. 1418–1420 (Bratton provides empirical evidence on shareholder activism championed by hedge funds, pointing out that such activism is about "shareholder value creation.").

6.5.1 Distressed Investors as Self-Interested Participants

When distressed investors set out to invest in distressed businesses, the objective is profit maximization.[78] Given their operational structures, there is in fact a heightened drive for profit maximization by distressed investors. As has been stated above,[79] these investors are often hedge funds or private equity firms that are typically structured as limited partnerships[80] with the general partners (GP) owing both fiduciary and contractual duties to their limited partners (the investors). This in effect means that the investors in the hedge funds or private equity firms are bound to seek the highest possible returns on the investments made in their portfolios.[81] Added to this is the fact that their compensation is performance based and often calculated as a percentage of the profit they make.[82] This means in many cases, that the distressed investors will take direct steps to see to the success of the businesses in which they are invested.[83]

The proper characterization of the distressed debt investor as a self-interested participant in the distressed business is also important for the discussion on value creation or maximization of the distressed business. However, it is important to distinguish value creation from value re-allocation or distribution. In the next section, this point is addressed especially as it pertains to the characterization of the distressed debt investor as a residual claimant.

---

[78] Baird and Rasmussen (2006), p. 1245 (the authors point out that the distressed debt investors are not charities and will seek to maximize their rate of returns when they act or exert their influence on the debtor); Harner (2008a), p. 103 (Distressed debt investors want to maximize the return on their investment in the debtor).

[79] See Sect. 6.3 above.

[80] Pekarek (2007), pp. 916–917 n.22 (noting most hedge funds are structured as limited partnerships).

[81] Macey (2008), p. 246 ("Hedge funds and private equity funds are highly motivated to make sure that their 'portfolio companies' succeed."); Franklin (2009), p. 13 ("... the [private equity] industry has a simple goal – to make investment capable of delivering returns to its investors that are significantly in excess of those they could obtain by investing in in the public equity markets."); Dai (2013), p. 566 (Commenting on hedge funds involved in distressed investing, author states that "Hedge fund managers also have greater incentives to generate positive abnormal returns because their compensation depends primarily on performance.").

[82] Gibson (2000), p. 684 (pointing out that "(t)he fund manager's compensation is based on the performance of the fund and ordinarily ranges from ten to twenty percent of the fund's profit."); see Dai (2013), p. 566 (pointing out that in addition to the 2% fixed fee charged by hedge funds, they typically charge a 20% performance fee which is based on the annual returns of the fund). See also Mietzner and Schweizer (2014), p. 184 (noting that the compensation structure achieves the alignment of the interests of the fund managers with those of the investors).

[83] Macey (2008), p. 248 (pointing out that distressed investors often use a "very hands-on approach to ensuring that their portfolio companies perform as well as possible.").

6.5.2 *Distressed Debt Investor as a "Residual Claimant": Value Creation or Re-allocation?*

In this section, it is essentially argued that the distressed debt investor as a residual claimant does not by itself create value for the distressed business. At best it allows for the redistribution of value from senior claimants to junior claimants. The residual claimant is considered to be that investor in a firm who receives additional value—in terms of returns on their investment—when the firm makes gains, or incurs a loss of value when the firm makes losses.[84] Residual claimants of the firm are believed by scholars to be better placed to look out for the best interest of the firm, as its self-interest coincides with that of the firm,[85] as such, identifying such actors have been advocated.[86] For this reason, scholars have hypothesized that the inefficiencies that inhere in the bankruptcy process may be overcome by the conferral of decision-making powers on residual claimants who enjoy a corresponding value increase or reduction as the assets of the distressed debtor increase or reduce against its liabilities respectively.[87]

As much as scholars agree on the positive role which the residual actor may play in the restructuring process,[88] in practical terms, it is not quite an easy task to determine which stakeholder in the firm to be restructured fits into the description of the residual actor.[89] When "the going is good" (i.e. when the firm is solvent), the shareholders of the corporation are generally regarded as the residual claimants.[90] As they strive to ensure the maximization of their residual (equity) interest in the business, the expectation is a corresponding increase in the value of the business, not just for themselves, as in the end all the stakeholders standing ahead of them will benefit

---

[84] LoPucki (2003), p. 661 ("The residual owner of a firm is the investor who will reap the marginal dollar of gain or suffer the marginal dollar of loss from the firm's activities"); see also Baird and Jackson (1988), p. 761 ("The dollar that is won or lost because of good or bad negotiating by definition is felt by the residual owner.").

[85] Goldschmid (2005), p. 196 ("… the residual actor's rational, self-motivated decision-making is so directly tied to the best interests of the firm as a whole that its self-motivated actions will also maximize that firm's overall wealth.").

[86] See Baird and Jackson (1988), p. 775 ("[T]he law of corporate reorganizations should focus on identifying the residual owner, limiting agency problems in representing the residual owner, and making sure that the residual owner has control over the negotiations that the firm must make while it is restructuring.").

[87] Jackson and Scott (1989), p. 159.

[88] Baird and Jackson (1988), p. 775 ("[T]he law of corporate reorganizations should focus on identifying the residual owner, limiting agency problems in representing the residual owner, and making sure that the residual owner has control over the negotiations that the firm must make while it is restructuring.").

[89] LoPucki (2004), pp. 1343–1347 (analyzing the concept of residual actor in bankruptcy as well as the challenge of identifying the stakeholder who serves as the residual actor).

[90] See Fama and Jensen (1983) (describing the residual claimant or residual risk bearers in the context of "healthy" firms, the authors point out that "the residual risk … is borne by those who contract for the right to net cash flows.").

from the increased value.[91] This basic assumption reinforces the protections which traditional corporate law bequeaths on shareholders, chief of which include fiduciary duties imposed on the managers of the corporation for the benefit of the shareholders, as well as the voting rights of shareholders.

The situation is quite different when the firm is in the region of insolvency. During this phase, the interest of the shareholders may be already worth next to nothing. The shareholders in the region of insolvency do not have much to lose, especially as shareholder value may have been greatly depleted or totally wiped out. Hence, the shareholders may be motivated to pursue investment strategies which may have higher hurdle rates but also involve higher risks. At this point, the survival of the distressed business will depend on the existence of a claimant who can think like shareholders would do in a solvent business.[92]

Standing on the other extreme, are senior secured creditors holding securitized debt in the business. These creditors may be even less motivated to participate in the restructuring of the distressed business of the debtor especially as they are better positioned to be paid their claim in full.[93] For good reason, they may be pro-liquidation of the business when it is in distress, or at best, advocate a hasty sale of the business.[94] This may even be the case, when pursuing a restructuring would yield a "higher expected return" for the stakeholders.[95] Furthermore, risk averse secured creditors may be particularly weary of the chances that the distressed business may pursue high-risk business strategies that may deplete the cushion on their collateral, or that may even deplete the collateral itself, leaving them worse off. The result of this apprehension by the senior creditors may therefore be an inefficient disposition of the assets of the distressed business.[96]

The divergent interests first manifest in the decision of what to do with a distressed business: liquidate the business or support a restructuring. The disagreement carries on into the process of restructuring, where the parties opt for it, leaving

---

[91] For the senior creditors, the benefit will be in terms of the assurance of the payment of the full value of their claims, while for junior claimants, this will mean that they receive increased value.

[92] Goldschmid (2005), p. 260 (suggesting that the solution to the residual actor problem is to identify the class of creditors who can step into the shoes of the shareholders in the solvent business).

[93] See LoPucki (2004), p. 1342. On the criticism that led to reform of the English receivership and the consequent reform under the Enterprise Act, 2002, see Armour et al. (2008), p. 158 ('…receivership led to excessive piecemeal liquidations and inflated costs on the theory that secured creditors (and, by extension, the receivers that they appointed) lacked the correct incentives to encourage them to maximize recoveries by favoring "going concern" outcomes and minimize the costs of their interventions.') A somewhat related problem, albeit on a larger scale, is faced by unsecured creditors in the case of big businesses that file under Chapter 11 (on corporate reorganization) of the US Bankruptcy Code. It has been argued that the consequence of the control exerted by secured creditors and their actions in exercising this control often results in the lack of incentive for those with power to recover any value for claims with lower priority. See Kuney (2005), p. 28.

[94] Ayotte and Morrison (2009), p. 514 ("Their [i.e. secured claimants'] claims may be paid in full during a quick sale, even if the firm is sold for less than its fundamental value; any delay--especially a lengthy reorganization process-could hurt them if firm value deteriorates over time.").

[95] Casey (2011), p. 761.

[96] Id.

junior claimants worse off.[97] This again points to the argument that the control of the firm in distress should be in the hands of creditors whose interests align with the interest of the firm as a whole.[98]

6.5.3 *Junior Creditors: The Role of Distressed Debt Investors as Residual Claimants*

The quest for the residual claimant whose interest coincides with that of the business therefore leads us in the direction of junior claimants who, by the design of most bankruptcy/insolvency legislations, enjoy similar legal rights and receive the same legal treatment in insolvency. The fact of the similarity in treatment therefore serves, as motivation for this class of claimants to seek the maximization of the value of the firm[99] for it is when the value of the firm is maximized that the chances of recovery are enhanced. This—as the theory goes—is particularly where the distressed debt investors come in.

Their participation in this tranche of debt, puts them in the mold of the champion of the junior creditors. One situation where distress investors stand up to the holders of senior debt is with regard to the valuation of the distressed business.[100] As is often the case, senior creditors may offer junior creditors low rates of recovery. Ordinarily, for these junior creditors, it is Hobson's choice: take the pittance offered, or go home empty-handed. With the participation of distress investors, the situation is quite different. A distress investor who seeks to profit from the arbitrage of trading in the distressed debt is more equipped with the resources to mount pressure on senior creditors by engaging the legal process in the restructuring process to possibly adjust the valuation in favor of junior claimants. Now, although the contestation of the valuation process is often done with its profit in mind, the distress investor challenges the tendency of senior lenders to extract higher value from the junior creditors and the distressed business.[101]

It is often the case that this characterization of the distressed debtor as a residual claimant is considered as a basis of its value creation.[102] As sound as the above char-

---

[97] "Junior creditors" or "junior claimant" is used in this chapter to refer to junior investments in the business, with equity occupying the lowest part of the tranche. This is consistent with the characterization of debt and equity as different tranches of investment. See Baird and Henderson (2008), pp. 1310–1311.

[98] LoPucki (2003), pp. 661–662 (the author casts doubt on the existence of a single residual actor as described by Baird and Rasmussen).

[99] See Baird and Rasmussen (2010), p. 654 ("Because they held the same kind of legal right subject to the same treatment, all had the same incentive to maximize the value of the estate.").

[100] On the valuation of the distressed business, see Roberts (2013), p. 170.

[101] Id. (advocating the contestation of the valuation of distressed businesses, as otherwise, "senior creditors would be free to extract even greater control discounts from the process.").

[102] See for instance, Jiang (2012), p. 514 (pointing out that the presence of hedge funds in corporate restructuring increases "the likelihood of a successful reorganization, which is usually associated with a higher recovery of junior claims.").

acterization of distressed debt investors may be, the narrative does not suffice to explain the underlying value creation that results from the activities of distressed investors for two reasons. This is because firstly, characterizing the distressed investor as a residual claimant (without more), presupposes at best that the distressed investor succeeds only in achieving the reallocation of value from the senior creditors of the distressed business to junior creditors. As desirable as value re-allocation may be, the benefit arising therefrom may only accrue to the distressed debt investor class, or to other similarly placed junior creditors, thereby inducing self-serving negotiation with senior creditors or the management of the distressed business. At best, what is theoretically achieved by the distressed investor in his characterization as a residual claimant, is a re-apportionment of value, so that value is taken from the senior claimants and spread to the junior claimants.[103] In sum, bearing in mind that the distressed debt investor is always motivated by its self-interest, it is not necessarily the case that its characterization as a residual claimant maximizes value for the firm. As shall be discussed much later in this chapter, its position as residual claimant may well be the basis for the destruction of value in the firm, or at best capturing firm value for itself.

Secondly, the characterization of the distressed investor as a residual claimant gives rise to an assumption that the distressed investor will always be invested in the junior debt of the distressed debtor i.e. the fulcrum debt. No doubt, distressed investors do invest in the junior claims of distressed businesses.[104] However, this is not always the case, and this is true across jurisdictions. In some cases, the distressed investor is invested in the senior debt and in some other cases, the debtor is invested across the different tranches of debt. Indeed, the decision of a distressed investor to invest in any particular tranche of the capital structure of the distressed business will depend on whether the distressed business has the capacity to fully settle its senior claims. Otherwise, the fulcrum debt may well reside with the senior creditors.[105] What this means therefore is that the distressed debtor may be invested in the senior or junior debt of the business.[106] The implication of the foregoing is that the dis-

[103] In other words, if the firm is viewed as a pie, and the size of the pie representing the value of the firm, the characterization of the firm as a residual claimant only "make[s] someone else's size smaller, thereby increasing the size of the investor's slice (even if the total size of the pie does not increase)." See Gilson (2010), p. 21.

[104] For instance, in the Chapter 11 filing of Allied Holdings and some of its subsidiaries, investment funds owned by Yucaipa (a distressed investor) owned over $ 98 Million of the $ 150 Million unsecured notes of Allied Holdings, making Yucaipa the largest debtholder before the filing. See Disclosure Statement for Joint Plan of Reorganization of Allied Holdings, Inc. and Affiliated Debtors Proposed by the Debtors, Yucaipa and the Teamsters National Automobile Transportation Industry Negotiating Committee at 20–21, *In re Allied Holdings, Inc.*, No. 05-12515 (Bankr. N.D. Ga. Mar. 2, 2007).

[105] See for instance Roberge (2013), p. 77 (pointing out that the fulcrum security of the debtor depends on the value of its collateral or assets).

[106] See the Chapter 11 filing of Tribune, where hedge funds Oaktree Capital Management and Angelo, Gordon & Co. were invested in the senior debt, while another hedge fund, Aurelius, was invested in the junior (bond) debts. See Confirmation Opinion *In re Tribune Co. et al* Case No. 08-13141 (KJC). Available at: http://www.deb.uscourts.gov/sites/default/files/opinions/judge-kevin-j.carey/kjc201101031-tribune.pdf Accessed 3 Feb 2018.

tressed investor may not necessarily be invested in the junior claim and therefore put them in the position of the champion of other junior claimants.

In any case, being a residual claimant may be relied upon to explain the motivation of distressed investors to reallocate or perhaps create value, however it does not explain the way distressed debtors create value. In the light of the foregoing, it does matter to ask: what underlies the value creation capacity of the distressed investor? Answering this question should explain why the distressed investor chooses to invest in a junior or senior debt. What follows is an explanation on why the investor may position itself in any part of the capital structure of the distressed business from which it may drive value creation in the distressed business. It is to this underlying consideration that we now turn.

It is important that the reader does not lose sight of the importance of this analysis. Recall that the book points to the value creation and reallocation role of distressed debt investors in the distressed business. It has been argued that the construct which suggests that the distressed debt investor is the residual claimant does not entirely capture the essential role of the distressed investor as a creator of value in the distressed business. At best, it points to the role of the investor as merely reallocating value. Besides, such a construct rests on the assumption that the distressed investor only invests in junior debt. Of course, as argued above, this is not necessarily true whether in the US, in the UK, or for German companies pursuing corporate restructuring in the UK. The degree of control or influence, which the distressed investor may wield, enabling it to engage in value creation is for the most part captured in three rubrics: the corporate restructuring regime, the contractual rights vested in the debts purchased, and the local legal culture.

6.6 Value Creation and the Goals of Corporate Restructuring Law

In the preceding section, the theoretical construct, which ties value creation by distressed debt investors to their role as the residual claimant in the distressed firm, has been challenged as not being sufficient to explain the role of distress investors in value creation. Indeed, the outcome of such a construct is the reallocation of value that would have been taken up by the senior creditors of the distressed business. But when value creation is the goal, it is important to be clear on what actually amounts to value creation. The goals of many corporate restructuring norms/legal regimes aspire to do more than reallocate value in the distressed business.

At the heart of corporate restructuring regimes is the maximization of value for the creditors of the business and the rehabilitation of the distressed business. In many cases, the expectation that the business will continue to provide jobs and continue as going concerns motivates the preference for restructuring over a liquidation of the business.[107] To achieve this, restructuring regimes (at least formal collective restructuring regimes) operate through structures that bring together the relevant stakeholders of the distressed debtor, so that through creative negotiations they can reach the best possible solutions for the stakeholders in the business.[108] The details of the restructuring process tend towards these goals.

The process of financial restructuring often goes hand in hand with organizational restructuring.[109] Reorganizing the financially distressed debtor encourages the distressed debtor to look more closely at its assets, and to determine the most appropriate combination of assets that will allow the business to operate efficiently

---

[107] Legislative policies tend in this direction. For instance, in the US, the legislative history of the Bankruptcy Code indicates that:

> The purpose of a business reorganization case, unlike a liquidation case, is to restructure a business's finances so that it may continue to operate, provide its employees with jobs, pay its creditors, and produce a return for its stockholders… It is more economically efficient to reorganize than to liquidate, because it preserves jobs and assets.

H.R. REP.NO. 95-595, at 220 (1977), reprinted in 1977 U.S.C.C.A.N. 5963, 6179.

See also Warren (1993), p. 355 (on the social and economic costs of liquidation authors argue that liquidation "affects employees who will lose jobs, taxing authorities that will lose ratable property, suppliers that will lose customers, nearby property owners who will lose beneficial neighbors, and current customers who must go elsewhere"); Lipson (2009), p. 1651 ("Chapter 11 negotiations are thus premised on the complex proposition that value can be maximized for all stakeholders in a debtor if the debtor is given reasonable opportunity to restructure its affairs."); Sprayregen et al. (2005) ("the ultimate goal of … [of Chapter 11 is] to maximize creditor recoveries.") In addition, in the UK, the IA 1986 for instance sets out clear policy goals for the administration process. These goals designed as the objectives of an administrator requires the office holder to rescue the company as a going concern or achieve better results for the creditors as a whole, realize property and make distribution to one or more secured or preferential creditors as the case may. These goals are set in a hierarchy, with the office holder implementing a subsequent objective where the prior objective is not reasonably practicable. See IA, 1986 Schedule B1 para 3(1). See also McCormack (2008), p. 3.

Similar sentiments have been echoed in the First Commission Report on Insolvency Law 1985. The Commission emphasized that: "The aim of the restructuring is to ensure the survival of the debtor company and ensure sustainable profitability." See Erster Bericht der Kommission für Insolvenzrecht 1985, Sentence 2.1.1, para. 1, p. 162. See also § 1 S. 1 InsO (the provision makes liquidation a goal equal to restructuring).

The same could be said of the normative restructuring regime known as the "London Approach", for which the underlying motive was to as much as possible, prevent "companies to be placed in receivership or liquidation unnecessarily for wider economic reasons [and wanting] viable jobs and productive capacities to be preserved. See Flood (2001), quoting Smith M, The London Approach, paper presented at the Wilde Sapte Seminar, London.

For the English Schemes of Arrangement, see *In the Matters of Apcoa Parking Holdings GmbH* & others [2014] EWHC 3849 (Ch) where the court agreed with the argument of the directors of the scheme companies (debtors) that without the restructuring (subject of the scheme), local insolvencies to be filed by the debtors will result in value destruction and loss of jobs.

[108] See Chap. 3 of the book. See also, Kamensky (2014), p. 237 (noting that through give and take between the debtor and its creditors, the parties may be able to "negotiate creatively to arrive at the best possible outcome for all parties in interest.").

[109] Wruck (1990), p. 420.

going forward.[110] With this restructuring, the distressed debtor is able to make operational changes where needed. For instance, it can do away with non-core assets with negative synergies and focus financial and managerial resources on its core business.[111] The underlying purpose of the participation of all of the key stakeholders may have the virtue of bringing to the table more interested stakeholders of the debtor, who may make critical input on how to improve the value of the business.

To be clear, the policy goals of corporate restructuring across most jurisdictions presupposes that value is created for the stakeholders of the distressed debtor. These goals go beyond the reallocation of existing value, but presupposes that value is created, sufficient to rehabilitate the business and improve creditors returns and to (possibly) keep the distressed debtor in business. The participation of distressed debt investors can drive the process of restructuring as investors come with characteristic qualities that can translate to value for the distressed debtor. To drive the process and add value, distressed debt investors will typically require control.

6.6.1 *Self-Interested Participants: How Distressed Investors are Positioned to Add Value*

A point which must not be lost is the concession that distressed debt investors are self-interested market participants. More than anything else, what matters to a distressed fund manager is the maximization of its profits. Their profit maximization goal notwithstanding, there still exists the possibility that their participation in the process of corporate restructuring yields benefits consistent with a goal of corporate restructuring which is the maximization of the value of the distressed business. This is because these investors have somewhat been shown to not only cooperate with other stakeholders, but also generally support the restructuring of the debtor.[112] What follows is a consideration of how the financial involvement of distressed debt investors contribute to value creation activities of distressed investors which in turn have salutary impacts on other stakeholders of the distressed business.

[110] Id (noting that restructuring of financially distressed businesses allow "resources to move to higher-valued uses by forcing managers and directors to reduce capacity and to rethink operating policies and strategy decisions.").

[111] Kaiser and Stouraitis (1995) (suggesting that firms gain from restructuring by eliminating negative synergies arising from diversification).

[112] Fuller (2006), p. 16 (2006) (suggesting that contrary to acting in a self-serving manner, distressed debt investors in the UK have worked with other lenders to drive the value proposition of the group).

6.6.2 Distress Investor Activism

The notion of activism used to be associated with institutional investors invested in corporations as shareholders, using their equity position to wrestle control from the management of the company.[113] Following the era of feverish takeovers in the 1980s in the US, distressed debt investors seem to achieve the same control results reached by the corporate raiders of those days. The difference being that rather than use equity, these investors use their debt positions in the capital structure of the debtor to effect the change in management of distressed companies. Within the frame of a loan-to-own strategy, the distressed debt investor purchases the debt of the distressed debtor or provides new financing to the distressed debtor. Through its debt position, the investor is able to pursue a debt-equity swap in the distressed business[114] with the aim of exerting management control over the debtor.[115]

First, instead of the outright purchase of equity participation in the distressed business, the investor goes for distressed debt, and uses its debt position to influence changes in the business, by the threat of, or actual invocation of rights accruing to their status as debtholders.[116] In other cases where the distressed debt investor provides new money to the distressed business, through the loan covenants, the investor has immense latitude to monitor the managers of the business, and exert pressure on the management to make certain decisions that may drive value for the business.[117] In other cases, distressed debt investors may orchestrate a change in management especially where the corporate failure is attributable to the lack of entrepreneurial creativity and poor leadership on the part of the extant management. Furthermore, distressed investors, through their activism are able to unlock corporate value which had been hitherto unharnessed or ignored by the extant managers of the business.[118] One must make haste to add that the distressed debt market will be able to effectively play this role of the distressed debt market is effectively tied to the existence of effective corporate law and litigation.

---

[113] This activism reached a feverish pitch in the 1980s with the takeovers orchestrated by investors known as "corporate raiders." For an overview of the activities of these investors, see Jensen and Chew (2011).

[114] Harner (2011), p. 157 (noting that distressed debt investors may provide new loans for the debtor or purchase its debt in order to acquire ownership of the debtor company).

[115] See for instance, The Vultures Take Wing (29 May 2007). ("Distressed-debt traders, who buy bonds no one else will touch, and turnaround specialists, who pull companies back from the brink, operate in a topsy-turvy world, where bad times are good and corporate wreckage yields rich rewards.").

[116] These rights may well be statutory, as provided for in the Bankruptcy/Insolvency legislation, or contractual rights as provided for in the distress loan agreement. For an examination of the rights accruing to a distressed debt holder in the context of US and UK corporate restructuring, see Harner (2008b), pp. 729–752.

[117] Harner et al. (2014), p. 245 (noting that such investors may pressure the company to dispose of weak divisions or to make cash distributions).

[118] Harner (2011), p. 158.

When the debtor becomes insolvent, the fiduciary duties of the managers of the distressed firm moves from protecting the interest of the shareholders to the maximization of value for the creditors in the business.[119] With this in mind, managers must make business decisions which ensure this objective. In this regard, the managers of the distressed firm will be expected to make key decisions pertaining to the form the financial restructuring should take or worst still, whether to go for an outright liquidation. Whatever the management settle on will especially turn on the appraisal of the firm, to determine how much value the firm is expected to yield. Needless to say, generally, junior creditors by their positioning are less empowered to take on senior creditors and their management "collaborators". It is here that the activism of distressed investors as junior creditors come to the rescue.

On a final note, the importance of the nature of activism undertaken by distressed investors is its strategic nature. Unlike typical investors such as mutual, and pension funds, activism by distressed investors is first informed by the distress opportunity, and the determination of whether the business in distress can benefit from activism.[120] For such typical investors (such as mutual fund and public pension fund), their activism:

> …if it occurs, tends to be incidental and ex post: when fund management notes that portfolio companies are underperforming, or that their governance regime is deficient, they will sometimes be active (footnote omitted). In contrast, hedge fund activism is strategic and ex ante: hedge fund managers first determine whether a company would benefit from activism, then take a position and become active.[121]

In the context of a distressed business, the activism of distressed investors is informed by the benefit that may arise from their activism in helping the business turn around its fortunes. As shown below, their reputation as sophisticated financial actors enhance their capacity to benefit the business.

6.6.2.1 Distressed Investors as Sophisticated Financial Actors

Distressed debt investors typically possess and exploit the requisite know-how about their target companies, which is important for engaging with the debtor and other stakeholders, in order to unlock the underlying value of the distressed business.[122] In the context of restructuring, value is created through the effective

---

[119] For the US perspective on this shift of fiduciary duties, see Ellias (2016). Although this may not be necessarily espoused in other jurisdictions without a debtor-in-possession type-arrangement, but the attitude of the court in nearly all jurisdictions will no doubt expect the management (insolvency practitioner or administrator) to act in ways that enhance the value of the firm for the creditors, when the firm is in distress.

[120] More will be said on this in the next subsection below.

[121] Kahan and Rock (2007), p. 1084.

[122] See Gilson (2012), p. 24 (noting that private equity firms invested in distressed businesses possess better information and a deeper understanding of the business which make them see opportunities where other investors see risk); see also Moya (2009) (reporting that "[a] US hedge fund once produced an 800-page report on Drax, Britain's largest power station, whose failure turned

recapitalization of the assets of the debtor.[123] The underlying assumption is that through the negotiations of the parties, the leverage on the capital structure of the debtor has been sufficiently downsized so that when new investments are made in the assets of the debtor, it can provide returns to the investors.[124] Indeed, this process does require new money, whether as debt or equity.[125] The new money may be particularly needed to help the company remain open and to continue to carry on its business.[126] Given their financial capacities, distressed investors can provide new money for the distressed debtor as a lender of last resort,[127] with a view to receive in exchange, equity stakes in the distressed debtor.

Furthermore, it is always very convenient to argue for the rescue of distressed firms. However, any rescue efforts must depend on the possibility that the distressed firm is viable but only financially distressed. Making this determination is not always an easy call. As sophisticated self-interested actors, distressed debt investors are better placed to determine which firms are viable and worthy of a rescue endeavor.[128] In all, the distressed debt investor not only provides financing to the distressed business, but it also provides the intelligence to guide the restructuring in a way that increases returns to the investor and other stakeholders of the distressed business.

6.6.2.2 Overcoming Senior Creditor Liquidation Bias

Given the interests of the distressed debt investor in the business—especially where there is a loan-to-own strategy—there is an increased likelihood that the intervention of such investors will be what stands between the liquidation of the business by the senior creditors, and the continuation of the business. This follows from the skilled investment decisions undertaken by the distressed investor, coupled with their self-interest, which aligns with the continued operation of the business. This is especially so when distressed investors take up positions as junior claimants in the distressed business.[129] Risk averse senior creditors who are protected by security

into multimillion-pound profits for funds such as BlueBay when its debt was converted into equity).

[123] Westbrook (2004), p. 825 (fn 113) (on value creation through restructuring).

[124] Id.

[125] Id.

[126] Gilson (2010), p. 55.

[127] See for instance, The Vultures Take Wing (29 May 2007) ("Indeed for many distressed borrowers, hedge funds have become the last, best hope of salvation.").

[128] Jiang (2012), p. 556 (showing that restructuring firms in which distressed debt investors were involved had strong operating performance, and are only distressed, echoing the view held by distressed debt investment practitioners that distressed investors target firms that have "good fundamentals" but "bad balance sheet.").

[129] Ibid at 540 (suggesting that the investment choices of distressed debt investors are more likely to offer desirable outcomes leading to emergence from the restructuring, as against liquidation favored by the senior claimants), as well as deviations from the absolute priority rule, for the benefit of junior claimants).

over the assets of the debtor may worry over the likely depletion of the value of the security. In some other cases where it appears the security is already depleting; senior creditors may opt for a hastened liquidation of the business. In addition to providing the distressed debtor with financing, the distressed debt investor can facilitate negotiations with the key stakeholders of the business, ensuring the emergence of the business from distress.

The English restructuring case of the German Apcoa Holding Group (Apcoa) is instructive in this regard. Apcoa, one of Europe's largest parking management company was nearing the maturity of a loan that was due in October 2014. The company was also still in need of new financing to help stabilize its operations. In the meantime, pre-distress lenders were actively offloading their claims in the secondary loan market, for fear of the outcome of the impending restructuring.[130] At the same time, Centerbridge, a distressed debt investor was buying up the loans on the market. Its agenda was clear, it wanted to be in a position to direct the restructuring of the distressed business. As it is typically the case, different pre-distress lenders have different strategies.

For some lenders, absent any legal basis for constraining their desire to quickly liquidate the borrower, that option is the first recourse, taking advantage of the financial pressures of the debtors, to extract value for themselves. So, it was with two of the senior lenders in this case. In this case, two assignees of pre-distress senior creditors were vehemently opposed to the restructuring scheme (plan), instead preferring a speedier liquidation of the indebtedness to them.[131] The involvement of Centerbridge, its controlling position, as well as its strategy was critical in driving a restructuring-focused negotiation. With the cooperation of several other senior creditors, the distressed debt investor was able to drive the negotiations in the direction of a successful restructuring of the business, providing initial new financing, and rallying other senior creditors to support the restructuring.

6.6.2.3 Driving Management Accountability, Discipline and Efficiency

Distressed debt investors may play a critical role in ensuring managerial accountability and efficiency in the conduct of the distressed business. One way in which it does this is to provide a much-needed market discipline on the distressed debtor, so that pre-distress lenders may dispose of their claims in a poorly run distressed

[130] See Ruckin (2013) (reporting "[b]anks are selling out of Apcoa and running for the door.").

[131] One of the assignees (FMS) had a reputation for pursuing strategies that improve their position and reaching a speedy liquidation when necessary. See para 22 of the decision of the court, where the court quoted the modus of FMS as follows:

> The experts from FMS...are always on the lookout ***for opportunities to accelerate the unwinding of the portfolio***. In restructuring work in particular they implement strategies in ongoing negotiations that improve FMS's position, examples include early repayment, an improved margin, higher collateral or a less complex financing structure... [Emphasis supplied].

The other dissenting lender (Litespeed) was a hedge fund. Although it was not represented in the convening and sanctioning of the scheme, it supported FMS in its submission.

debtor, and distressed investors on their part, may take control of the restructuring, or as an alternative, drive the process for the liquidation of the distressed debtor.

In cases where the distressed debt investor supports the restructuring process, its promotion of efficiency is particularly tied to the time which the distressed firm may spend in the course of (especially formal) restructuring. With control over the process, the distressed debt investor is able to set timelines within which the business should restructure. The formal restructuring of Kmart is oft cited to explicate this point.[132] The company had experienced significant delays in the negotiation of its restructuring plan, incurring huge costs in the monthly payments associated with the professionals involved in the restructuring. Then along came ESL as a distress investor who bought a significant stake in Kmart's debt. ESL also offered the debtor exit financing. Typically, this financing was not without conditions, chief among them being the early exit from formal restructuring, with the threat of rescinding the exit financing offered.[133] Similarly, ESL took swift steps to negotiate financing settlement with a trade creditor who had threatened and in fact had the capacity to further delay proceedings through a hold-up of the plan confirmation, being a large unsecured trade creditor.[134] Eventually, the company experienced a tremendous increase in its share value following the restructuring.[135]

The above exemplifies a distressed investor involvement in a formal restructuring. Given their interest in speedy conclusion of the restructuring process, it is argued—especially in the context of formal restructuring—that compared to traditional lenders, distressed debt investors are better placed to balance restructuring benefits with the direct and indirect costs that result from lengthy formal restructuring proceedings.[136] Similar results may be achieved in informal restructuring or through a prepack, if the distressed investor appears before the debtor files for formal restructuring.

[132] For a detailed explanation of the involvement of a distressed debt investor in the formal restructuring of Kmart, see Harner (2008b), p. 725.

[133] Ibid, pp. 724–726.

[134] Id.

[135] See generally, Berkowitz (2006) https://thehedgefundjournal.com/kmart-a-case-for-the-bankruptcy-history-books/ (accessed Aug. 10, 2017) (pointing out that the prices of common stock issued to pre-distress creditors as part of the formal restructuring plan peaked tremendously risen to 543% within an 18-month holding period).

[136] See Goldschmid (2005), p. 217 (author points out that this way, distressed debt investors can reduce transaction costs and achieve economic efficiency in large bankruptcies).

6.7 When Distressed Investor Self Interest Becomes Value Destructive

The case made above regarding the capacity of distressed investors to create value for the business, like many things in life is not an absolute truth. This is because distressed debt investors also have their downsides, so that a relativist approach can be taken on the question of value creation by the distressed debt investors.[137] Apart from this relativist approach, one must not lose sight of the settled fact that distressed debt investors are first profit oriented and act as rational economic actors to drive value for themselves, and at best incidentally, for the other stakeholders of the distressed business.[138]

Recall that the distressed investor creates value through the means of control which it exercises over the process of restructuring. This control when solely used in the pursuit of the distressed investors' self-interest could have negative results for the distressed business and its broader stakeholders.[139] When a distressed investor acts like this, the result is often not only the extraction of existing value in the business, but also possible destruction of it. This value destruction manifests in different ways. Furthermore, given that it is not all the time that the self-interest of the distressed investor aligns with creating value which manifests in the successful restructuring of the distressed debtor, the pertinent question will border on how the courts should react to such value destruction or diversion. This of course will be as it pertains to formal (or in-court restructurings).

The role of the court will be examined, in the light of particular situations where distressed investors have sought to push their profiteering agenda in ways that do not maximize value for the other stakeholders. These value destructive tendencies are analyzed below in the light of investor's strategic hold-up of the restructuring and the use of multiple restructuring positions of the restructuring.

6.7.1 Strategic Hold-Up of Restructuring

As part of its involvement in the process of corporate restructuring, distressed debt investors have the capacity to hold-up the process of restructuring in two situations that both have detrimental consequences for the distressed business. The first relates to hold up of the restructuring process by way of ransom demands, the purpose

[137] See Harner et al. (2014), p. 169 (noting that whether the activities of distressed debt investors in the business may be considered value creating will depend on the part of the capital structure from which the proponent or opponent makes the argument).

[138] Id (noting that sometimes, distressed debt investors will adopt corporate decisions which enhance the value of their claims against that which maximizes firm value).

[139] Lipson (2009), p. 1639 ("There is also the possibility that [the involvement of distressed debt investors] permits sophisticated player to obtain transitory control, and to exercise that control, in ways that may benefit the holder at the expense of the debtor and its stakeholders.").

being to negotiate leverage to improve their profits.[140] This will be typical amongst claim traders who in their quest to improve their profit, they become irritants, creating nuisance value, to the detriment of the restructuring process.[141] The second relates to investors who in a bid to execute a loan-to-own strategy, enter into long-drawn conflicts to consolidate on their position of control over the business. The consequence can be worsened when there are several distress investors invested in different parts of the capital structure of the debtor.[142]

The investors with (control in mind) may propose different approaches to the restructuring, while offering financing for the restructuring, and in a bid to ensure that they assume control, the distressed business suffers the consequences. Investors may set out for an "all-out-war" in their quest to improve their returns.[143] These contests could be detrimental as they are typically characterized by long-drawn, and expensive litigation which result in loss of value for the distressed business.

6.7.2 *Multiple Positions in Capital Structure and Consequent Perverse Incentive*

Distressed debt investors often have the capacity to strategically invest in different parts of the capital structure of the business. For instance, in addition to purchasing a stake in different positions of the debt structure, such an investor may also hold an equity position, either through actual purchase of the shares or through short selling,[144] or investment in derivatives.[145] The rationale for such strategy will be that where as a result of the restructuring plan, there is a dilution or elimination of equities, the investor profits from the debt, as well its short position.[146] When an investor holds multiple positions, it may well serve as an incentive for value destruction to the detriment of the other stakeholders of the business.[147] For instance, an investor

[140] Lipson (2009), p. 1617 ("This leverage might, in turn, enable the investor to extract rent from other stakeholders of the debtor who are committed to supporting the plan.").

[141] See Murray-Watson (2005) (recounting how Centaurus and other distressed debt investors tried to hold up the takeover of a financially distressed Energies by Cable and Wireless).

[142] Chasan (2009) (recounting how disagreements by distressed debt investors over valuation of the company lengthened the restructuring).

[143] Harner et al. (2014), p. 178 ("Critics of [distressed debt investors] point to their scorch-earth tactics....").

[144] Short selling involves the sale of stock which in this context does not belong to the investor. The goal of short selling is to enable the seller reap profits from a fall in the price of the underlying stock.

[145] Credit derivatives may be used to limit the exposure of an investor in the event that an event such as a default or failure occurs.

[146] Lipson (2009), p. 1654.

[147] For a description of events leading to the decline of Tower Automotive, a US truck frame supplier to the auto industry, see Sender (2005), p. Cl. See below the English case of *Re Colt Telecom Group*.

who takes a short or derivative position on the failure of the restructuring or a fire sale of its assets may act in ways that yield such results.[148] In such situation, the investor no doubt maximizes value for its own investment, plays no part in improving the governance of the company,[149] while producing undesirable consequences for other stakeholder classes.[150]

When distressed debt investors use their multiple positions in this way, the perception of their investment as having the capacity to maximize value for the business becomes difficult to justify. However, even more than that, it is doubtful that such investors will provide financing for the distressed business, neither do such investors have in mind the creation of value in the long term. Such multiple positions held by a distress investor may provide an indication of a short-term investment horizon which may well be inconsistent with value maximization.

6.8 Fear of Value Destruction and Investor Exclusion: "Throwing Away the Baby with the Bathwater"?

The contentious litigation and other strategic behavior often spearheaded by distress investors come at huge financial costs for the already distressed business. In some cases where the business is unlucky to have several distress investors in its capital structure, it may even run out of cash as the investors engage in contentious litigation.[151] In some other cases, a distressed debt investor aggression may stem from its desire to own the distressed business, either through a debt-equity swap, or through the ownership of key assets of the debtor's business. As a result, business owners and managers (borrowers) still fear the involvement of distressed debt investors in their capital structure, especially where the debt is bought in the secondary market without the knowledge of the debtor.[152] One manifestation of this fear was the use of certain clauses that formed part of standard loan agreements, restricting the transfer of loans or participation in it to specified third parties as well as requiring

---

[148] See Partnoy and Skeel (2007), pp. 1034–1035 (noting that shorts selling and the use of other derivatives have the tendency to incentivize the investor to force the borrower into a default).

[149] Ibid, at 1033 (noting that this is so especially because the possibilities of maximizing their value dulls the incentive to actively monitor the borrower).

[150] Lipson (2009), p. 1661 (holders of multiple positions may "reduce recoveries for other stakeholders, destroy going concern value, and needlessly eliminate jobs").

[151] Peress and Prinzhorn (2006), pp. 57–58. (author cites the case of America Remanufacturers Inc. involving three distressed investors, investing in senior and 2nd lien tranches of the debt of the company. While Black Diamond Capital Finance LLC, the senior debt holder offered financing with terms favoring the disposition of the business with itself as a lead bidder, the other two investors, which controlled the second liens (DDJ Capital Management LLC and Airlie Opportunity Master Fund Ltd) offered financing which favored the restructuring of the debtor. The result of the ensuing litigation was the conversion of the case to a liquidation in Chapter 7).

[152] For concerns on the use of new financing as a guise for aggressive loan-to-own strategy by distressed debt investors in Europe, see Weijs and Baltjes (2018), p. 230.

borrower consent before such transfers. As it particularly concerns the specification of third parties, the preferred transferees are typically "banks and other financial institutions."[153] In one of such cases, the US district court excluded a distressed debt investor from voting on a formal restructuring plan, holding that it fell outside the class of eligible assignees as contemplated in the loan agreement.[154]

Contractual restrictions do have their shortcomings and may indeed produce mixed results. Giving effect to such restrictions may discount the potentially valuable contribution of distressed debt investors in the successful restructuring of distressed business. In addition, given the important financing role which distressed debt investors have taken on, it will be increasingly difficult to exclude such investors from the class of "other financial institutions."[155] This is particularly in view of their capacity to serve as a key source of new financing. Furthermore, the fear that the distressed debt investor may be more aggressive to deal with may yield no different result if it is held on the portfolio of the original lender or another financial institution who is unwilling to participate in the restructuring.

In the light of the foregoing and in the context of formal restructuring, it becomes important to delicately balance the self-interested profit maximization goals of

---

[153] Gullifer succinctly opines that such clauses are inserted as a result of concerns that:

> ...were the loans to be assigned to, for example, hedge funds specializing in distressed debt, it would be enforced in a much more aggressive way than it would be by a bank. It also stems from the concern that the loan might be sold to one of the competitors of the borrower.

See Gullifer (2015), p. 65. See the English cases of *Re Olympia Securities Commercial Plc v. WDW 3 Investments Limited & ors* [2017] EWHC 2807 (Ch); *McKillen v Maybourne Finance Ltd and anor.* [2012] EWCA Civ 864; *Barbados Trust Company Ltd v Bank of Zambia and another* [2007] EWCA Civ 148. *Essar Steel Ltd v The Argo Fund Ltd* [2006] EWCA Civ 241).

[154] See *Meridian Sunrise Village v NB Distressed Debt Investment Fund Ltd (2014) WL 909219,*at 4:

> ...[i]f the parties had intended "financial institutions" to mean what the Funds claim it means—any entity that manages money—then Bank of America was free to assign the loan to virtually any entity that has some remote connection to the management of money—up to and including a pawnbroker.

[155] See *Essar Steel Ltd*, at para 43, Lord Justice Auld of the English Court of Appeal construed other financial institutions as follows:

> In my judgment, the Judge correctly concluded that the term "other financial institution" in the expression "bank or other financial institution" need not be a bank or even akin to a bank. Clearly, the disjunctive form of the contractual expression, "bank or other financial institution", allowed for a financial institution that was not a bank, certainly not in the narrow conventional sense of lending money and/or accepting deposits for investment.

But contrast the decision of the US district court in *Meridian Sunrise Village v NB Distressed Debt Investment Fund Ltd (2014) WL 909219,* at 4:

> ...[i]f the parties had intended "financial institutions" to mean what the Funds claim it means—any entity that manages money—then Bank of America was free to assign the loan to virtually any entity that has some remote connection to the management of money—up to and including a pawnbroker.

distressed debt investors, to the equally important policy goals of corporate restructuring i.e. the maximization of value for creditors, to which they may contribute. One way to do so is to ensure that the self-interest pursuit of distressed debt investors is circumscribed within firm value creation/maximization as the overarching motif of the restructuring. In the light of this, a "**collateral purpose and effect**" rule is proposed below.

6.9 The "Collateral Purpose and Effect" Rule

The formulation of the collateral purpose and effect rule has its origins in the English common law, involving the grant of a petition for winding up (or bankruptcy) proceedings.[156] It rests on the pillars of the collective nature of the proceedings and the need to prevent the abuse of the winding up (or bankruptcy) proceedings for a purpose, other than the need to receive payment for the debt (collateral purpose). Such proceedings are typically collective, in the sense that it allows for the realization of the assets of the company or individual and the disbursement of the proceeds in the order of priority. The courts have held that where a party seeks the involuntary winding up or bankruptcy of the debtor, then it is important that majority of the other creditors, especially of the same class are agreeable to, or are in support of the petition filed. In the old case of *Re Crigglestone Coal Company Limited*,[157] Buckley J. opined that:

> If a majority of the class are opposed to his view, and consider that they have a better chance of getting payment by abstaining from seizing the assets, then, upon general grounds … the Court gives effect to such right as the majority of the class desire to exercise. This is no exception. It is a recognition of the right but affirms that it is the right not of the individual, but of the class; that it is for the majority to seek or to decline the order as best serves the interest of their class.[158]

The above is only one pillar of the derived collateral purpose and effect rule i.e. the collective nature of the proceedings. The second pillar which is considered more cogent for the proposed rule is the collateral purpose which has informed the action of the petitioner. In this sense, the English courts have restrained or denied petitioners an order to wind up a distressed debtor, even where the debt in question is still unpaid and unchallenged by the debtor. The rationale for this hesitance by the courts have been to decipher the purpose for which the petition is brought. In *Re a*

[156] Winding up applies to companies while bankruptcy applies to individuals in the English law context. Although the proceedings are somewhat different, the English court has held that they are similar in terms of their collective nature. See *Cambridge Gas v. Official Committee of Unsecured Creditors of Navigator Holdings plc* [2007] 1 AC 508 at para 14–15.

[157] [1906] 2 Ch 327.

[158] Ibid, 331–332. The English Court of Appeals in *Re P & J Macrae Limited* [1961] 1 WLR 229 (at 232, per Willmer LJ and at 238–239 per Upjohn LJ); Re *Leigh Estates (UK) Limited* [1994] BCC 292, at 294.

Company,[159] the court pointed out that when faced with a winding up petition, the relevant question is: "for what purpose does the petitioner wish to wind up the company."[160] If the purpose is for its own rather than for the class tow which it belongs, then the petition has not been properly brought before the court.[161] Thus, creditor who petitioned for the winding up of the debtor, for the purpose of taking over the lease of the debtor's business premises was denied a winding up order.[162]

The proposed rule as a normative framework deviates from and extends the English rule as applied in the winding up context, to situations where courts are faced with the presence of distressed debt investors in the capital structure of a financially distressed business undergoing formal restructuring. In a much wider sense, the rule can be applied in situations where distressed debt investors seek to influence the outcome of the restructuring process to solidify their loan-to-own strategy. This strategy by itself will qualify as a collateral purpose. It will therefore remain to determine what effect the collateral purpose will have on the other creditors or how the strategy of the investor fits into the overall policy of restructuring.

When faced with the involvement of distressed debt investors in the restructuring of distressed debtors, it may be necessary in such situations, that the court, examining the entire circumstances of the case, look out for two things: the existence of a collateral purpose; and how the collateral purpose measures up against the goals of the restructuring. The loan-to-own strategy adopted by distressed debt investors is indeed a classic case of a collateral purpose: thus, the distressed debt investor either purchases the debt of the distressed company, or provides it with a loan, with a view to acquiring the company. In the same vein, trading in the claims of distressed businesses to profit from their nuisance value is also a collateral purpose. To achieve these ends, the distressed investor employs all manner of strategies to attain its own profit maximization goal. It is, however, not enough to argue that the distressed debtor is motivated by a collateral purpose, thus prejudging its involvement as unpleasant or reprehensible. It also must be shown that the collateral purpose only achieves a reallocation of value to the distressed debt investor, leaving all other claimants worse off. Two English court cases, and a US decision will be used to expatiate on typical collateral purposes and to show that the courts have somehow incorporated this approach to distressed debt investors involvement in the capital structure of restructuring businesses.

Re Leigh Estates (UK) Ltd[163] shows how the English court has addressed the collateral purpose of a creditor exercising a strong-arm tactic. Although the claimant was not a distressed debt investor, the case demonstrates how a court can refuse to lend its authority to the coercive behavior on the part of claimant. The petitioning claimant, (a local council) brought a petition to wind up the debtor company which

---

[159] (No. 001573 of 1983) [1983] BCLC 492.

[160] Id.

[161] Id.

[162] Id. See also *Bryanston Finance Ltd v De Vries (No 2)* [1976] Ch 63; *Ebbvale Limited v Hosking* [2013] UKPC 1.

[163] [1994] BCC 292.

was undergoing administrative receivership, as a result of unpaid rates in respect of an unoccupied premises owned by the debtor company. The administrative receiver had been appointed by secured creditors whose claims against the debtor company were higher than that of the petitioning claimant. The strategy of the petitioning claimant was that if the court granted a winding up order, the receivers or possibly the banks would become liable for the rates on the premises. Opposing the order sought, the secured creditors took the position that an order to wind up the debtor company would negatively affect the realisation efforts of the administrative receiver. More so, it would negatively impact the general body of creditors. Dismissing the petition, the court first identified the collateral purpose underlying the behaviour of the petitioning claimant. This was apparently to improve the value of its claim. However, the result of improving the value of its claim was not to maximize the value of the estate of the debtor, neither was it to improve the value accruing to other unsecured creditors. Instead, the petitioning creditor sought a preference over other creditors.[164]

In *Re: Glenn Maud*,[165] the English court examined the coercive tendency of a distressed debt investor employing a loan-to-own strategy, one of the results of its strategy being the statutory order which the plaintiff sought to set aside.[166] Although the case was one for personal bankruptcy, it is instructive first because it illustrates the coercive tendencies of distressed debt investors desirous of taking control of the business through a loan-to-own strategy.[167] Secondly it emphasizes how the existence of a collateral purpose by an investor does not by itself render the conduct of the investor reprehensible. The court examined investors' coercive behavior as tending towards an abuse of court process in two situations. In this regard, the court pointed out as follows:

> … the pursuit of insolvency proceedings in respect of a debt which is otherwise undisputed will amount to an abuse in two situations. The first is where the petitioner does not really want to obtain the liquidation or bankruptcy of the company or individual at all, but issues or threatens to issue the proceedings to put pressure on the target to take some other action which the target is otherwise unwilling to take. The second is where the petitioner does want to achieve the relief sought but he is not acting in the interests of the class of creditors

---

[164] In the words of the court:

> I find that [the petitioning claimant's] reason for seeking to wind up the company is not to swell the estate of the company or otherwise to improve the lot of the unsecured creditors but rather to gain for themselves a preference over the secured and unsecured creditors alike. It might reasonably be said that this attitude is not acting in the interests of the class of unsecured creditors.

Ibid at 295.

[165] *Edgeworth Capital Luxembourg Sarl, Aabar Block Sarl v Glenn Maud* [2016] EWHC 1016 (Ch).

[166] According to the evidence of the applicant, part of the strategy of the respondents (distressed investors) was to render him bankrupt, which would trigger the pre-emptory right in the company charter to enable them get full control over the business. Ibid para 17 of the judgment.

[167] The petition creditors had purchased participation in the debts which they now hold from Royal Bank of Scotland (RBS) following the default of the borrower.

> of which he is one or where the success of his petition will operate to the disadvantage of the body of creditors.[168]

Similarly, in a recent US case,[169] the distressed debt investor did not hide its collateral purpose which was to effect ownership of the business of the distressed debtor through a credit bid,[170] instead of to have its loan repaid to it. On the effect of the investor's collateral purpose on the stakeholders of the distressed debtor, the court pointed out as follows:

> [the distressed debt investor] has tried to depress the sales price of the Debtors' assets, not to maximize the value of those assets. A depressed value would benefit only [the distressed debt investor], and it would do so at the expense of the estate's other creditors.[171]

These three cases exemplify the principled approach to distressed debt investing which places the value creation or maximization—which is the hallmark of formal restructuring regimes—before the judge as the overarching policy, against which investor action is to be measured. It is important to state here that the loan-to-own strategy (which has been identified as motivating distressed debt investor coercive behavior) ought not be considered as of itself to be reprehensible, as to form the sole basis on which the courts may frown at the involvement of distressed debt investors. The coercive behavior of a creditor may not of itself be reprehensible as to deprive the investor of the remedy which it seeks before the court. However, the remedy sought ought to be measured against how much broader value will result from granting the claim of the creditor.

The English court was faced with this situation in the Scheme of Arrangement confirmation case of the German company Apcoa Parking Holding Gmbh. In this case,[172] the opposing creditor by assignment—FMS Wertmanagement Anstalt Öffentlichen Rechts ("FMS")—argued tenuously that Centerbridge Partners, a distressed debt investor was championing the restructuring of the distressed group because it was pursuing its own objective as a specialist in distressed debt investment with a loan-to-own strategy.[173] The Scheme court was not impressed by this

---

[168] See para 29.

[169] *In re The Free Lance–Star Publishing Co. of Fredericksburg, VA* 512 BR 798 (E.D. Virginia, Richmond Division. April 14, 2014).

[170] A credit bid under Chapter 11 allows a secured creditor to bid for the asset over which it has a security interest in a sale of the asset, so that the debt owed is offset against the purchase price of the asset. See 11 U.S.C. 363(k)a.

[171] Id at 806.

[172] *Re Apcoa Parking Holdings GmbH* [2014] EWHC 3849 (Ch).

[173] Ibid at para 17:

> Centerbridge is the real mastermind and driving force of the Schemes, and that it has contrived them and their urgency in pursuit of its own commercial objectives as a specialist in distressed debt investment with a "loan-to-own" strategy or model of buying distressed loans at a significant discount and then seeking to swap the debt for equity in a restructuring which enables a profit to be made on the exit from its equity investment.

characterization of the Centerbridge Partners, given the particular circumstances of the case. It was clear to the court that an overwhelming majority of the creditors had consented to the scheme. Also, Centerbridge had provided new monies to the distressed business, which had sustained the distressed debtor until the time which the debtor now sought another round of financing. Furthermore, as the court found, unless the scheme was approved, the distressed entity was condemned to a certain liquidation under German law. The result was a greater economic loss for the creditors as a whole. This, in addition to the attendant economic loss to the broader stakeholders of the business. Although the court did not deem it necessary to weigh in on the loan-to-own strategy, its attitude to the greater good to be served by the restructuring[174] supports the collateral purpose and effect principle proposed in this book. In the words of the court: '[i]t may well be that Centerbridge has been pursuing a "loan-to-own" strategy and may have driven a hard bargain; but the fact is that the other sophisticated creditors consider the prescription to offer a cure.'[175] This is instructive in the context of distressed investors in a restructuring. When such investors seek to arm-twist the management of the business in furtherance of their self-interest, the court must be able to look at the consequence of granting the claim which they seek, and how widespread the fruits of their coercion will be in terms of the maximization of the value of the distressed debtor.

To further clarify the principle stated above, it is needful to restate that the approval of a coercive conduct must be examined in the light of the value creation/maximization that will result from the order sought from the courts. The emphasis should not be merely on value reallocation but on the creation or maximization of the value of the distressed business. This explains the reasoning of the English court in *Re Colt Telecom Group Plc.*[176]

In *re Colt*, distressed debt investors, had at different times, purchased Notes issued by Colt Telecom, significantly discounted over the face value. At the time of bringing the petition to place Colt Telecom in administration, the distressed investor held Notes of Colt Telecom to the tune of £75m, representing 7% of the Notes issued by Colt Telecom. As its strategy, the distressed debt investor took "short" positions in the equity of their targets expecting a fall in the price of its shares, while acquiring the debt of their targets at a discount, in the expectation that it could negotiate for higher value for the debts.[177] Interestingly, although Colt Telecom had not defaulted on the bonds, the distressed debt investor sought to put the Colt Telecom in administration, arguing that Colt Telecom was distressed and was likely to be insolvent in the nearest future. While there were clear indications to show that Colt

[174] The court noted that the alternative for the company was an insolvency proceeding under German law would be extremely damaging in value terms for the other creditors, given that such will yield abysmally low realization values. See para 33 of judgment.

[175] See para 118.

[176] [2002] EWHC 2815 (Ch).

[177] Ibid at 14 ("The initial approach to Colt suggested a 100% payment of the face value of the Notes, even though repayment of capital was years away and [distress investor] had obviously bought the notes at a discount. They were obviously after a large and quick profit.").

Telecom was still relatively stable,[178] the distressed debt investor based its petition on a plunge in the price of the equities of Colt Telecom, operational losses, and negative cashflows. If the distressed debt investor had succeeded in persuading the court to commence administration proceedings, the investor would have made a quick profit on its 7% debt holding.[179]

The court recognised the coerciveness of the move of the distressed debt investor. In other words, the court recognized the **collateral purpose** as being to compel the borrower to take a cause of action. However consistent with the proposed principle, it was also important to decipher what the **effect** of the collateral purpose will be on the business. On the effect, it was clear to the court that although the distressed debt investor proposed to enter into formal restructuring (administration), it indeed sought to achieve an unjustified reallocation of value from the shareholders to itself. In the words of the court:

> What is not issue in is that a key object of the proposed administration is to achieve what [distressed debt investor] call "a restructure." What they actually mean is *a transfer of value in the company from the shareholders to the bondholders* — either by conversion of debt to equity or simply by payment from Colt's cash or both. The initial approach to Colt suggested a 100% payment of the face value of the Notes, even though repayment of capital was years away and [the distressed debt investor] had obviously bought the notes at a discount. *They were obviously after a large and quick profit.* [Emphasis supplied][180]

In the *Colt* case, it was quite clear what the intentions of the distressed debt investor were and especially as the effect was to bring about a value transfer in favour of bond holders and to the detriment of the stakeholders.

Identifying the **collateral purpose and effect rule** of an investor's strategy on the restructuring process presents the court with an opportunity to determine how much it is willing to allow the involvement of the investor in directing or driving the restructuring process. So far, the analysis has been focused on markets with advanced restructuring regimes, with courts conversant with the law and practice of distressed debt restructuring, and with at least an appreciable presence of distressed debt investors, coupled with a wide margin of discretion. The distressed debt market is examined, from the perspective of frontier markets, with particular reference to Nigeria.

---

[178] At the time of the application, Colt was a FTSE mid-250 member, with a market capitalization in excess of £550m and its latest balance sheet showed net assets of £977m.

[179] Recall that the distressed debt investor took a short position in the stock. Hence, a decline in the price of the shares of the borrower means that the investor earns a profit. On the other hand, exerting the pressure of a potential administration proceeding had the potential to force the borrower to avoid negotiations with the investor on its notes.

[180] See para 14.

6.10 Managing Distressed Debt in Frontier Markets: The Nigerian Example

Many frontier markets are characterized by their low liquidity, immature capital markets,[181] low market capitalization as well as fledgling formal restructuring regime.[182] When businesses operating in such markets are distressed, they have limited options when sourcing for new financing to facilitate their restructuring. Also, whether the distressed business survives through distress is a function of the disposition of the lender towards the restructuring of the debtor, coupled with the regulatory constraints such lenders face. The traditional lenders who typically provide financing in this market may not be in the position to provide the financing required by the debtor to steer itself away from troubled waters, especially in situations where the lenders themselves are struggling with huge non-performing loans of their own. This means that the availability of a secondary market for such loans will not only be beneficial for the distressed businesses themselves, but also for the traditional lenders within the market.[183]

There is no thriving distressed debt market in frontier markets. Given the characteristics of frontier markets already noted above, and the domination of the market by traditional bank lenders, non-performing loans (NPLs) in the portfolio of these bank lenders is the most likely entry point for distressed debt investors. This section focuses on Nigeria, a frontier market, arguing that such a market for NPLs can have a salutary impact on the value of distressed firms within the country, and pointing out perceived regulatory missteps that may further hamper entry of such investors.

6.10.1 *Nigeria's Distressed Debt: Post-2008*

Although commercial bank lenders within Nigeria had had quite a checkered history, the period after 2008 marked a watershed in the handling of bad loans. At this time, it is reported that most of the banks had to make huge provision for the bad loans on their balance sheet, impacting their capital and their lending capacity to businesses in need of financing.[184] Indeed, it was difficult to provide financing to healthy borrowers, not to mention businesses which were already in distress. In fact,

[181] See Chap. 1, Sect. 1.3 on the characteristics of frontier markets.

[182] See Wielebinski and Hardt (2017).

[183] Levy (2017) (noting that an expanded role for the secondary market for distressed debt is a constructive strategy and as such, a priority for emerging markets).

[184] See Echebiri (2012) ("The provisions ate deep into the capital of most of the banks and considerably reduced their credit creation capacity."); see also Nwagbaraji (2010) ("These bad business deals are weighing on the balance sheets of these banks and have impacted on their abilities to be effective financial intermediaries, hence, the commercial bankers' inability to lend funds to consumers and the business communities.").

the lenders themselves were in desperate need of a market for their NPLs, if they would have a chance to stabilize. It was clear that an intervention was necessary.

In spite of the uncertainties and challenges that characterized the Nigerian market at the time, the bank lenders were hesitant to sell the distressed debt it their portfolio. First, the bank lenders were unwilling to discount the already non-performing assets in their portfolio.[185] Secondly, as with distressed claims generally, bank lenders are often wary and unwilling to give representations, warranties and indemnities to potential buyers of the distressed assets, especially for non-standard risks[186] which may be passed on to the buyers of the loan.[187] As the Nigerian government sensed the existential threat posed by the NPLs to the economy at large, it took important steps to set up an entity to manage the situation. This entity is the Asset Management Corporation of Nigeria (AMCON).

6.10.2 AMCON as Sole Trader in Nigeria's Secondary Loan Market

AMCON was established under the AMCON Act.[188] Its mandate was essentially to mop up NPLs of Nigerian financial institutions that had been rescued by the Nigerian Central Bank, as well as the relatively stable financial institutions which had huge NPLs as a result of margin loans.[189] The expectation was that through its intervention, stability would be restored to the banking and financial sectors of the country.[190]

---

[185] Simon Mundy (2010) ("We thought the banks would welcome us with open arms, but they were unwilling to give a discount…"A company might not have paid [the bank lenders] in two or three years, but if we express an interest, it suddenly has value for them.").

[186] In practice, standard liabilities which may be incurred by the distressed debt investor will include the risk that the courts refuse part or all of the claims of the bank lender, the risk of lower recovery arising from the overvaluation of the loan, or that the purchaser of the portfolio may have further legacy obligations of the seller, e.g. funding an unfunded portion of a letter of credit. The purpose of the representations, warranties, and indemnities is to protect the purchaser of the loan from any risk or liability not falling into the class of standard liabilities, which may well arise as a result of wrongdoing by the bank lender especially given that less information exist regarding such private debts. See Gilson (2010), p. 35. See also Fortgang and Mayer (1990), p. 19 (stressing the crucial importance of representations, warranties and indemnities and how a large number of deals failed because of them, even when the parties had agreed on the economic terms).

[187] Id ("obtaining representations, warranties, or indemnities can be difficult, however, because creditors who sell their claims most often wish to rid themselves of all ties to the [distressed debtor])".

[188] See AMCON Act 2010. The Act was amended in 2015.

[189] Margin loans are loans collateralized by the stock of the borrower trading on the Nigerian stock exchange. This was particularly a major cause of the spike in NPLs during the period leading up to the creation of AMCON. See *Transcript: Interview with Nigeria's new central bank governor* FT (Jun. 21, 2009).

[190] See Mike Igbokwe, *Receivership under the AMCON Act: Scope and Application.* Text of paper

In addition to its other roles under the AMCON Act, AMCON played the role of Nigeria's distressed debt investor in NPLs. How so? By virtue of the legislation establishing it, AMCON was empowered to buy the debt claims[191] held by commercial lenders[192] pursuant to a valuation or pricing guideline to be issued by the Central Bank of Nigeria from time to time.[193] Upon purchasing any debt claims from the bank lender, AMCON generally assumes all the rights of the lender, to the exclusion of all others who may be interested in the debt claim and any asset securing the claim.[194] Furthermore, upon assuming the debt and the contractual assignment of the claim, AMCON effectively trumps any contractual stipulation restricting such a transfer, or any consent, notification, registration or licensing requirement.[195] The only restraint to the transfer of the debt and the asset securing it which is recognized under the statute is the existence of a subsisting valid court order of which the bank lender has been made aware.[196]

As a statute-backed corporation, AMCON is set ahead of private investors willing to invest in distressed debt. Although there is no statutory prohibition of private players, it might have been difficult for such private debt investors to compete in the difficult Nigerian market with a statute-backed corporation like AMCON. Apart from its first-mover advantage, the statutory protection enjoyed by AMCON took care of two of the most important challenges which distressed debt investors typically faced with the bank lenders i.e. the refusal of the bank lenders to discount the debts, and the unwillingness to provide buyers with representations, warranties and indemnities.[197] In addition, in practice, the debt sale agreements between AMCON and bank lenders were drafted in such a way that AMCON excluded standard risks

presented at the 6th AMCON interaction with Federal High Court, Court of Appeal, and Supreme Court Justices held on March 27–28 at the National Judicial Institute, Abuja.

[191] Described in the AMCON Act as eligible bank assets (EBA). See s. 24 AMCON (Act (as amended).

[192] Described in the AMCON Act as eligible financial institutions (EFIs).

[193] The Guidelines are to be issued pursuant to the provisions of s. 28 AMCON Act (as amended). The Guidelines for the Operations of the Asset Management Corporation of Nigeria, 2010.

[194] See s.34 (1) AMCON Act. The earlier legislation required AMCON to also assume the obligations of the lenders, however any reference to obligations have been deleted in the amended legislation.

[195] See s. 34(2)(a) and (b). In the light of the current personal property security regime in Nigeria, it is not clear what happens if an issue of priority arises between AMCON and another creditor, where the bank lender had failed or neglected to perfect the movable asset prior to the transfer of the asset to AMCON. For an analysis of the current personal property security law regime in Nigeria, see Iheme and Mba (2017).

[196] See s. 34(2) (c) AMCON Act (as amended).

[197] See s. 42(c) AMCON Act (as amended) (which holds the bank lender liable in damages for undisclosed representations made by it); s. 43(1)(a) AMCON Act (as amended) (excludes AMCON from any liability arising from any wrong doing committed by the bank lender); and s. 44 AMCON Act (provides for the indemnification of AMCON for any liability or loss arising before the date of the debt transfer).

which are typically borne by distressed debt investors.[198] These were privileges not available to private distressed debt investors, who would be left to bargain for them.

6.10.3 How Will Distressed Debt Investors Intervention Help?

As has been pointed out earlier, commercial banks carrying huge non-performing loans on their books have a downside for the banks themselves.[199] One must bear in mind that bank lenders, more than anything else, seek the liquidation of the debt owed. In view of this, liquidity in the capital market not only inures in favor of the banks, helping them dispose of the distressed debt,[200] but it also benefits borrowers as such liquidity reduces the cost of capital.[201] As part of the strategy adopted by distressed debt investors, new money may be provided for viable distressed debtors in need of new financing. In an economy that is largely dependent on regulated commercial banks and institutional investors that are largely risk averse, it is not typical to find such investors throwing good money after bad. Specialized investors willing to take a chance in the market will not only ease liquidity constraints for the distressed business, but also provide an exit route for pre-distress investors unwilling to remain invested in the debtor. Such lenders may go on to further provide lending to other businesses in need of funding.

One of the strongest criticisms about business debtors in Nigeria is their unwillingness to pay their debt.[202] Other things being equal, the participation of private distressed debt investors in the Nigerian distressed debt market may serve the purpose of ensuring that management the management of such businesses are left at the mercy of distressed investors. The underlying value of the distressed business may

---

[198] See for instance, the **Loan Purchase and Limited Service Agreement between AMCON and First Bank of Nigeria Plc. (FBN) dated January 2, 2012** in respect of the defaulted loan of **Seawolf Oilfield Services Limited**. The agreement provided in pertinent parts as follows:

> AMCON shall acquire and buy from FBN which sold and assigned to AMCON absolutely, all FBN's rights, title, interest, benefits, receivables and proceeds arising from and in connection with FBN's Loan(s) to, and Loan Agreement(s) with, Seawolf including without limitation, the proceeds of, cash in or under, right to or chose in action in relation to, such loan(s) and all rights, title, interest, benefits and proceeds arising from and in all security interest(s) pertaining to the loan(s) and loan agreement(s) and collateral documents connected therewith (being "the eligible bank assets"), *excluding any obligation or liability of FBN under the loan agreement(s) or the collateral document(s)*. [Emphasis supplied]

[199] See Sect. 6.2.2 above.

[200] Miller and Waisman (2004), pp. 181–182 (commenting on how distressed debt traders help financial institutions by providing them liquidity and lower risks).

[201] See Levy (2017) (noting that disposal of NPLs can help advance "financial deepening and inclusion as *banks become more prepared to lend to riskier clients*. [Emphasis supplied]").

[202] See Dumo (2011) (quoting the Managing Director of AMCON as saying that Nigerians hate paying back debt).

be better unlocked by a strategic investor pursuing a loan-to-own strategy. Such an investor may through its debt position, wrest control from the extant management and oversee a successful turnaround of the business. Given that they have a skin in the game, it is unlikely that such investors will mismanage the distressed business. This may be exactly what the debtor needs to be successfully restructured and returned to productivity.

6.10.4 Should Policymakers be Worried About Asset Stripping?

As has been already pointed out, one of the key misgivings against financing emanating from the distressed debt market is the possibility of value destruction.[203] In the case of Nigeria, this fear is grounded in the possible stripping of the distressed business of its assets. It is not incorrect to say that part of the strategy of the distressed debt market may entail stripping the distressed business of its assets. Coming from the rather unfortunate experiences from the privatization of State-owned enterprises,[204] there appears to be a cautiousness on the part of policymakers to prevent reoccurrence. Two arguments may be made in this regard. First, Nigeria has since had a similar system of debt resolution which is primarily focused on the stripping of the assets of the distressed business through the appointment of a receiver over the affairs of the business. This power is until now, the primary tool in the arsenal of secured bank lenders and also AMCON, in the quest for seeking the repayment of debt owed by distressed debtors. The argument or fear of distressed investors acting as "vultures" does therefore seem to be a particularly valid one. However, it is arguable that management-oriented distressed investors bring more to the table and may very well pursue a relatively longer-term approach to the sale of the assets of the company, as against a fire sale that has been the hallmark of the Nigerian receivership system. Whatever the case, the decision of the investor will be driven by the maximization of the value of asset.

Secondly, the intervention of distressed investors helps to diffuse (even if momentarily), the specter of insolvency which may be hanging over the head of the distressed debtor. This certainly does have implication for the value at which the market will price the assets of the business. During the intervening period, a distressed investor in the quest to derive higher value for the distressed business may make an informed wager, based on its knowledge of the company, on when, and whether to sell the assets the business individually or as a whole. Besides, it could be argued that such informed sale driven by value maximization will yield a better payoff than a fire-sale orchestrated through the appointment of a receiver/manager.

---

[203] See Sect. 6.8 above.

[204] Etieyibo (2011) (noting that only about 10% of over 400 privatized companies were still functioning and that "[s]ome of the privatized enterprises were underhandedly undervalued and divested to investors who made quick profits off them by aggressive asset stripping.").

What is more? In cases where the distressed debt investors seek an equity stake in the distressed business, (such as a private equity firm choosing to invest in a distressed portfolio company), the distressed investor has a skin in the game. Hence, it will be counterintuitive for the distressed investor to take steps which will be detrimental to the overall survival of the distressed debtor as profits for the investing fund is tied to the value created out of the distressed business.

6.10.5 Promoting Wider Participation: A Case for the Liberalization of Nigeria's Distressed Debt Market

As if the financial crisis that peaked in 2008 was not enough, tougher times were yet to come for many Nigerian businesses and also for their bank lenders. Following the crash of oil prices in the international market, coupled with a foreign exchange crisis, as well as underhand dealings by some bank boards, it became difficult for businesses to fulfil their obligations to their bank creditors. This triggered another round of fresh NPLs. Primary lenders once again came under the strains of huge non-performing loan portfolios.[205] In the light of this, there cannot be any delusion that the creation of statutory incentives in the insolvency law regime will automatically result in the willingness of bank lenders to finance the distressed businesses.

There are even more reasons why an insolvency law regime providing for financing incentives for new money lenders may not altogether resolve the need for financing distressed Nigerian businesses.[206] This is because the administration of the legal regime will be faced with extant systemic obstacles prominent among them being issues of corruption, a pervasive mistrust[207] as well as poor appreciation of insolvency law amongst both practitioners and judges.[208] Even more concretely, Nigeria is yet to enact a corporate insolvency legislation, with mostly defective restructuring regimes scattered in different legislative instruments.[209] Although this is still in the works, there is still a long way to go in fine-tuning the several grey areas in the draft legislation. More so, the draft law does not provide for any concrete sweeteners for

---

[205] See for instance, Holodny (2016) (reporting the changes in the board of Skye Bank Plc, a 2nd tier Nigerian bank and 8th largest lender by assets, following the failure of the bank to meet capital adequacy ratio and its huge non-performing loan portfolio).

[206] Adebola (2014), p. 316 (see author's proposal that prospective new money lenders in Nigeria may be offered superpriority and junior liens with the consent of the court).

[207] Ibid at 315 (on the prevailing situation, the author's investigation showed that "no one trusts anyone else: judges do not believe the practitioners, the bankers or the debtors; no other party believes the other.").

[208] Id.

[209] For the existing restructuring regimes in Nigeria and the reform efforts, see Part II of Chap. 3 above.

new money financers of the distressed debtor.[210] While the process of corporate insolvency reform runs its course, the distressed debt market may have so much to offer in the interim, and even after the enactment of the law. In view of the foregoing, the distressed debt market presents an alternative source of value creation for businesses undergoing financial distress and in need of financial restructuring. Such investors particularly present an alternative for businesses yet to enter into formal insolvency.

Where these businesses have not already entered into insolvency, the issues which the distressed investor will have to face will be more of informal restructuring that follows the path of basic contract and corporate law. The courts and legal practitioners have a longer history and possibly deeper knowledge of contract and corporate law related issues more than of complex insolvency rules. As such, it is arguable that navigating corporate law compared to insolvency law is relatively easier. Take the example of a distressed investor willing to provide financing for a distressed business through a share deal.[211] Typically, apart from executing key contractual agreements,[212] the investor may be required to comply with practical corporate law requirements.

Furthermore, the involvement of distressed debt investors has its own value for the distressed business. In addition to the availability of new financing that comes with their investment, in some instances, they also come with operational know-how that may be useful for the distressed business as it restructures. Furthermore, in some cases, they may not be subjected to exactly the same regulatory supervision both in terms of the investments they may pursue, or the limits within which an investment may be pursued, as it is the case with commercial banks.[213]

---

[210] See Chap. 4, Sect. 4.7.1.

[211] A share deal here entails buying into the share capital of the business so that on the one hand, the investor assumes ownership of corporate assets and on the other hand, assumes equivalent liabilities.

[212] The typical agreements will include an Investment Agreement, detailing the amount of investment and the asset class in which the investor wishes to invest; a Deed of Share Charge, creating a security over the shares in favor of the investor to secure the acquisition of the shares by the investor; a Share Purchase Agreement, recording the terms and conditions relating to the sale of the sale of the shares to the investor; and a Shareholders Agreement, detailing the relationship between and among the shareholders following the investment to be made by the distress investor.

[213] See for instance, Berman and Brighton (2007) (citing the example of hedge funds, the authors point out that: "hedge funds can be particularly useful in the restructuring context because they are not constrained to make only a single type of investment and [are] not bound by banking regulations, which make them much more nimble than traditional lenders.").

6.10.6 PAMC: Limiting the Role of Investors as Distress Financers

Given the magnitude of Nigeria's distressed debt holding, the Central Bank of Nigeria (CBN) has started a process of liberalizing the space for distressed debt investment in the country. Through the exposure draft of the framework for licensing private assets management companies in Nigeria,[214] the draft framework proposes a very cautious involvement of distressed debt investors in the Nigerian market. In fact, it is a strict regulatory regime for distressed debt investors who may be interested in participating in the non-performing loan component of Nigeria's distressed debt market. Describing these investors as **private assets management companies** (PAMC), the strictness of the regime is deducible from the list of activities which the PAMCs are specifically prohibited from engaging in under the framework. Two prominent issues that arise pertain to the restriction of the provision of financing to the distressed businesses as well as a blanket prohibition of fund management services by the PAMCs. Two key prohibitions are analyzed below. The first is a prohibition on lending and the second is a prohibition on the carrying out of fund management services to third parties.

The Regulation expressly prohibits the PAMCs from providing credit to their "customers".[215] Indeed, it is not clear who "customers" in the Regulation refers to: the traditional lender from whom the debt is bought, or the borrower over which the PAMC now holds a claim. A prohibition of the extension of credit to the former (after the payment of the purchase price of the loan) may not raise any concerns in the context of financing the distressed business. In the case of the latter however, it becomes somewhat problematic. As has been highlighted in the earlier parts of this chapter, distressed debt investors do have an important role to play in the provision of liquidity for distressed businesses. As it is often the case, Nigerian businesses with defaulted loan portfolios are typically in a bad place especially when they have a history of defaulted loans. In developed economies, the result of default may be an increased cost of capital. However, in the case of Nigeria, increased bank regulation means that traditional lenders exhibit so much risk aversion, so that it will be in very rare cases that they will lend to such businesses.

An outright ban on the provision of financing to distressed businesses by distressed debt investors has the effect of excluding the distressed investors from playing a role in the provision of financing for distressed businesses. Indeed, it ignores the value creation or maximization role which distressed investors can play in a firm which is distressed and in need of the professional management capacity that may be offered by distressed debt investors, as they are known to do. It may well have been possible to bypass the restriction on the prohibition of financing by the PMACs

[214] See Circular from the Financial Policy and Regulation Department detailing a draft framework for the licensing, regulation and supervision of private asset management companies in Nigeria (PAMC Regulation) Document on file with author.

[215] See Clause 4.2 (a) PMAC Regulation.

to distressed businesses. For instance, the distressed business may procure new facility on the strength of a guarantee by the PAMC. However, the Regulation also prohibits PAMCs from standing as guarantors for loans.[216] With this, alongside the financing prohibition, the Regulation essentially isolates a potential lender and driver of value from being involved with the distressed business.

There is also a blanket prohibition of fund management services by PAMCs to third parties under the proposed Regulation.[217] This prohibition should raise concerns, given the nature of the players typically involved in the distressed debt market. Recall as discussed above that the players in the distressed debt market are typically fund managers. The organizational structure of both entities typically includes a GP who amongst other things, is responsible for seeking out investment opportunities, raising financing, and managing the portfolios in which they are invested. It also includes a limited partner comprising investors who provide funds for investment by the GP. With this prohibition, it is not really clear whether hedge funds/private equity debt investors who manage funds on behalf institutional investors or high net worth individuals will be allowed to participate as PMACs.

With this Regulation, the distressed debt market in Nigeria is likely to be a heavily regulated one and is likely to hinder entry into the market by distressed debt investors. It may even well be that the regulation is designed to restrict entry into the Nigerian market, or to at least ensure that entry is routed through AMCON.[218] Unless this the case, it is doubtful if distressed businesses in Nigeria will be able to reap from the valuable role which the distressed debt investors can potentially offer, both as lenders and value creators in distressed businesses.

6.11 Conclusion

The distressed debt market has been broadly examined. The purpose is to expose its role as financers of distressed businesses. Not only does the distressed debt market demonstrate this promise of providing financing, it also shows great promise in creating or maximizing value for businesses that restructure. Deducible from this chapter is the difference in penetration of distressed debt investors. A thriving secondary market for assets, a time-tested restructuring regime one of its key goals being the maximization of value for the stakeholders and the existence of court manned by judges with sufficient knowledge to appreciate the intricacies of the cases when brought in the context of formal restructuring. It is upon these pillars

[216] See Clause 4.2(c) of the Regulation.

[217] Clause 4.2(f) of the Regulation.

[218] In 2016, Duet Private Equity, an investor with distressed investing strategy, partnered with AMCON to invest an initial USD 400 million and a subsequent USD 200 million. The investment is "focused on turnaround and distressed situations where companies require additional capital and debt restructuring." see AMCON News, Duet Private Equity teams with AMCON to launch Nigeria FMCG Fund. Available at: https://amcon.com.ng/news-story.php?n=5 (accessed 5 Dec 2017).

that the collateral purpose and effect rule proposed in the chapter rests as a litmus test for the actions of the distress debt investor. Of course, in the broader context of regulating distressed debt investors, different approaches including disclosure of investor positions may be necessary.[219] The proposal in the book focuses on the courts.[220]

It is obvious that the proposed collateral purpose and effect approach advocated in the book is fitted to formal restructuring as the implementation of the approach is designed to be effected by the courts. This is true because formal restructuring frameworks by their design typically allow for the invocation of the jurisdiction and consequently, the coercive powers of the court in order to achieve the purpose of the restructuring. Unfortunately, informal restructuring regimes do not give the court much role to play, unless an aggrieved party approaches the court, and there exists a cause of action. In this case, it is arguable that the court can apply the proposed approach to resolving the dispute, in view of the policy goals of corporate financial restructuring, especially that which seeks to ensure the maximization of value for the stakeholders and of the distressed firm. Other than in such cases, it will appear that the proposed approach has limited applicability to informal restructuring.

Another challenge to the proposed principled approach is its overt reliance on the powers of the courts in a formal restructuring, to identify collateral incentives and measure the implication of such incentive against the policy goals of a restructuring. It would appear that too much faith is reposed on the ability of the courts to control the predilection of a distressed investor to act in a manner that could be value destructive and detrimental to a debt restructuring.[221] After all, "judges like the rest of us are prone to error."[222] A response to this likely attack will require a reiteration of the theme of this chapter. Distress debt investors can play a valuable role in the financing of corporate debt restructurings. However, as self-interested actors, their interests can interfere with the policy goals of corporate restructuring. Indeed, the pursuit of their self-interest may be value destructive for the financially distressed firm. Reposing faith in the judge involved in the financial restructuring to intervene is justified on two key grounds. The first is that although the proposed approach is principle-based rather than prescriptive, there is a measurable yardstick against which the consequence of the investor's collateral purpose may be measured. This yardstick is the goal of the restructuring. Secondly, without prejudice to the likelihood of error on the part of the judge, the judge has the support of all the relevant documents, and representations of relevant stakeholders and their experts involved in restructuring. Hence, no other person is better placed to make a judgment call on

[219] See generally, Lipson (2009), at Section III.

[220] On the concern that reliance on the courts could lead to further complicating the restructuring process, see Weijs and Baltjes (2018), p. 230.

[221] For a somewhat similar criticism, see the Baird (1987), pp. 820–821 (criticizing the reliance on the role of the bankruptcy judge to limit the rights of creditors in order to increase the chances of a successful restructuring).

[222] Ibid, at 821.

the effect of the collateral purpose of the restructuring, more than the judge before whom the formal restructuring procedure is instituted.

For frontier markets like Nigeria, there appears to be a cautious movement towards opening up the distressed debt market to participation by distressed debt investors. Driving participation in the loans offered on the market will require that such investors enjoy similar treatments enjoyed by the flagship trader in the distressed debt market. Regulatory regimes need not be unduly restrictive as to impose constraints on participation by distressed investors especially as financers of the restructuring. It also becomes the more imperative that the restructuring regime is quickly enacted, and the judiciary is properly positioned to understand what issues are at stake in effecting high stake restructuring of distressed businesses.

References

Agarwal V, Meneghetti C (2011) The role of hedge funds as primary lenders. Rev Deriv Res 14:241–261

Adebola B (2014) Unpublished PhD dissertation. University College London. Available at: http://discovery.ucl.ac.uk/1385156/7/1385156_Thesis.pdf

Altman EI (2014) The role of distressed debt markets, hedge funds and recent trends in Bankruptcy on the outcomes of Chapter 11 reorganizations. Am Bankr Inst Law Rev 75–123

Anabtawi I (2006) Some skepticism about increasing shareholder power. UCLA Law Rev 53:561–600

Armour J, Hsu A, Walters A (2008) Corporate insolvency in the United Kingdom: the impact of the enterprise act 2002. Eur Company Financ Law Rev 2:149–171

Australian Prudential Regulation Authority (APRA) Alerts (2003) Super Industry to the Drawbacks of Hedge Funds, Media Release No. 03.25, 5 March 2003

Ayotte KM, Morrison ER (2009) Creditor control and conflict in Chapter 11. J Legal Anal 1:511–551

Baird DG (1987) Loss distribution, forum shopping, and bankruptcy: a reply to warren. Univ Chic Law Rev 54(3):815

Baird DG, Henderson MT (2008) Other people's money. Stan Law Rev 60:1309–1344

Baird DG, Jackson TH (1988) Bargaining after the fall and the contours of the absolute priority rule. Univ Chicago Law Rev 55:738–789

Baird DG, Rasmussen RK (2006) Private debt and the missing lever of corporate governance. Univ Pa Law Rev 154:1209–1251

Baird DG, Rasmussen RK (2007) The prime directive. Univ Cincinnati Law Rev 75:921–942

Baird DG, Rasmussen RK (2010) Antibankruptcy. Yale Law J 119:648

Berkowitz DM (2006) Kmart: a case for bankruptcy history books? Hedge Fund J. Available at: https://thehedgefundjournal.com/kmart-a-case-for-the-bankruptcy-history-books/. Accessed 10 Aug 2017

Berman M, Brighton J (2007) Will the sunlight of disclosure chill hedge funds? Am Bankr Inst J 24

Bianchi RJ, Drew ME (2014) Hedge fund regulation and systemic risk. Griffith Law Rev 19(1):6–29

Bratton WW (2007) Hedge funds and governance targets. Geo Law J 95:1375

Casey A (2011) The creditors' bargain and option-preservation priority in Chapter 11. Univ Chicago Law Rev 78:759–807

Chasan E (2009) Fight over what six flags is worth could get ugly. Reuters. Available at: https://www.reuters.com/article/us-sixflags/fight-over-what-six-flags-is-worth-could-get-ugly-idUSTRE5B30AR20091204. Accessed 10 Aug 2017

Chassany A, Sender H (2013) US distressed debt investors target Europe. FT. Available at: https://www.ft.com/content/0322d550-6f0b-11e3-9ac9-00144feabdc0. Accessed 10 Aug 2015
Dai N (2013) Hedge fund activism and corporate governance. In: Wright DM et al (eds) The Oxford handbook of corporate governance. Oxford University Press, Oxford, pp 564–580
Dixit V (2007) Private equity, now in 3D. Stan Bus Rep
Donegan T (1998) Note, covering the "Security Blanket": regulating bankruptcy claims and claim-participations trading under the federal securities laws. Bankr Dev J 14:381–424
Dumo E (2011) Analysis: Amcon, bad debtors and moral hazard. Available at: https://www.vanguardngr.com/2011/02/analysis-amcon-bad-debtors-and-moral-hazard/. Accessed 10 Aug 2017
Echebiri R (2012) Rage of the risk god: a reportage of the Lamido Sanusi banking reforms. Xlibris Corp
Ellias JA (2016) Do activist investors constrain managerial moral hazard in Chapter 11?: Evidence from junior activist investing. J Legal Anal 8(2):493–547
Etieyibo E (2011) Privatization in Nigeria, social welfare, and the obligation of social justice. J Econ 2(1):37–44
Fama EF, Jensen MC (1983) Separation of ownership and control. J Law Econ 26(2):301–325
Flood C (2017) New US liquidity rules strain mutual funds. Available at: https://www.ft.com/content/b23cea60-7c4c-11e7-9108-edda0bcbc928. Accessed 10 Oct 2017
Flood J (2001) The vultures fly east: the creation and globalisation of the distressed debt market. In: Nelken D, Feest J (eds) Adapting legal cultures. Hart, Oxford, pp 257–278
Franklin T (2009) What private equity investors look for: investments, managers, advisers and professionals. In: Soundy M et al (eds) A practitioner's guide to private equity. Thomas Reuters, London, pp 13–29
Fortgang CJ, Mayer TM (1990) Trading claims and taking control of corporations in chapter 11. Cardozo Law Rev 12:1
Fuller M (2006) The distressed debt market-a major force that's here to stay. Recovery, 15
Gibson WE (2000) Is hedge fund regulation necessary? Temp Law Rev 73:681
Gilson S (2001) Creating value through corporate restructuring: case studies in bankruptcies, buy-outs and breakups. John Wiley & Sons, New York
Gilson S (2010) Creating value through corporate restructuring: case studies in bankruptcies, buy-outs, and breakups, 2nd edn. John Wiley & Sons, New York
Gilson S (2012) Coming through in a crisis: how Chapter 11 and the debt restructuring industry are helping to revive the U.S. economy. J Appl Corp Financ 24(4):23–35
Goldschmid P (2005) More phoenix than vulture: the case for distressed investor presence in the bankruptcy reorganization process. Colum Bus Law Rev 191–267
Gullifer L (2015) Should clauses prohibiting assignment be overridden by statute? Penn State J Law Int Aff 4(1):47
Hammer DL et al (2005) US regulation of hedge funds. ABA, Chicago
Harner M (2008a) Trends in distressed debt investing: an empirical; study of investors' objectives. Am Bankr Inst Law Rev 16:69–107
Harner MM (2008b) The corporate governance and public policy implications of activist distressed debt investing. Fordham Law Rev 77:703–772
Harner MM (2011) Activist distressed debtholders: the new barbarians at the gate? Wash Univ Law Rev 89:155–206
Harner MM et al (2014) Activist investors, distressed companies, and value uncertainty. Am Bankr Inst Law Rev 22:167–194
Henriques DB (1992) The vulture game. New York Times, 1
Holodny E (2016). Available at: http://www.businessinsider.com/central-bank-of-nigeria-taking-over-skye-bank-2016-7. Accessed 10 Aug 2017
Holzman D (2007) Shopping for distressed companies. Weil. Available at: https://www.weil.com/articles/shopping-for-distressed-companies. Accessed 10 Aug 2017

Hsu DH, Kenney M (2005) Organizing venture capital: the rise and demise of American Research & Development Corporation, 1946–1973. Ind Corp Change 14:579–616

Iheme WC, Mba SU (2017) Towards reforming Nigeria's secured transactions law: the Central Bank of Nigeria's attempt through the back door. J Afr Law 61(1):131–153

Insol International (2007) Economic and geographical implications of hedge funds in distressed debt

IPE Real Estate (2014) German distressed debt on the rise – study. Available at https://realestate.ipe.com/german-distressed-debt-on-the-rise-study/10003173.fullarticle. Accessed 8 Sept 2017

Jackson TH, Scott RE (1989) On the nature of bankruptcy: an essay on bankruptcy sharing and the creditors' bargain. Virginia Law Rev 75:155–204

Jensen MC (1996) Corporate control and the politics of finance. In: Bhandari JS, Weiss LA (eds) Corporate bankruptcy: economic and legal perspectives. Cambridge University Press, Cambridge, pp 329–335

Jensen MC, Chew D (2011) US Corporate Governance: Lessons from the 1980's. Available at https://papers.ssrn.com/sol3/papers.cfm?abstract_id=146150. Accessed 28 Jan 2018

Jiang KL, Wang W (2012) Hedge funds and Chapter 11. J Financ 67:513

Jiang W (2012) Hedge funds and Chapter 11. J Financ 37(2):513–559

Johnson M, Fortado L (2017) US hedge funds start to bet big on Europe. FT. Available at: https://www.ft.com/content/a570cbf8-e962-11e6-893c-082c54a7f539. Accessed 10 Aug 2017

Kahan M, Rock E (2009) Hedge fund activism in the enforcement of bondholder rights. Northwest Law Rev 103:281–314

Kaiser K, Stouraitis A (1995) Value creation through corporate restructuring: European divestitures. Eur Manage J 13(2):164–174

Kahan M, Rock EC (2007) Hedge funds in corporate governance and corporate control. Univ Pa Law Rev 155:1021

Kamensky DB (2014) Furthering the goals of Chapter 11: considering the positive role of hedge funds in the reorganization process. Am Bankr Inst Law Rev 22:235–246

Kashyap A et al (2011) The macroprudential toolkit IMF. Econ Rev 59:145–161

KPMG (2016) European debt sales: loan portfolio advisory. Available at: https://assets.kpmg/content/dam/kpmg/pdf/2016/06/european-debt-sales.pdf. Accessed 10 May 2016.

Krasoff J, O'Neill J (2006) The role of distressed investing and hedge funds in turnarounds and buyouts and how this affects middle-market companies. J Priv Equity 9(2):17–22

Kuney GW (2005) Hijacking Chapter 11. Emory Bankr Dev J 21:19–112

Landler M (2005) U.S. Balks at German chancellor's call for global regulations to curb hedge funds. New York Times

Levitin AJ (2007) Finding Nemo: rediscovering the virtues of negotiability in the wake of Enron, 2007. Colum Bus Law Rev 83

Levy J (2017) Why distressed asset resolution is important to development finance. The World Bank. Available at: https://blogs.worldbank.org/voices/why-distressed-asset-resolution-important-development-finance. Last accessed 30 Jan 2018

Lipson JC (2009) The shadow bankruptcy system. Boston Univ Law Rev 89:1609–1669

LoPucki LM (2003) The nature of the bankrupt firm: a reply to baird and Rasmussen's the end of bankruptcy. Stan Law Rev 56:645–671

LoPucki LM (2004) The myth of the residual owner: an empirical study. Wash Univ Law Q 82(4):1341–1374

Macey J (2008) Corporate governance: promises kept, promises broken. Princeton University Press, Princeton

McCormack G (2008) Corporate Rescue law: an Anglo-American perspective. Edward Elgar, Cheltenham

Mccahery JA, Vermeulen EPM (2008) Corporate governance in non-listed companies. Oxford University Press, New York

McNee A (2005) NPL trading takes off in Germany. The Banker. Available at http://ec2-54-72-50-240.eu-west-1.compute.amazonaws.com/Markets/Capital-Mkts/NPL-trading-takes-off-in-Germany?ct=true. Accessed 10 Aug 2017

Mietzner M, Schweizer D (2014) Hedge funds versus private equity funds as shareholder activists in Germany—differences in value creation. J Econ Financ 38:181–208

Miller HM (2007) Chapter 11 in transition – from boom to bust and into the future. Am Bankr Law J 81:375–403

Miller HR, Waisman SY (2004) Does Chapter 11 reorganization remain a viable option for distressed businesses for the twenty-first century? Am Bankr Law J 78:153–200.

Miller HR, Waisman SY (2007) Is Chapter 11 bankrupt? Boston Coll Law Rev 47:129–181

Moya E (2009) Meet the bankruptcy barons who turn bust into boom. The Guardian. Available at: https://www.theguardian.com/business/2009/jan/27/profit-struggling-firms. Accessed 11 Aug 2017

Mundy S (2010) Distressed assets: brothers go for broke, distressed assets: brothers go for broke. FT. http://www.ft.com/cms/s/0/5488f652-ca97-11df-a860-00144feab49a.html#axzz3l2uTtvLB. Accessed 18 Aug 2015

Murray-Watson A (2005) We stood up to the get-rich-quick opportunists. The Telegraph. Available at: https://www.telegraph.co.uk/finance/2920944/We-stood-up-to-the-get-rich-quick-opportunists.html. Accessed 17 June 2016

Neyens RL (2002) Principles of corporate restructuring and asset resolution. Law Bus Rev Am 8:371–394

Nwagbaraji AE (2010) Amcon, distressed assets, and the future of investing. Vanguard Nigeria. Available https://www.vanguardngr.com/2010/10/amcon-distressed-assets-and-the-future-of-investing-2/. Accessed 10 Aug 2017

Partnoy F, Skeel DA (2007) The promise and perils of credit derivatives. Univ Cincinnati Law Rev 75:1019–1051

Paterson S (2014) Bargaining in financial restructuring: market norms, legal rights and regulatory standards. J Corp Law Stud 14(2):333–365

Paterson S (2016) The paradox of alignment: agency problems and debt restructuring. Eur Bus Org Law Rev 17:497–521

Pekarek E (2007) Pruning the hedge: who is the "client" and whom does an adviser advise? Fordham J Corp Financ Law 12(5):913–975

Peress D, Prinzhorn TC (2006) Nontraditional lenders and the impact of loan-to-own strategies on the restructuring process. Am Bankr Inst J 48–49, 57–58

Peterman NA et al (2014) Credit bidding challenges in bankruptcy. Financier Worldwide. Available at: https://www.financierworldwide.com/credit-bidding-challenges-in-bankruptcy/#.Wh7WuGhSzIU. Accessed 10 May 2018

Protess B (2011) Banks face obstacles with Volcker rule, report finds. New York Times (DEAL BOOK). Available at: https://dealbook.nytimes.com/2011/08/05/banks-face-obstacles-with-volcker-rule-report-finds/. Accessed 10 Nov 2017

Rasmussen RK (2007) Where are all the transnational bankruptcies? The puzzling case for universalism. Brooklyn J Int Law 32(3):983–1003

Roberge S (2013) Maneuvering in the shadows of the bankruptcy code: how to invest in or take over bankrupt companies within the limits of the bankruptcy code. Emory Bankr Dev J 30:73–104

Roberts MT (2013) The bankruptcy discount: profiting at the expense of others in Chapter 11. Am Bankr Inst Law Rev 21:157–187

Rosenberg H (2000) The vulture investors. Wiley, New York

Ruckin C (2013) Centerbridge buys up Apcoa's debt before restructuring. Reuters. Available: https://uk.reuters.com/article/uk-apcoa-loans/centerbridge-buys-up-apcoas-debt-before-restructuring-idUKBRE9A40UI20131105. Accessed 11 Aug 2017

Sakoui A, Jones S (2010) Distressed debt fund to list. FT

Schmies C et al (2017) Germany. In: Nassiri A (ed) The lending and secured finance review, 4th edn. Business Research Ltd, London, pp 92–101

Schwartz PA, Breslow SR (2016) Private equity funds: formation and operation, 2nd edn. Practising Law Institute, New York

Sender H (2005) Hedge-fund lending to distressed firms makes for gray rules and rough play. Wall Street J, C1

Shaked I, Michel A (1999) Value & cents: valuing the financially distressed firm. Am Bankr Inst J 18:34

Sharfman K, Warner GR (2014) Hedge funds in bankruptcy 22. Am Bankr Inst Law Rev 22:61

Sprayregen JHM et al (2005) Chapter 11: not perfect but better than the alternatives. J Bankr Law Prac 6

Stevenson A (2014) Distressed debt hedge fund commits $530 million to Europe. Deal Book. Available at: https://dealbook.nytimes.com/2014/01/27/distressed-debt-hedge-fund-commits-530-million-to-europe/. Accessed 17 Aug 2017

Stulz RM (2007) Hedge funds: past, present, and future. J Econ Perspect 21(2):175–194

The Vultures Take Wing (2007) The Economist. Available at: https://www.economist.com/finance-and-economics/2007/03/29/the-vultures-take-wing. Accessed 10 Aug 2017

Thomas RD (2010) Tipping the scales in Chapter 11: how distressed debt investors decrease debtor leverage and the efficacy of business reorganization. Emory Bankr Dev J 27:213–253

Tung F (1996) Confirmation and claims trading. Northwest Univ Law Rev 90:1684

US Securities Exchange (2003) Implications of the growth of hedge funds. Available at: https://www.sec.gov/news/studies/hedgefunds0903.pdf. Accessed 16 Mar 2017

Warren E (1993) Bankruptcy policymaking in an imperfect world. Mich Law Rev 92:336–387

Westbrook JL (2004) The control of wealth in bankruptcy. Tex Law Rev 82:795

Weijs R, Baltjes M (2018) Opening the door for the opportunistic use of interim financing: a critical assessment of the EU draft directive on preventive restructuring frameworks. Int Insol Rev 27:223–254

Widows R (2008) Look here to invest in distressed assets. The Street. Available at: http://www.thestreet.com/story/10422276/1/look-here-to-invest-in-distressed-assets.html. Accessed 8 Aug 2017

Wielebinski JJ, Hardt M (2017) Special report: financial restructuring and insolvency challenges in emerging markets. Financier Worldwide. https://www.financierworldwide.com/financial-restructuring-and-insolvency-challenges-in-emerging-markets/#.W1_6VtIzbIU. Accessed 7 Sept 2018

Wollaston A (2005) The growing importance of debt in European corporate transactions. Insol Int 18(10):147

Wruck KH (1990) Financial distress, reorganization and organizational efficiency. J Financ Econ 21:419–444

Yap S (1995) Investing in Chapter 11 companies: vultures or white knights. Southwest J Law Trade Am 2:153

Chapter 7
Conclusion and Final Remarks

As this book has shown, restructuring has assumed heightened importance as a means of resolving financial distress for viable businesses. Indeed restructuring (whether as an aspect of bankruptcy law, company law or even informally), will continue to be relevant so long as the phenomenon of financial distress exists, whether as a result of internal factors such as faulty corporate strategy, the indiscretions of extant management, or other exogenous factors relating to cyclical economic downturns.[1] In such situations where the fortunes of the business begin to dwindle, the existence of a restructuring regime suited to facilitating the continuation of the distressed debtor as the process of restructuring is underway. Efforts continue across jurisdictions to fine-tune restructuring regimes by strengthening bankruptcy legislations, to make them the more restructuring-friendly. What is often still in debate is the exact shape which the reform should take.[2] For instance, questions may arise, regarding whether the pre-distress management be retained in place, or whether a new official is appointed I their place, or whether a mid-course that allows the management to remain in place but supervised by an official, may be appropriate. Or, as the book has largely focused on, whether new financing is to be incentivized by prescribing incentives as part of the restructuring regime or allowing market participants to sort out this issue for themselves.

The provision of financing for the distressed debtor implicates at least three cogent requirements on which this book have touched on. **The first** is the need for a regime against which debt is renegotiated between the distressed business and its key stakeholders. This regime must be such that facilitates liquidity for the restructuring business. One of the fallouts from the analysis of jurisdictional restructuring regimes is that other than the US, it is not common amongst the other jurisdictions analyzed, to find any one regime that incorporates all of the identified restructuring

[1] See Chap. 1, Sect. 1.5.1 on the meaning and causes of financial distress.

[2] See for instance, Jennifer Payne, *The Future of UK Debt Restructuring*, 9 (October 5, 2016). Available at SSRN: https://ssrn.com/abstract=2848160 (accessed Feb. 10, 2018) (on the debate on what precise form the reform restructuring in the UK ought to take).

S. U. Mba, *New Financing for Distressed Businesses in the Context of Business Restructuring Law*, https://doi.org/10.1007/978-3-030-19749-0_7

tools within a single legislation.[3] The US Chapter 11 from which most restructuring regimes draw inspiration provide for a stay of creditor action, the preparation of a plan, a mechanism to bind unwilling stakeholders to the plan, and provide circumstances upon which extant management may be retained or ousted.[4] Of course, it also addresses restructuring financing through what has been addressed in the book as incentives.[5] In the UK, multiple restructuring regimes incorporating one or more of the above tools have led parties to resort to the so-called "twinning" of procedures to ensure that parties are able to enjoy the best of both procedures. This of course comes with its own costs too.

An important lesson that can be drawn from the German restructuring regime touches on how suited its current restructuring regime may be for distressed borrowers who seek to avert a looming insolvency. Given the much talked about high bankruptcy stigma in Germany, it may be of some concern that the restructuring regime is still a part of the legislative regime which deals with the liquidation of insolvent businesses. In that situation, it may be difficult for distressed companies which wish to restructure to enter into a proceeding which in the eyes of the public may still be similar to liquidation proceedings. This therefore makes a case for the need to reconsider the status quo by instead providing for a standalone restructuring regime, distinct from the InsO itself. Countries too with high bankruptcy stigma can draw from this, as they rework their restructuring regime.

In the same vein, new financing will continue to be a critical component of the restructuring toolkit in any restructuring regime as its availability may be a critical determinant of the success of the restructuring process. In this regard, the book has identified the rules that incentivize new lending and identified two main articulated approaches that have been pervasive: to wit, a **market-based approach** on the one hand, and a **prescriptive approach** on the other. The book has not necessarily preferred one jurisdictional approach over another. Countries which seek to avail distressed businesses of new financing through incentives for new lenders within their formal restructuring will first need to understand and understudy the financial actors within the market, the ease with which new financing is accessible, and the capacity of the pre-distress lender to shut out competitive new financing owing to its bargaining power. This, as the book has argued, will be most apt in the context of smaller businesses or single lender cases, hence requiring regulatory intervention, justifying some form of incentive prescription in the restructuring framework.

In the above sense, the book has argued that a prescriptive approach is consistent with the need to make competitive financing accessible especially to SMEs which when compared to the bank lenders, are the weaker parties. This also applies in frontier markets where there are more SMEs operating within the markets and for whom prescriptive incentives for new lenders will be most beneficial. The prescriptive approach will also be important to allow new lenders to participate in deciding on the viability of the distressed businesses. Consistent with the market-based

[3] See Chap. 3, Sect. 3.4 on the key requirements of restructuring.

[4] Ibid.

[5] See Chap. 4 above.

approach, the decision remains one to be decided by prior lenders who unless there is the certainty of increased value for them may starve the debtor of funds and prevent outside financing.

Furthermore, regarding new financing whether by lenders with prior lending relationship or even coming from the distressed debt market, it continues to be of critical importance that the policy goals of restructuring continue to be the lodestar and the courts become more involved. It is against such policy goals that lender self-interest can be measured and curtailed, in the interest of a successful restructuring.

7.1 Rethinking Approach to Law Reform in Nigeria: A Case for an Organic Restructuring Law

One of the most important lessons that can be drawn for Nigeria is in its approach to law reform, which is particularly atypical of the process of law reform that should ideally involve broad consultations across the spectrum of interests that will be impacted by the reform. A cursory look at the restructuring framework that presently exists reveals a mix between an outdated system provided for by the present CAMA regime, and the increasingly restructuring oriented regimes of the "new generation" legislations, as well as others that are before the legislature for passage into law.[6] Two key issues impact the toolkits of the Nigerian restructuring package. The first pertains to the proliferation of restructuring toolkits in different statutes. The second and equally pertinent issue relates to the reform process which itself betrays a top-down approach to reform.

There presently exist different regimes scattered across different laws and draft laws that speak or will speak to the question of distressed debtor restructuring in Nigeria.[7] On the one hand is the extant CAMA regime which as clearly canvased is a carryover of English legislative efforts. Thus while Nigerian businesses groan under the hangover of the borrowed model that the present CAMA represents, English law reform has moved along in the light of the realities of its market. Admittedly, current reform efforts of CAMA, however limited, marks a forward-looking approach in capturing some of the restructuring toolkits pertinent to restructuring.[8] The AMCON Act, through its recently enhanced receivership equally captures within the legislation, restructuring tools to facilitate the restructuring of

---

[6] See generally, Chap. 3, Sect. 3.8.

[7] Going by the provision of the law, which sets up the Nigerian Law Reform Commission, one of the remits of the Commission is the reduction in the number of enactments that regulate any given issue. In the same vein, the Commission is saddled with the responsibility of "... conduct[ing] such seminars and, where appropriate, hold such public sittings concerning any programme for law reform as it may consider necessary from time to time." See s. 5(1) and (5) of the Nigerian Law Reform Commission Act. The provision of the legislation notwithstanding, this is hardly ever the case. The Commission appears to play no role whatsoever in the reform efforts of key business legislations.

[8] See generally, Chap. 3, Sect. 3.8.

distressed businesses within AMCON's portfolio. The draft BIA also envisages within its provision a restructuring regime that incorporates some of the tools. The proliferation of these regimes is either suggestive of a lack of coordination amongst the drivers of restructuring reform, or it represents the absence of a clear policy direction on what the outlook of distressed debtor restructuring should be and consequently, what should facilitate that policy. In this light, it becomes obvious why there is first no mention of new financing, a key tool for restructuring. In other words, it may account for the default market-based approach to incentivizing new financing, which is to assume that it will be considered a cost of administering the estate of the borrower, if such financing becomes contentious.

While argument has been made in this book for the consolidation of the restructuring regime in one statute,[9] there is still the problem that the process of lawmaking in Nigeria today essentially follows a top-down approach. There appears to be a growing trend that is suggestive of law reform that is hardly inclusive of consultation of stakeholder groups in the process through which proposed legislations eventually make their way to the legislature for passage into law. This ought not to be the case, given that it mirrors a top-down approach to law making which has its own consequences for the efficacy of the laws passed.[10] On the one hand, it deprives the enabling law of the robust local content that should determine the direction of the reform effort. Furthermore, it becomes increasingly difficult for researchers to understand the rationale for such reform in the first place, given the lack of official comments or publicly available records of the debate proceeding.

Borrowing a leaf from the UK with which Nigerian law is mostly affiliated, there continues to be a robust engagement and consultation on what should (or should not) be included in the restructuring regime,[11] in addition to how the liquidity constraints of the distressed business may be eased. During this engagement, it has continuously been made abundantly clear that the choice of a market-based approach to incentivizing new financing is reflective of the thinking of at least a sizable segment of the stakeholders. This engagement has also revealed hesitance to the creation of heightened priority in the nature of the creation of superpriority position for providers of new financing.[12] Whether these choices are consistent with the economic arguments that suggest a prescriptive approach and superpriority position for new lenders, and whether there are any signs suggestive of regulatory capture, the input of the relevant actors in shaping the direction of the law cannot be discounted.

[9] See Chap. 3, Sect. 3.8.5.

[10] For a critique of the top-down lawmaking approach in the context of EU member states, see McCormack (2017), p. 192.

[11] See Chap. 4, Sect. 4.6.2.2.

[12] The most recent efforts being in 2016. See also, A Review of The Corporate Insolvency Framework: A Consultation on Options for Reform, section 10 (The Insolvency Service, 2016). The results of the 2016 consultations showed that **73%** of the respondents were opposed to a US-style DIP financing which in this book follows the prescriptive approach. See A Review Of The Corporate Insolvency Framework: A Summary of Responses (The Insolvency Service, 2016).

In view of the foregoing, it becomes even the more imperative that an elaborate process of reform is undertaken, which would consider different stakeholder interests. This should also include the conduct of broader surveys across the spectrum of business stakeholders on the propriety or otherwise of such issues as the approach to new financing for distressed businesses in the formal restructuring framework.[13] What this book has done, is to provide the groundwork on the talking points that may support the reforms one way or the other, even though a preference for the prescriptive approach to new financing has been advocated.

Finally, the proposals in the book have largely been constructed around the role of the courts in seeing through the process of restructuring. This requires expertise and familiarity with the restructuring. For instance, the resolution of claims and the adequate protection of lenders in a prescriptive regime, regarding the incentive structure and balancing of the concerns of pre-distress lenders with the need for new financing. These are quite technical matters that will involve questions of claim valuation for which the Nigerian judge does not have the expertise. It therefore behooves the government in conjunction with the regulatory body of insolvency professionals to organize training sessions that will help keep the judges up to date on the happenings in the restructuring universe. Absent such training and retraining, it will be nearly impossible to navigate the process of restructuring in a way that optimally balances the aspirations of the stakeholders with the policy goals of restructuring.

Reference

McCormack G (2017) Business restructuring law in Europe: making a fresh start. J Corp Law Stud 17(1):167–202

[13] Although reference is made to the formal restructuring framework, it is important to keep in mind that the formal restructuring framework will typically be the backdrop against which informal restructurings will be conducted.

Kolibri 360 GmbH
Ferdinand-Jühlke-Straße 7
99095 Erfurt, Deutschland
produktsicherheit@kolibri360.de